@FULL MOON

1

Sanami Matoh

Translated by
Andria Cheng

Lettered by
Janice Chiang

KC
KODANSHA
COMICS

CONTENTS

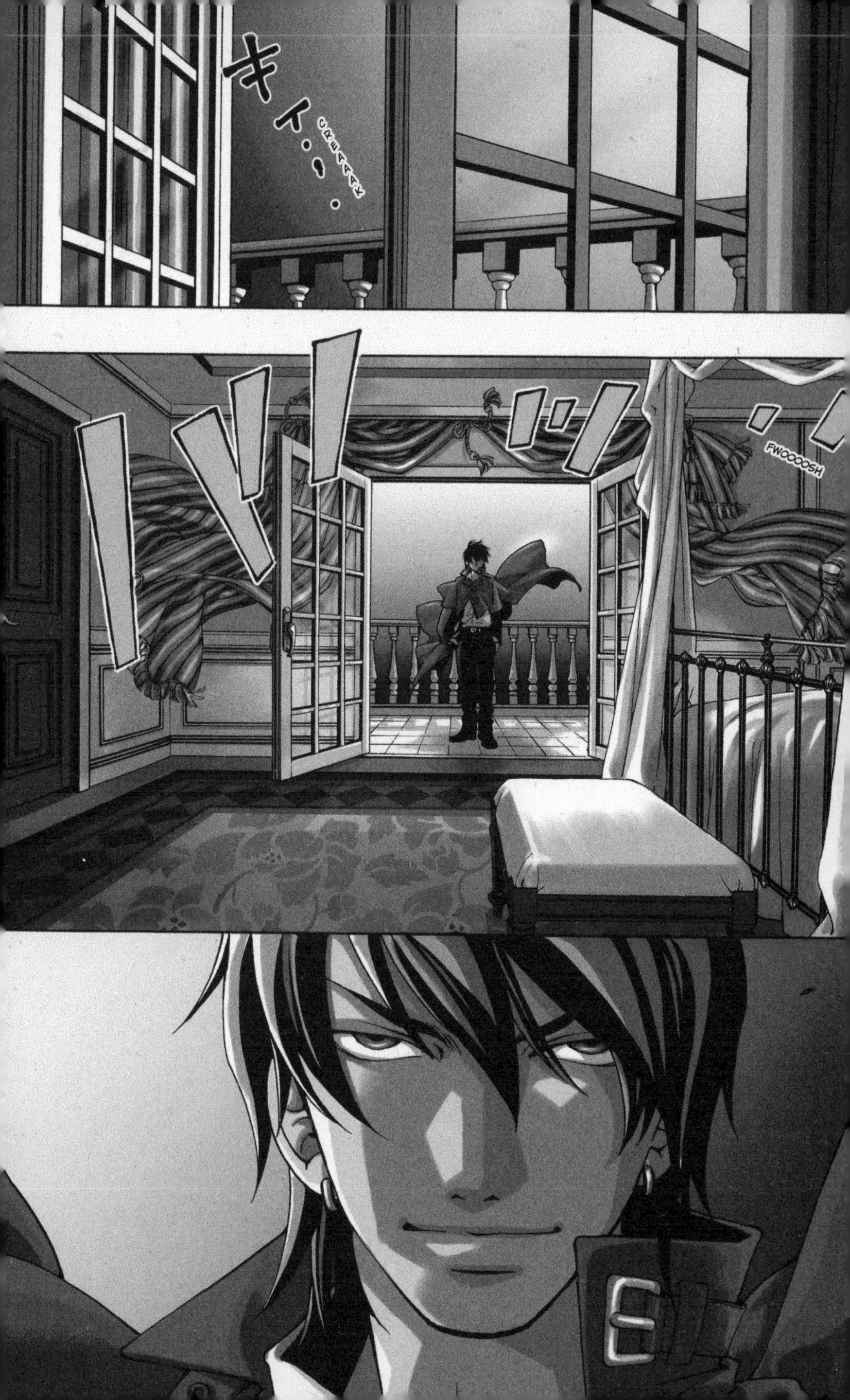
キィ・・・
CREAAAK
バババッ・・・
FWOOOOOSH

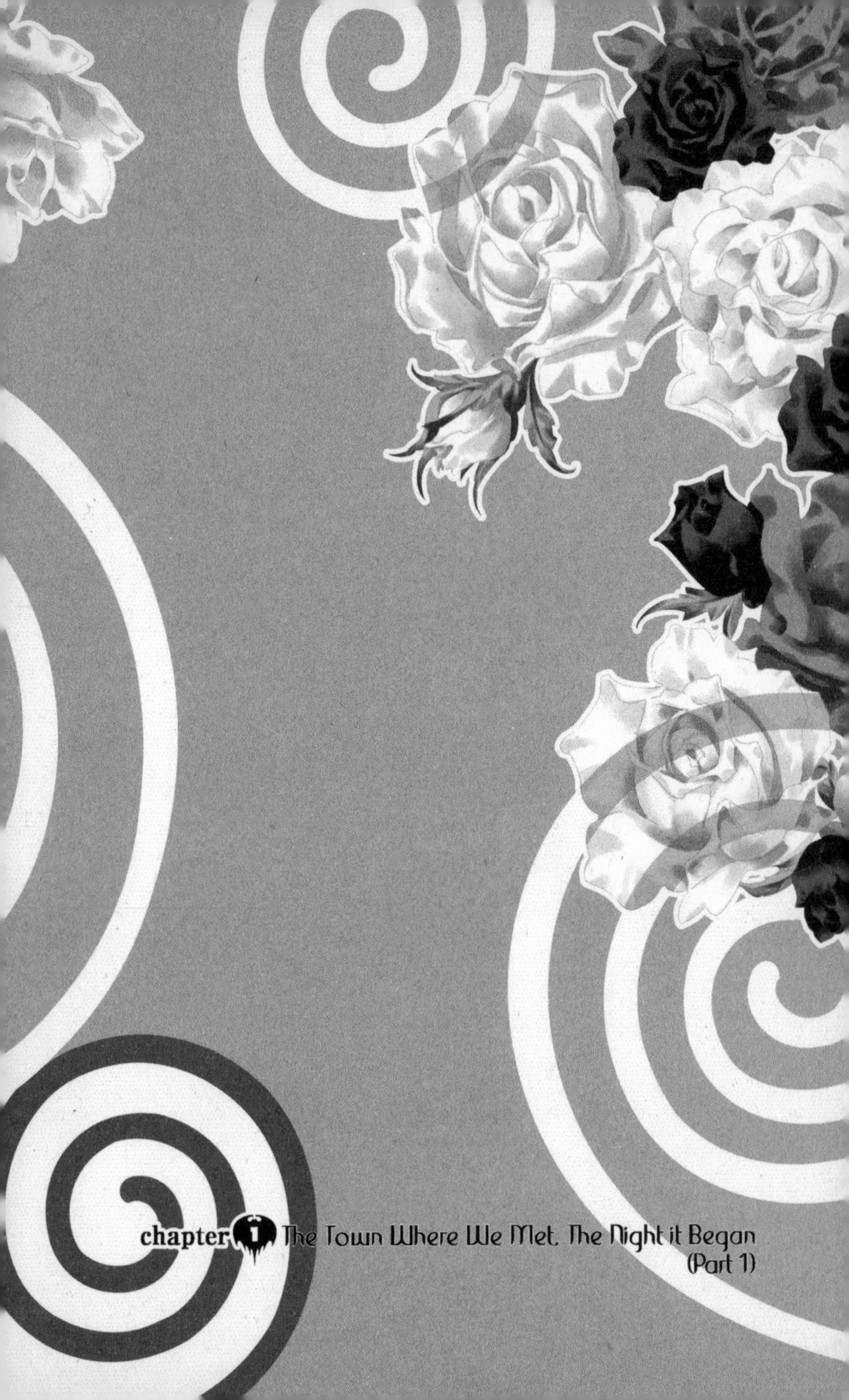

chapter 1 The Town Where We Met, The Night it Began (Part 1)

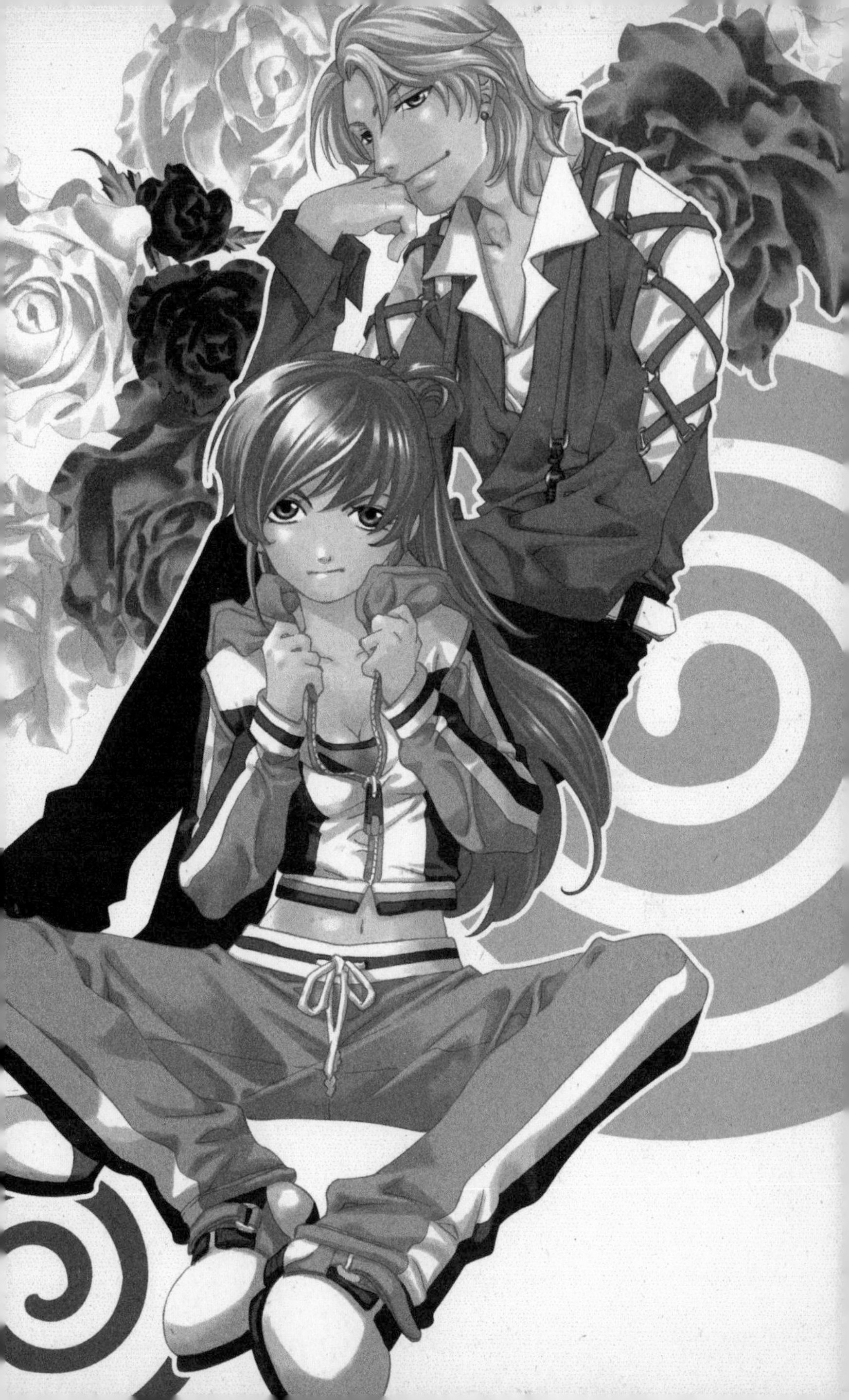

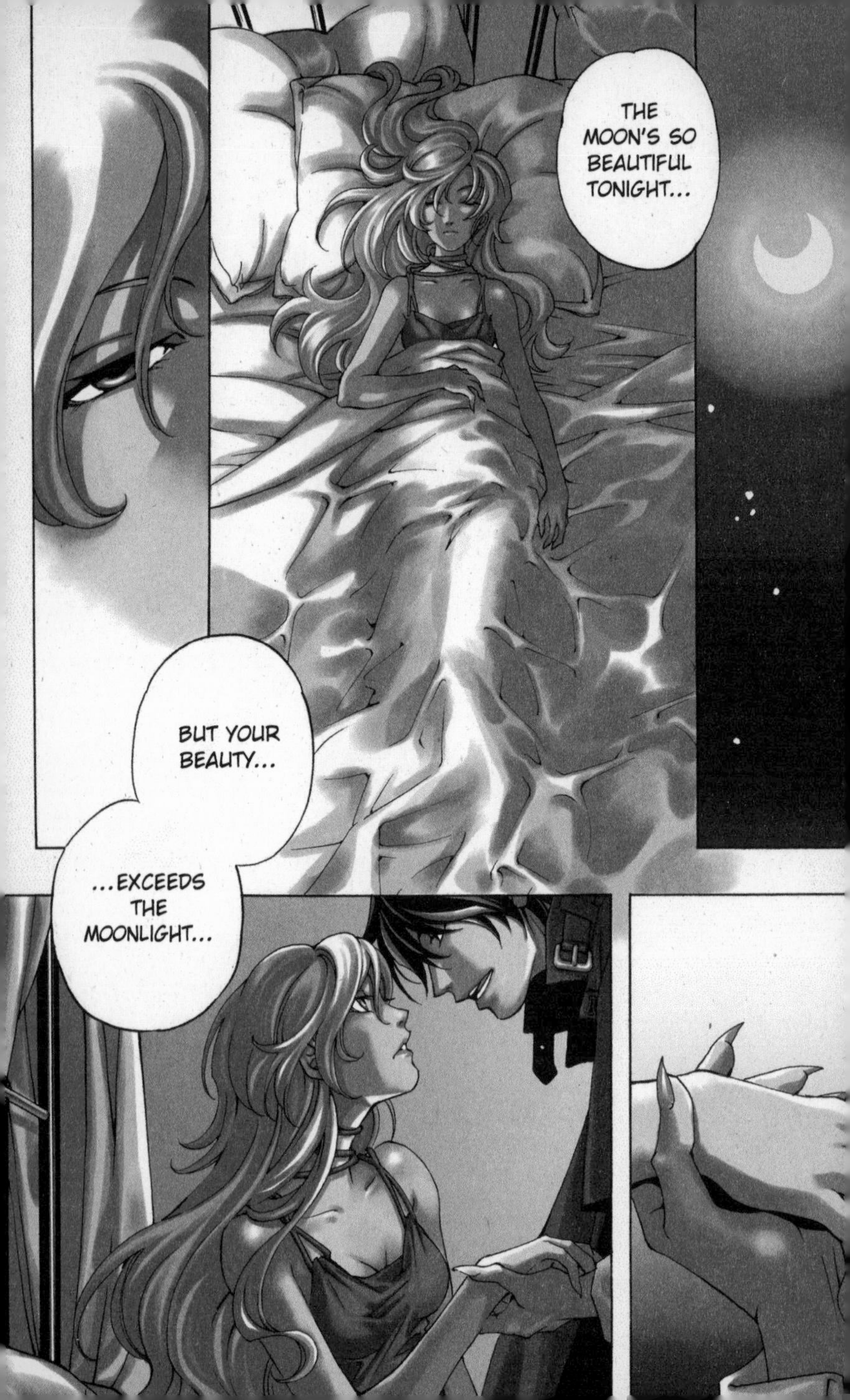
THE MOON'S SO BEAUTIFUL TONIGHT...
BUT YOUR BEAUTY...
...EXCEEDS THE MOONLIGHT...

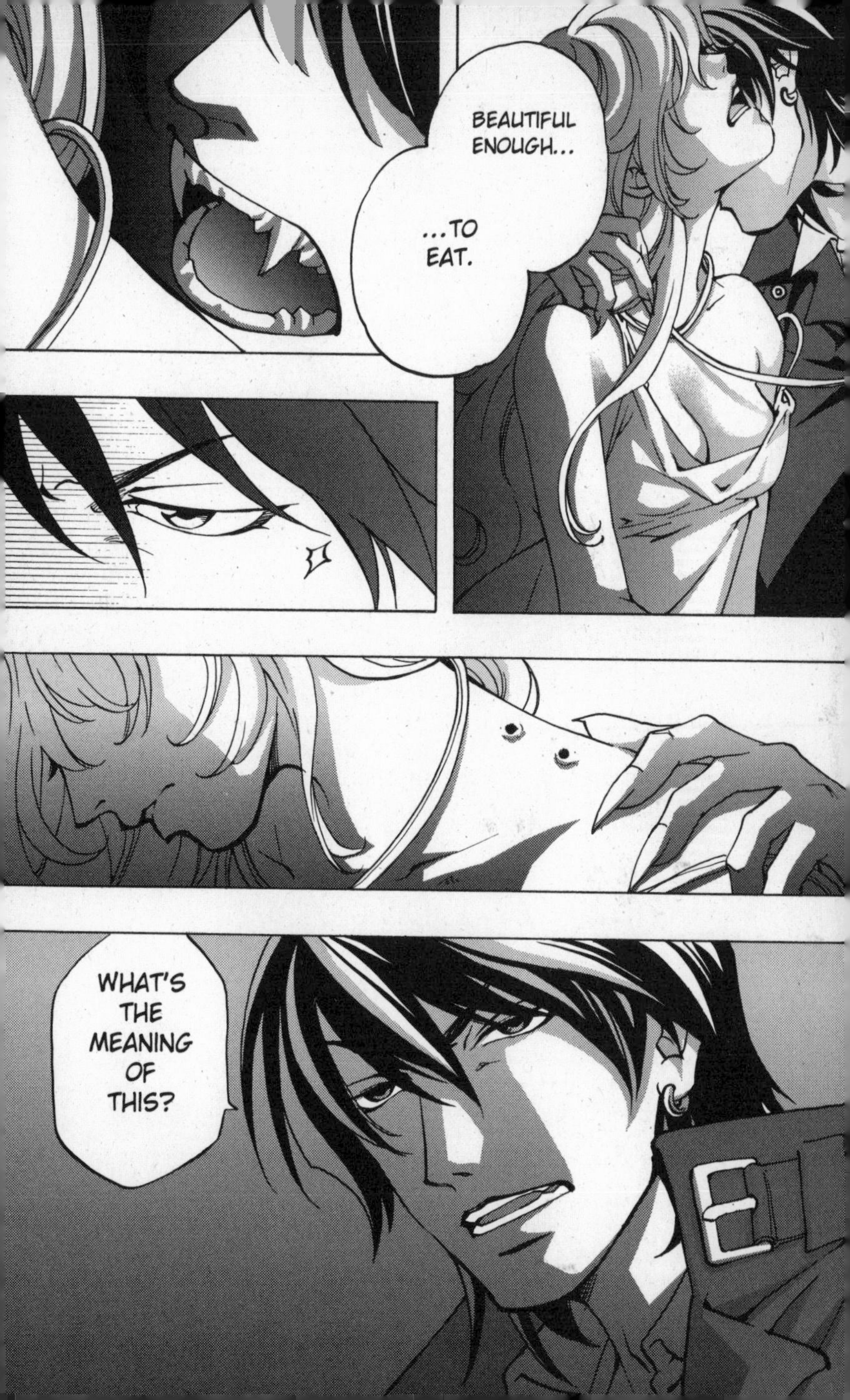
BEAUTIFUL ENOUGH...
...TO EAT.
WHAT'S THE MEANING OF THIS?

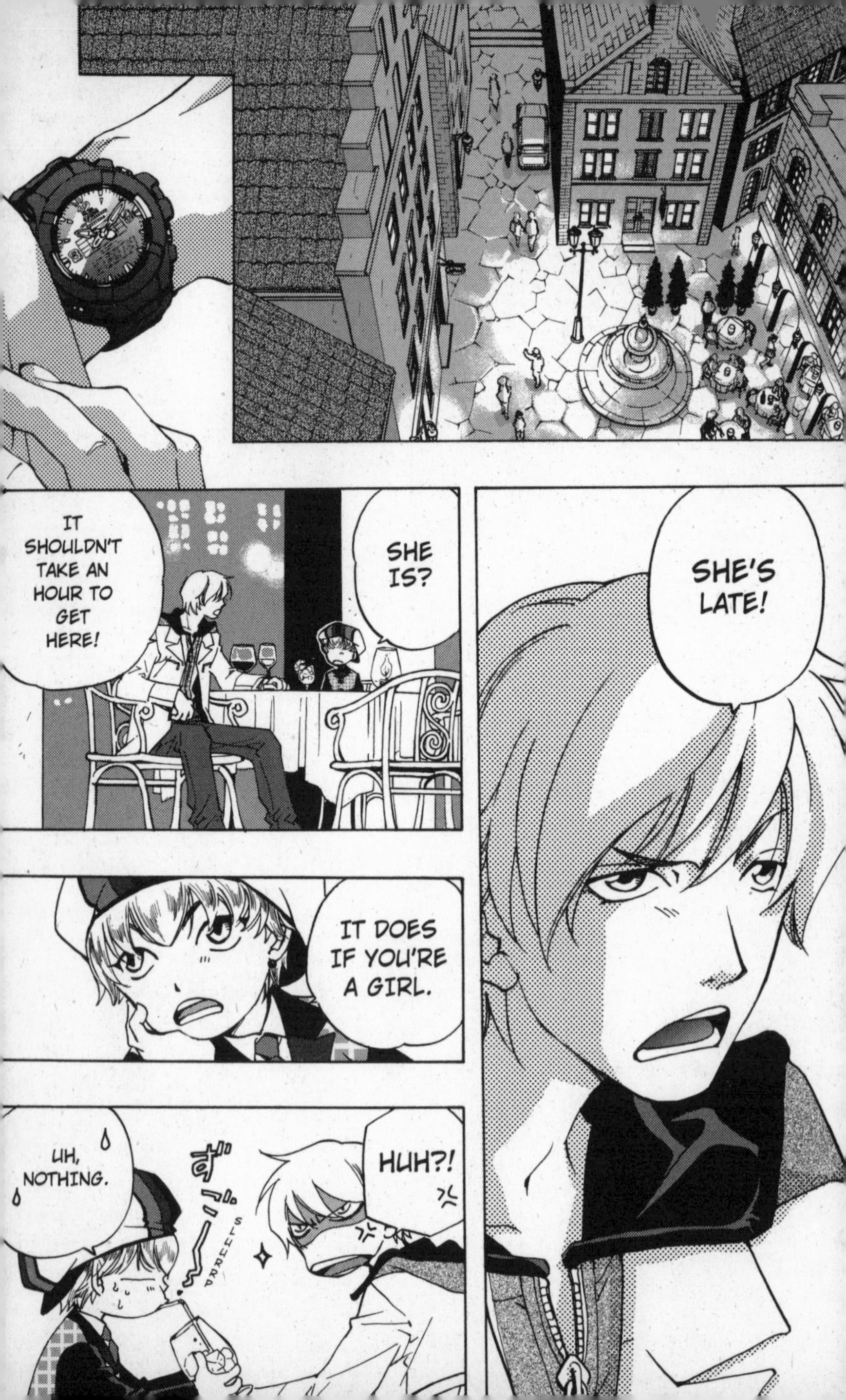
SHE'S LATE!
SHE IS?
IT SHOULDN'T TAKE AN HOUR TO GET HERE!
IT DOES IF YOU'RE A GIRL.
HUH?!
SLURRP
UH, NOTHING.

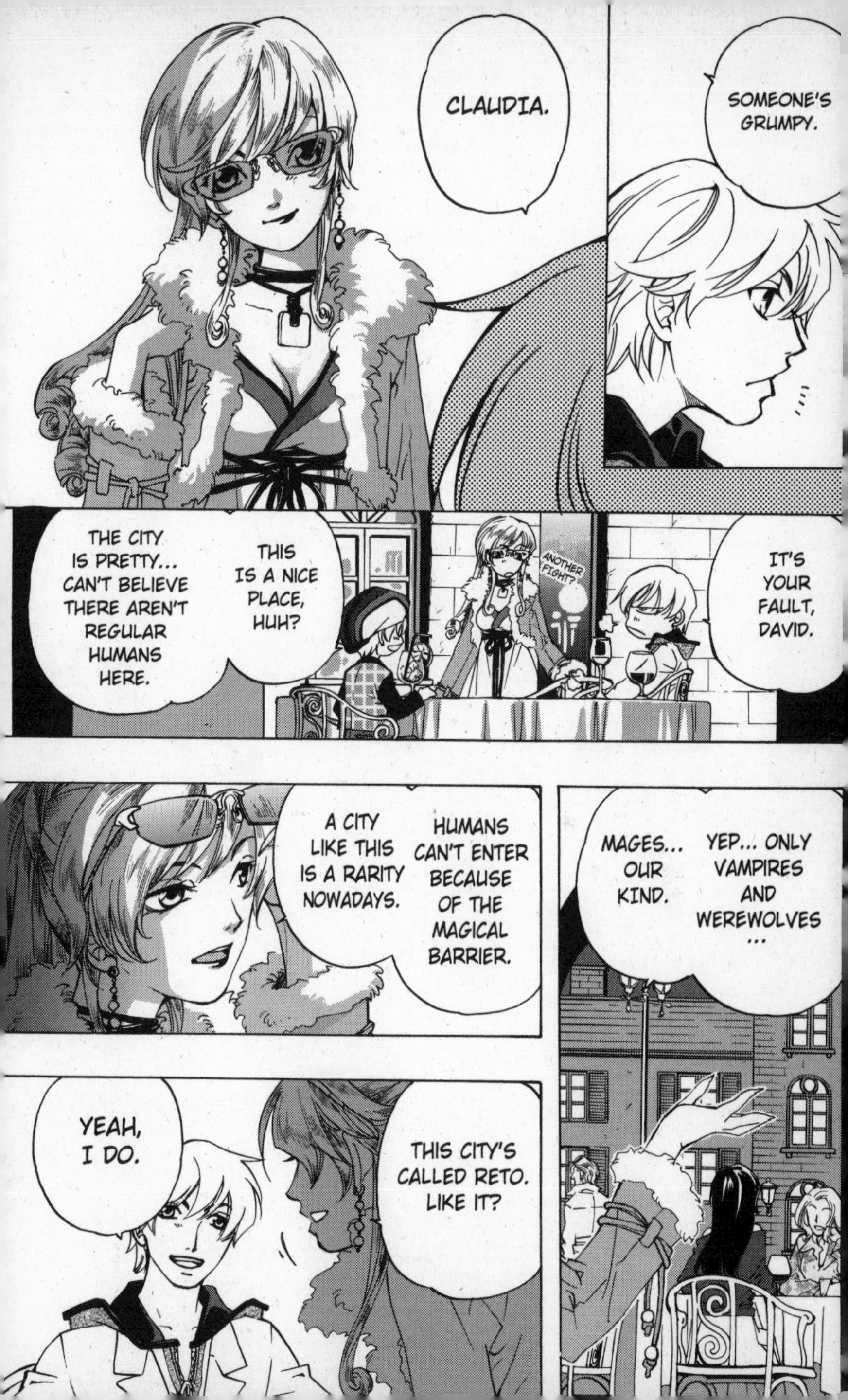
SOMEONE'S GRUMPY.
CLAUDIA.
IT'S YOUR FAULT, DAVID.
ANOTHER FIGHT?
THIS IS A NICE PLACE, HUH?
THE CITY IS PRETTY... CAN'T BELIEVE THERE AREN'T REGULAR HUMANS HERE.
YEP... ONLY VAMPIRES AND WEREWOLVES ...
MAGES... OUR KIND.
HUMANS CAN'T ENTER BECAUSE OF THE MAGICAL BARRIER.
A CITY LIKE THIS IS A RARITY NOWADAYS.
THIS CITY'S CALLED RETO. LIKE IT?
YEAH, I DO.

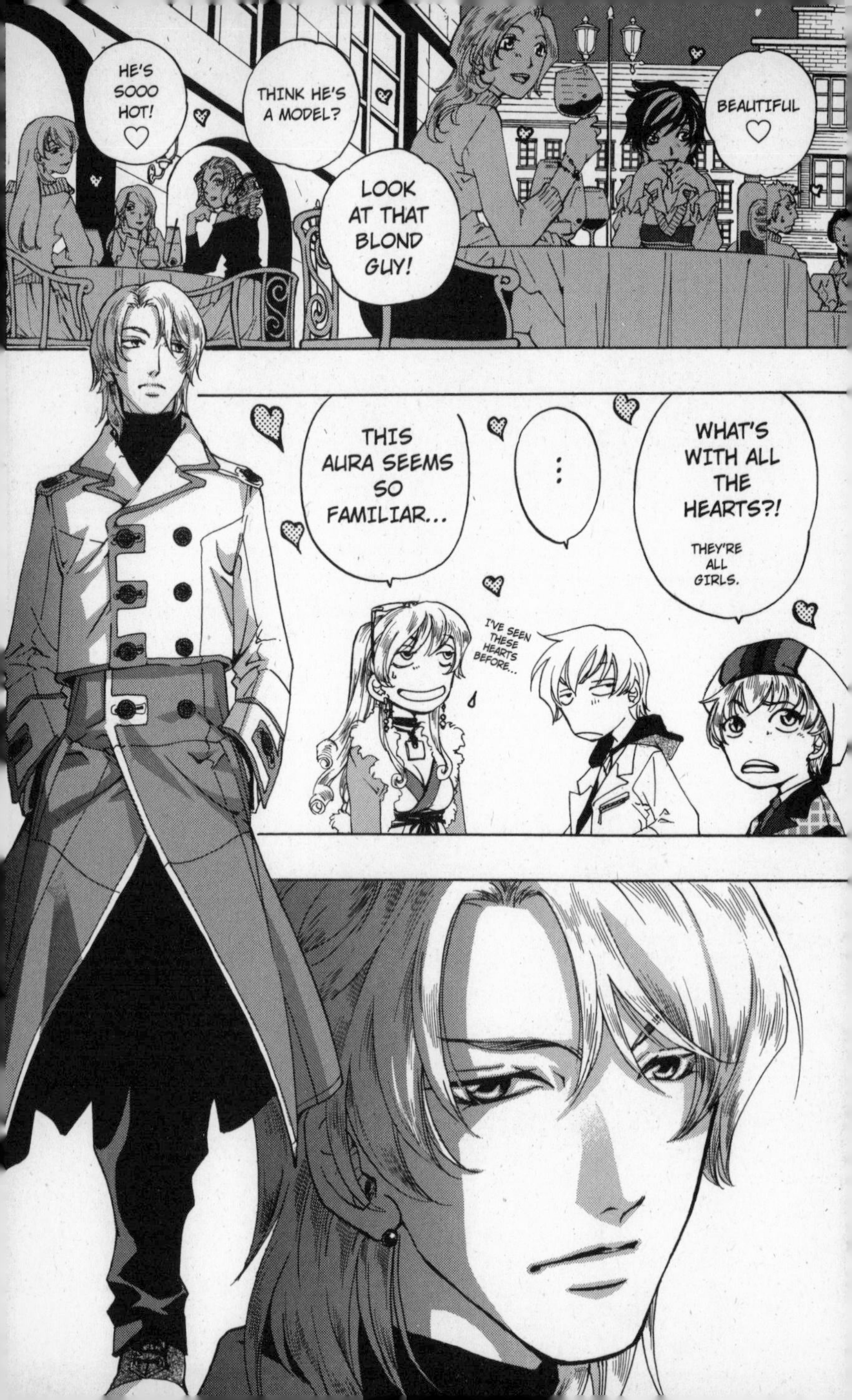

BEAUTIFUL
LOOK AT THAT BLOND GUY!
THINK HE'S A MODEL?
HE'S SOOO HOT!
WHAT'S WITH ALL THE HEARTS?!
THEY'RE ALL GIRLS.
...
I'VE SEEN THESE HEARTS BEFORE...
THIS AURA SEEMS SO FAMILIAR...

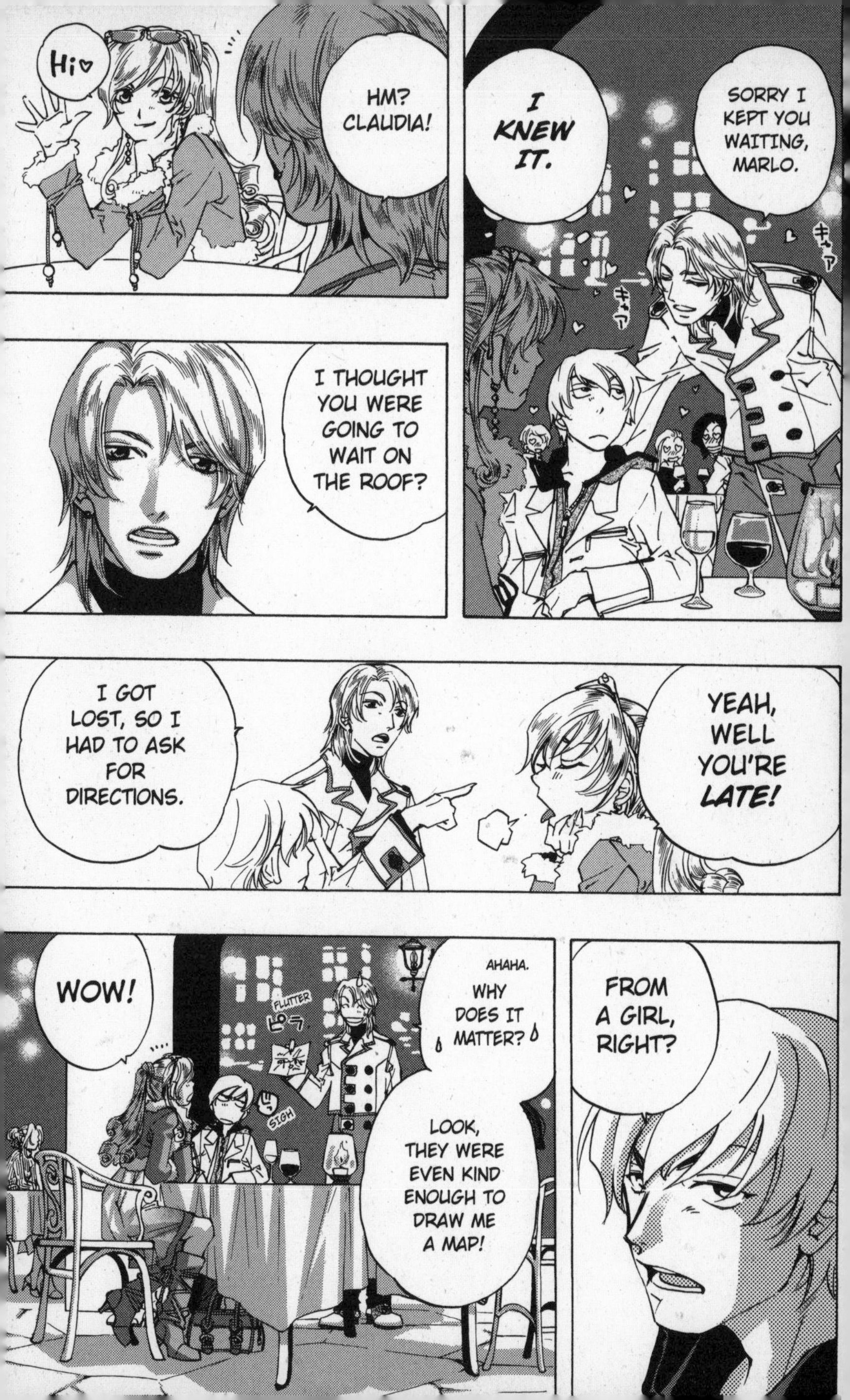
SORRY I KEPT YOU WAITING, MARLO.
キャア
キャア
I KNEW IT.
Hi♥
HM? CLAUDIA!
I THOUGHT YOU WERE GOING TO WAIT ON THE ROOF?
YEAH, WELL YOU'RE LATE!
I GOT LOST, SO I HAD TO ASK FOR DIRECTIONS.
FROM A GIRL, RIGHT?
AHAHA.
WHY DOES IT MATTER?
LOOK, THEY WERE EVEN KIND ENOUGH TO DRAW ME A MAP!
FLUTTER
ピラ
SIGH
WOW!

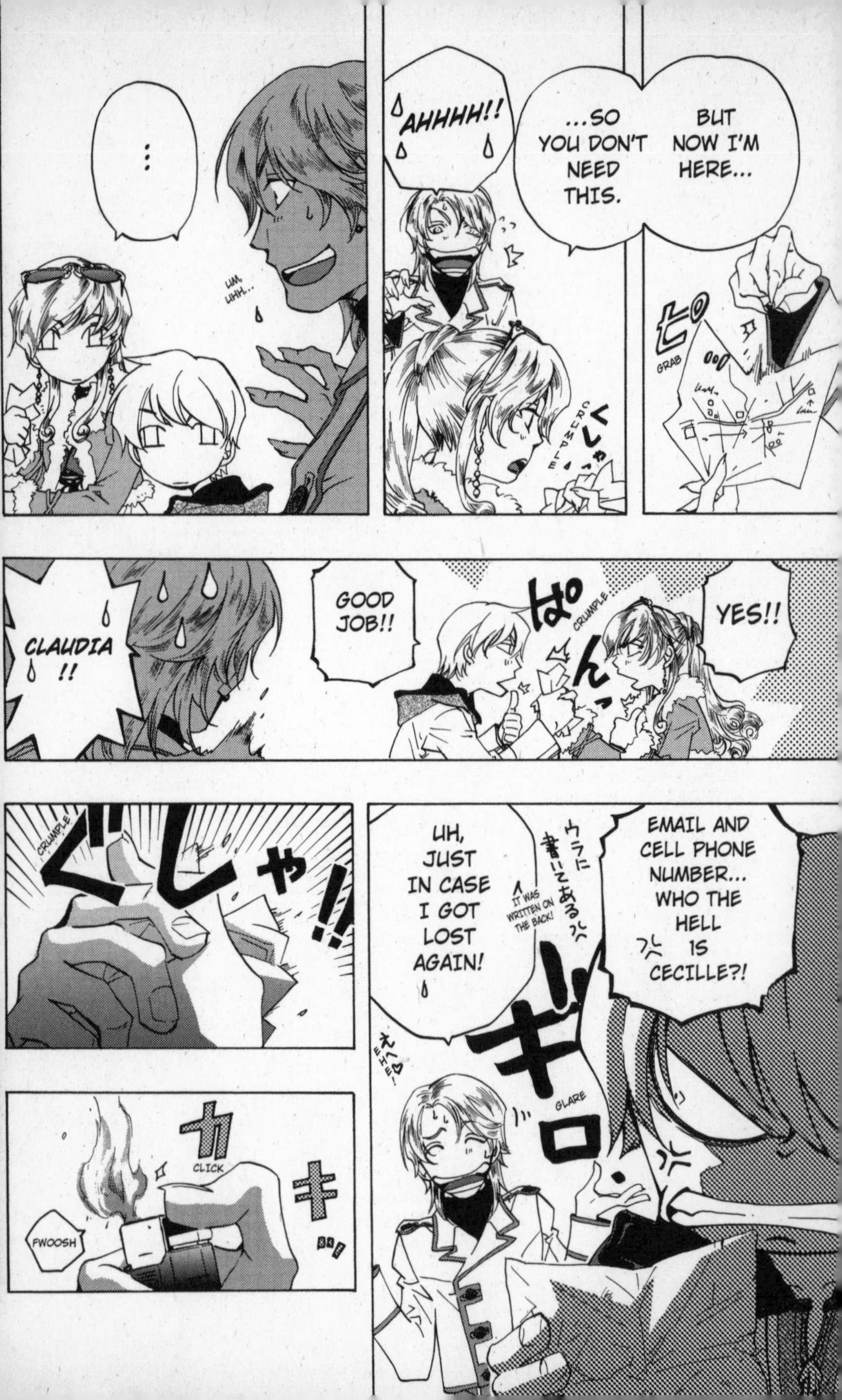
BUT NOW I'M HERE...
...SO YOU DON'T NEED THIS.
GRAB
AHHHH!!
CRUMPLE
…
UM, UHH...
YES!!
GOOD JOB!!
CRUMPLE
CLAUDIA !!
EMAIL AND CELL PHONE NUMBER... WHO THE HELL IS CECILLE?!
ウラに書いてある
IT WAS WRITTEN ON THE BACK!
UH, JUST IN CASE I GOT LOST AGAIN!
GLARE
EHE
CRUMPLE
CLICK
FWOOSH

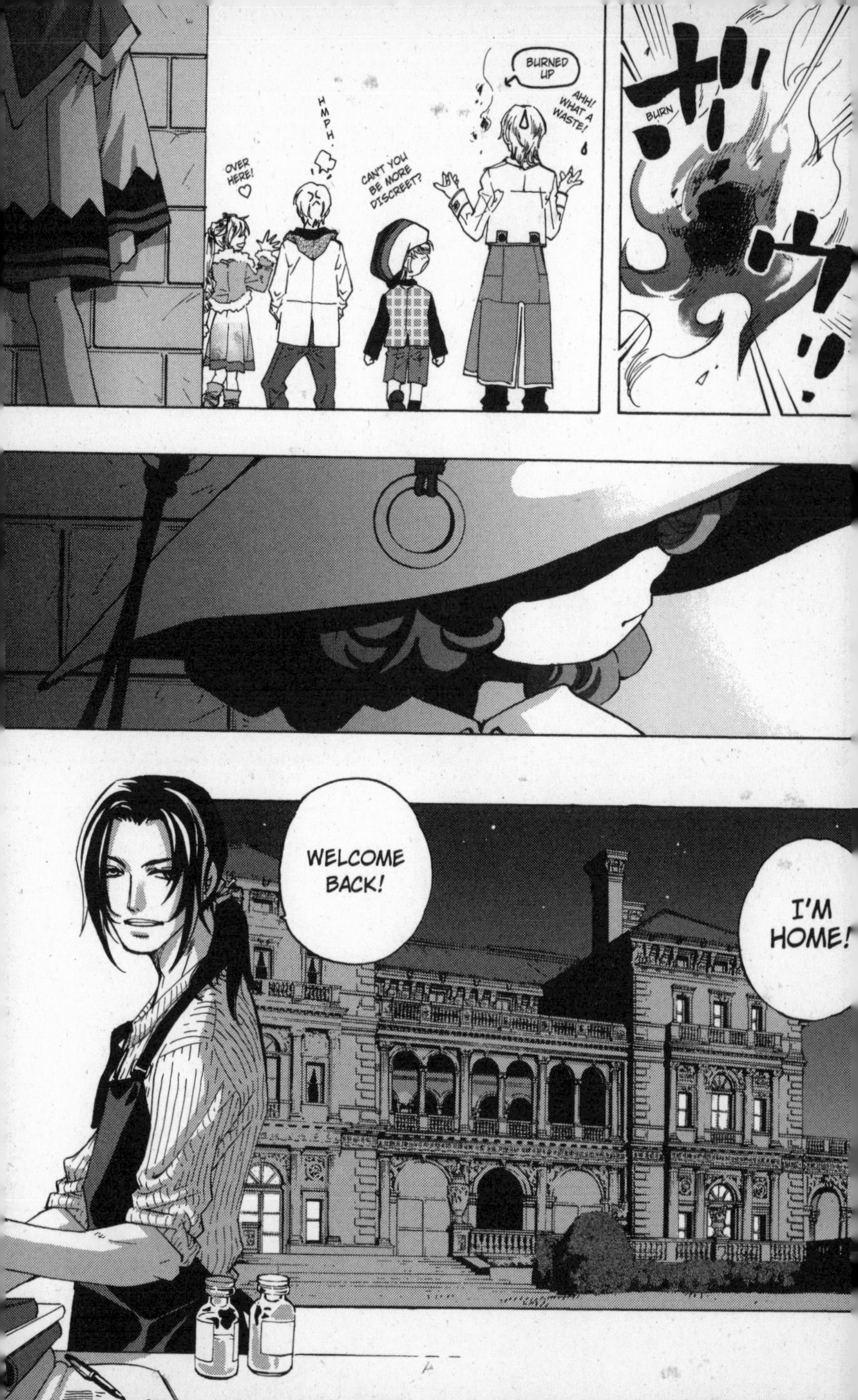
BURN
BURNED UP
AHH! WHAT A WASTE!
HMPH.
CAN'T YOU BE MORE DISCREET?
OVER HERE!
I'M HOME!
WELCOME BACK!

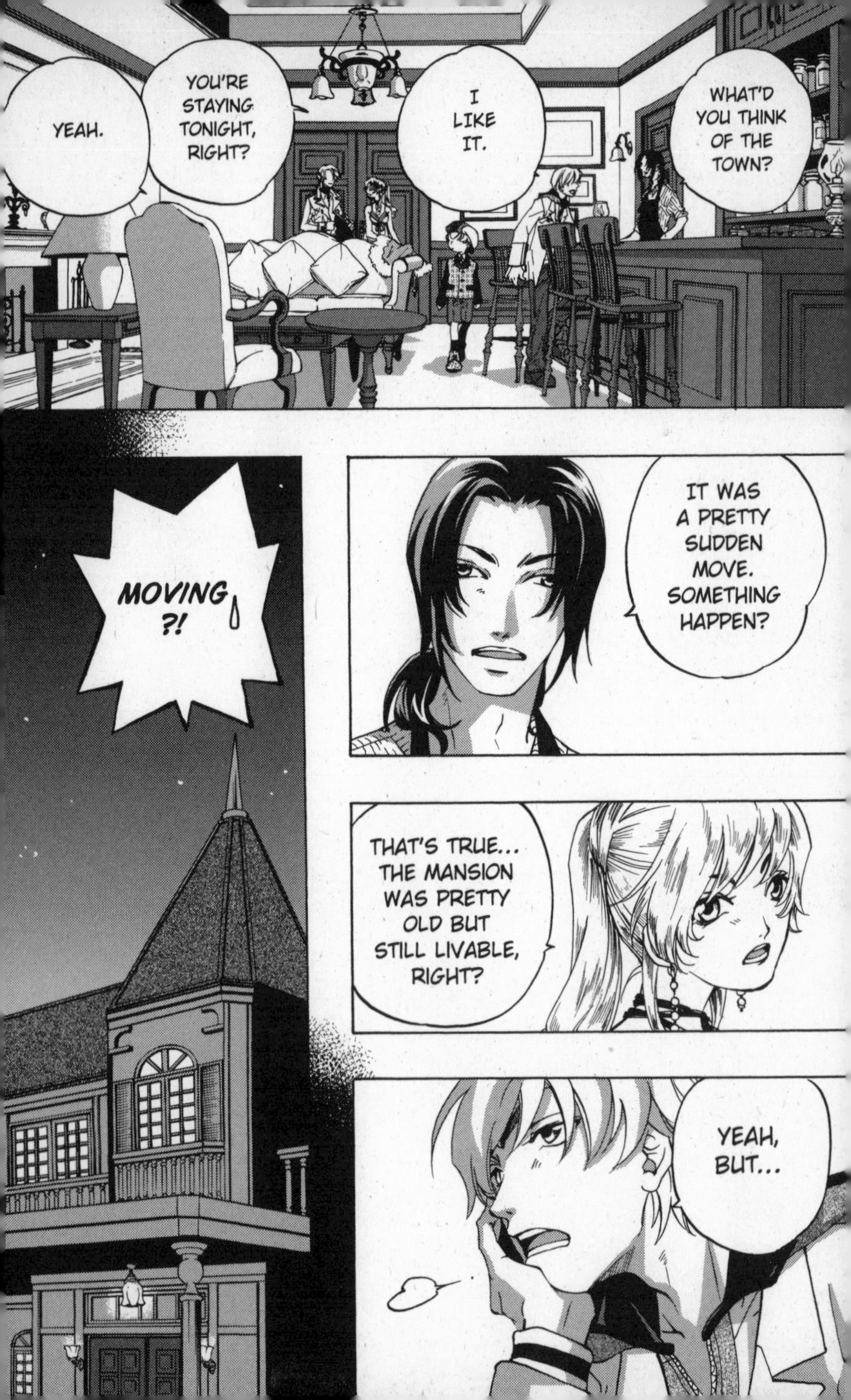
WHAT'D YOU THINK OF THE TOWN?
I LIKE IT.
YOU'RE STAYING TONIGHT, RIGHT?
YEAH.
IT WAS A PRETTY SUDDEN MOVE. SOMETHING HAPPEN?
THAT'S TRUE... THE MANSION WAS PRETTY OLD BUT STILL LIVABLE, RIGHT?
YEAH, BUT...
MOVING ?!

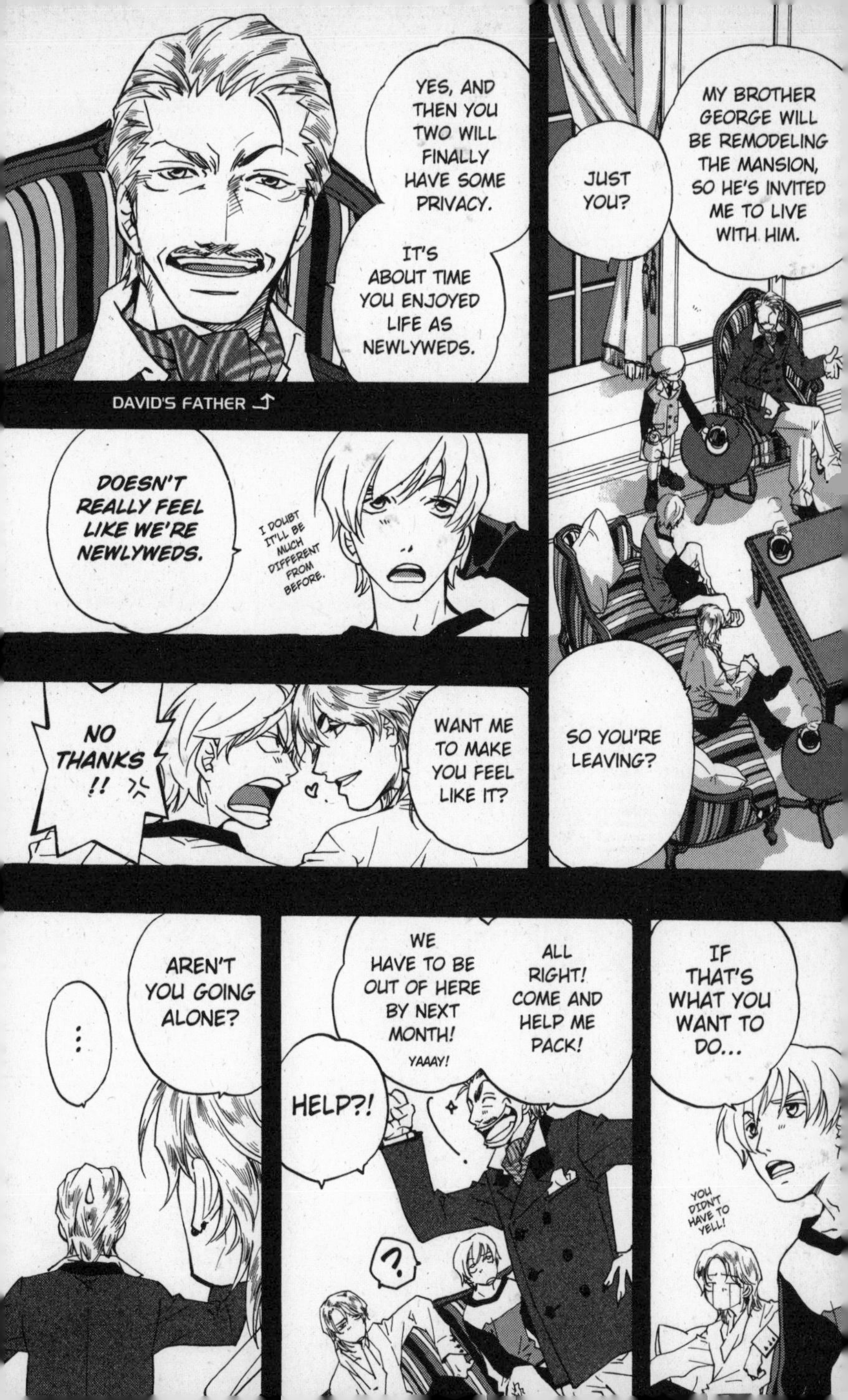
MY BROTHER GEORGE WILL BE REMODELING THE MANSION, SO HE'S INVITED ME TO LIVE WITH HIM.
JUST YOU?
SO YOU'RE LEAVING?
YES, AND THEN YOU TWO WILL FINALLY HAVE SOME PRIVACY.
IT'S ABOUT TIME YOU ENJOYED LIFE AS NEWLYWEDS.
DAVID'S FATHER
I DOUBT IT'LL BE MUCH DIFFERENT FROM BEFORE.
DOESN'T REALLY FEEL LIKE WE'RE NEWLYWEDS.
WANT ME TO MAKE YOU FEEL LIKE IT?
NO THANKS!!
IF THAT'S WHAT YOU WANT TO DO...
YOU DIDN'T HAVE TO YELL!
ALL RIGHT! COME AND HELP ME PACK!
WE HAVE TO BE OUT OF HERE BY NEXT MONTH!
YAAAY!
HELP?!
?
AREN'T YOU GOING ALONE?
...

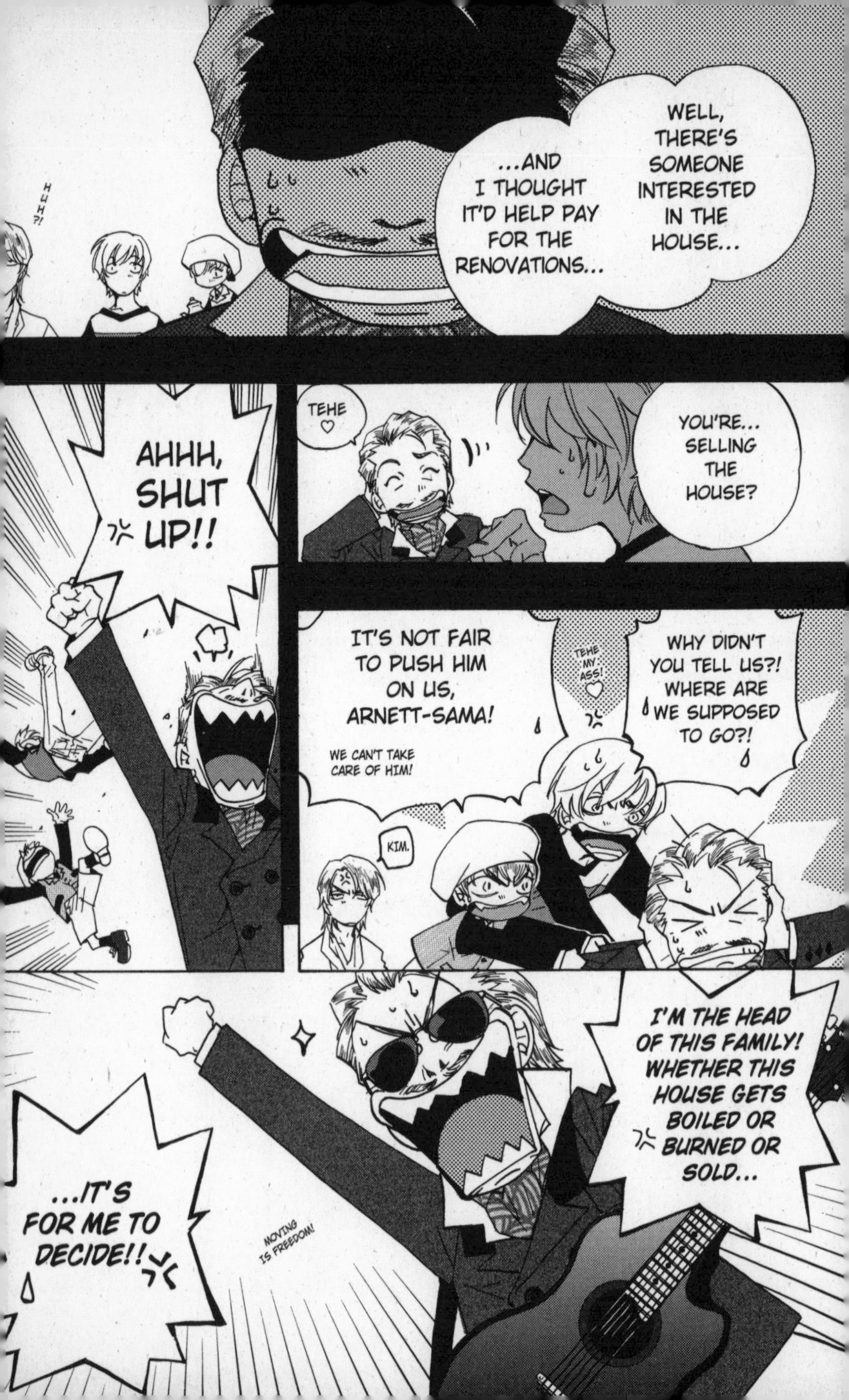

WELL, THERE'S SOMEONE INTERESTED IN THE HOUSE...
...AND I THOUGHT IT'D HELP PAY FOR THE RENOVATIONS...
HUH?!
YOU'RE... SELLING THE HOUSE?
TEHE ♡
WHY DIDN'T YOU TELL US?! WHERE ARE WE SUPPOSED TO GO?!
TEHE MY ASS! ♡
IT'S NOT FAIR TO PUSH HIM ON US, ARNETT-SAMA!
WE CAN'T TAKE CARE OF HIM!
KIM.
AHHH, SHUT UP!!
I'M THE HEAD OF THIS FAMILY! WHETHER THIS HOUSE GETS BOILED OR BURNED OR SOLD...
MOVING IS FREEDOM!
...IT'S FOR ME TO DECIDE!!

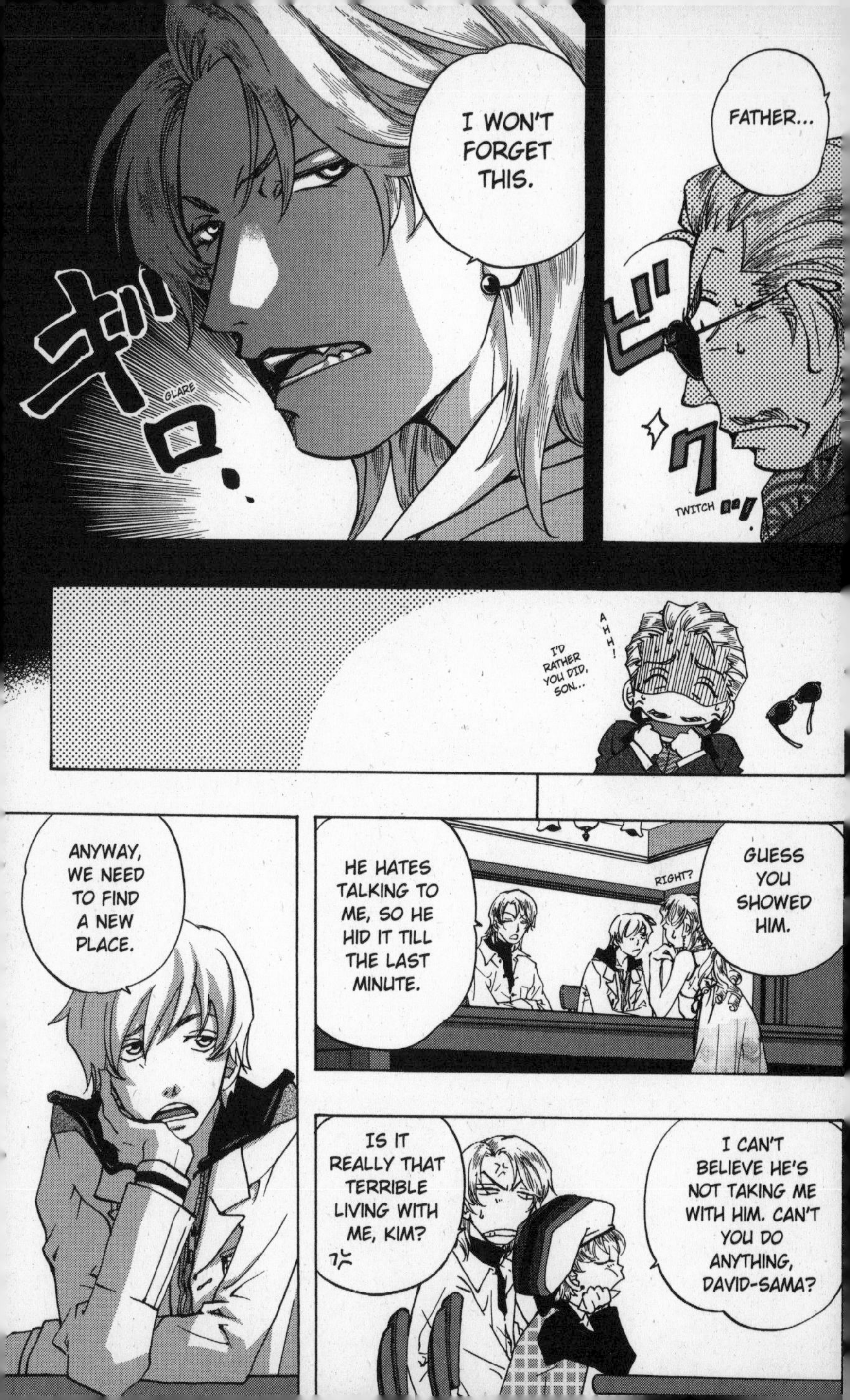
FATHER...
TWITCH
I WON'T FORGET THIS.
GLARE
I'D RATHER YOU DID, SON...
AHH!
GUESS YOU SHOWED HIM.
RIGHT?
HE HATES TALKING TO ME, SO HE HID IT TILL THE LAST MINUTE.
I CAN'T BELIEVE HE'S NOT TAKING ME WITH HIM. CAN'T YOU DO ANYTHING, DAVID-SAMA?
IS IT REALLY THAT TERRIBLE LIVING WITH ME, KIM?
ANYWAY, WE NEED TO FIND A NEW PLACE.

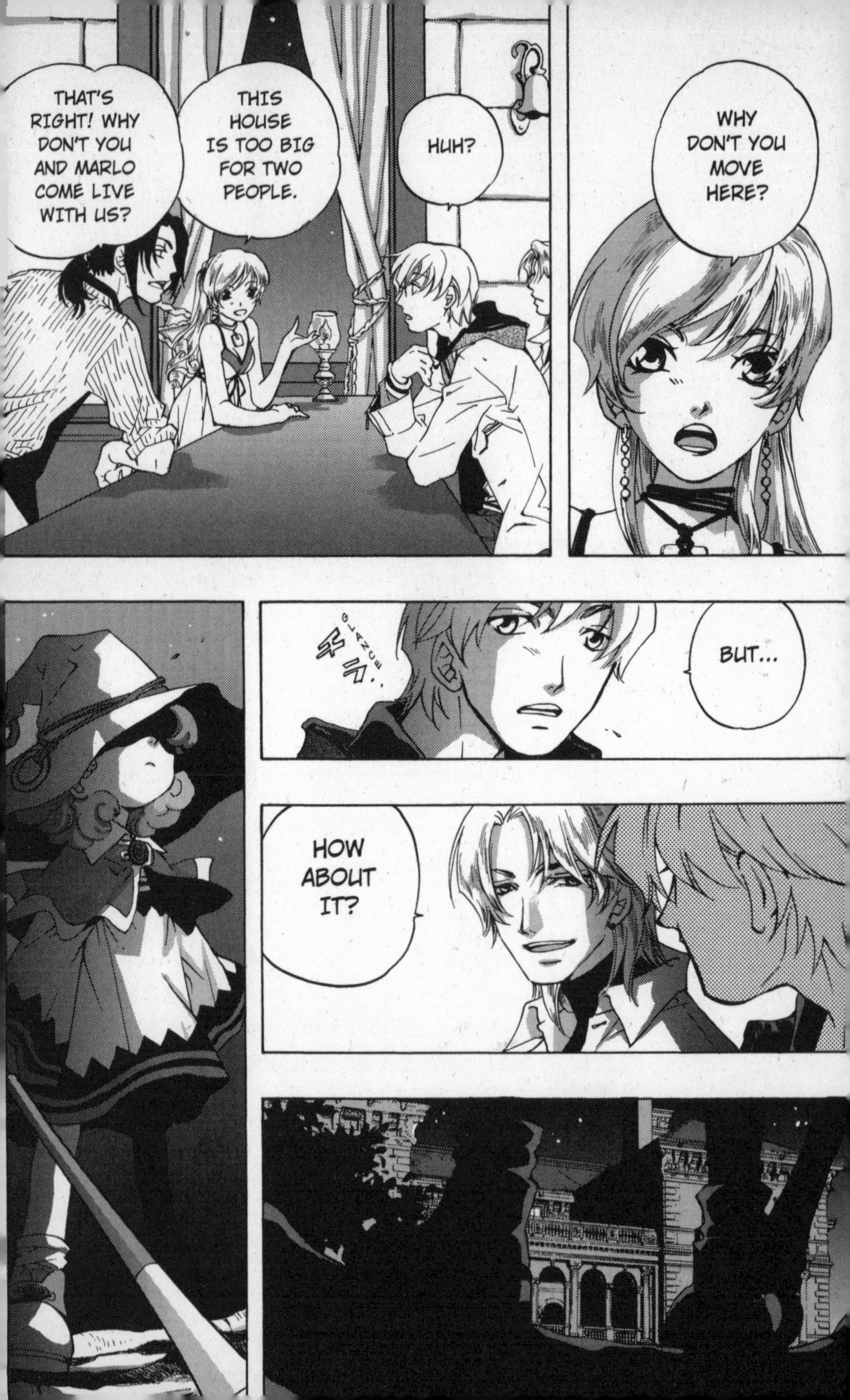
WHY DON'T YOU MOVE HERE?
HUH?
THIS HOUSE IS TOO BIG FOR TWO PEOPLE.
THAT'S RIGHT! WHY DON'T YOU AND MARLO COME LIVE WITH US?
BUT...
GLANCE
HOW ABOUT IT?

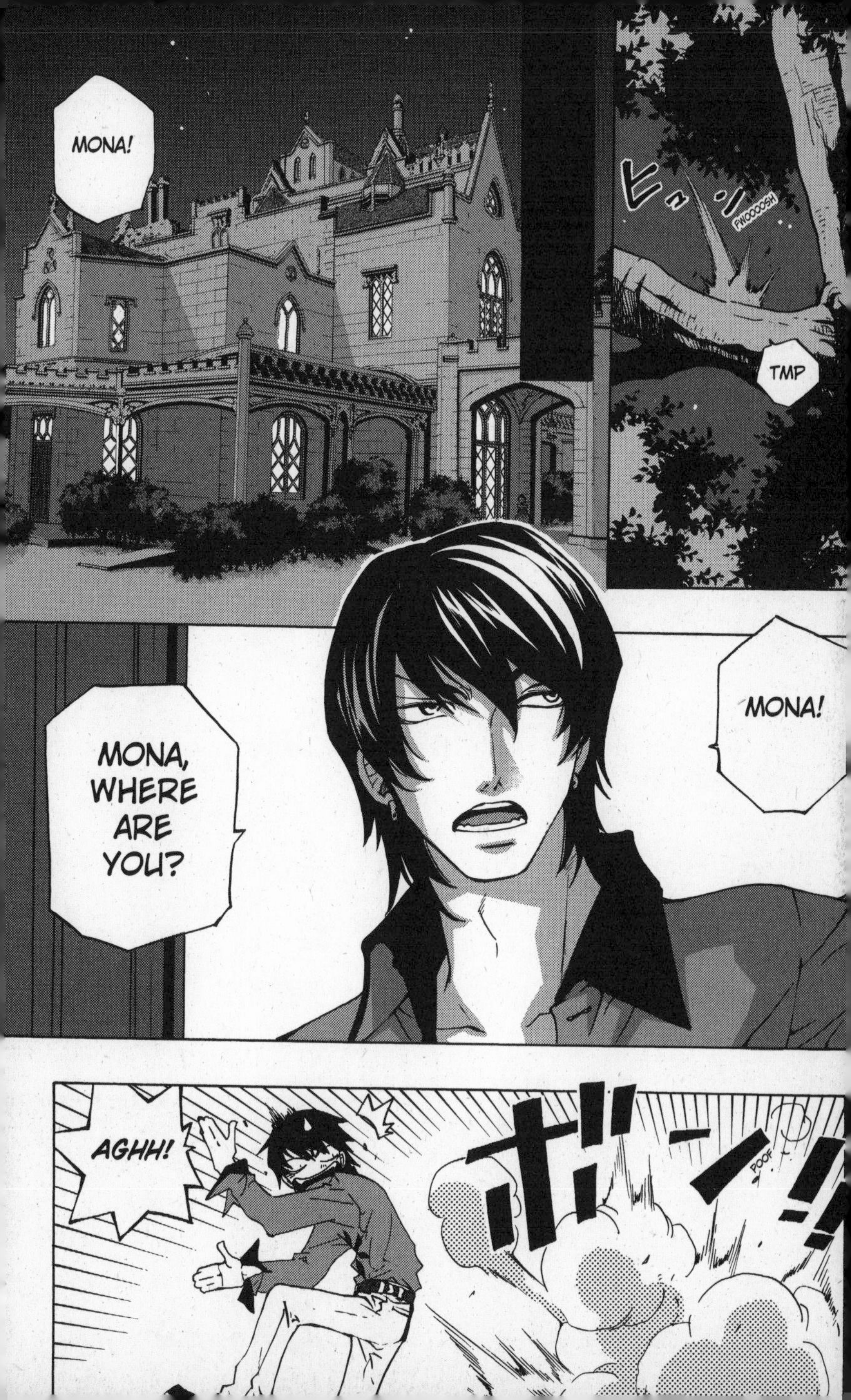

ヒュン
PWOOOOSH
TMP
MONA!
MONA!
MONA, WHERE ARE YOU?
ボーン!!
POOF
AGHH!

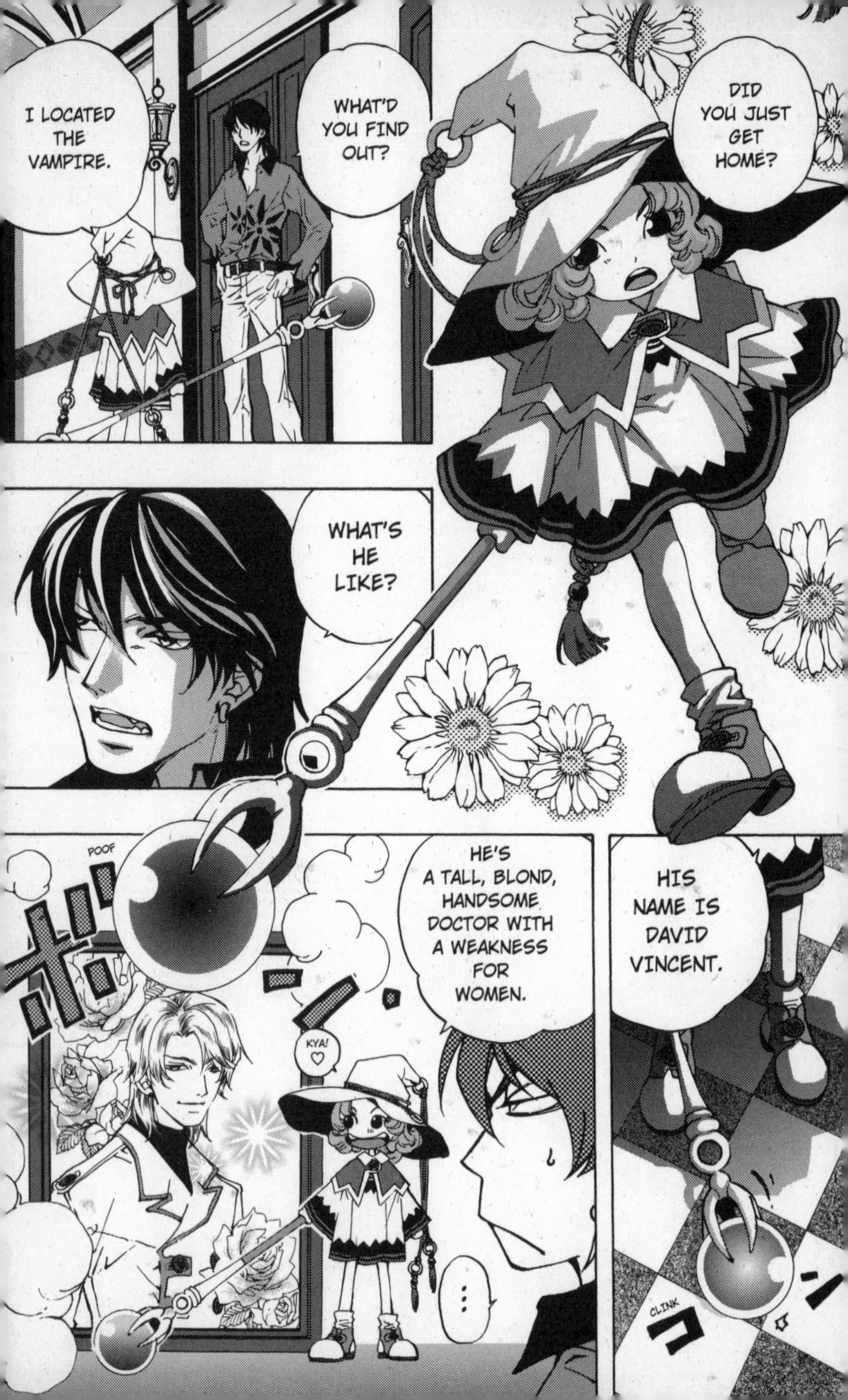
DID YOU JUST GET HOME?
WHAT'D YOU FIND OUT?
I LOCATED THE VAMPIRE.
WHAT'S HE LIKE?
HIS NAME IS DAVID VINCENT.
CLINK
HE'S A TALL, BLOND, HANDSOME DOCTOR WITH A WEAKNESS FOR WOMEN.
POOF
KYA! ♡
...

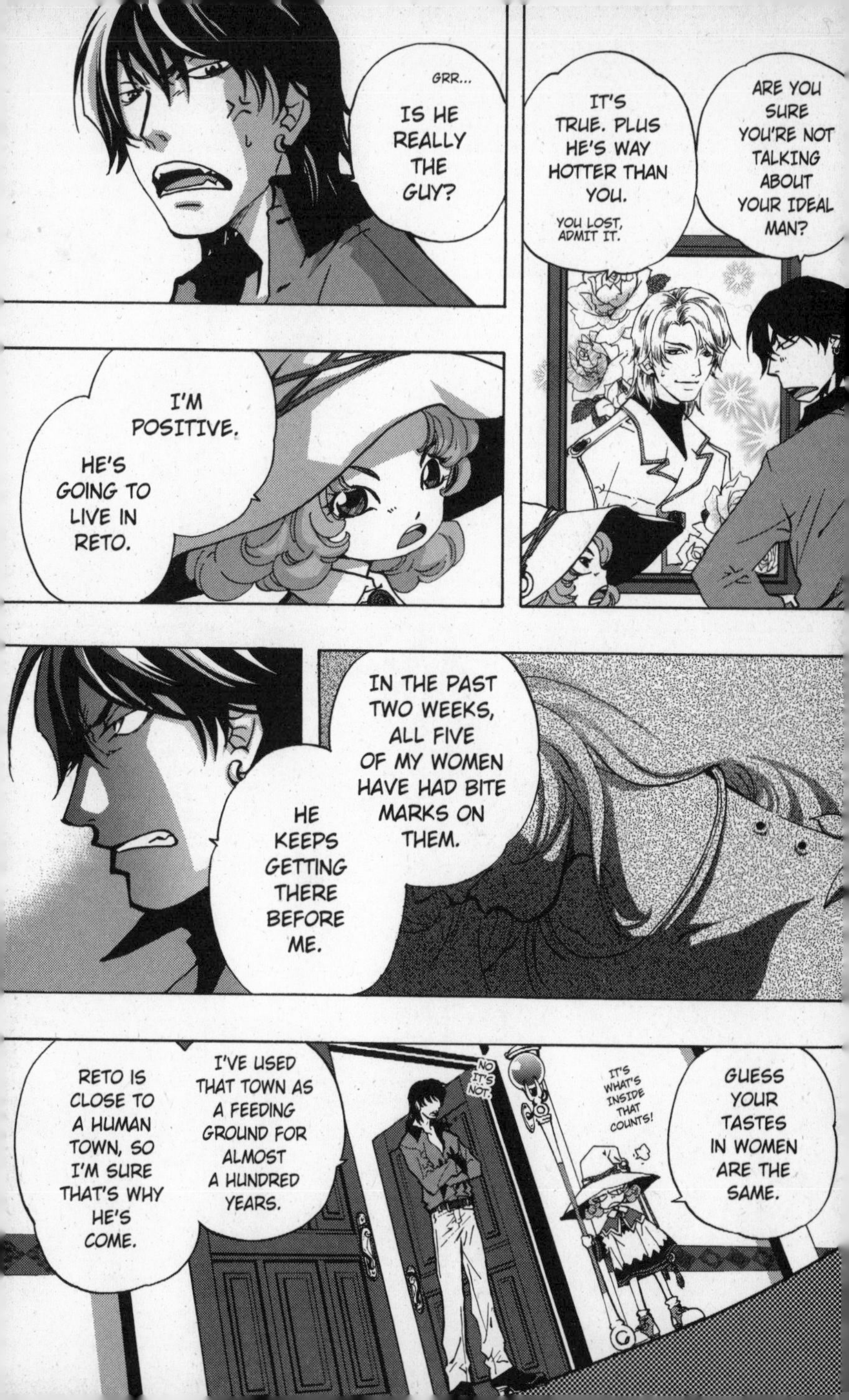
ARE YOU SURE YOU'RE NOT TALKING ABOUT YOUR IDEAL MAN?
IT'S TRUE. PLUS HE'S WAY HOTTER THAN YOU.
YOU LOST, ADMIT IT.
GRR...
IS HE REALLY THE GUY?
I'M POSITIVE.
HE'S GOING TO LIVE IN RETO.
IN THE PAST TWO WEEKS, ALL FIVE OF MY WOMEN HAVE HAD BITE MARKS ON THEM.
HE KEEPS GETTING THERE BEFORE ME.
GUESS YOUR TASTES IN WOMEN ARE THE SAME.
IT'S WHAT'S INSIDE THAT COUNTS!
NO IT'S NOT.
I'VE USED THAT TOWN AS A FEEDING GROUND FOR ALMOST A HUNDRED YEARS.
RETO IS CLOSE TO A HUMAN TOWN, SO I'M SURE THAT'S WHY HE'S COME.

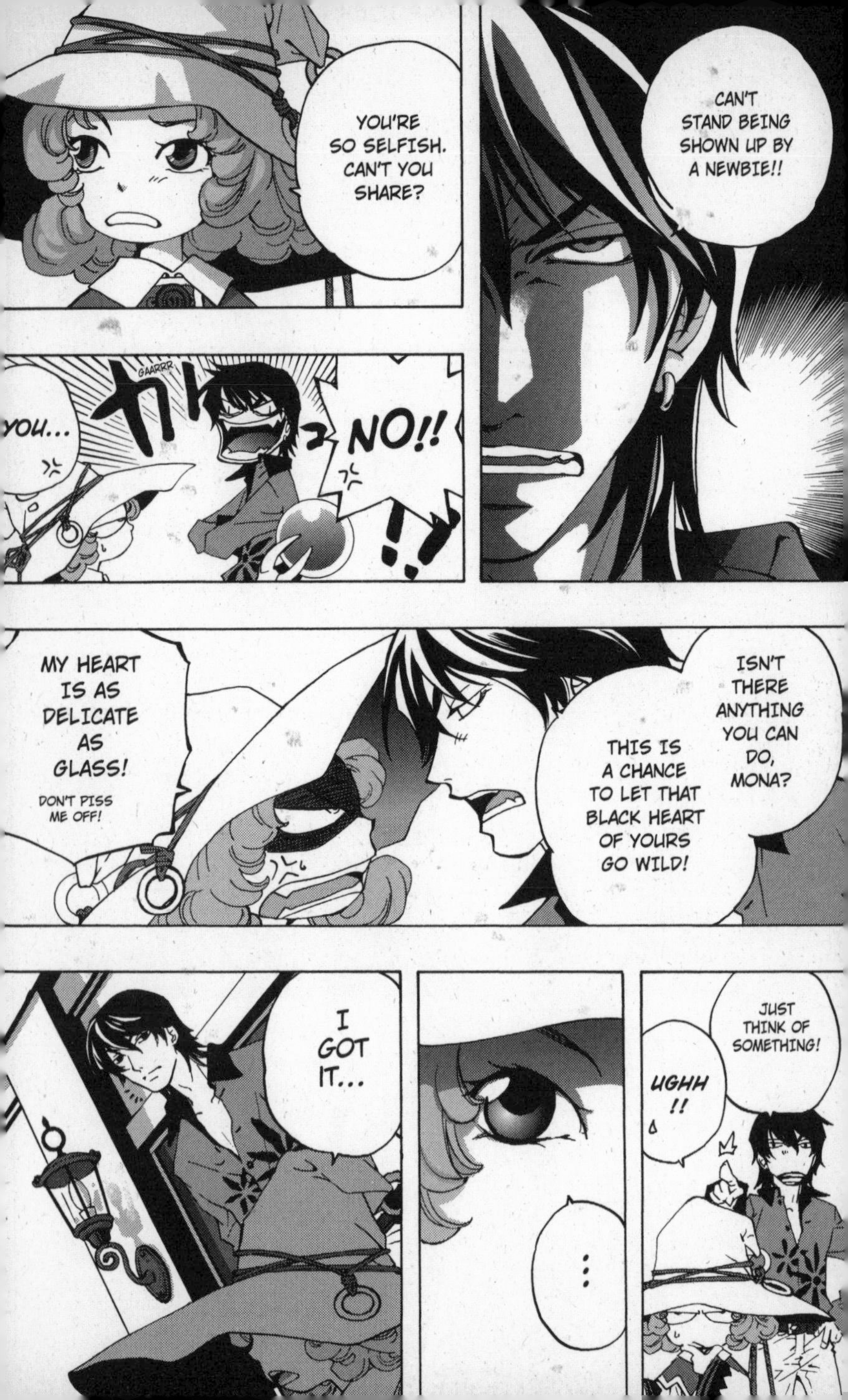
CAN'T STAND BEING SHOWN UP BY A NEWBIE!!
YOU'RE SO SELFISH. CAN'T YOU SHARE?
NO!!
GAARRR
YOU...
ISN'T THERE ANYTHING YOU CAN DO, MONA?
THIS IS A CHANCE TO LET THAT BLACK HEART OF YOURS GO WILD!
MY HEART IS AS DELICATE AS GLASS!
DON'T PISS ME OFF!
JUST THINK OF SOMETHING!
UGHH!!
...
I GOT IT...

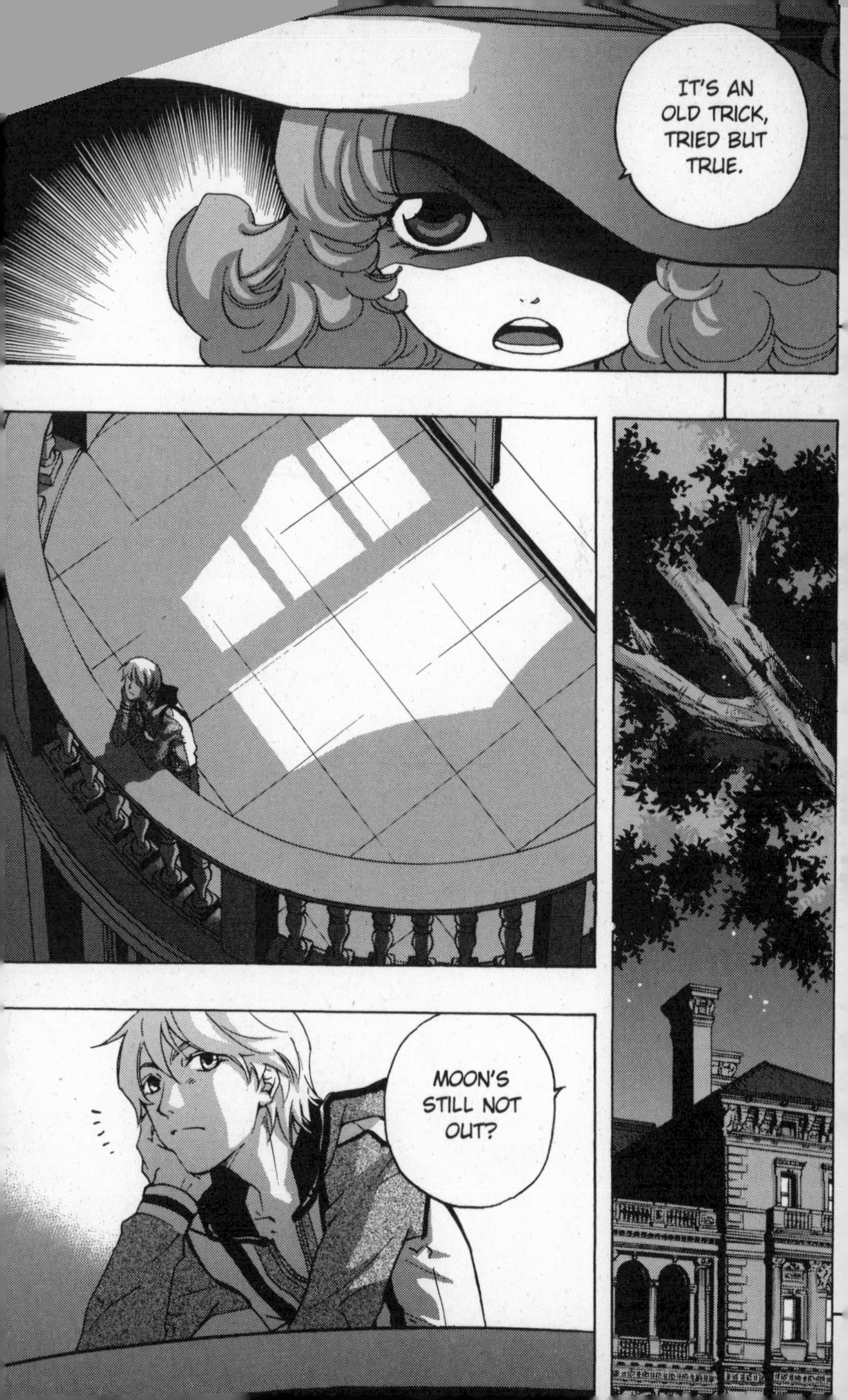
IT'S AN OLD TRICK, TRIED BUT TRUE.
MOON'S STILL NOT OUT?

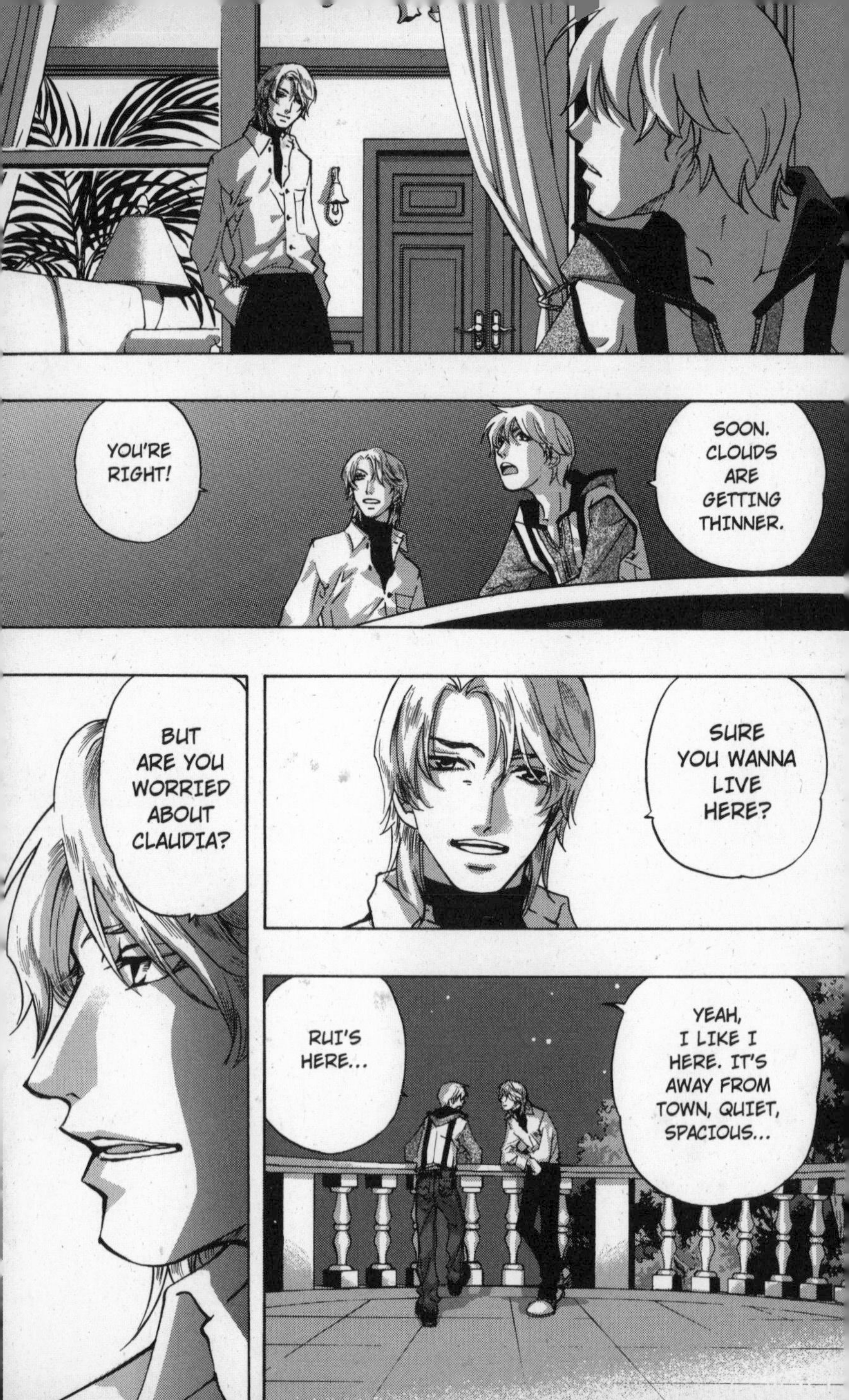
SOON. CLOUDS ARE GETTING THINNER.
YOU'RE RIGHT!
SURE YOU WANNA LIVE HERE?
YEAH, I LIKE I HERE. IT'S AWAY FROM TOWN, QUIET, SPACIOUS...
RUI'S HERE...
BUT ARE YOU WORRIED ABOUT CLAUDIA?

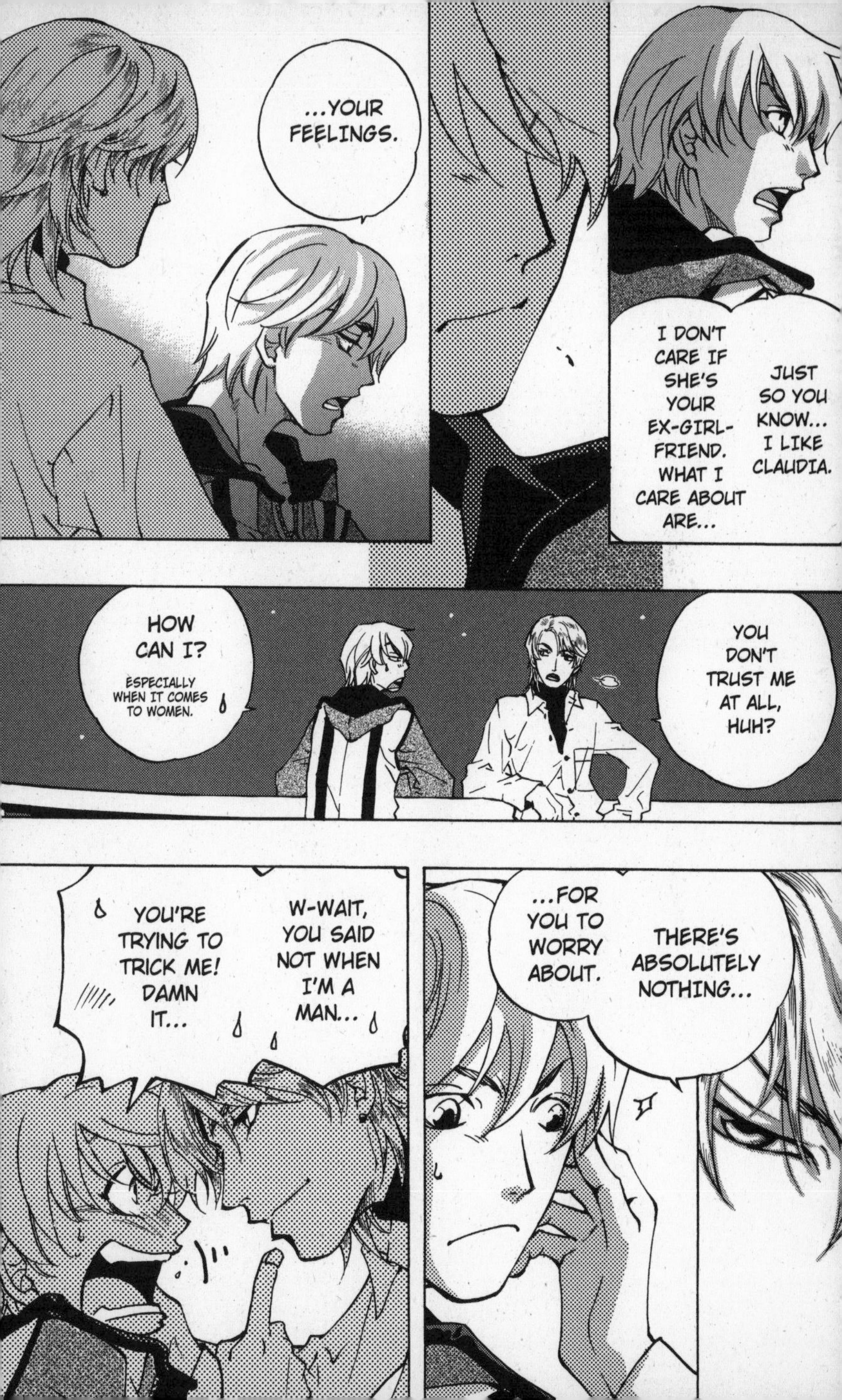
JUST SO YOU KNOW... I LIKE CLAUDIA.
I DON'T CARE IF SHE'S YOUR EX-GIRL-FRIEND. WHAT I CARE ABOUT ARE...
...YOUR FEELINGS.
YOU DON'T TRUST ME AT ALL, HUH?
HOW CAN I?
ESPECIALLY WHEN IT COMES TO WOMEN.
THERE'S ABSOLUTELY NOTHING...
...FOR YOU TO WORRY ABOUT.
W-WAIT, YOU SAID NOT WHEN I'M A MAN...
YOU'RE TRYING TO TRICK ME! DAMN IT...

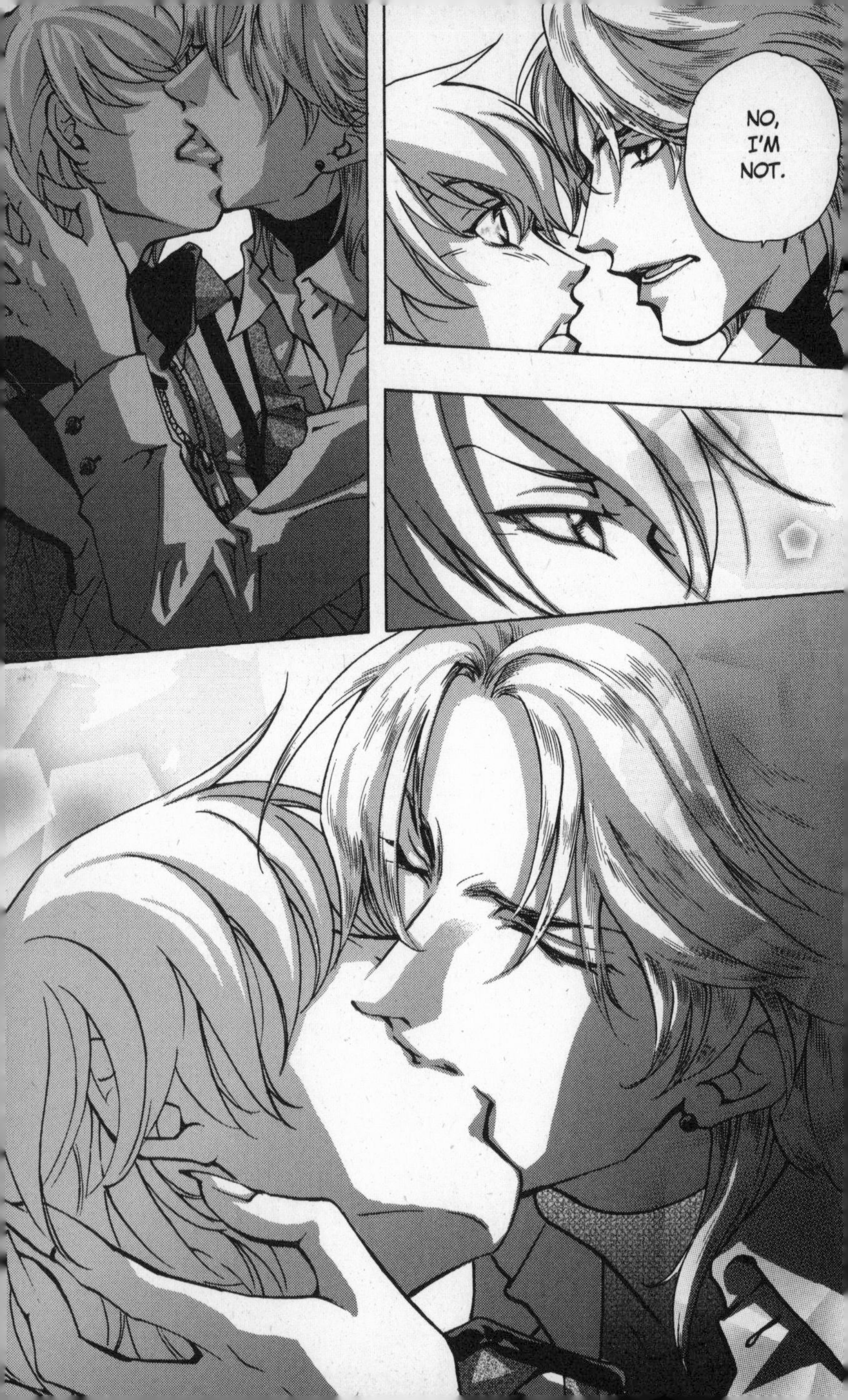
NO, I'M NOT.

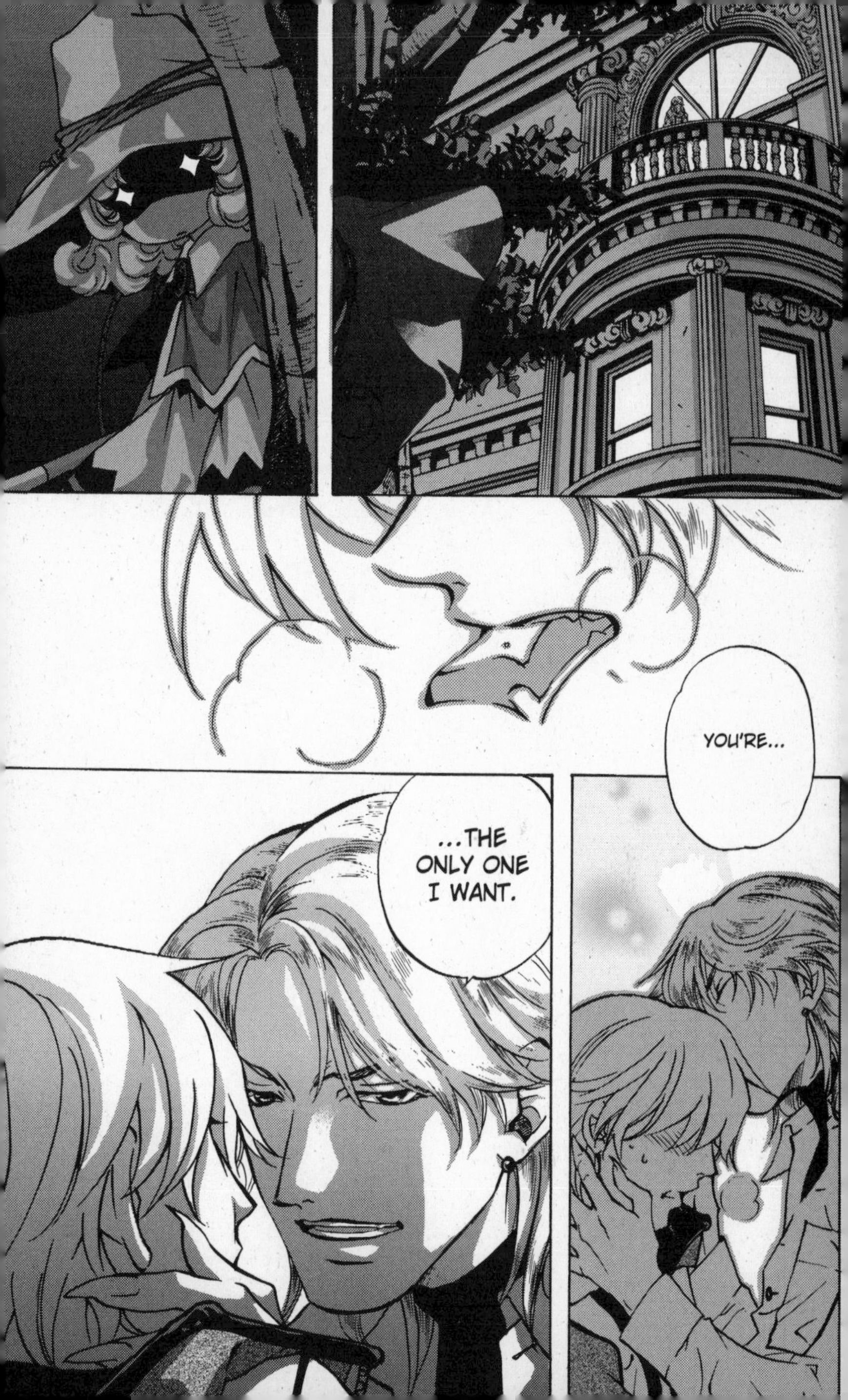
YOU'RE...
...THE ONLY ONE I WANT.

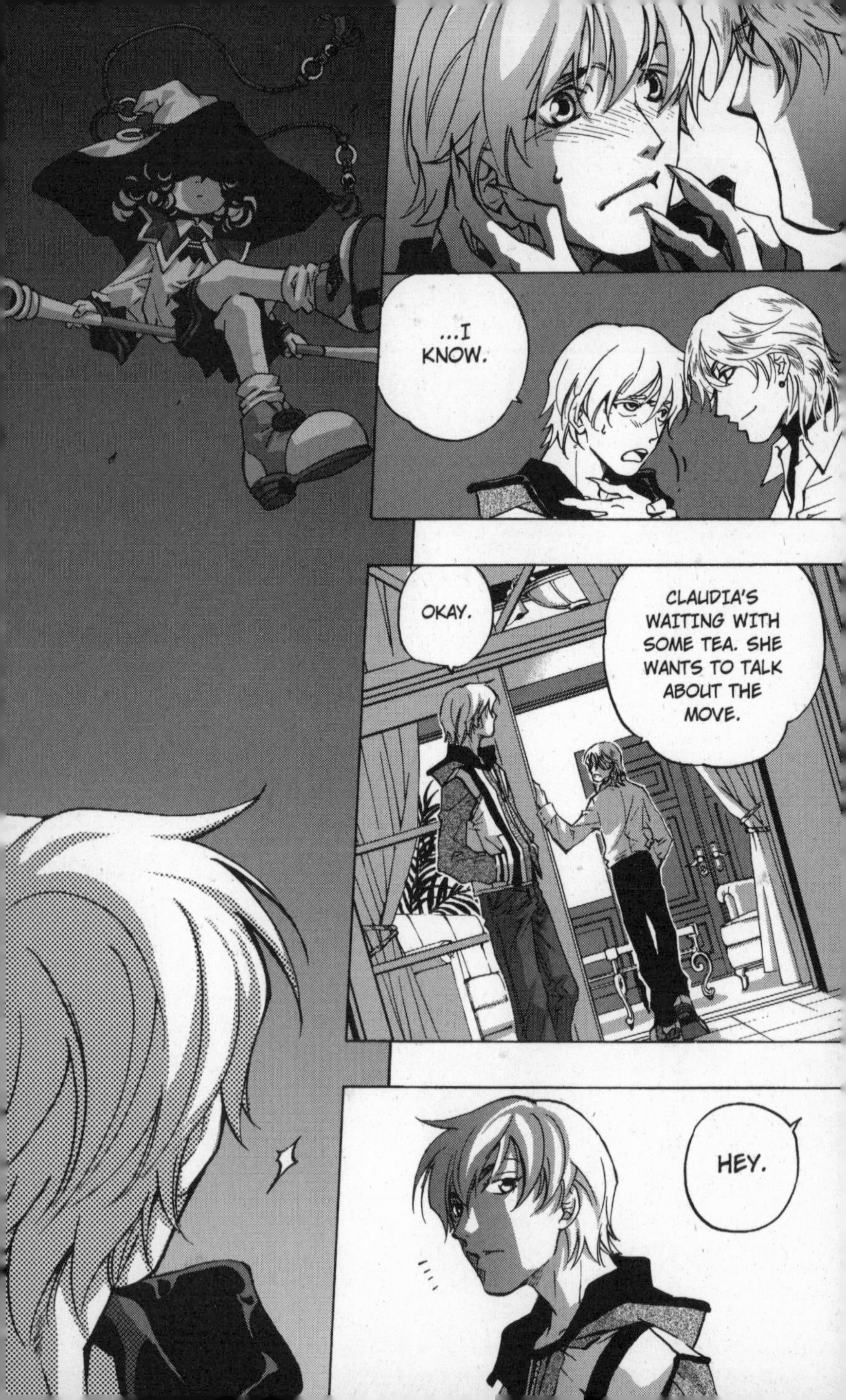
...I KNOW.
CLAUDIA'S WAITING WITH SOME TEA. SHE WANTS TO TALK ABOUT THE MOVE.
OKAY.
HEY.

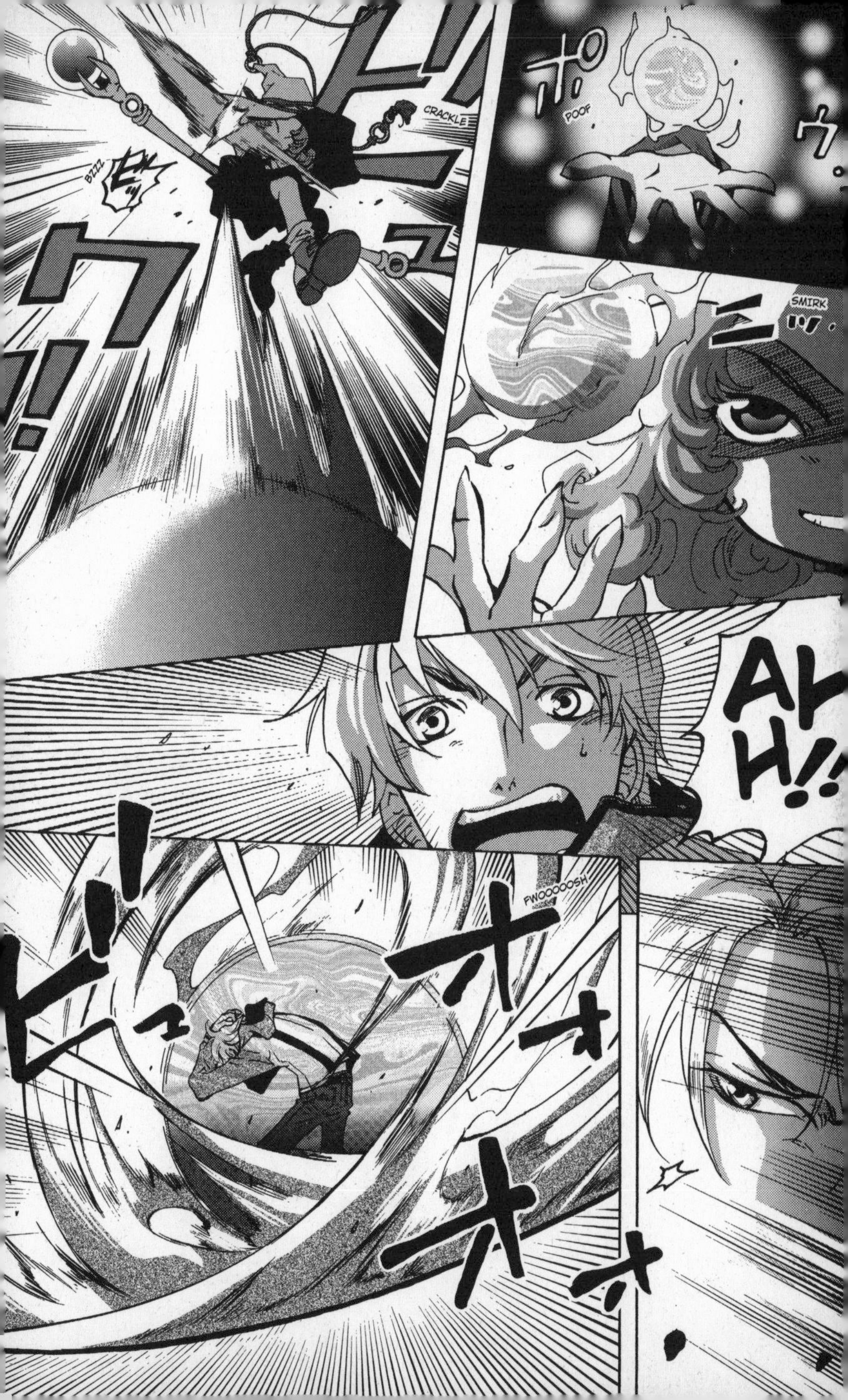
POOF
SMIRK
CRACKLE
BZZZ
AH!!
FWOOOOOSH

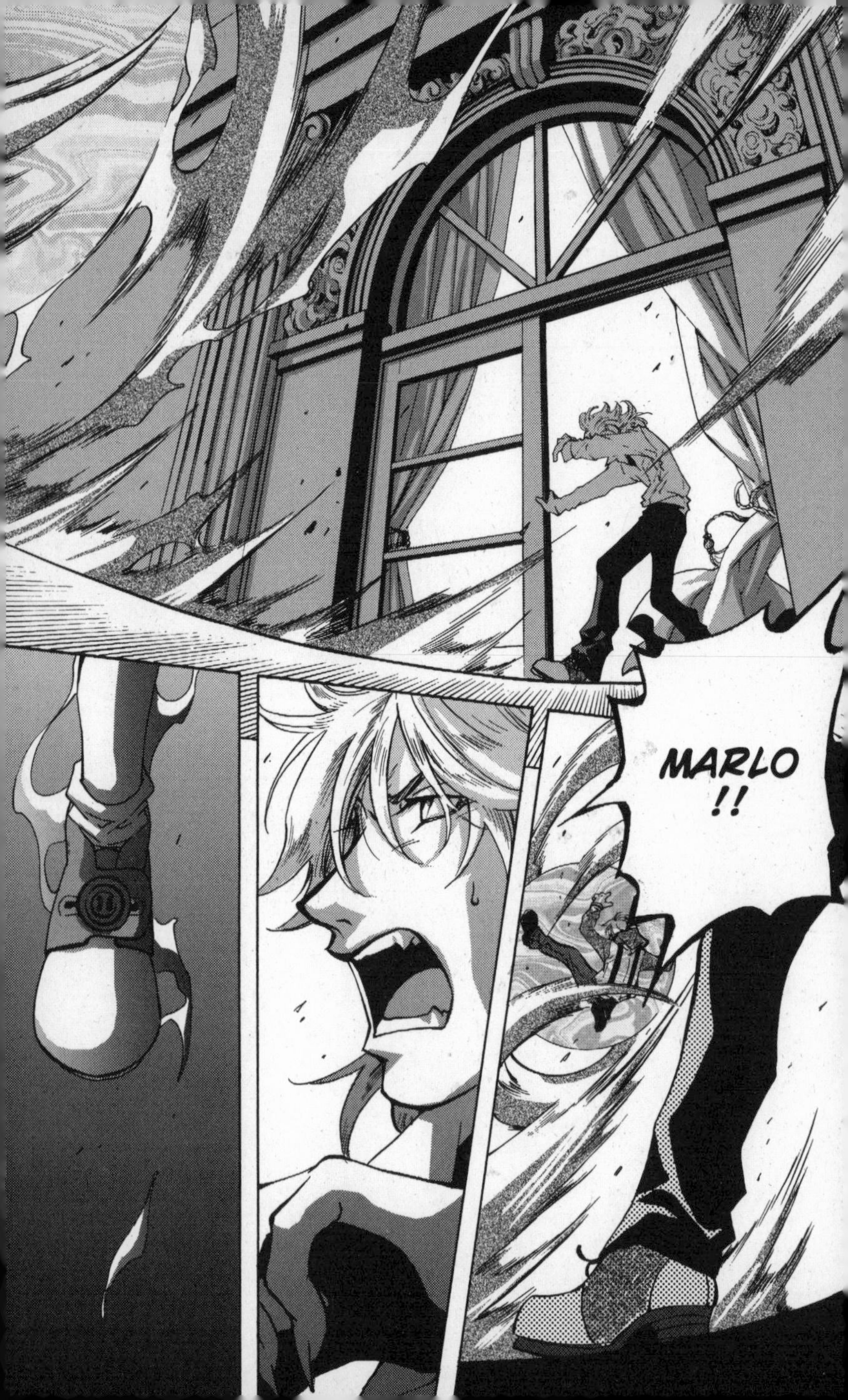
MARLO !!

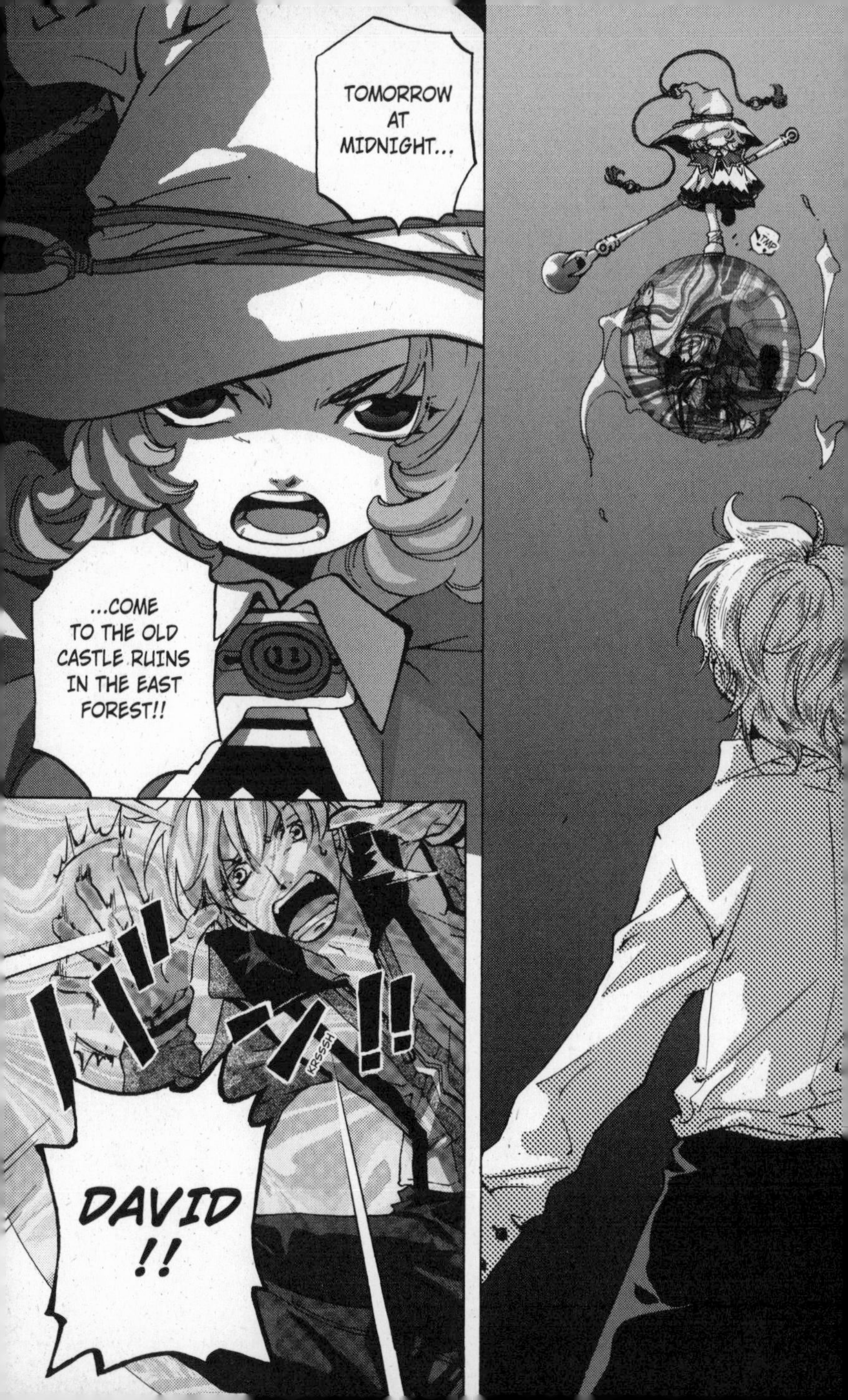
TMP
TOMORROW AT MIDNIGHT...
...COME TO THE OLD CASTLE RUINS IN THE EAST FOREST!!
KRSSSH
DAVID !!

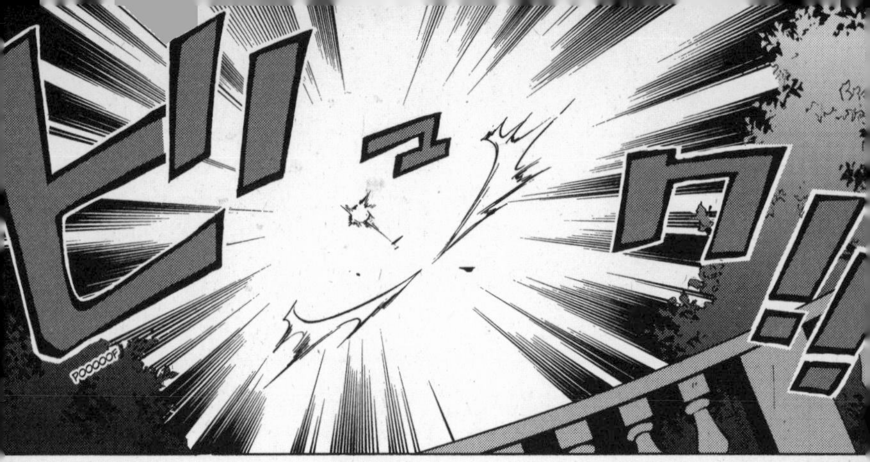
ビューウ!!
POOOOOF

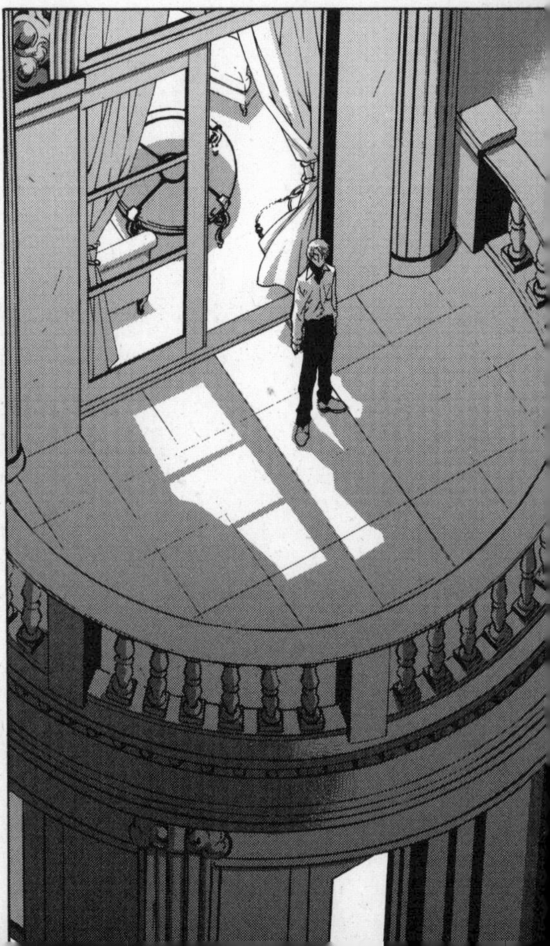

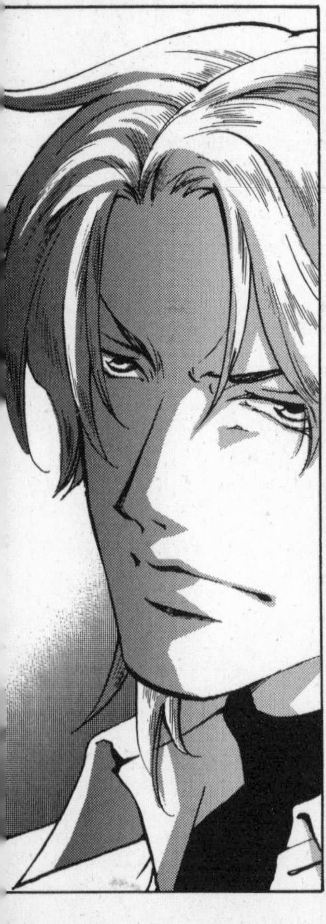

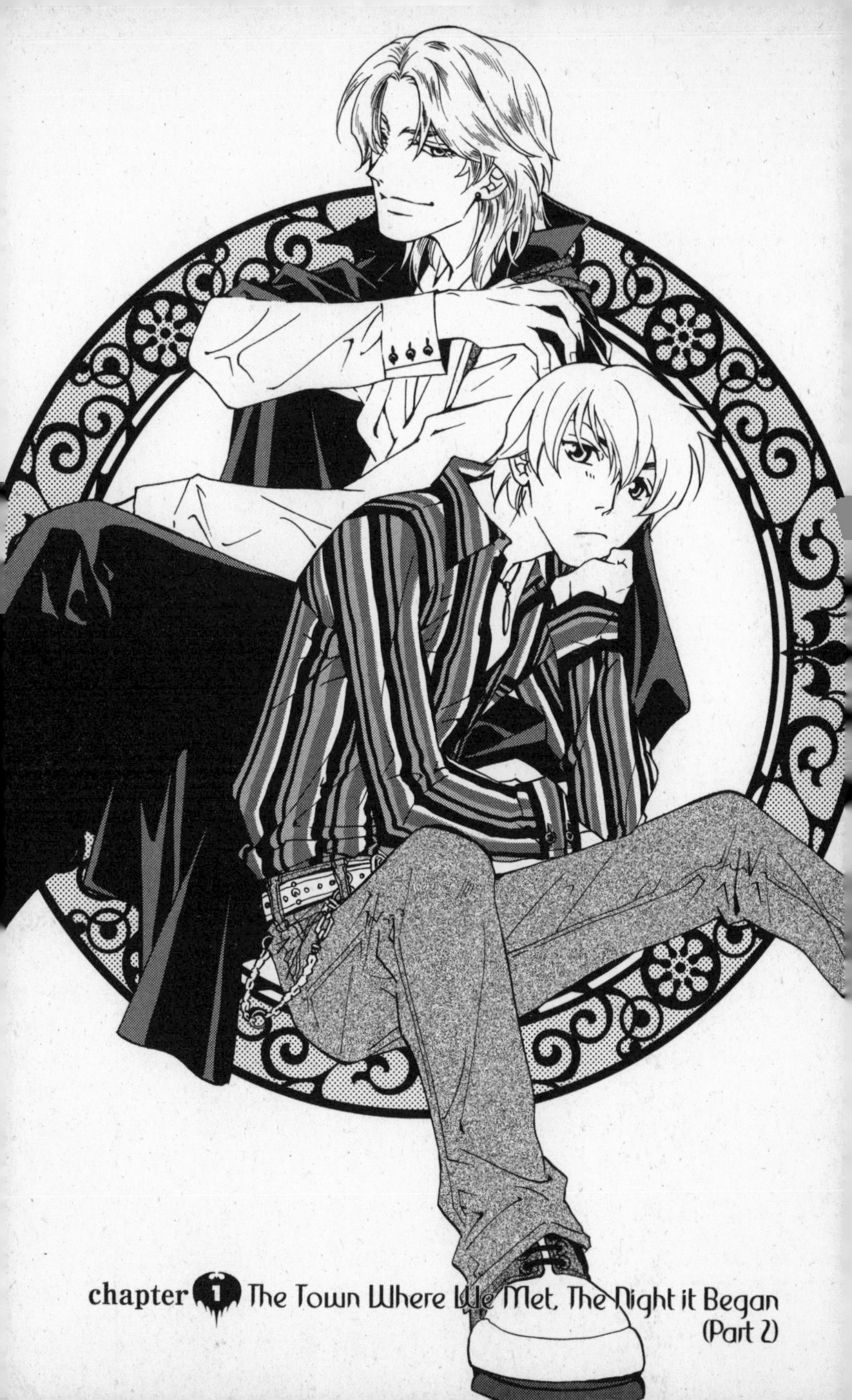

chapter 1 The Town Where We Met, The Night it Began (Part 2)

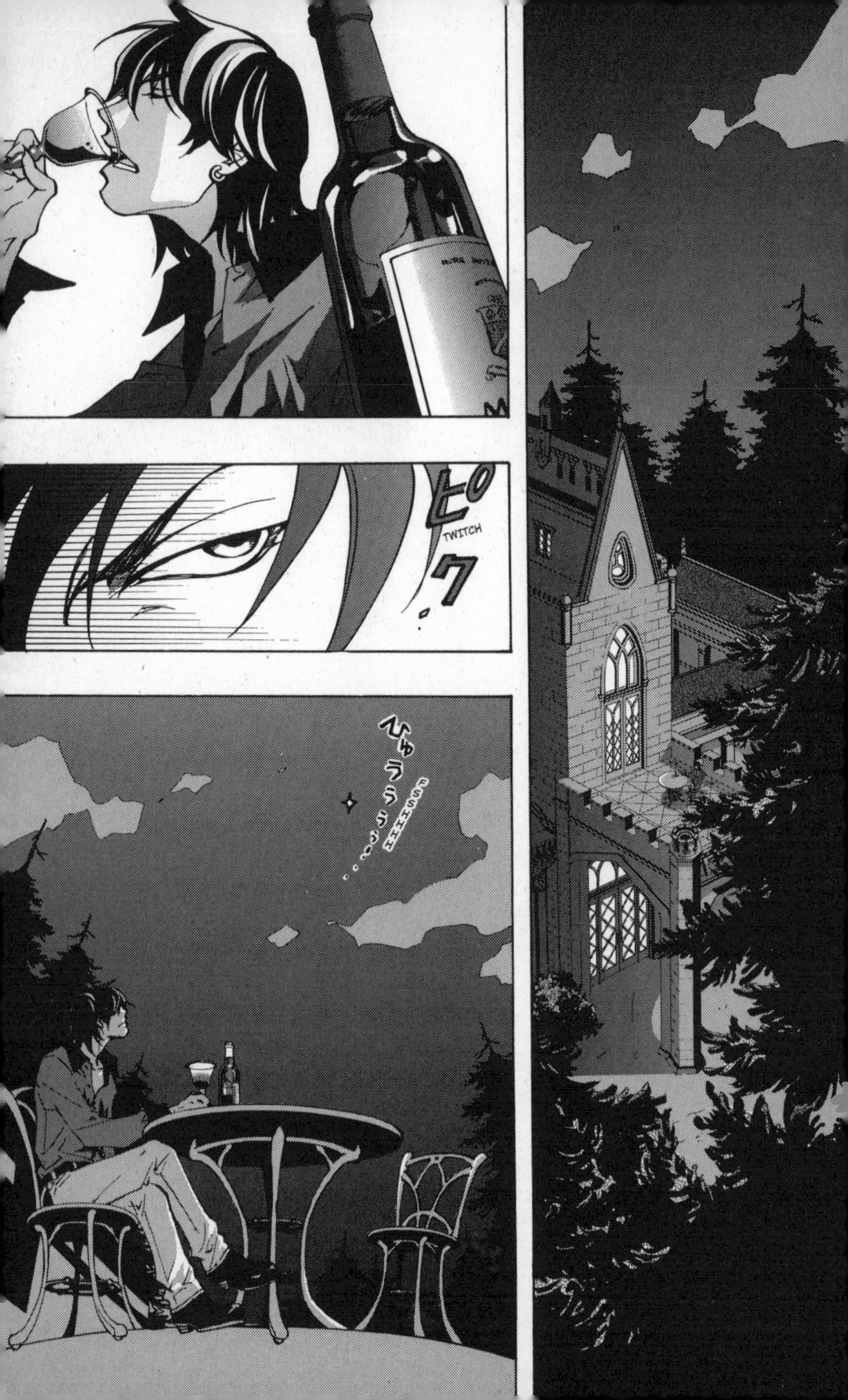
ピク
TWITCH
ひゅううう……
FSSHHHH

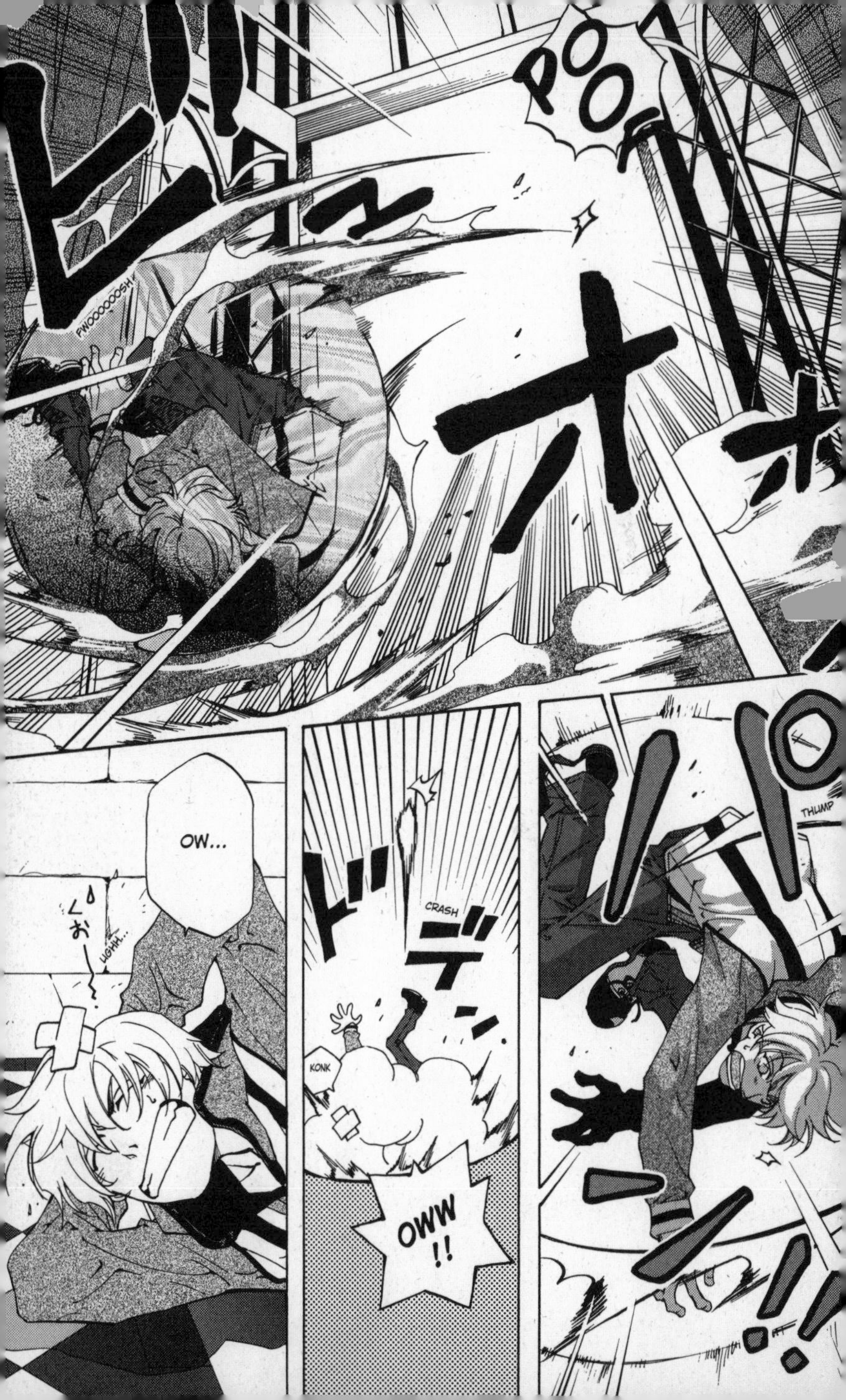
POOF
PWOOOOOOSH
THUMP
CRASH
KONK
OWW !!
OW...
UGHH...
くぉ～～

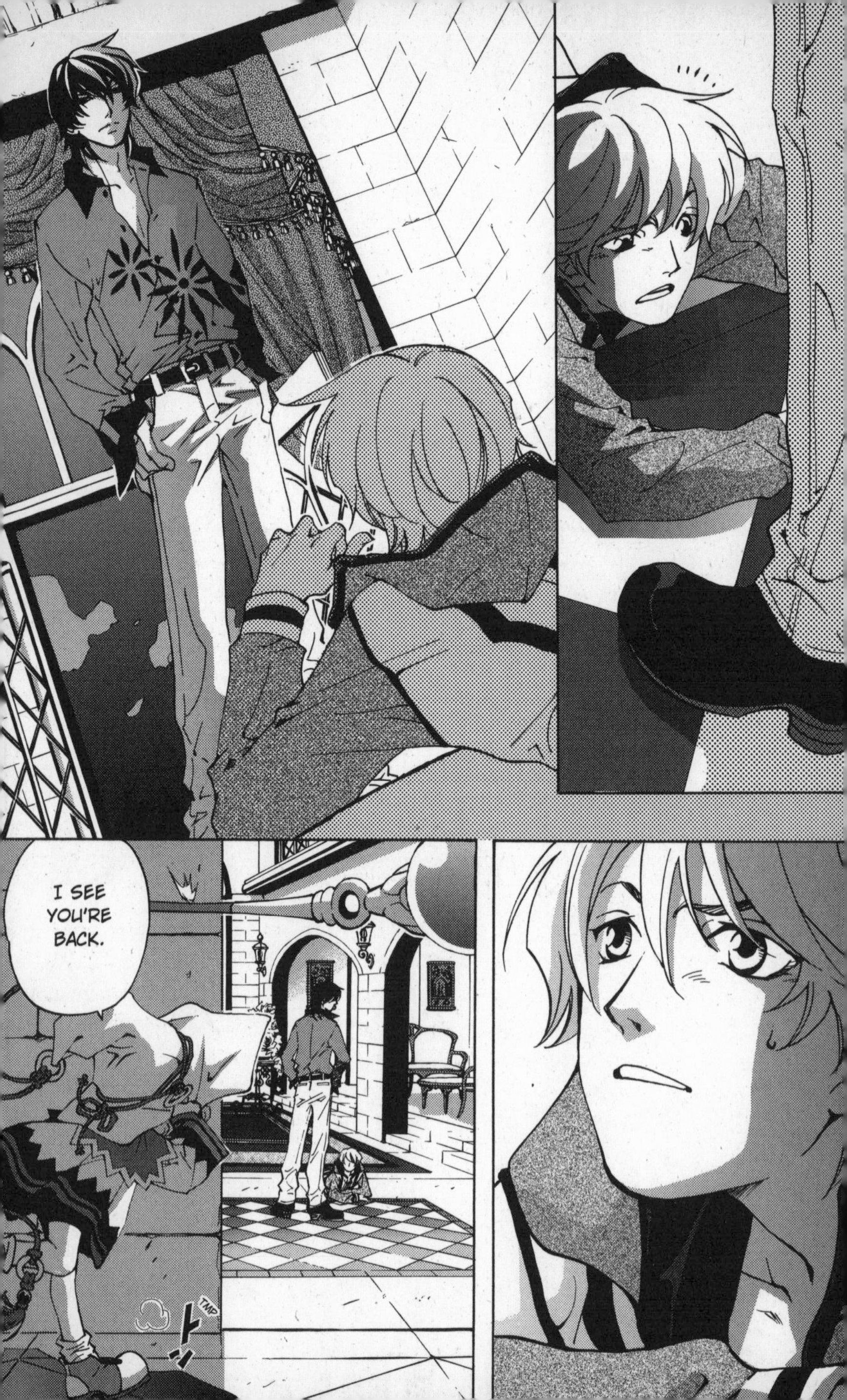
I SEE YOU'RE BACK.
TMP

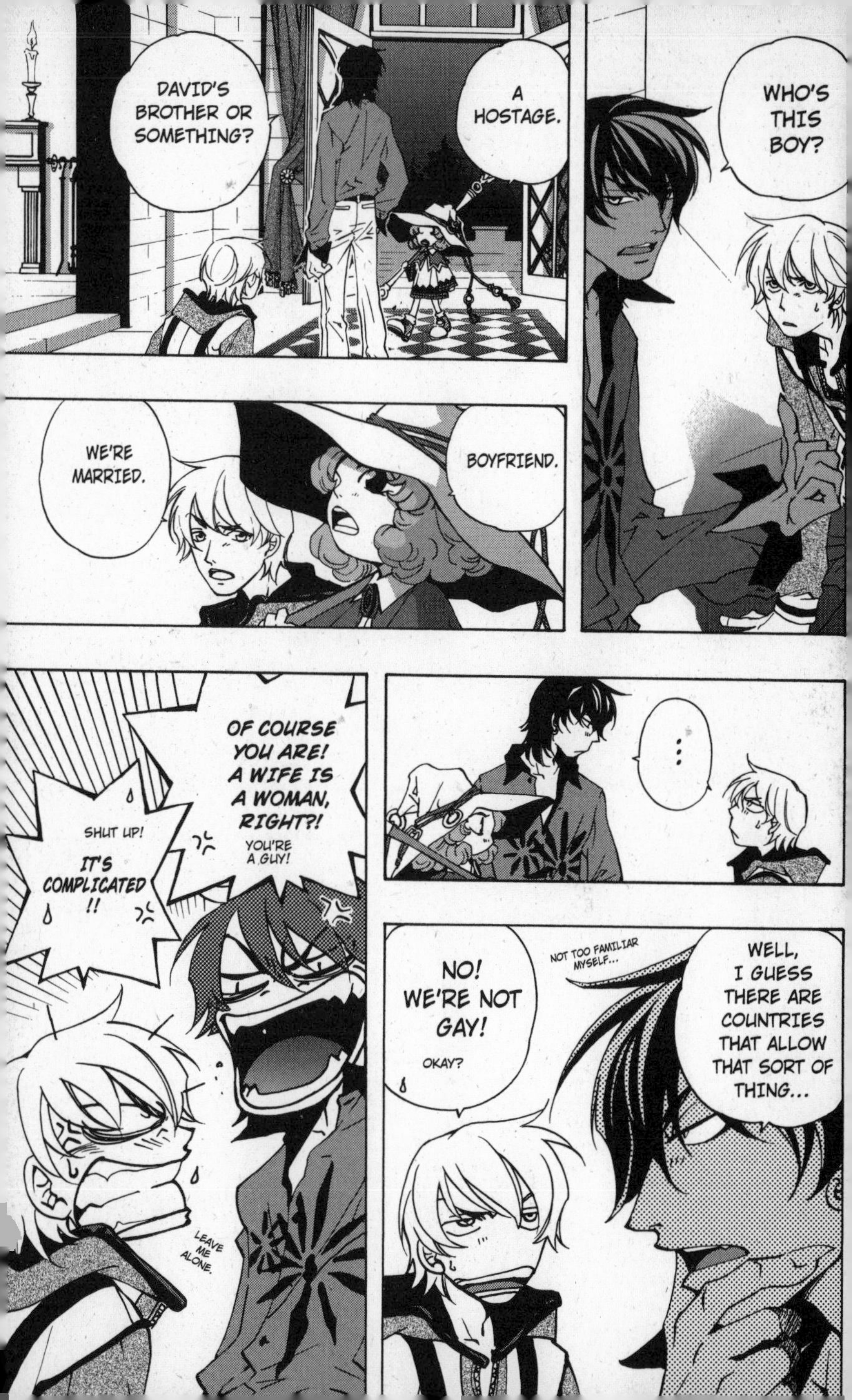
WHO'S THIS BOY?
A HOSTAGE.
DAVID'S BROTHER OR SOMETHING?
BOYFRIEND.
WE'RE MARRIED.
...
WELL, I GUESS THERE ARE COUNTRIES THAT ALLOW THAT SORT OF THING...
NOT TOO FAMILIAR MYSELF...
NO! WE'RE NOT GAY!
OKAY?
OF COURSE YOU ARE! A WIFE IS A WOMAN, RIGHT?!
YOU'RE A GUY!
SHUT UP!
IT'S COMPLICATED!!
LEAVE ME ALONE.

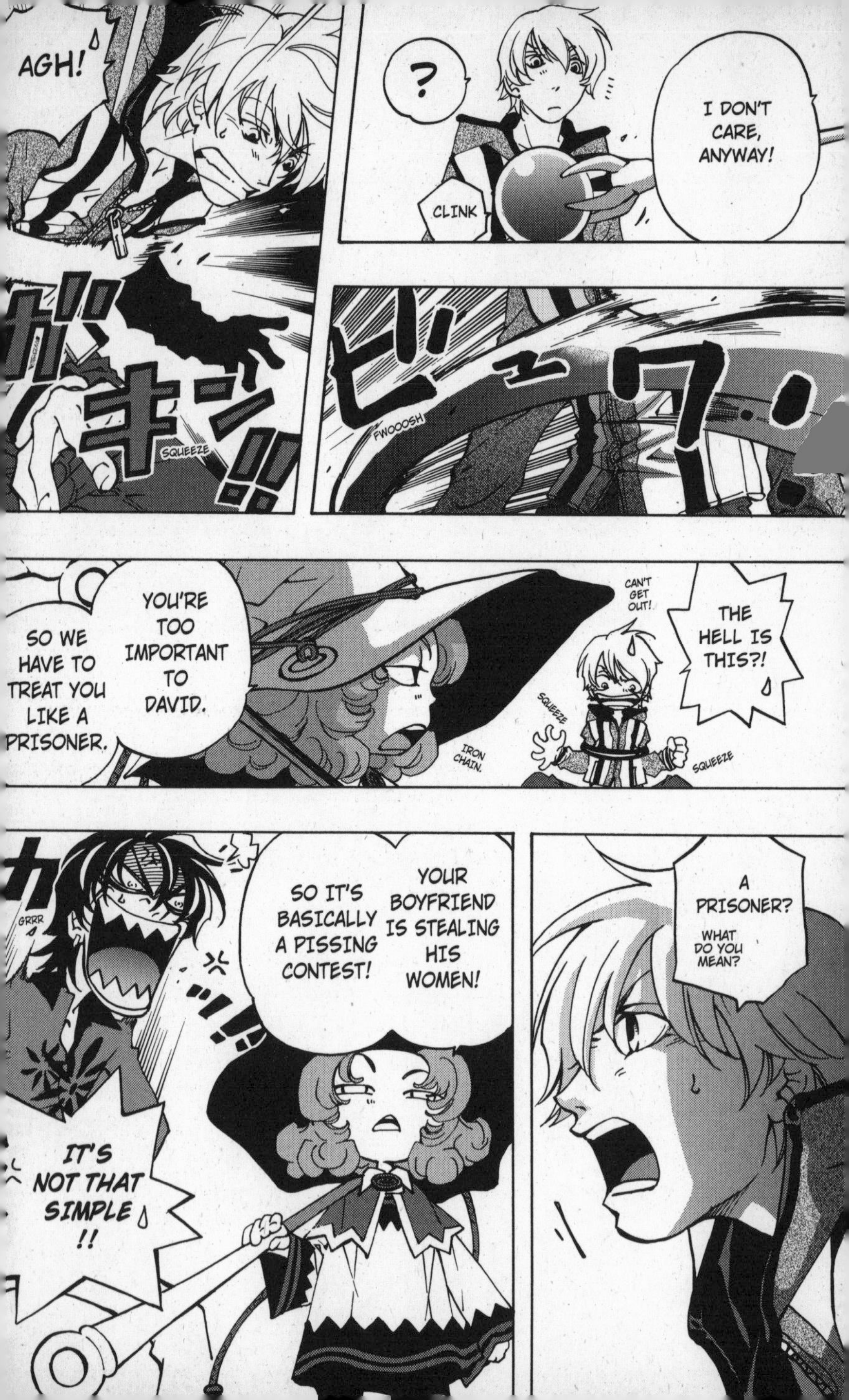
I DON'T CARE, ANYWAY!
?
CLINK
AGH!
FWOOOSH
SQUEEZE
CAN'T GET OUT!
THE HELL IS THIS?!
SQUEEZE
SQUEEZE
IRON CHAIN.
YOU'RE TOO IMPORTANT TO DAVID.
SO WE HAVE TO TREAT YOU LIKE A PRISONER.
A PRISONER?
WHAT DO YOU MEAN?
YOUR BOYFRIEND IS STEALING HIS WOMEN!
SO IT'S BASICALLY A PISSING CONTEST!
GRRR
IT'S NOT THAT SIMPLE!!

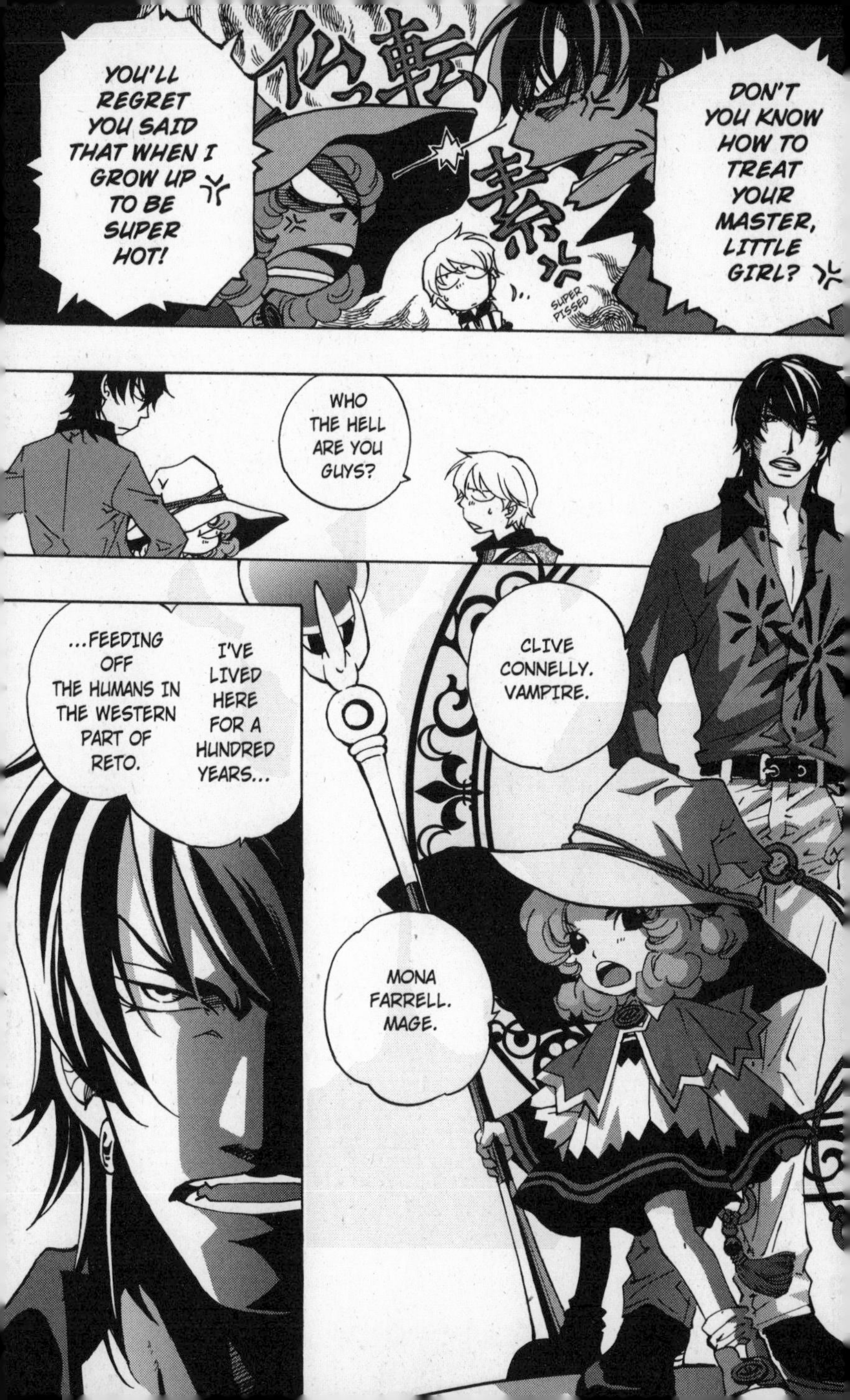
DON'T YOU KNOW HOW TO TREAT YOUR MASTER, LITTLE GIRL?
SUPER PISSED
YOU'LL REGRET YOU SAID THAT WHEN I GROW UP TO BE SUPER HOT!
WHO THE HELL ARE YOU GUYS?
CLIVE CONNELLY. VAMPIRE.
MONA FARRELL. MAGE.
I'VE LIVED HERE FOR A HUNDRED YEARS...
...FEEDING OFF THE HUMANS IN THE WESTERN PART OF RETO.

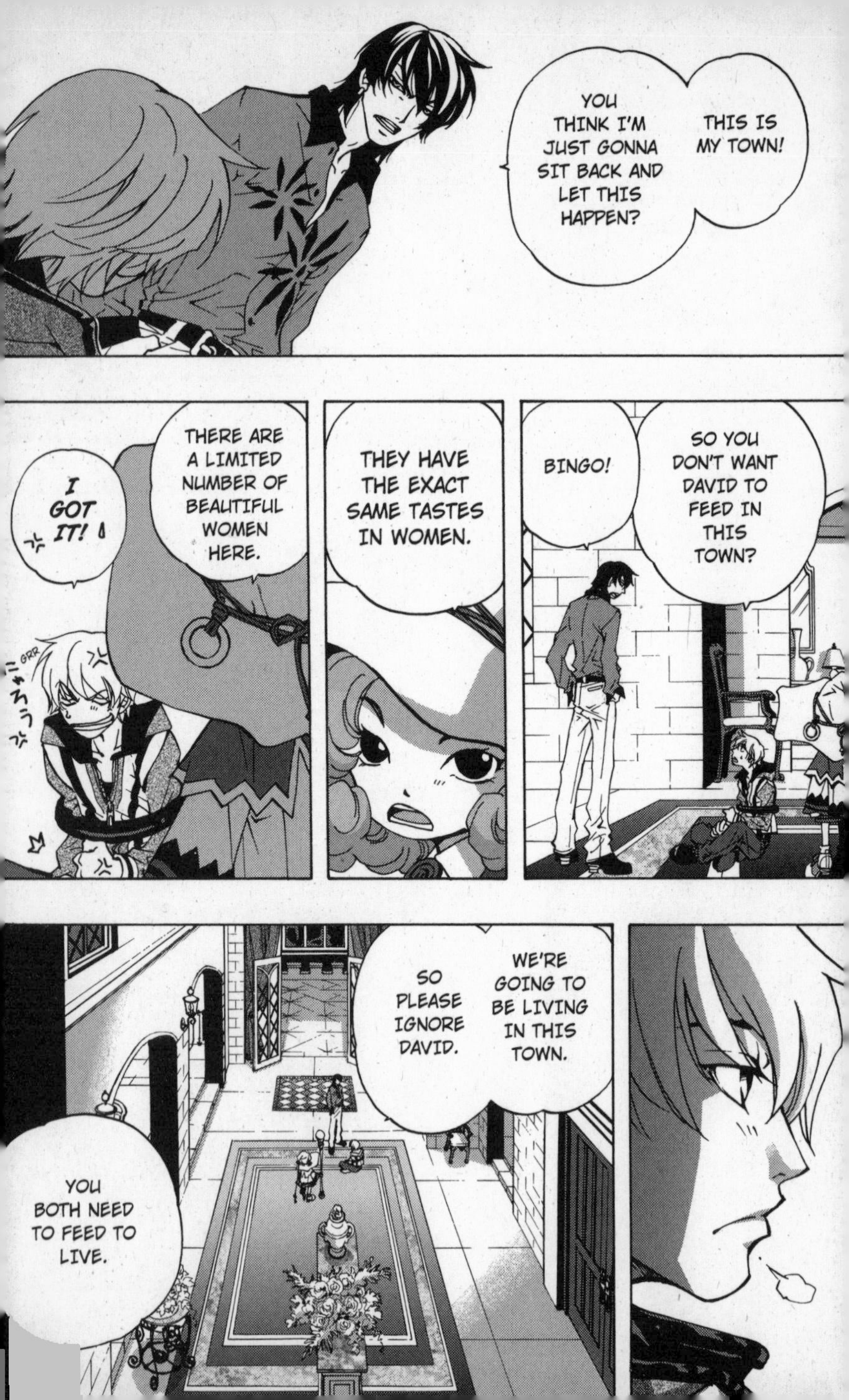
THIS IS MY TOWN!
YOU THINK I'M JUST GONNA SIT BACK AND LET THIS HAPPEN?
SO YOU DON'T WANT DAVID TO FEED IN THIS TOWN?
BINGO!
THEY HAVE THE EXACT SAME TASTES IN WOMEN.
THERE ARE A LIMITED NUMBER OF BEAUTIFUL WOMEN HERE.
I GOT IT!
GRR
WE'RE GOING TO BE LIVING IN THIS TOWN.
SO PLEASE IGNORE DAVID.
YOU BOTH NEED TO FEED TO LIVE.

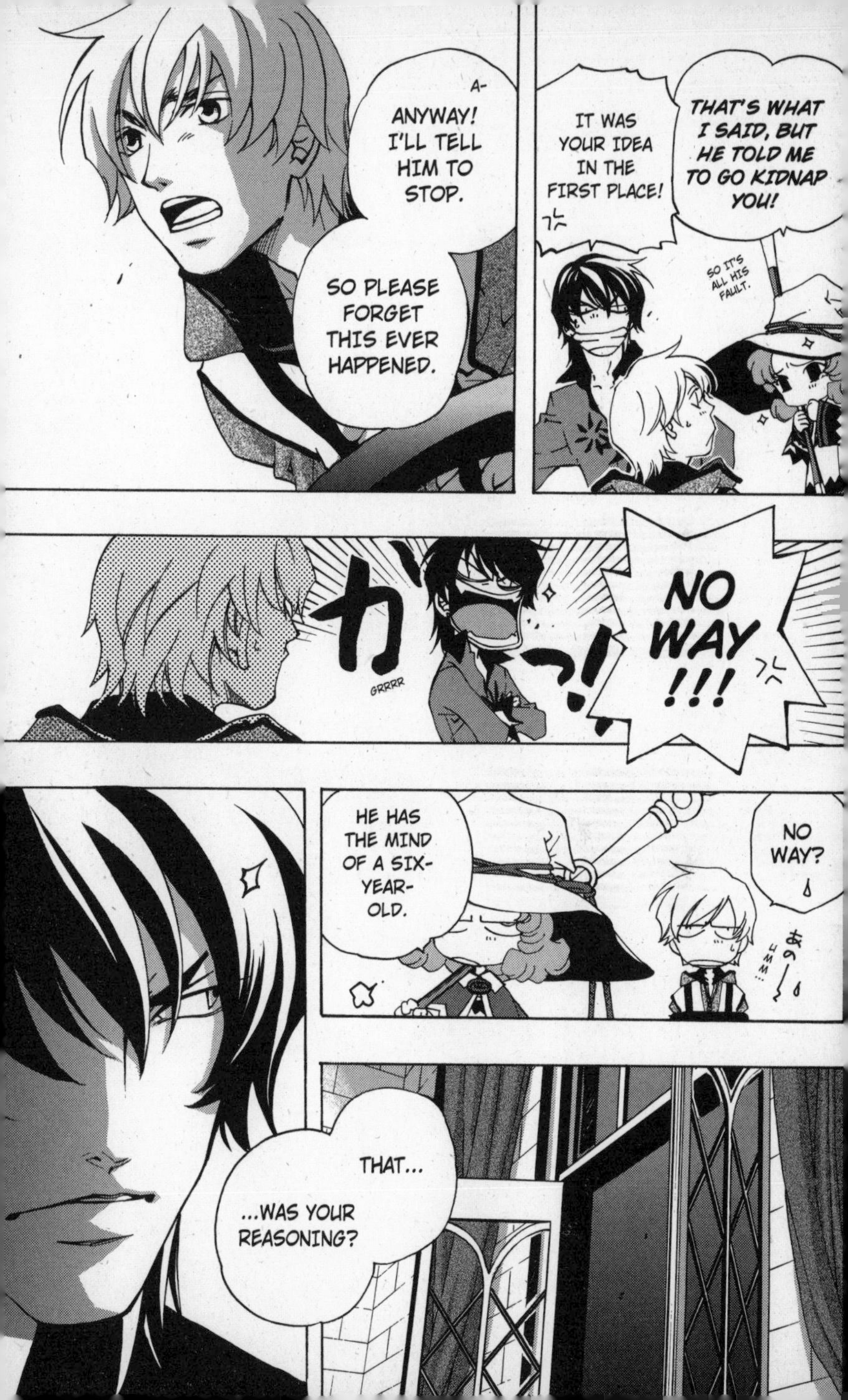
THAT'S WHAT I SAID, BUT HE TOLD ME TO GO KIDNAP YOU!
IT WAS YOUR IDEA IN THE FIRST PLACE!
SO IT'S ALL HIS FAULT.
A- ANYWAY! I'LL TELL HIM TO STOP.
SO PLEASE FORGET THIS EVER HAPPENED.
NO WAY!!!
かっ!
GRRRR
NO WAY?
あの~
UMM...
HE HAS THE MIND OF A SIX-YEAR-OLD.
THAT... ...WAS YOUR REASONING?

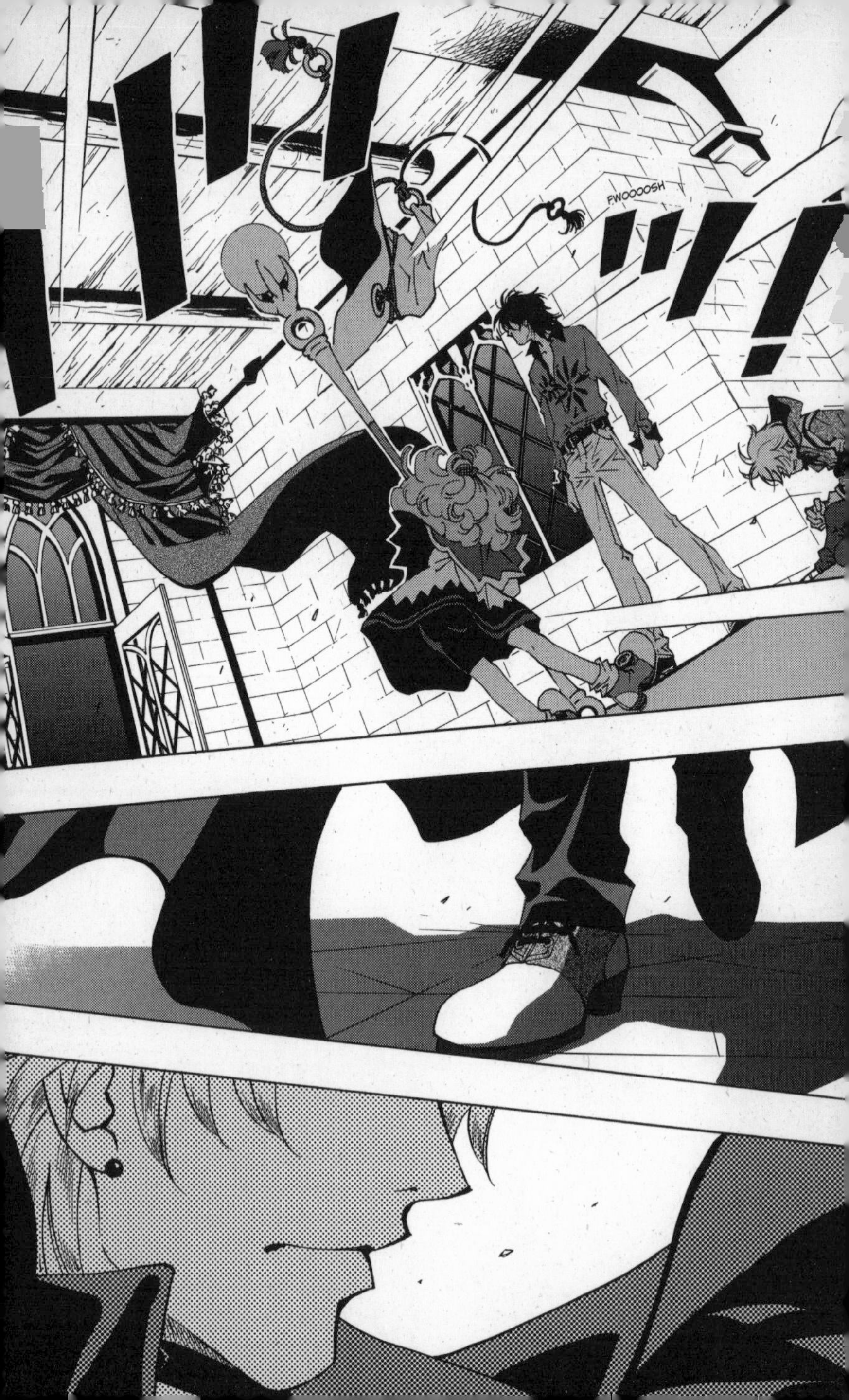
FWOOOOSH

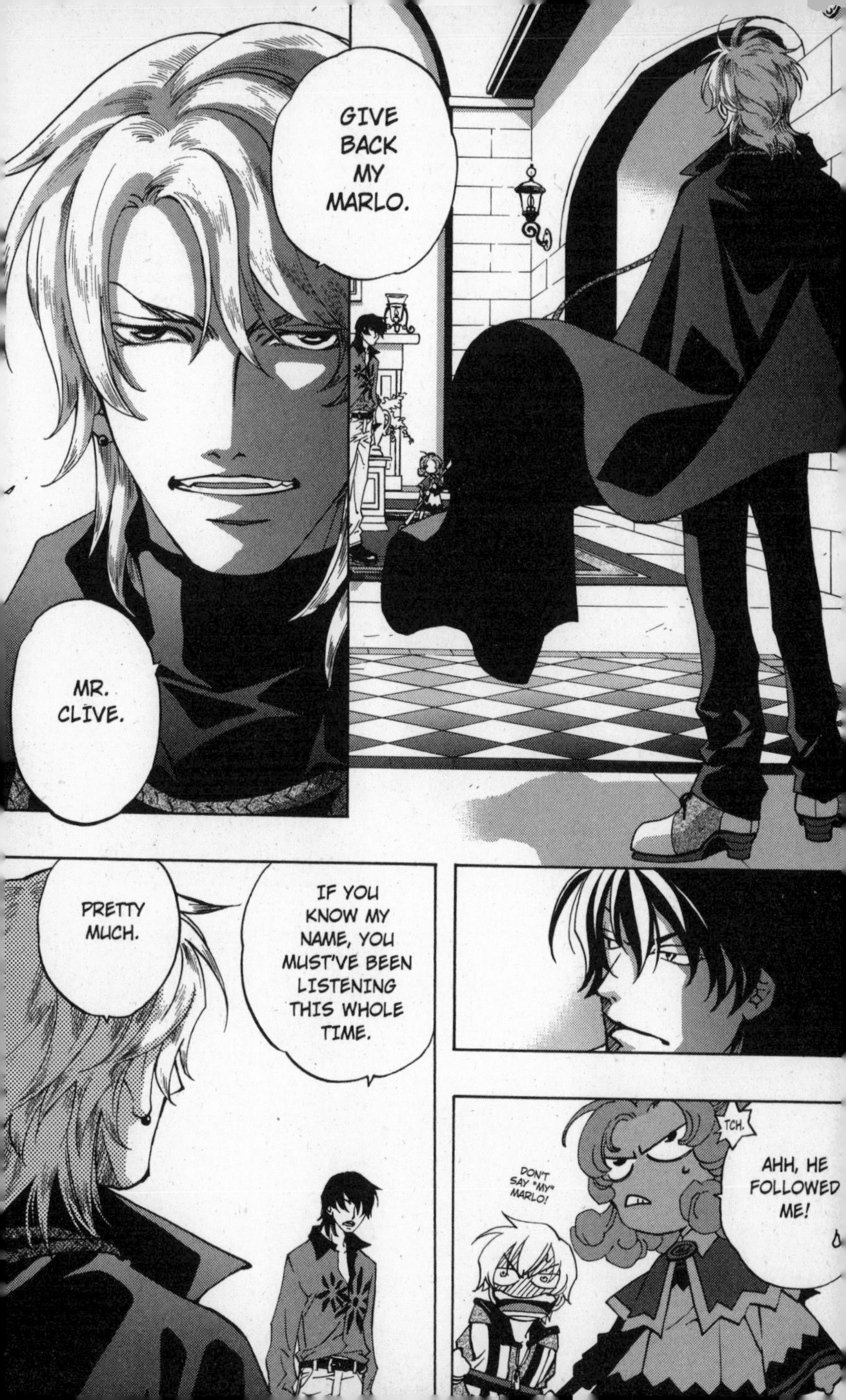
GIVE BACK MY MARLO.
MR. CLIVE.
TCH.
AHH, HE FOLLOWED ME!
DON'T SAY "MY" MARLO!
IF YOU KNOW MY NAME, YOU MUST'VE BEEN LISTENING THIS WHOLE TIME.
PRETTY MUCH.

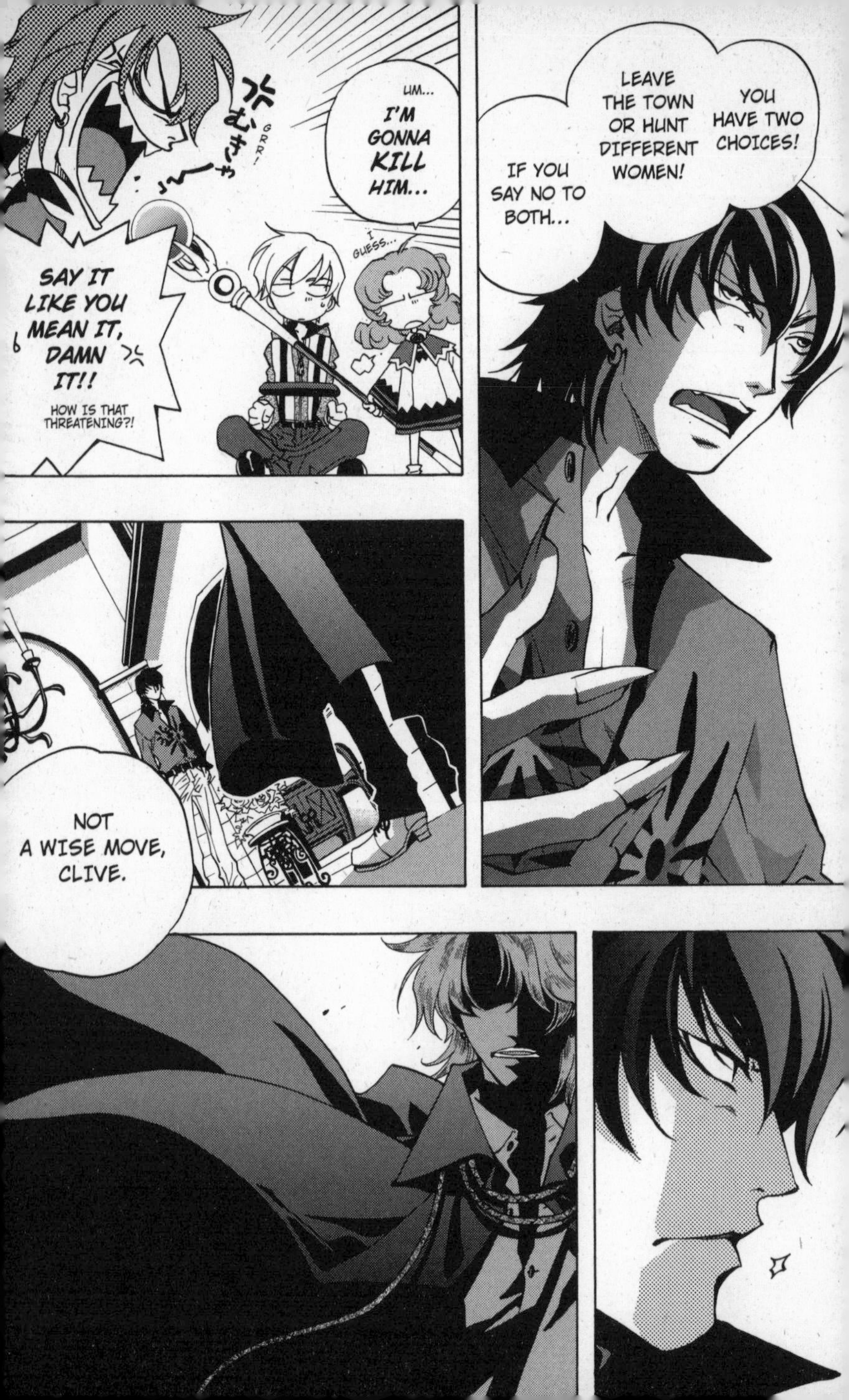
YOU HAVE TWO CHOICES!
LEAVE THE TOWN OR HUNT DIFFERENT WOMEN!
IF YOU SAY NO TO BOTH...
UM... I'M GONNA KILL HIM...
I GUESS...
GRR!
SAY IT LIKE YOU MEAN IT, DAMN IT!!
HOW IS THAT THREATENING?!
NOT A WISE MOVE, CLIVE.

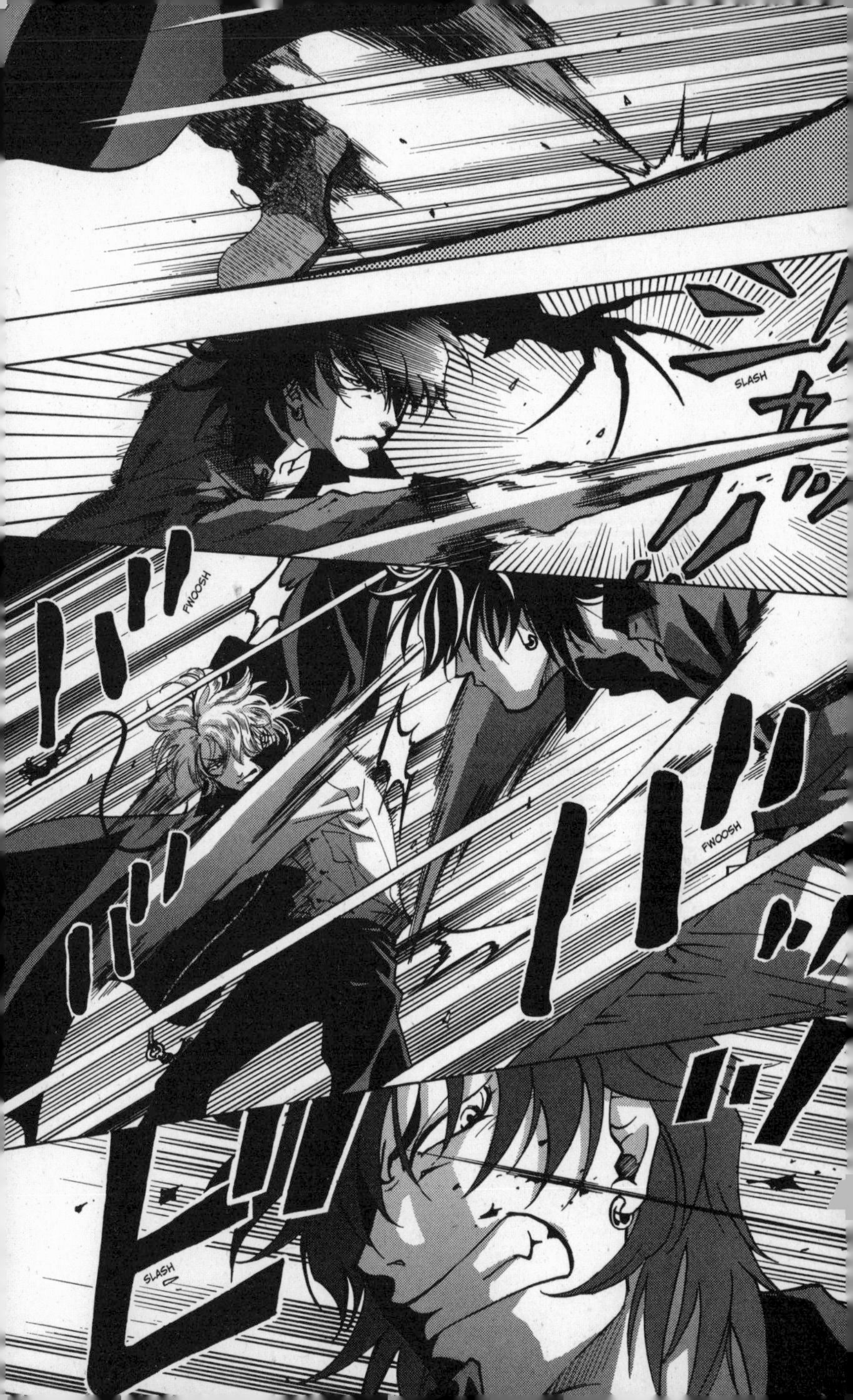
SLASH
FWOOSH
FWOOSH
SLASH

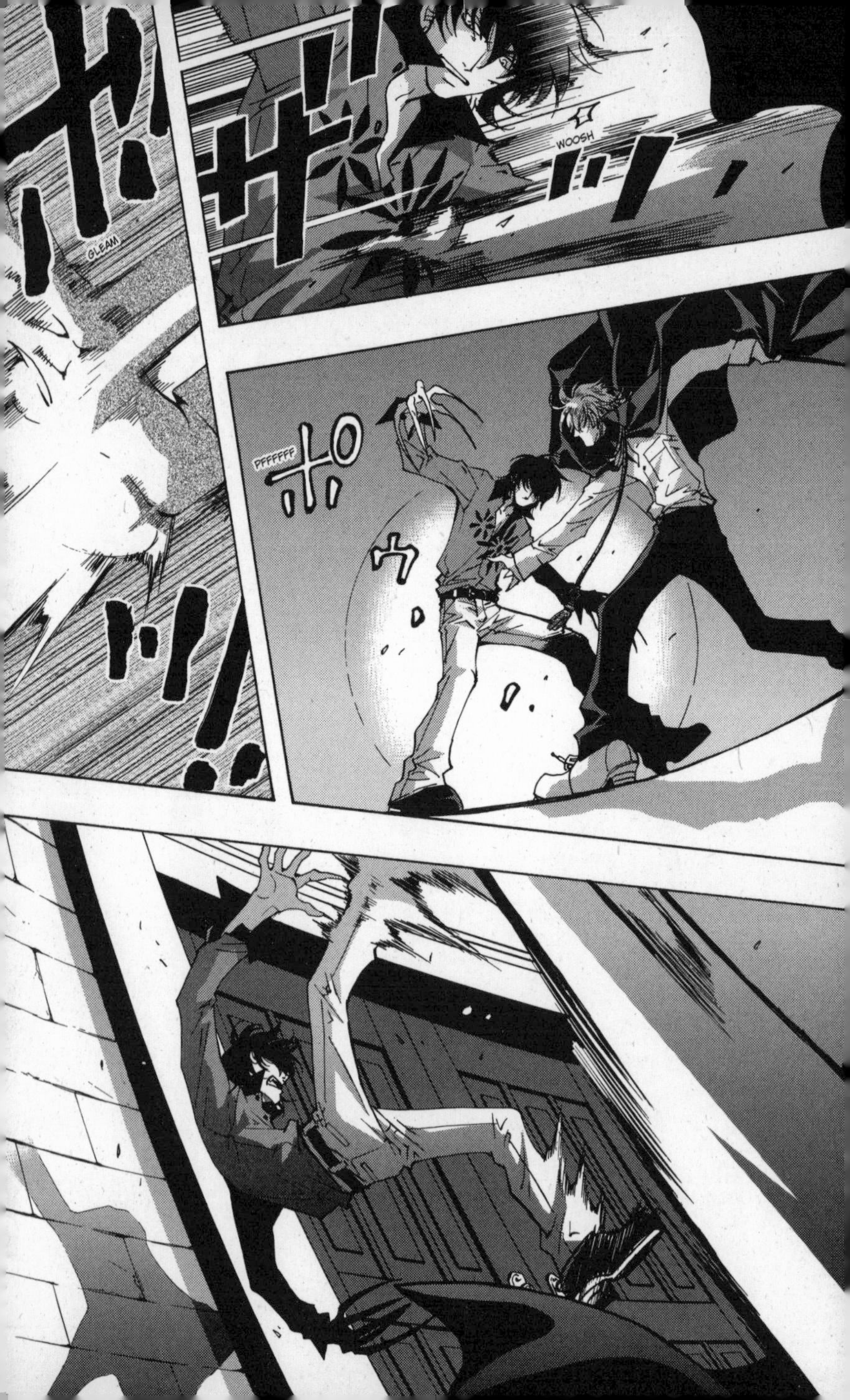
WOOSH
PFFFFFF
GLEAM

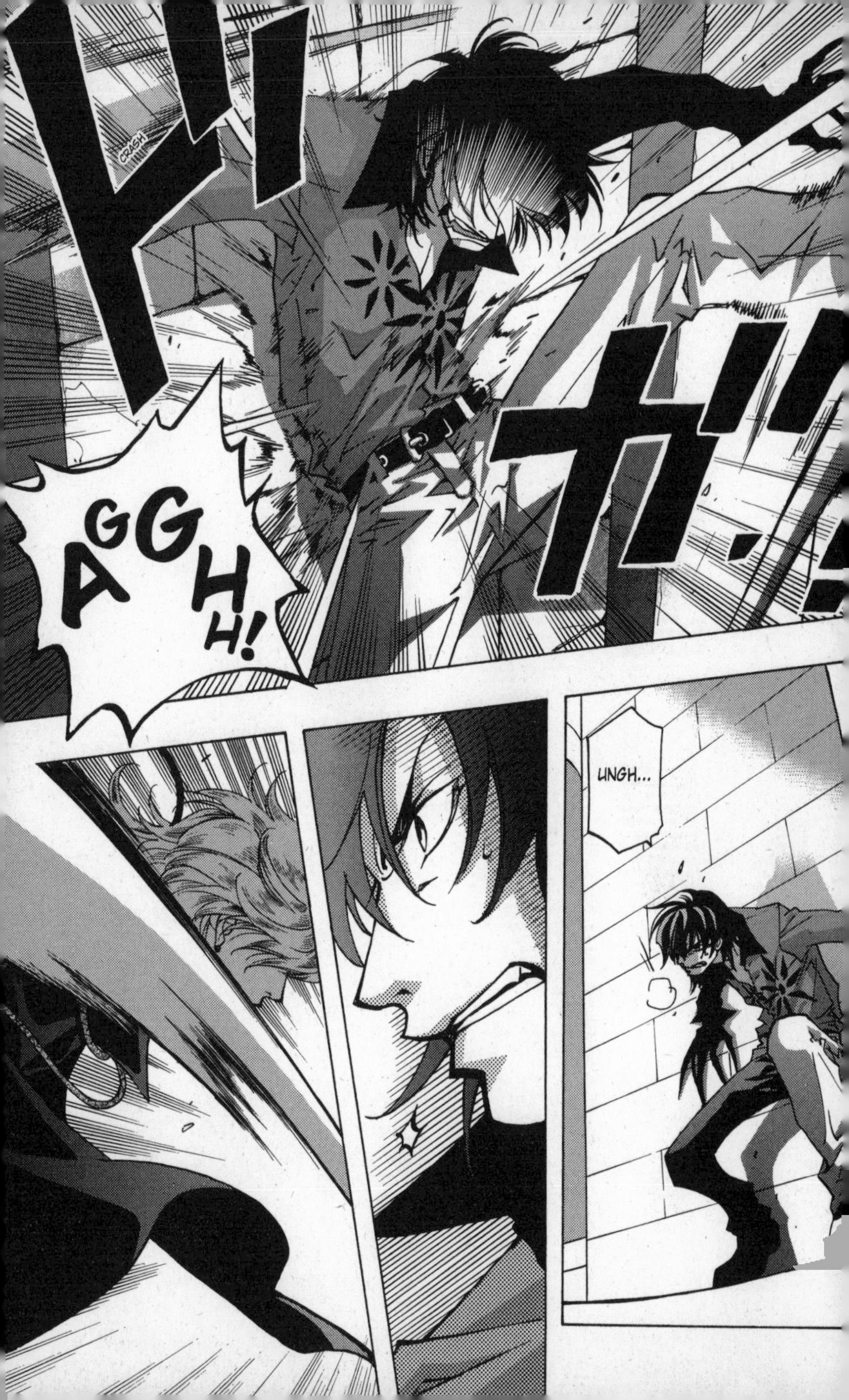
CRASH
AGGHH!
UNGH...

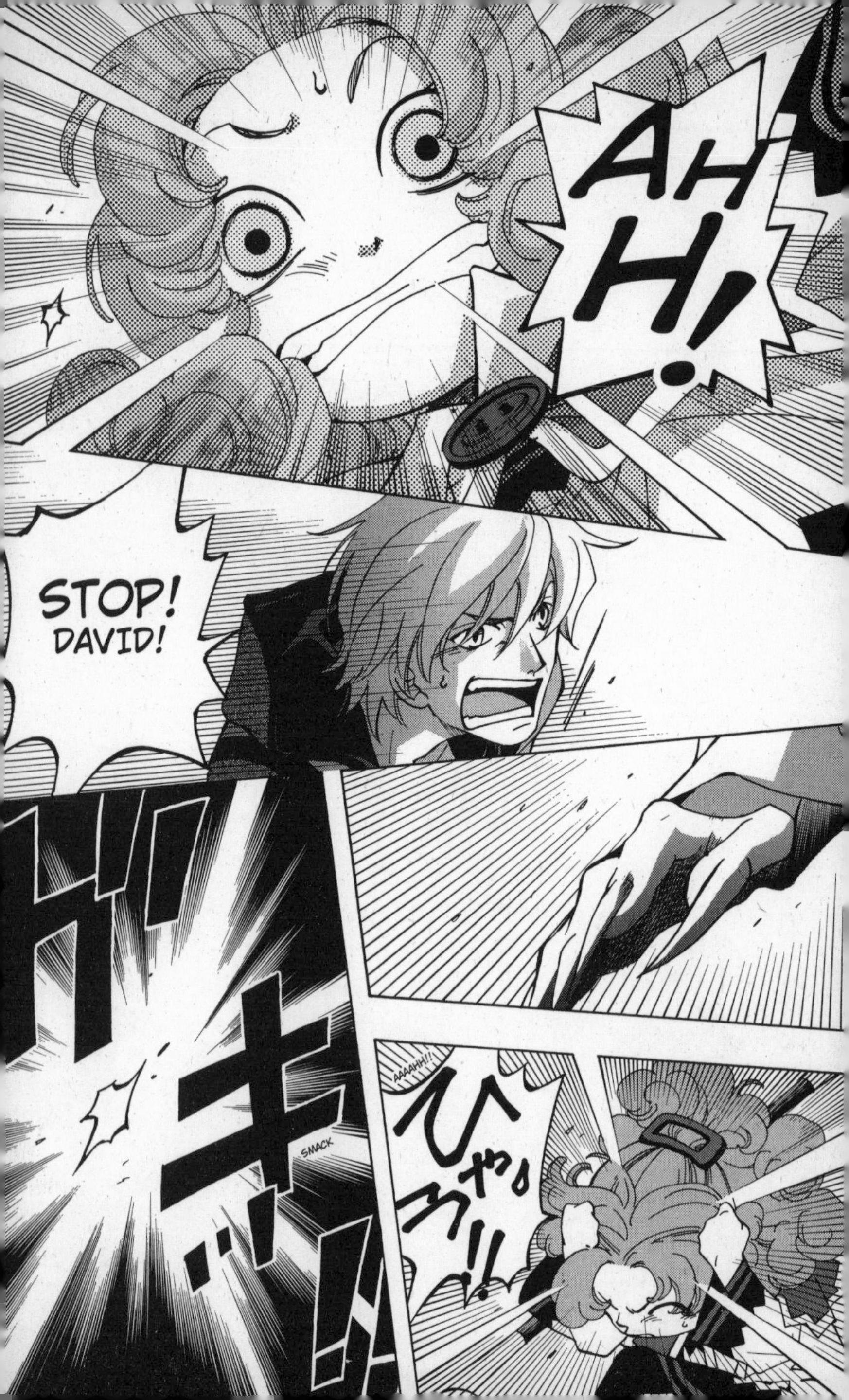
AHH!
STOP! DAVID!
AAAAHH!!
SMACK

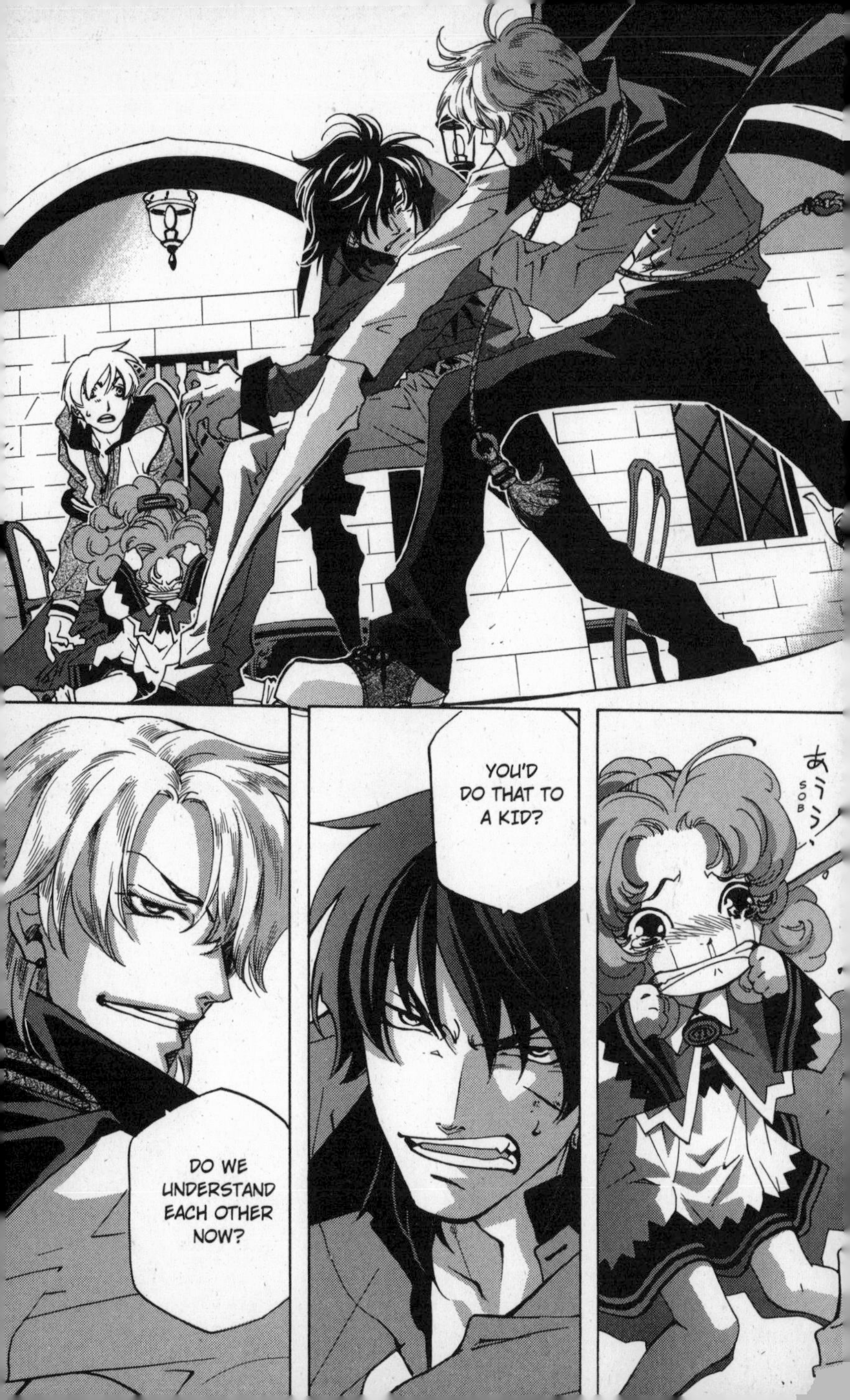
SOB
YOU'D DO THAT TO A KID?
DO WE UNDERSTAND EACH OTHER NOW?

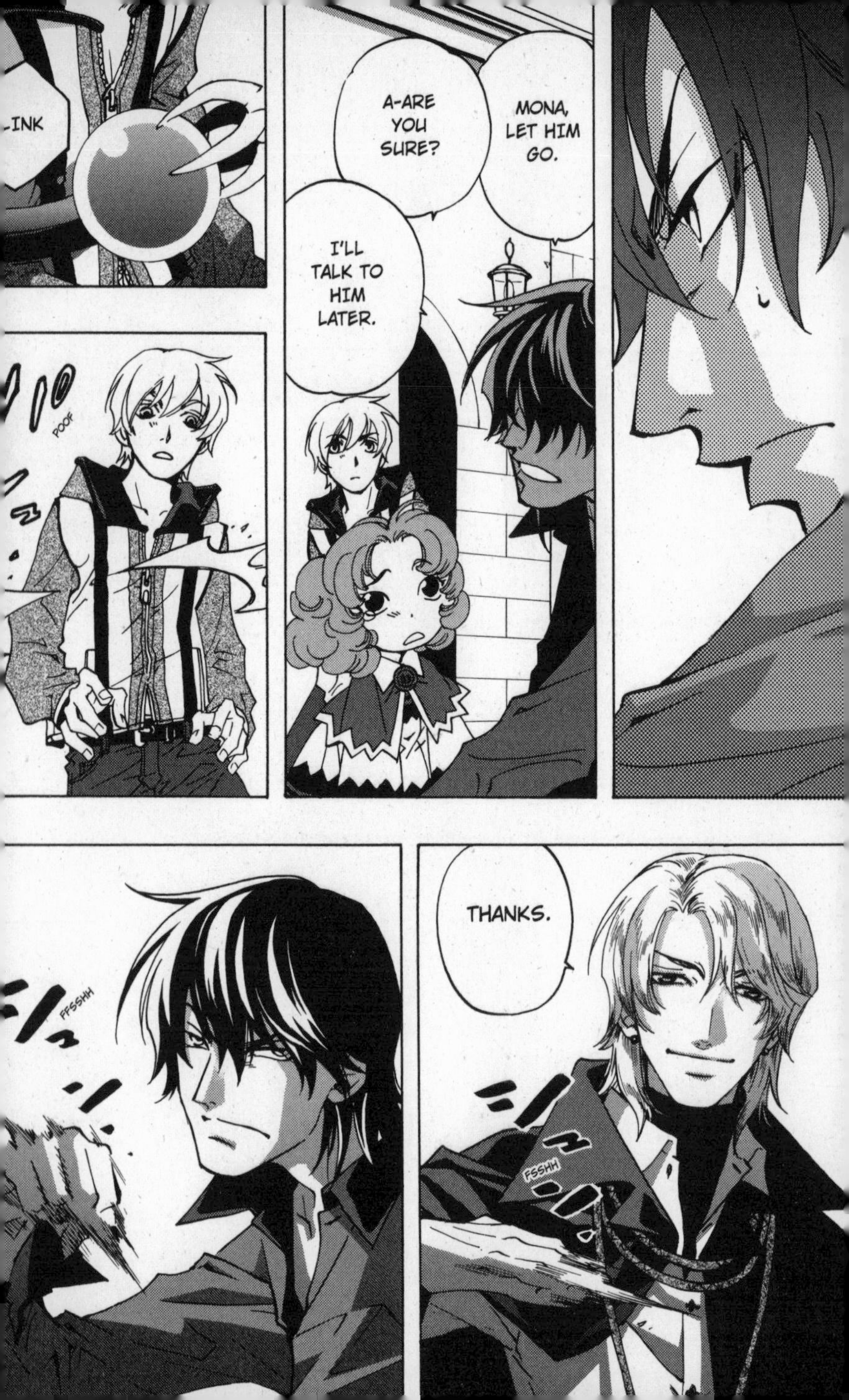
MONA, LET HIM GO.
A-ARE YOU SURE?
I'LL TALK TO HIM LATER.
-INK
POOF
THANKS.
FSSHH
FFSSHH

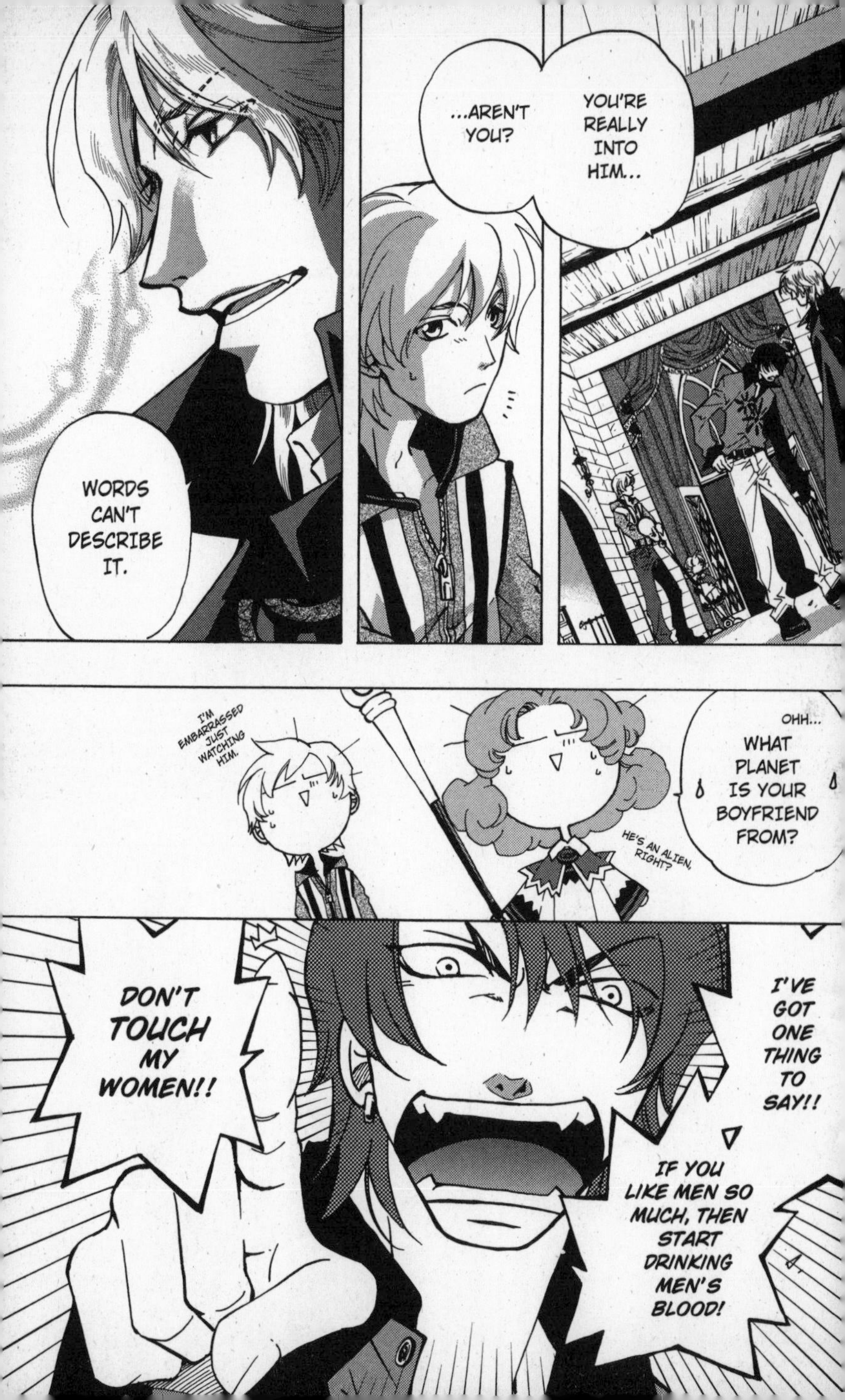
YOU'RE REALLY INTO HIM...
...AREN'T YOU?
WORDS CAN'T DESCRIBE IT.
OHH... WHAT PLANET IS YOUR BOYFRIEND FROM?
HE'S AN ALIEN, RIGHT?
I'M EMBARRASSED JUST WATCHING HIM.
I'VE GOT ONE THING TO SAY!!
IF YOU LIKE MEN SO MUCH, THEN START DRINKING MEN'S BLOOD!
DON'T TOUCH MY WOMEN!!

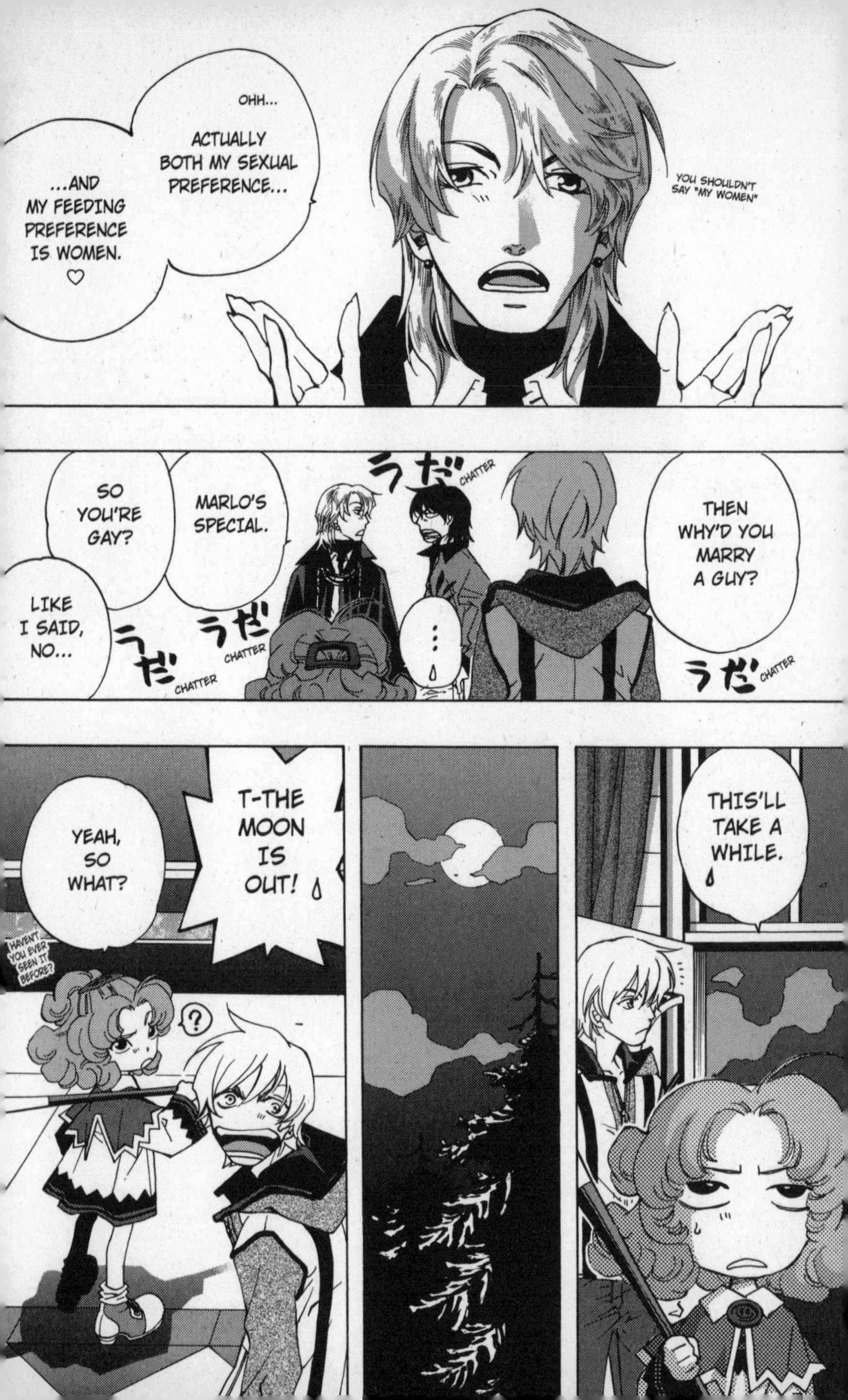
OHH... ACTUALLY BOTH MY SEXUAL PREFERENCE... ...AND MY FEEDING PREFERENCE IS WOMEN. ♡
YOU SHOULDN'T SAY "MY WOMEN"
THEN WHY'D YOU MARRY A GUY?
ラだ CHATTER
ラだ CHATTER
...
MARLO'S SPECIAL.
SO YOU'RE GAY?
LIKE I SAID, NO...
ラだ CHATTER
ラだ CHATTER
THIS'LL TAKE A WHILE.
T-THE MOON IS OUT!
YEAH, SO WHAT?
HAVEN'T YOU EVER SEEN IT BEFORE?
?

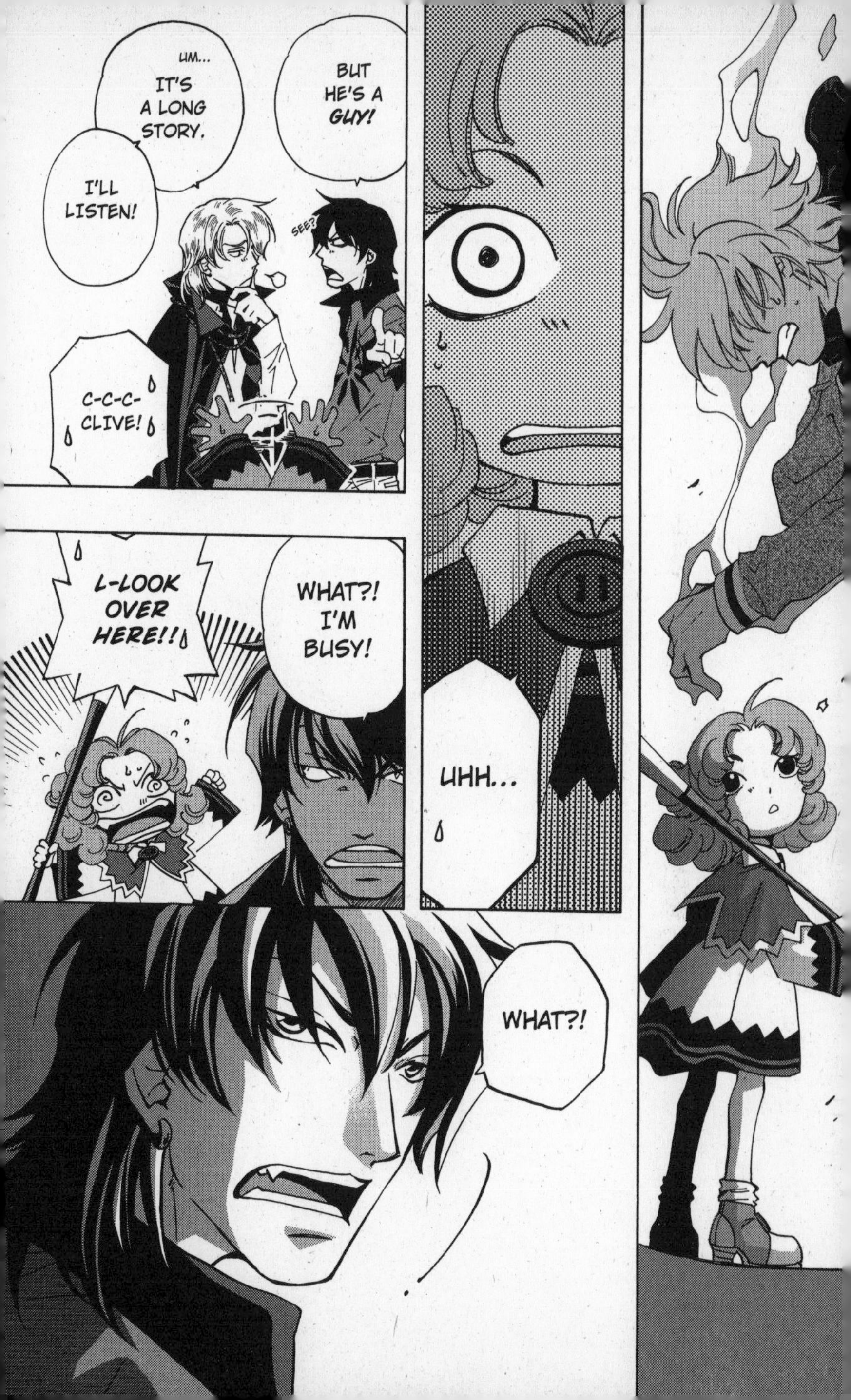
UHH...
BUT HE'S A GUY!
SEE?
UM... IT'S A LONG STORY.
I'LL LISTEN!
C-C-C-CLIVE!
WHAT?! I'M BUSY!
L-LOOK OVER HERE!!
WHAT?!

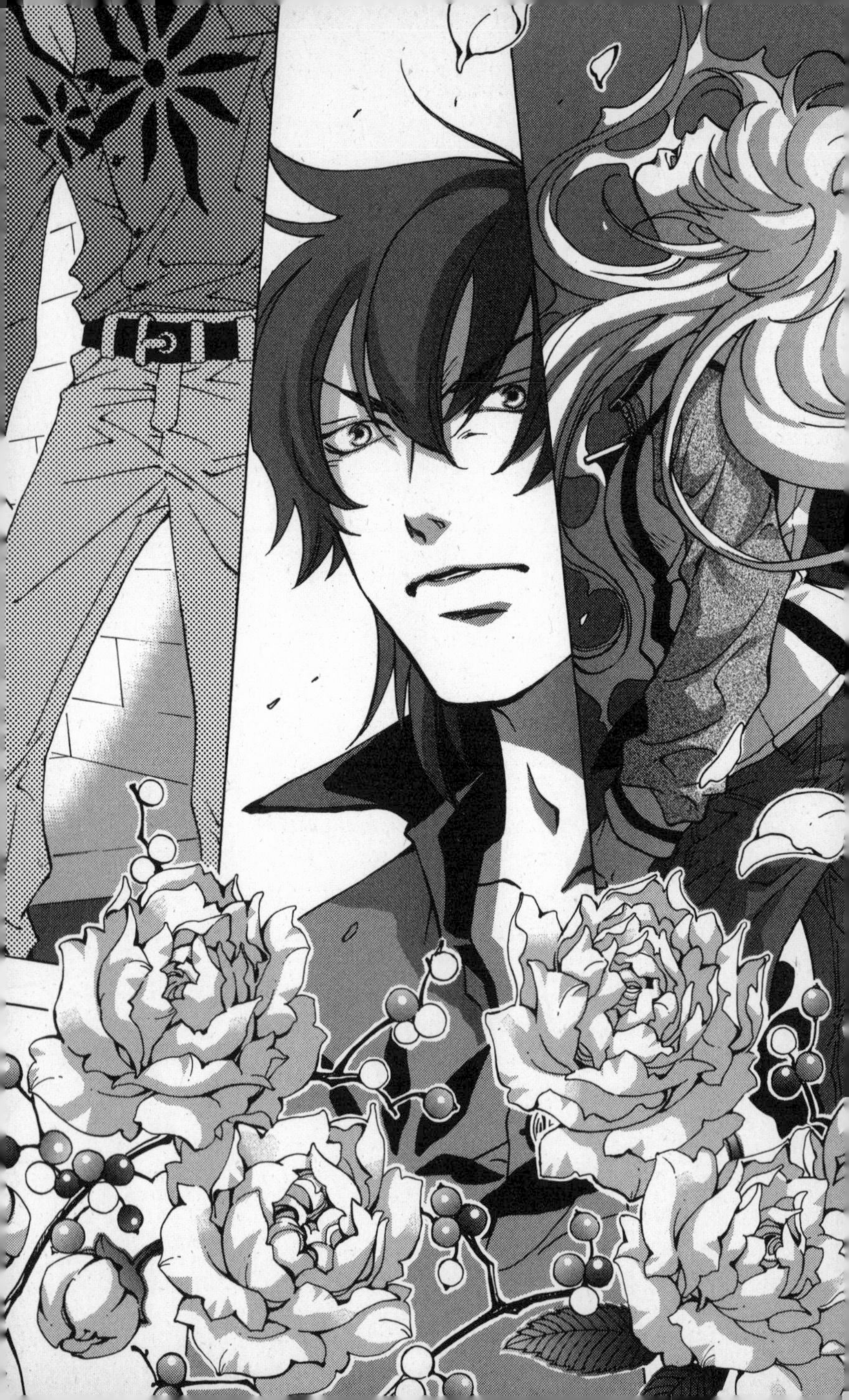

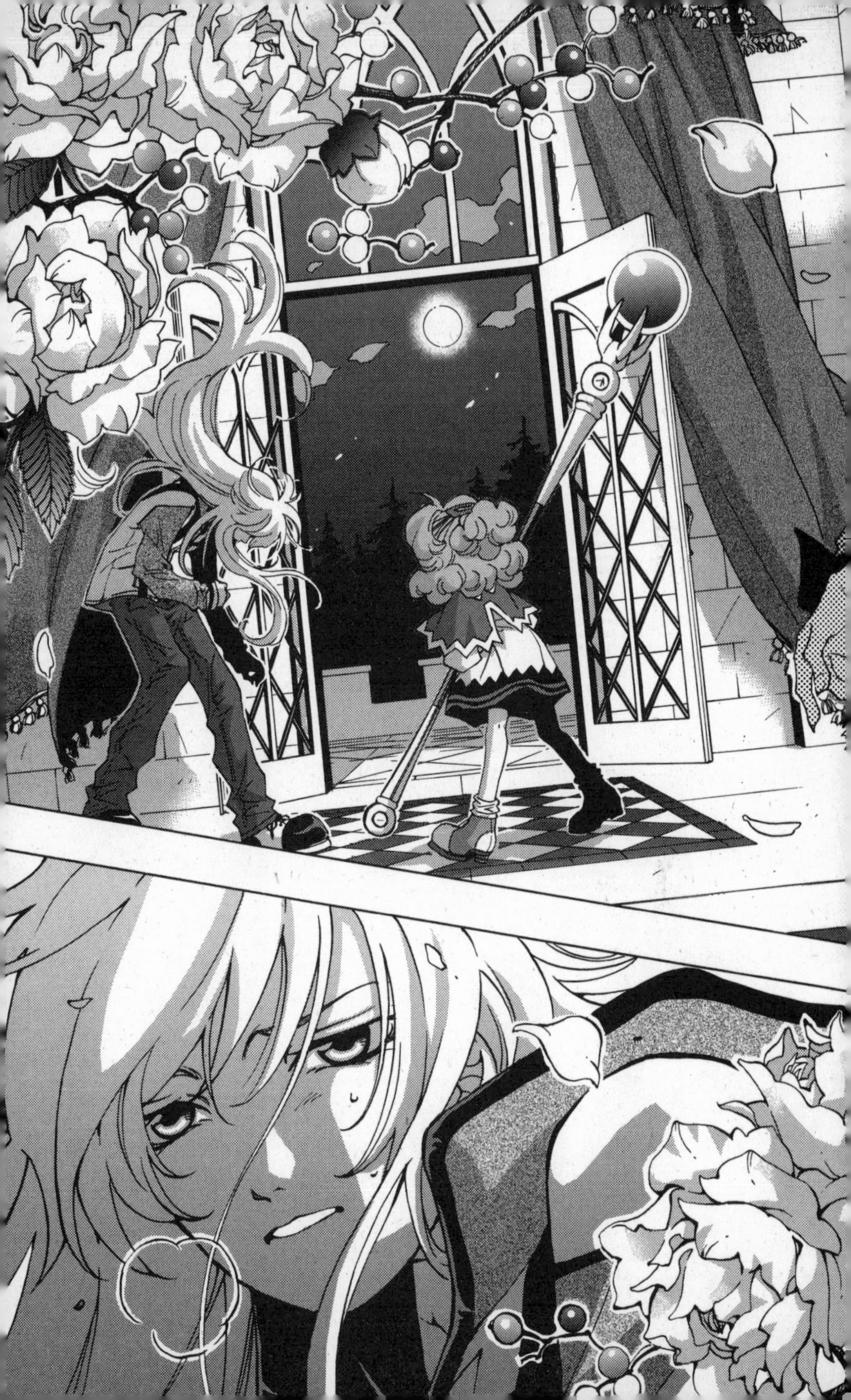

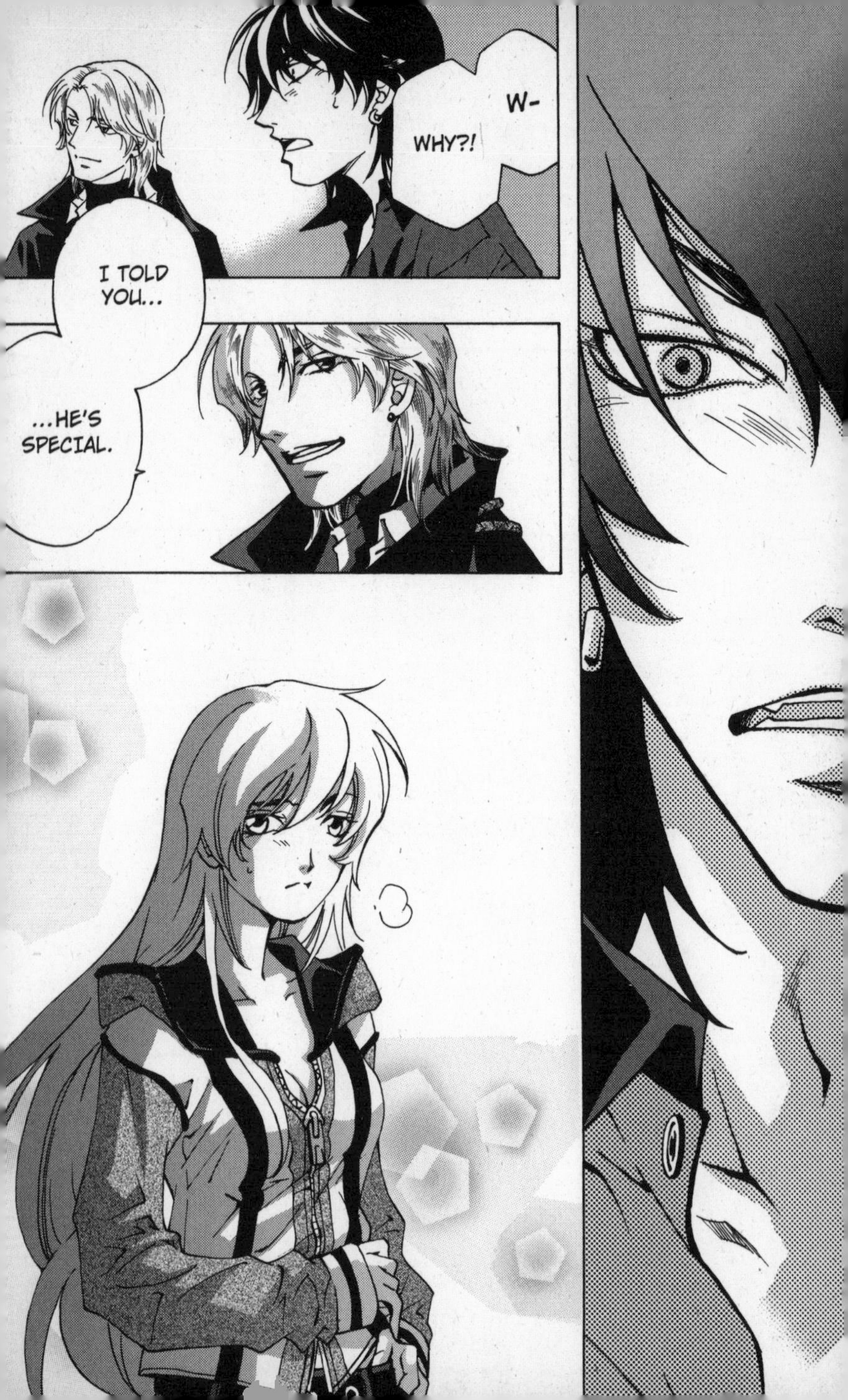
W- WHY?!
I TOLD YOU...
...HE'S SPECIAL.

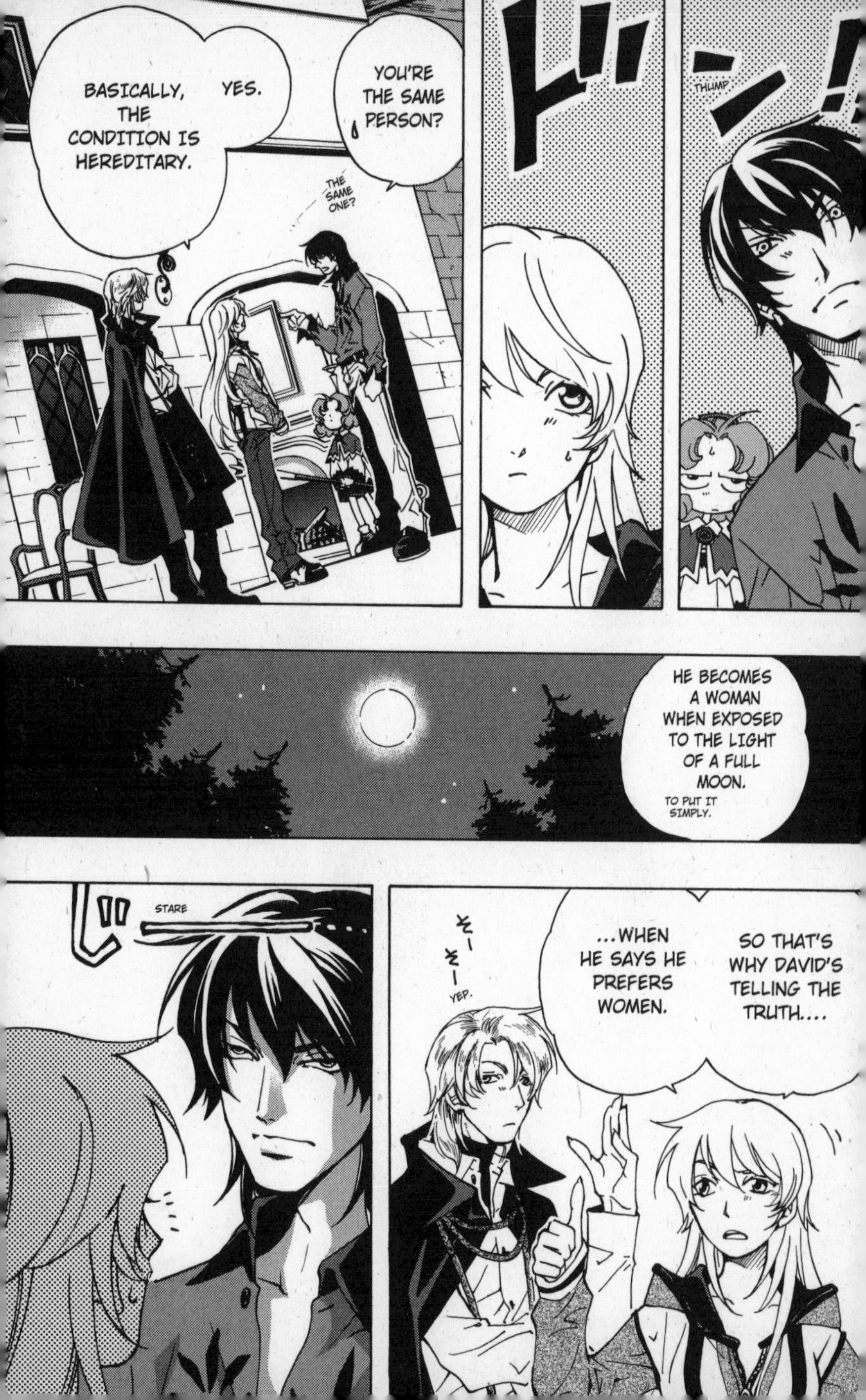
ドーン!
THUMP
YOU'RE THE SAME PERSON?
THE SAME ONE?
YES.
BASICALLY, THE CONDITION IS HEREDITARY.
HE BECOMES A WOMAN WHEN EXPOSED TO THE LIGHT OF A FULL MOON.
TO PUT IT SIMPLY.
SO THAT'S WHY DAVID'S TELLING THE TRUTH....
...WHEN HE SAYS HE PREFERS WOMEN.
そーそー
YEP.
STARE

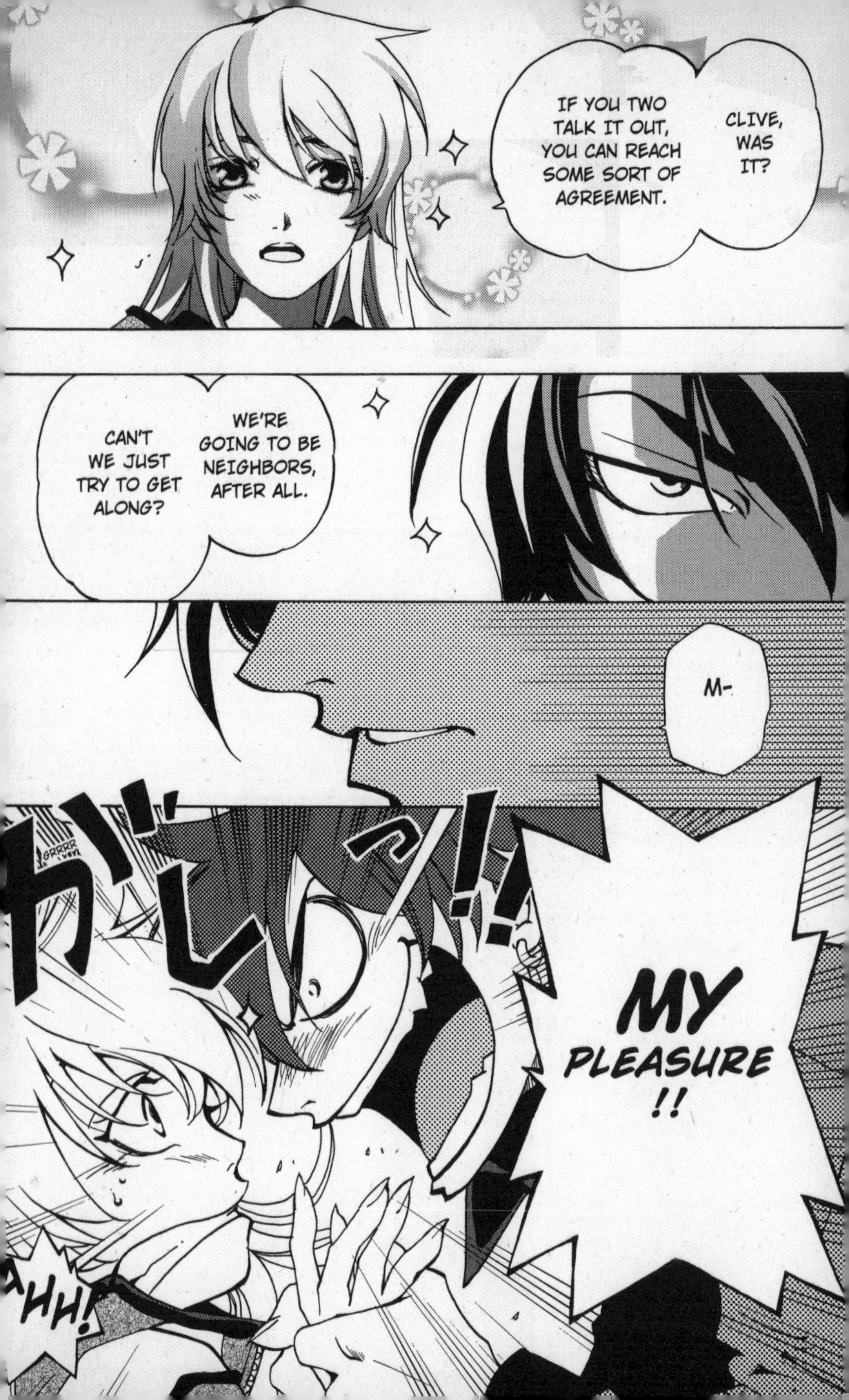
CLIVE, WAS IT?
IF YOU TWO TALK IT OUT, YOU CAN REACH SOME SORT OF AGREEMENT.
WE'RE GOING TO BE NEIGHBORS, AFTER ALL.
CAN'T WE JUST TRY TO GET ALONG?
M-
MY PLEASURE !!
がじっ!!
GRRRR

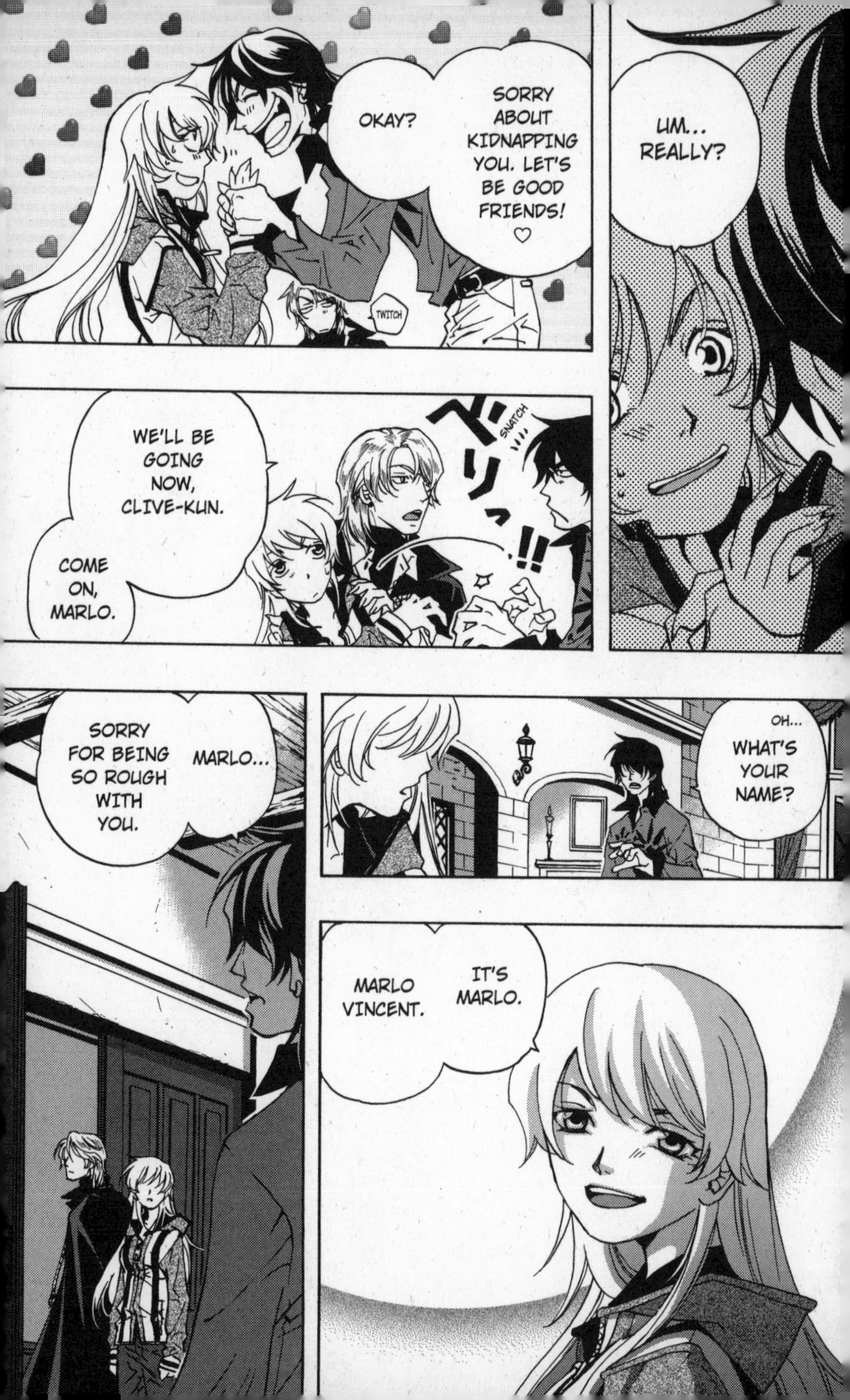
UM... REALLY?
SORRY ABOUT KIDNAPPING YOU. LET'S BE GOOD FRIENDS! ♡
OKAY?
TWITCH
SNATCH
!!
WE'LL BE GOING NOW, CLIVE-KUN.
COME ON, MARLO.
OH... WHAT'S YOUR NAME?
MARLO...
SORRY FOR BEING SO ROUGH WITH YOU.
IT'S MARLO.
MARLO VINCENT.

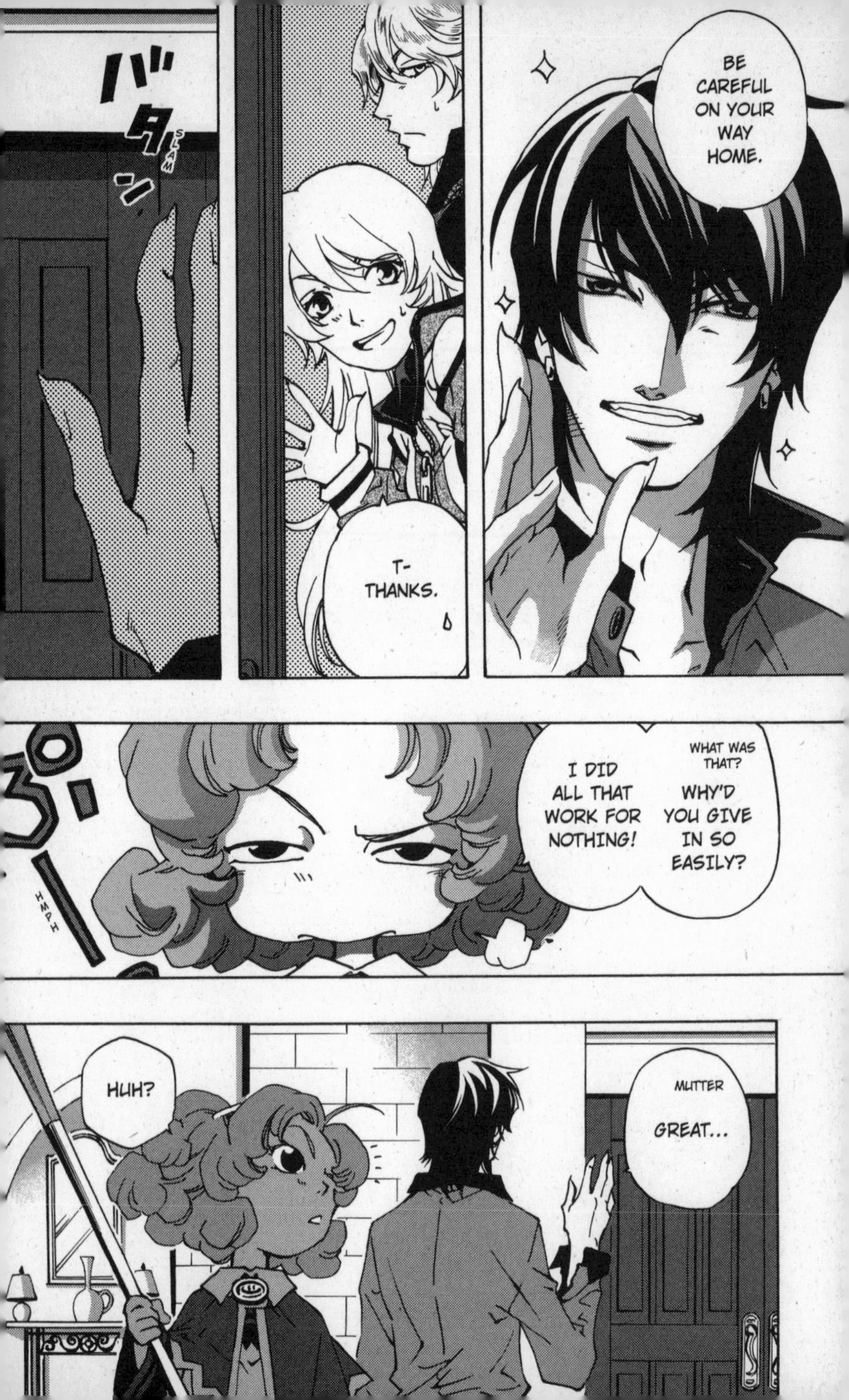

BE CAREFUL ON YOUR WAY HOME.
T-THANKS.
SLAM
WHAT WAS THAT?
WHY'D YOU GIVE IN SO EASILY?
I DID ALL THAT WORK FOR NOTHING!
HMPH
MUTTER
GREAT...
HUH?

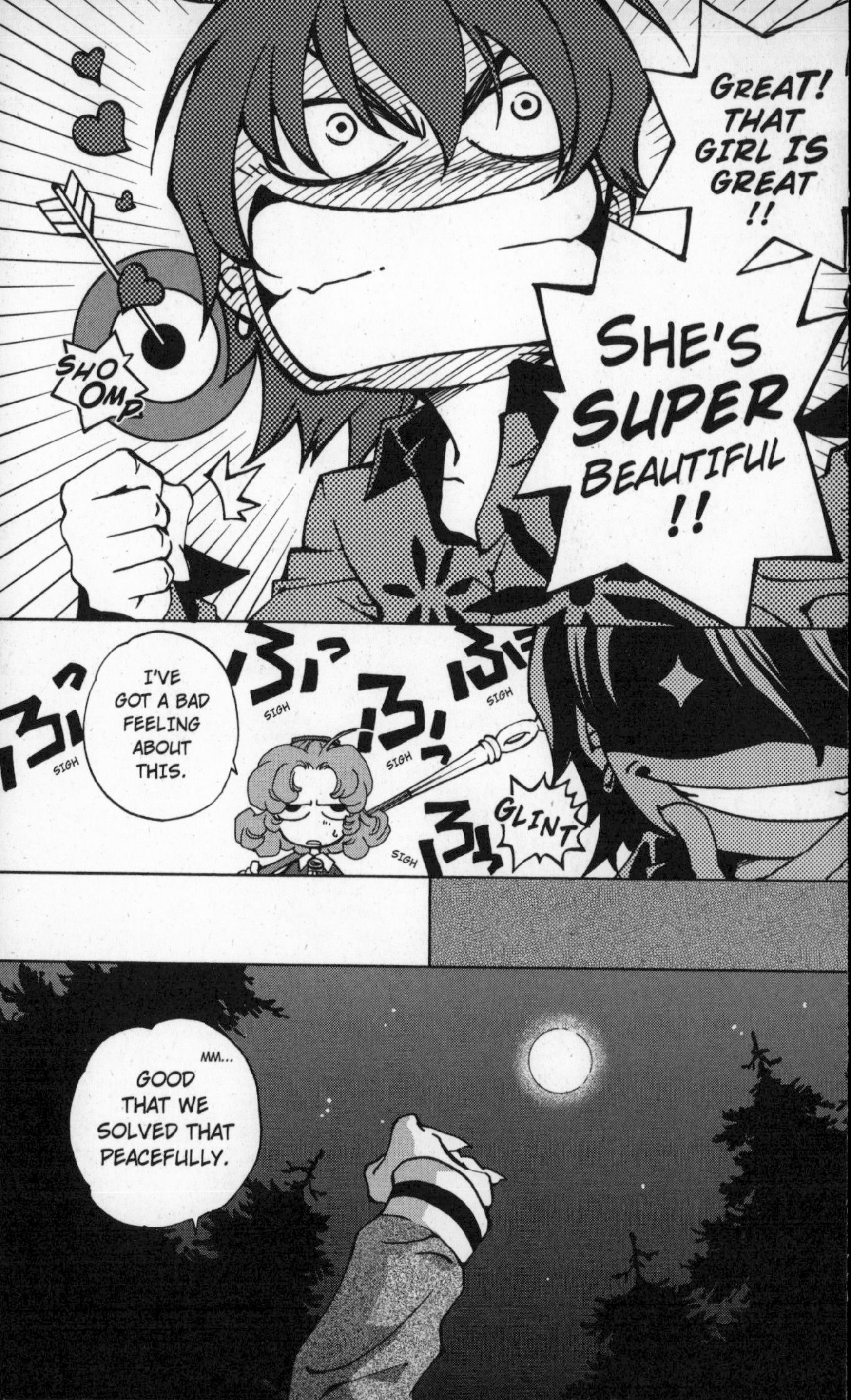
GREAT! THAT GIRL IS GREAT !!
SHE'S SUPER BEAUTIFUL !!
SHOMP
GLINT
SIGH
SIGH
SIGH
SIGH
SIGH
I'VE GOT A BAD FEELING ABOUT THIS.
MM... GOOD THAT WE SOLVED THAT PEACEFULLY.

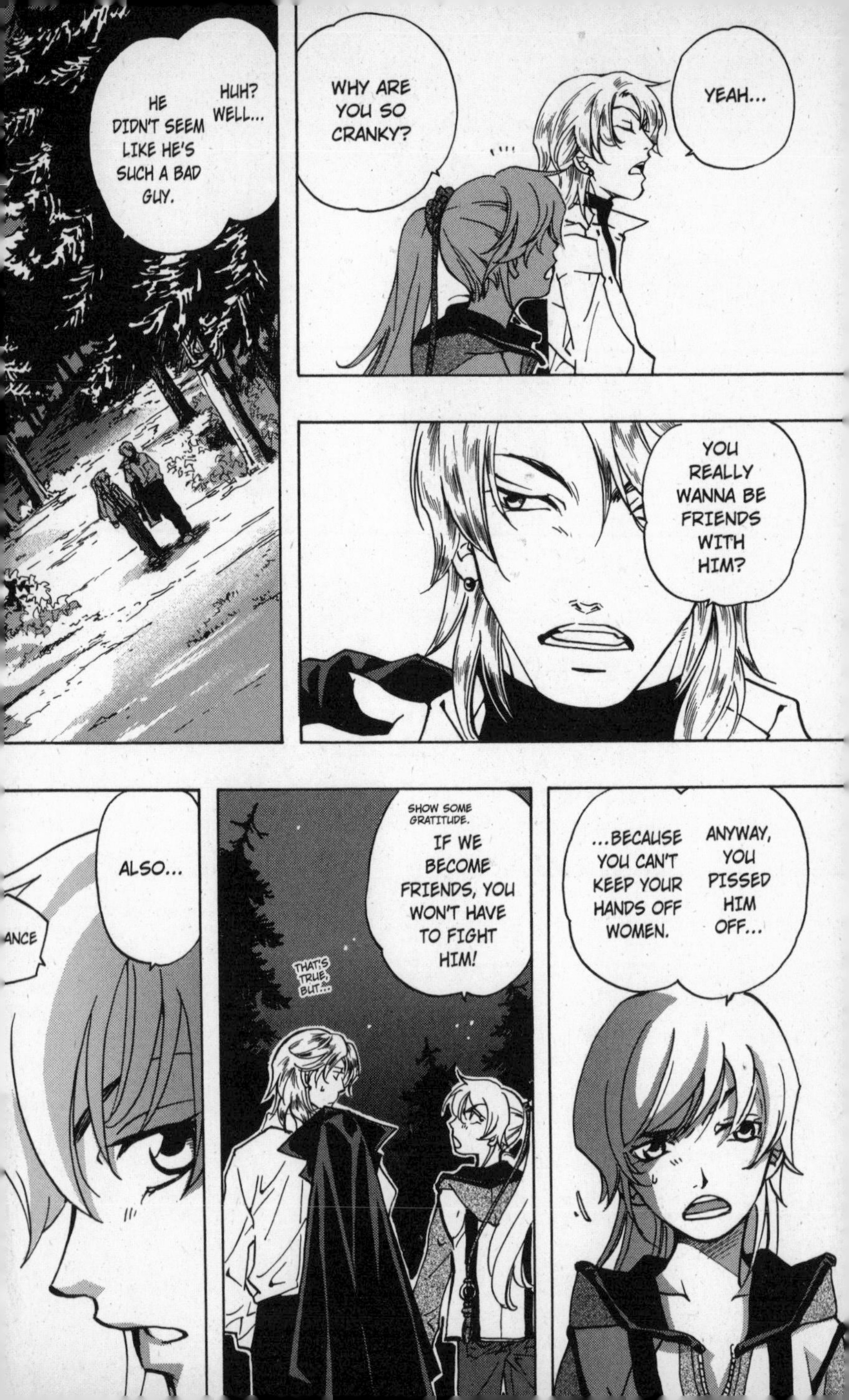
YEAH...
WHY ARE YOU SO CRANKY?
YOU REALLY WANNA BE FRIENDS WITH HIM?
HUH? WELL...
HE DIDN'T SEEM LIKE HE'S SUCH A BAD GUY.
ANYWAY, YOU PISSED HIM OFF...
...BECAUSE YOU CAN'T KEEP YOUR HANDS OFF WOMEN.
IF WE BECOME FRIENDS, YOU WON'T HAVE TO FIGHT HIM!
SHOW SOME GRATITUDE.
THAT'S TRUE, BUT...
ALSO...
ANCE

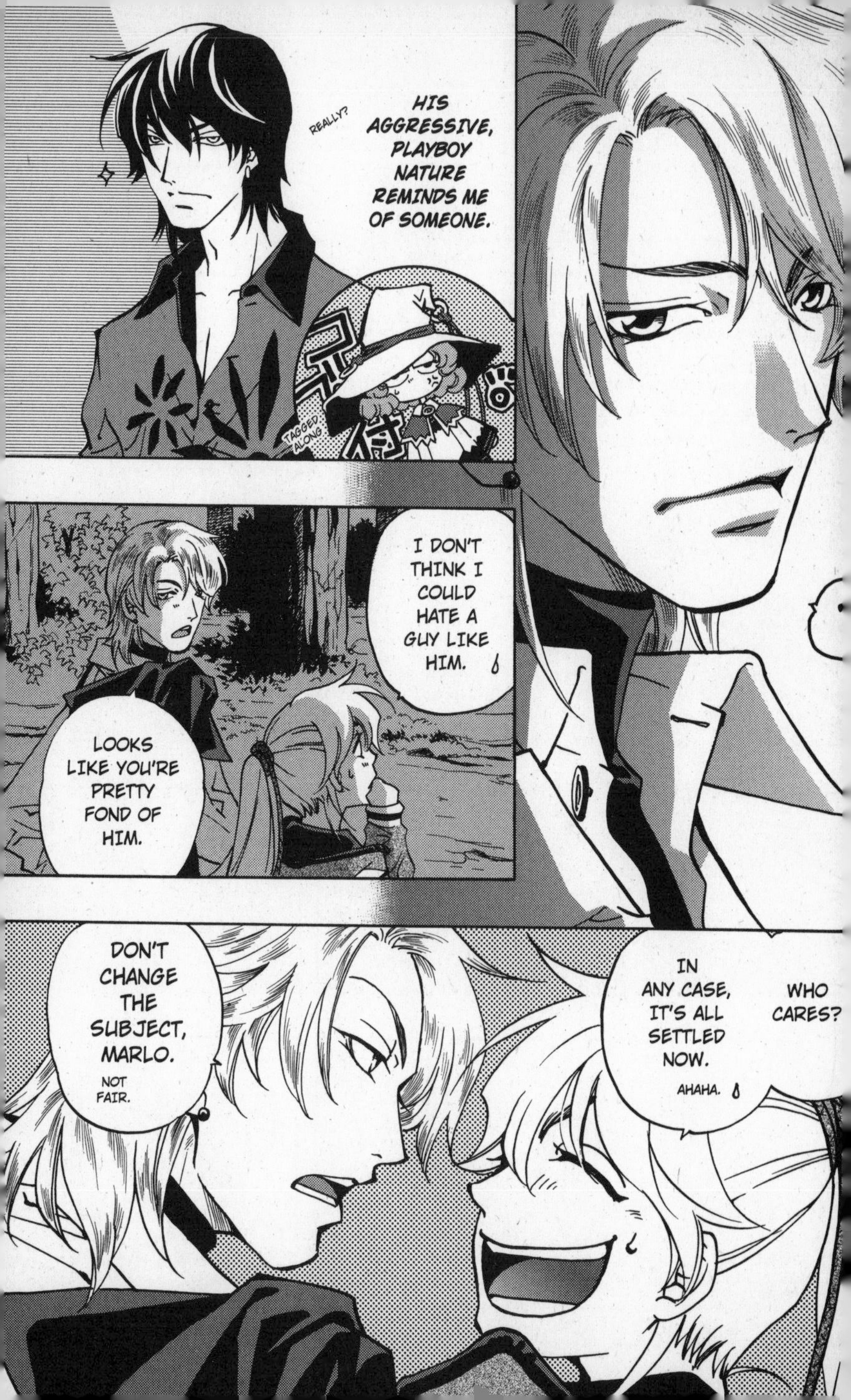
HIS AGGRESSIVE, PLAYBOY NATURE REMINDS ME OF SOMEONE.
REALLY?
TAGGED ALONG
I DON'T THINK I COULD HATE A GUY LIKE HIM.
LOOKS LIKE YOU'RE PRETTY FOND OF HIM.
WHO CARES?
IN ANY CASE, IT'S ALL SETTLED NOW.
AHAHA.
DON'T CHANGE THE SUBJECT, MARLO.
NOT FAIR.

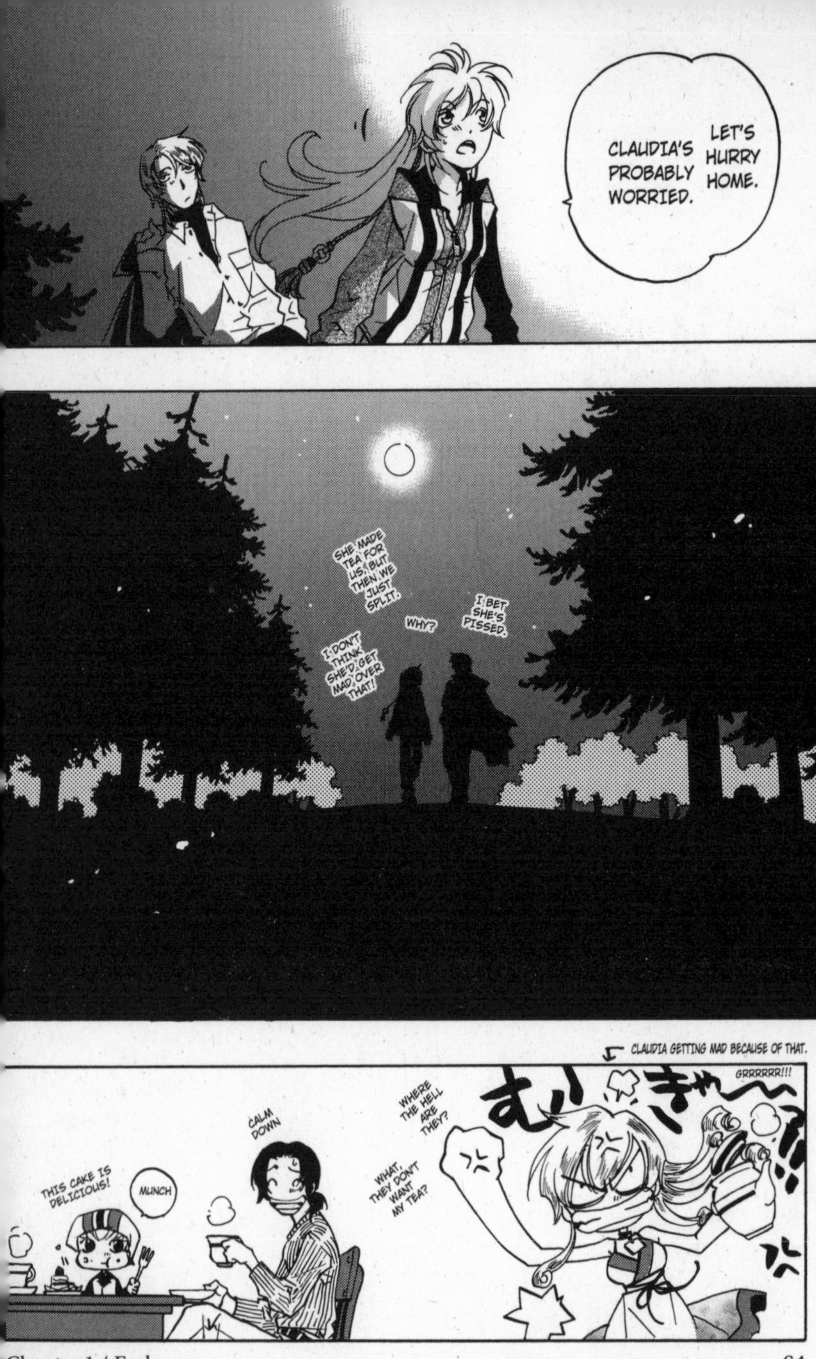
LET'S HURRY HOME. CLAUDIA'S PROBABLY WORRIED.
I BET SHE'S PISSED.
WHY?
SHE MADE TEA FOR US, BUT THEN WE JUST SPLIT.
I DON'T THINK SHE'D GET MAD OVER THAT!
CLAUDIA GETTING MAD BECAUSE OF THAT.
GRRRRRR!!!
む〜きゃ〜〜!!
WHERE THE HELL ARE THEY?
WHAT, THEY DON'T WANT MY TEA?
CALM DOWN
MUNCH
THIS CAKE IS DELICIOUS!

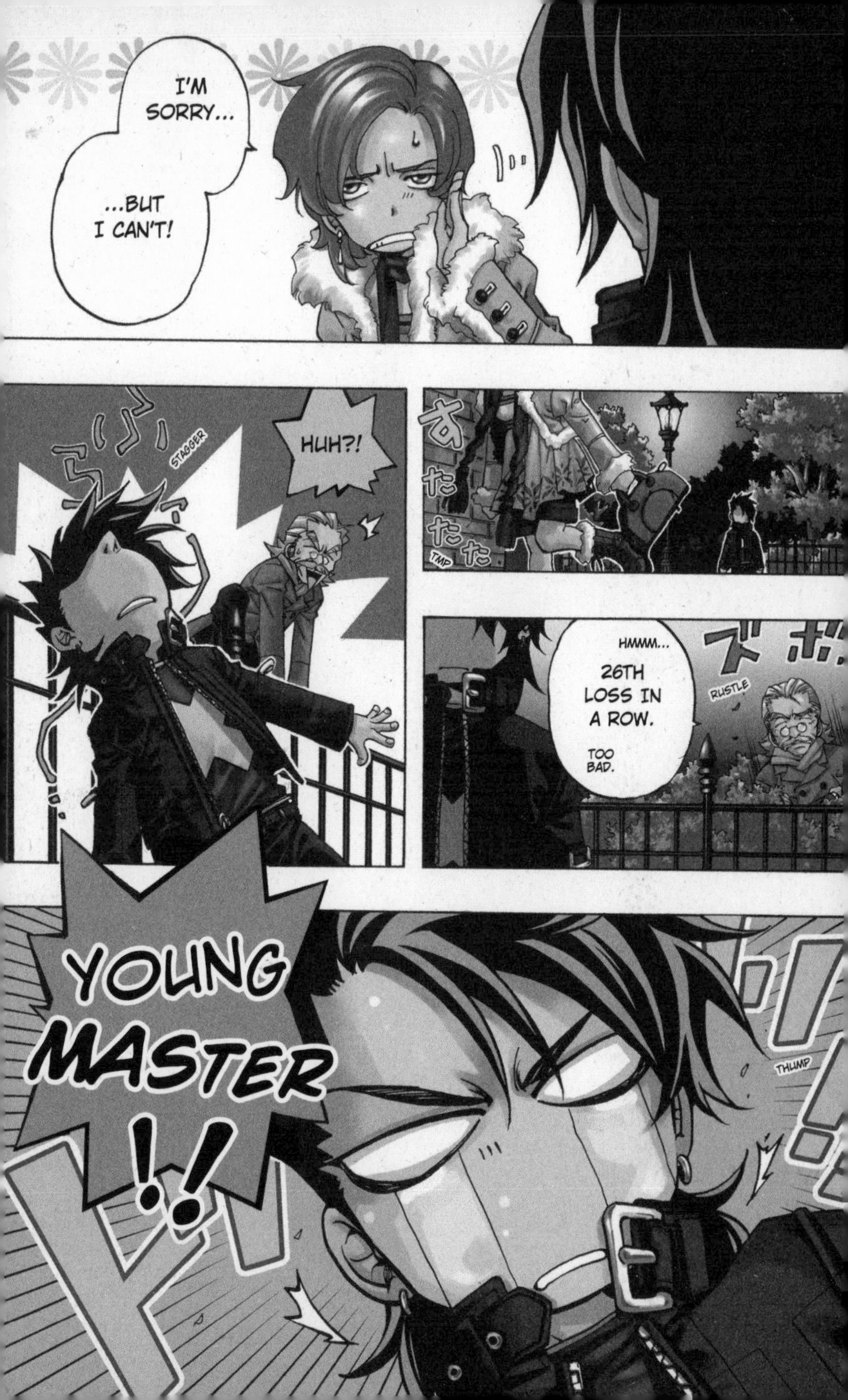
I'M SORRY...
...BUT I CAN'T!
TMP
HMMM...
26TH LOSS IN A ROW.
TOO BAD.
RUSTLE
HUH?!
STAGGER
THUMP
YOUNG MASTER!!

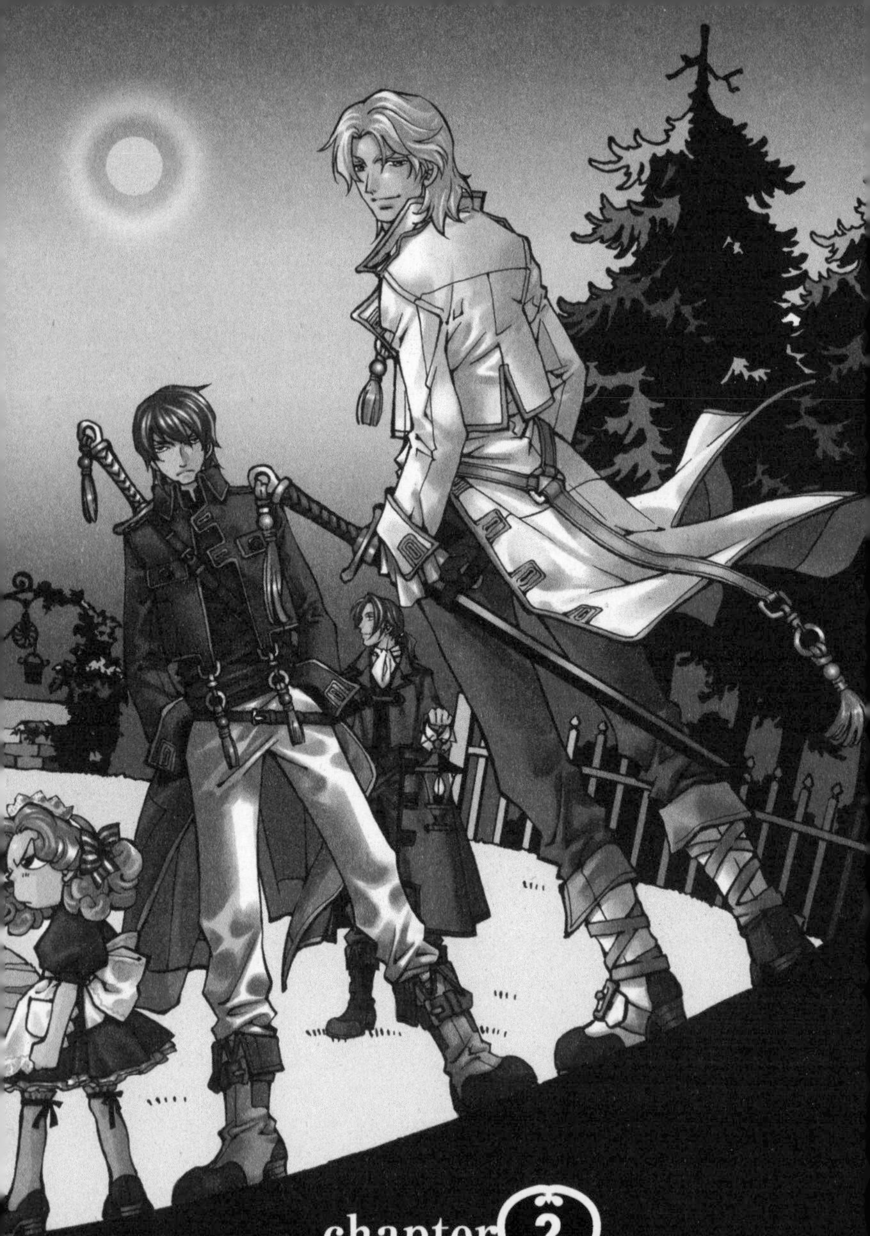

chapter 2
Scrambled Night (Part 1)

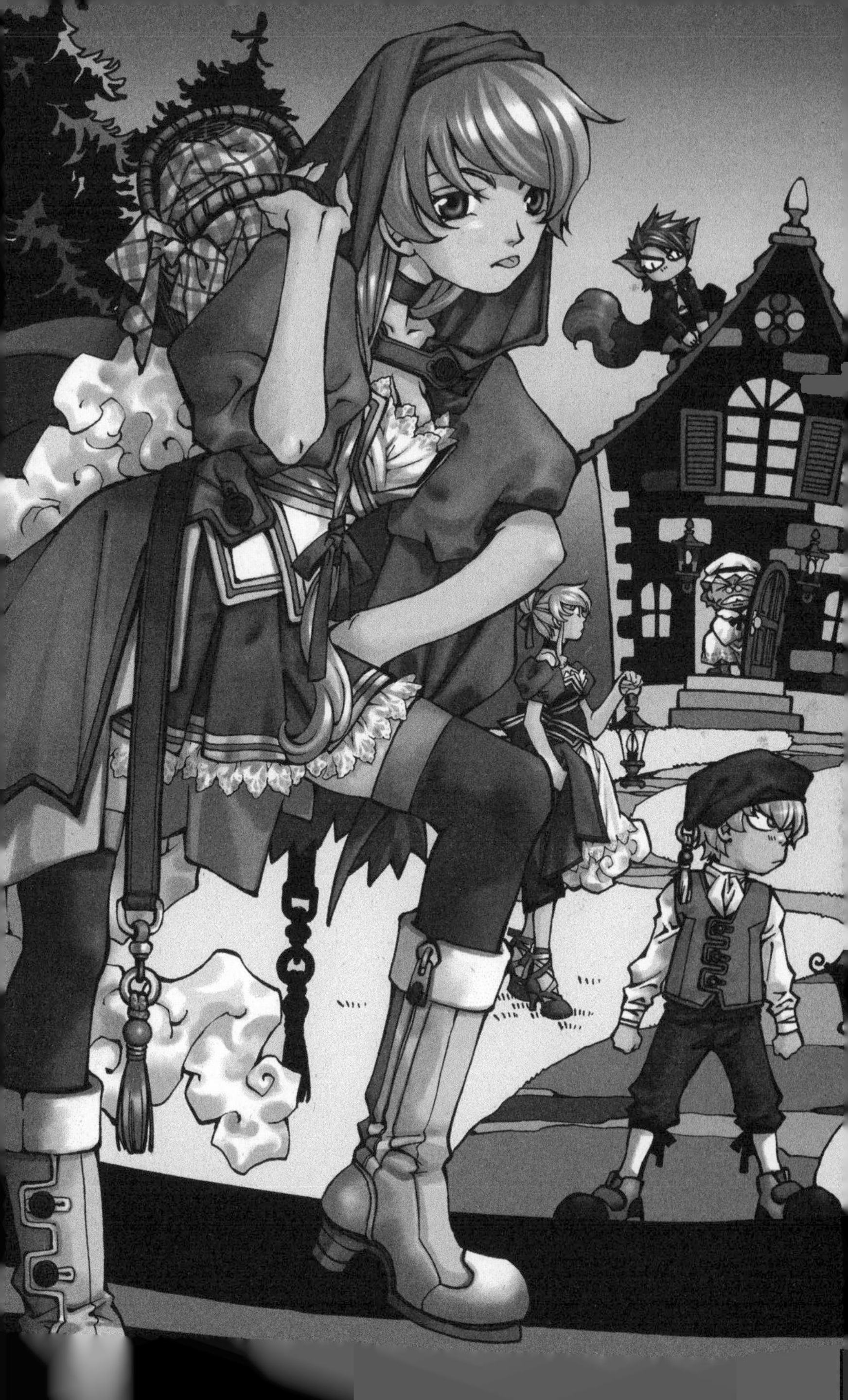

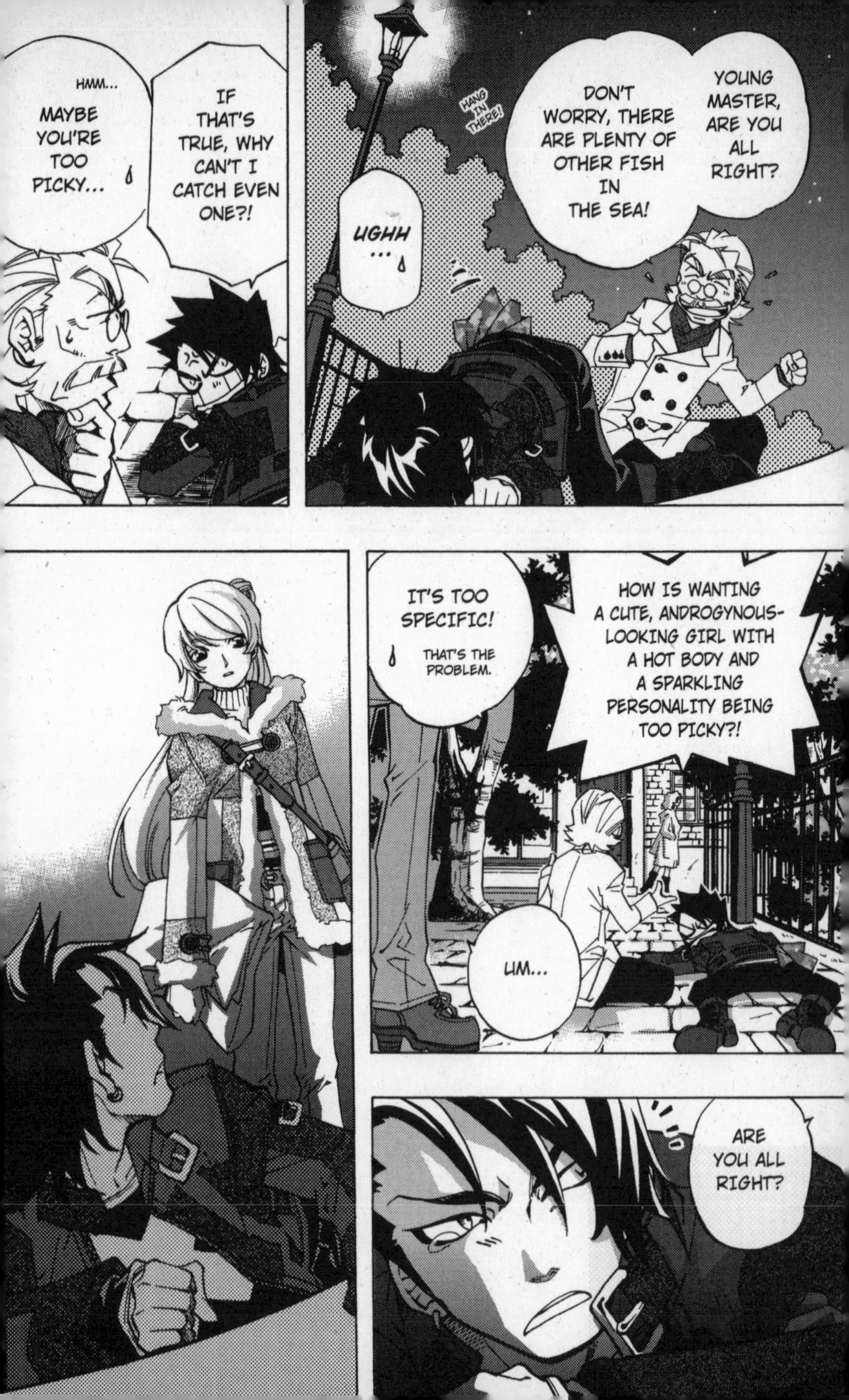
YOUNG MASTER, ARE YOU ALL RIGHT?
DON'T WORRY, THERE ARE PLENTY OF OTHER FISH IN THE SEA!
HANG IN THERE!
UGHH...
IF THAT'S TRUE, WHY CAN'T I CATCH EVEN ONE?!
HMM... MAYBE YOU'RE TOO PICKY...
HOW IS WANTING A CUTE, ANDROGYNOUS-LOOKING GIRL WITH A HOT BODY AND A SPARKLING PERSONALITY BEING TOO PICKY?!
IT'S TOO SPECIFIC!
THAT'S THE PROBLEM.
UM...
ARE YOU ALL RIGHT?

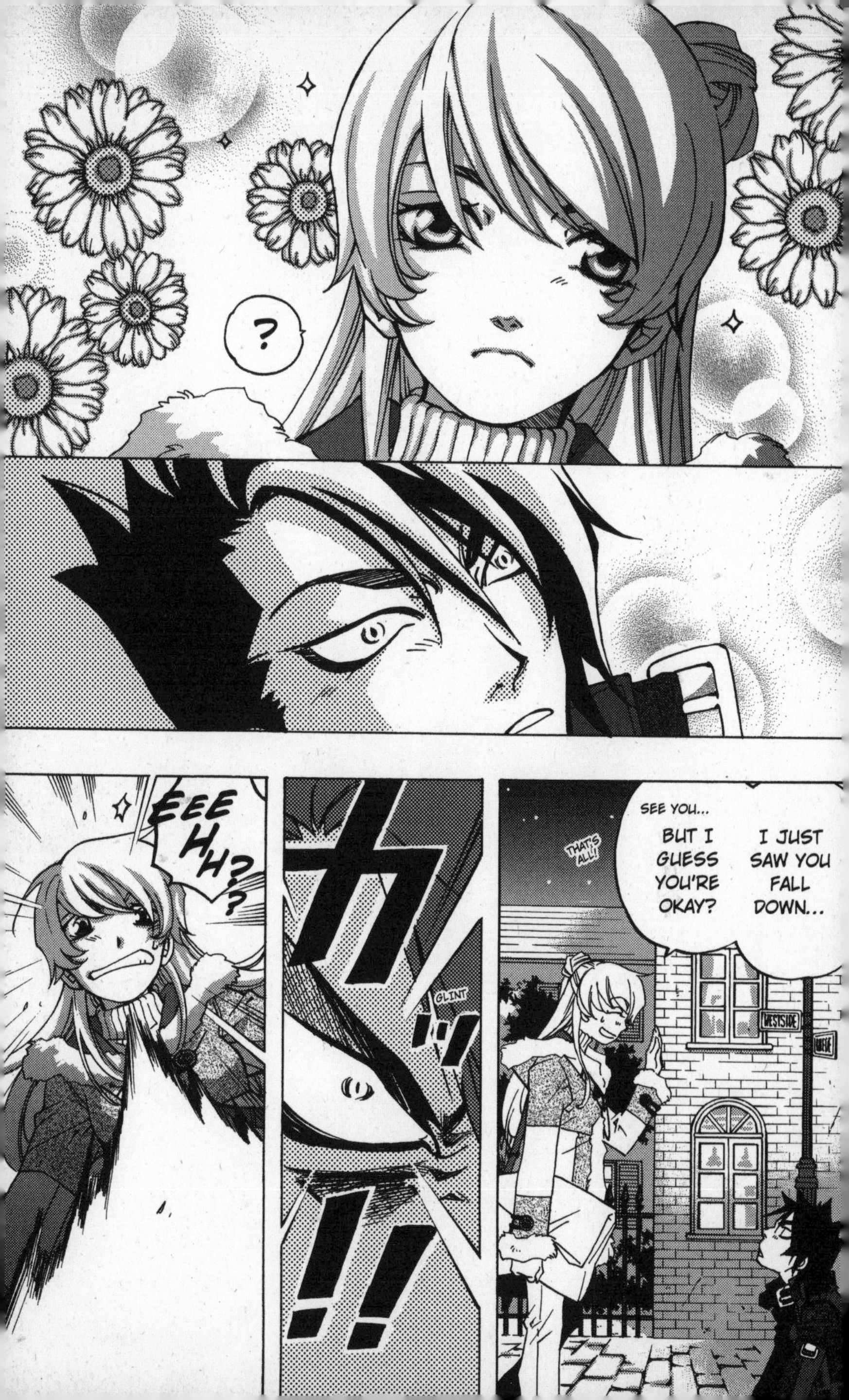
?
I JUST SAW YOU FALL DOWN...
BUT I GUESS YOU'RE OKAY?
SEE YOU...
THAT'S ALL!
WESTSIDE
GLINT
!!
EEEHH??

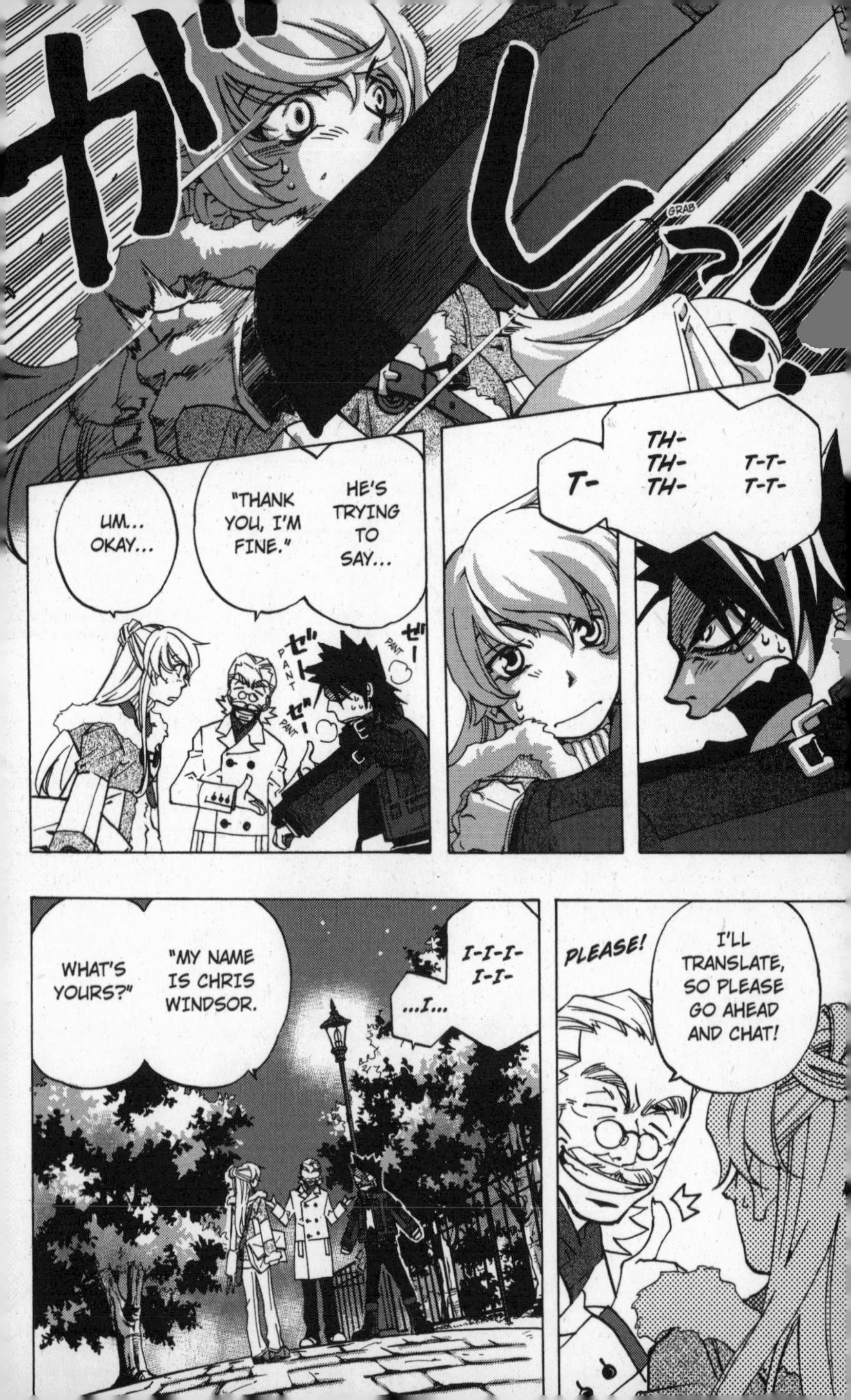
ガしっ!!
GRAB
!?
T-T- T-T-
TH- TH- TH-
T-
HE'S TRYING TO SAY...
"THANK YOU, I'M FINE."
UM... OKAY...
ゼー PANT
ゼー PANT
ゼー PANT
I'LL TRANSLATE, SO PLEASE GO AHEAD AND CHAT!
PLEASE!
I-I-I- I-I-
...I...
"MY NAME IS CHRIS WINDSOR.
WHAT'S YOURS?"

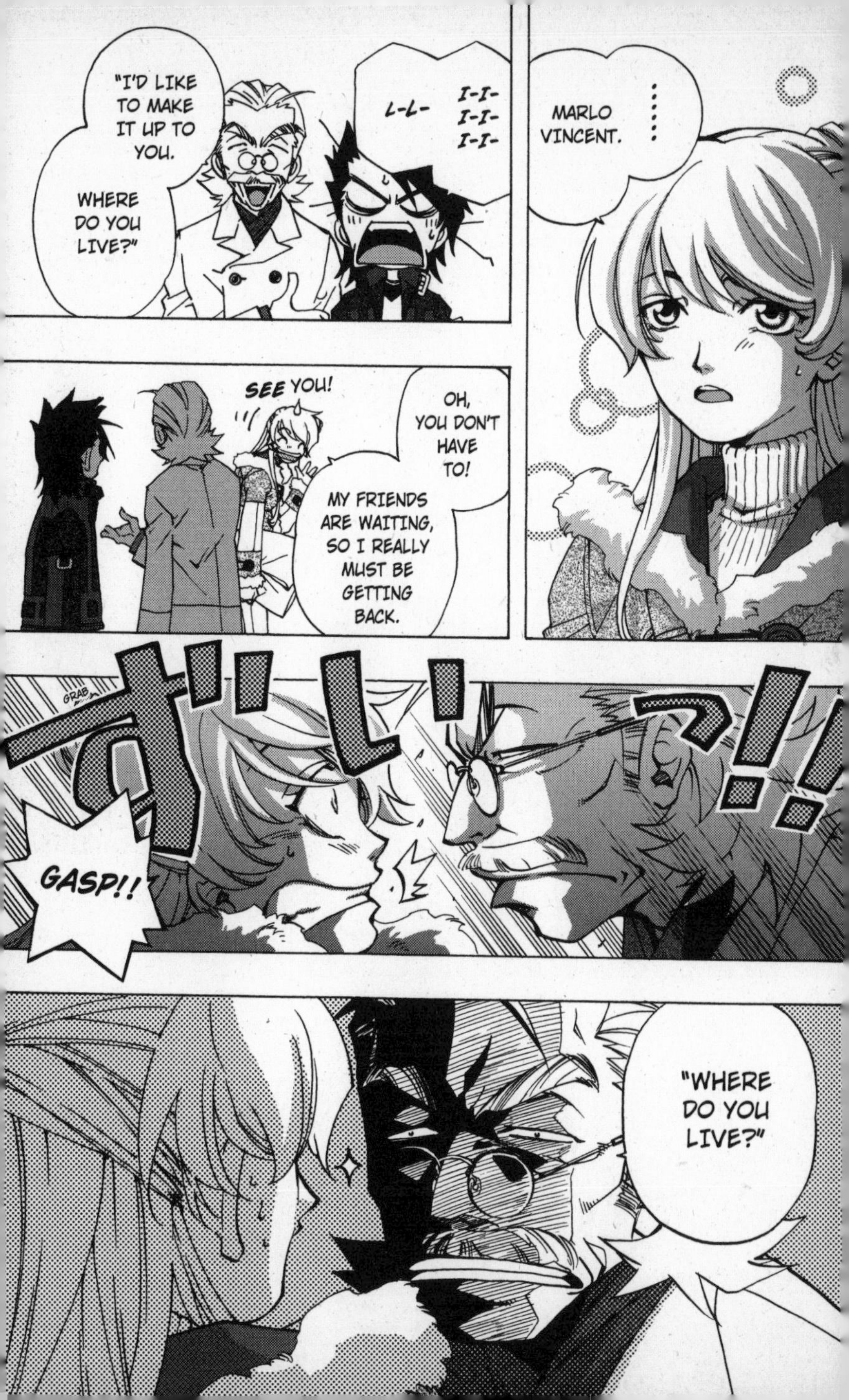
......
MARLO VINCENT.
I-I- I-I- I-I-
L-L-
"I'D LIKE TO MAKE IT UP TO YOU.
WHERE DO YOU LIVE?"
OH, YOU DON'T HAVE TO!
MY FRIENDS ARE WAITING, SO I REALLY MUST BE GETTING BACK.
SEE YOU!
GRAB
GASP!!
"WHERE DO YOU LIVE?"

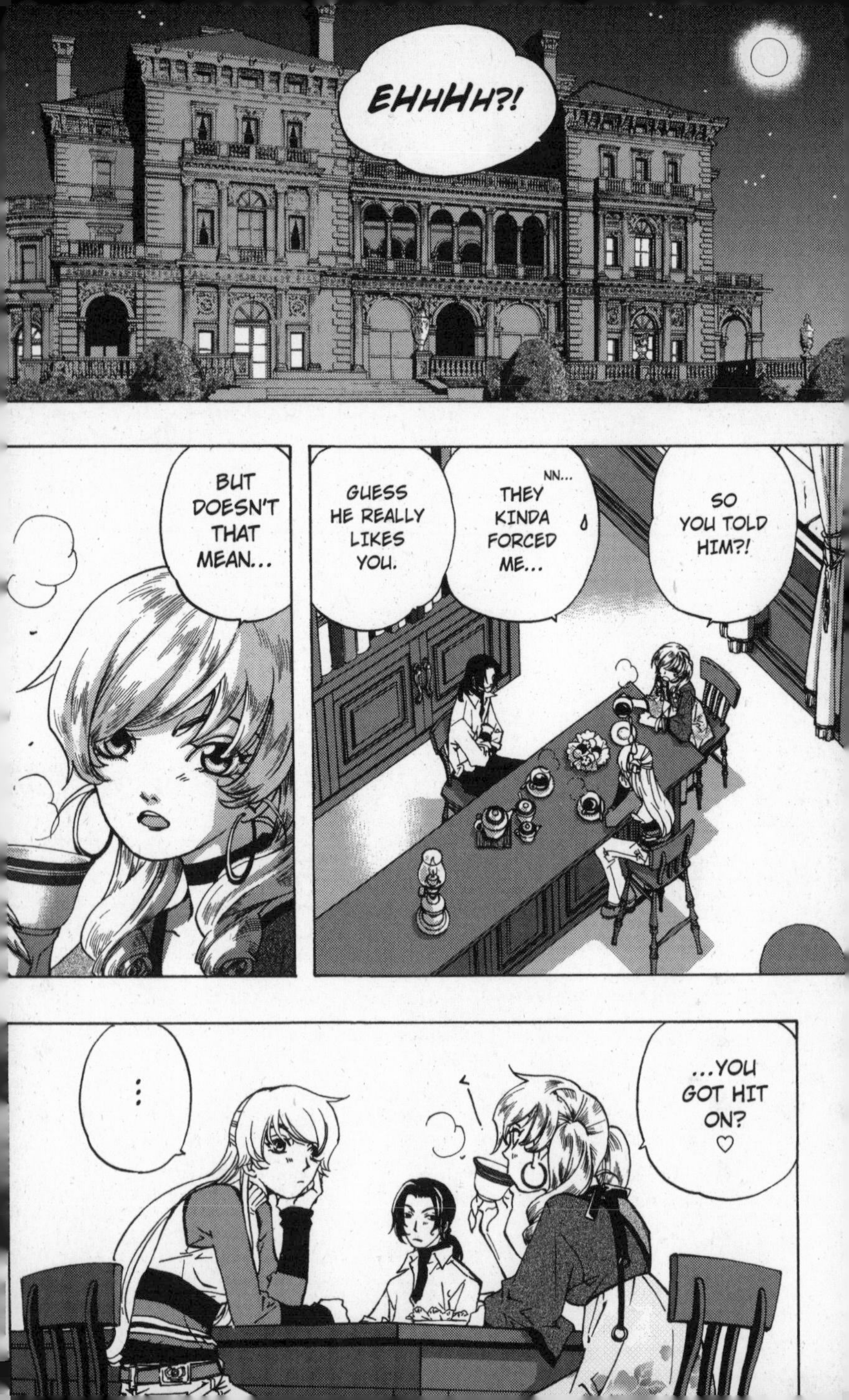
EHHHh?!
SO YOU TOLD HIM?!
NN...
THEY KINDA FORCED ME...
GUESS HE REALLY LIKES YOU.
BUT DOESN'T THAT MEAN...
...YOU GOT HIT ON? ♡
...

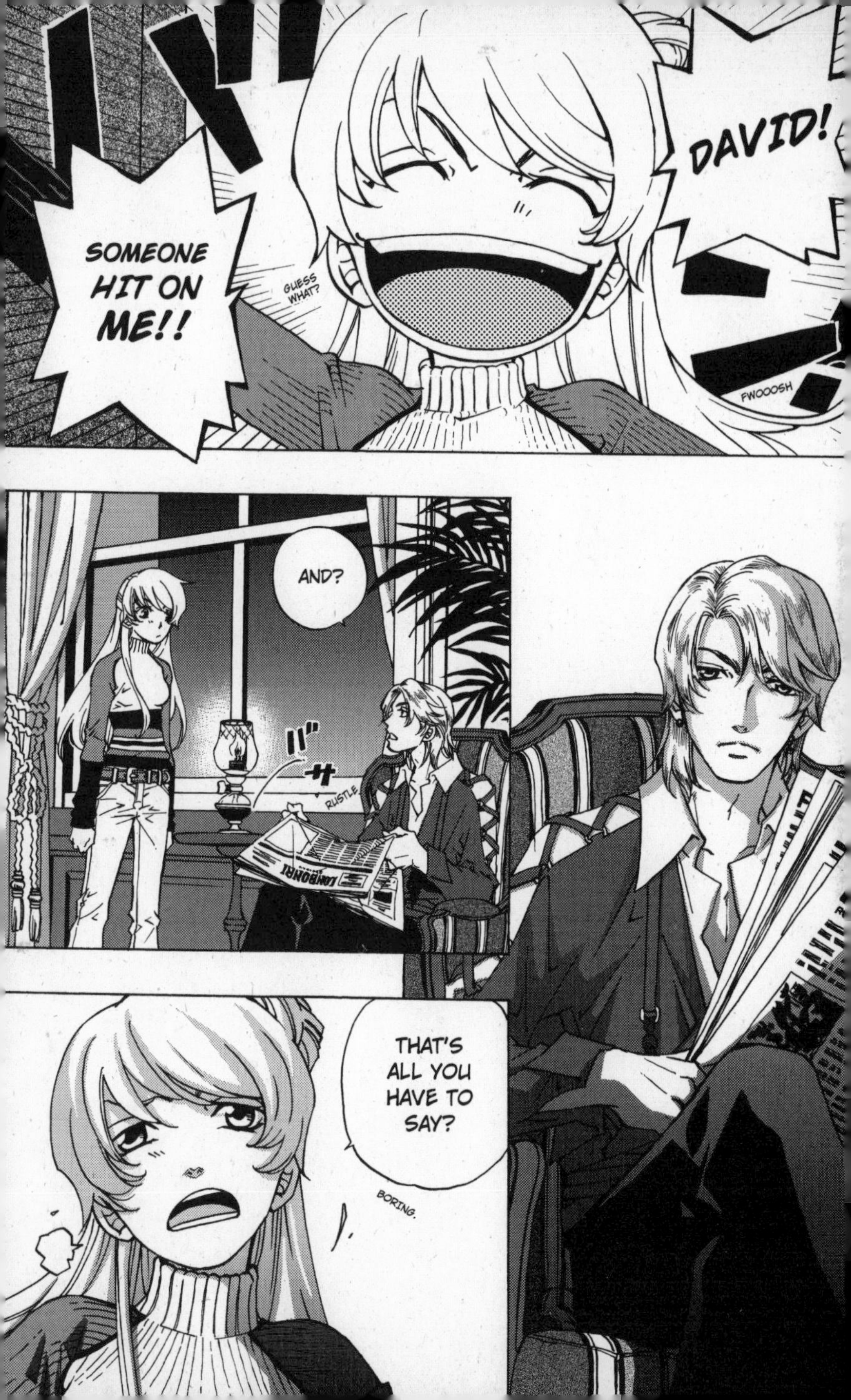
DAVID!
SOMEONE HIT ON ME!!
GUESS WHAT?
FWOOOSH
AND?
RUSTLE
THAT'S ALL YOU HAVE TO SAY?
BORING.

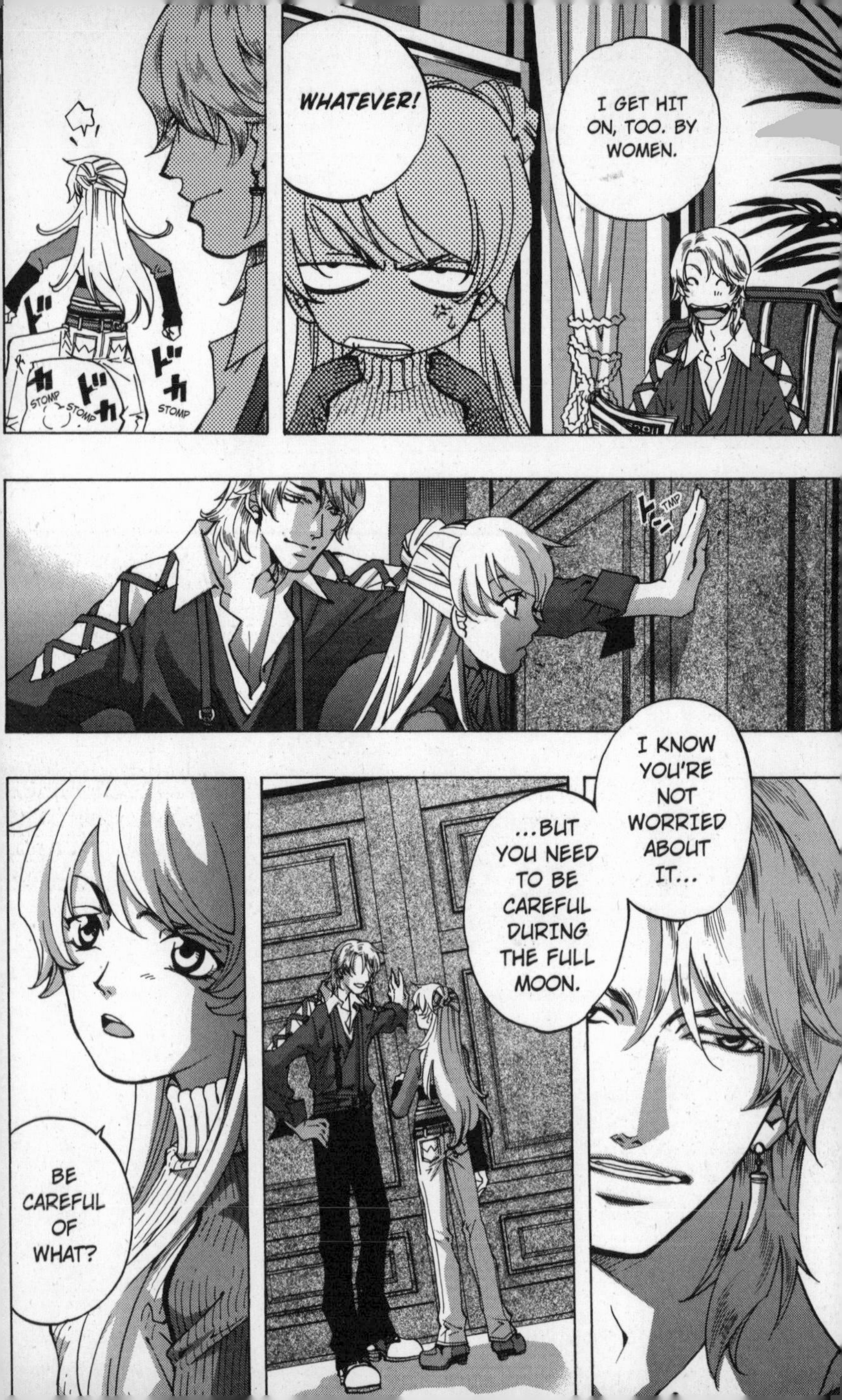
I GET HIT ON, TOO. BY WOMEN.
WHATEVER!
ドカ ドカ ドカ
STOMP STOMP STOMP
ト TMP
I KNOW YOU'RE NOT WORRIED ABOUT IT...
...BUT YOU NEED TO BE CAREFUL DURING THE FULL MOON.
BE CAREFUL OF WHAT?

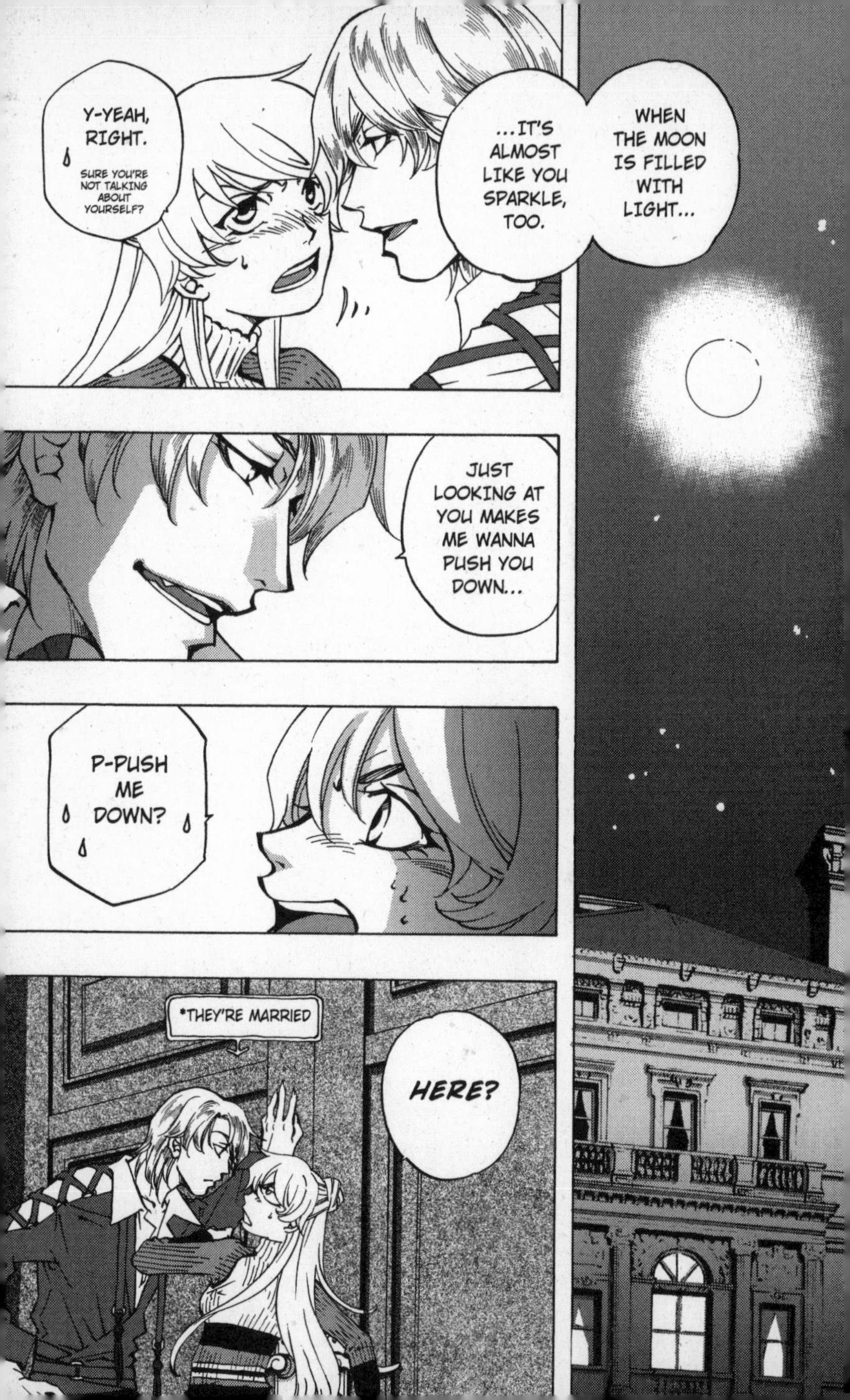
WHEN THE MOON IS FILLED WITH LIGHT...
...IT'S ALMOST LIKE YOU SPARKLE, TOO.
Y-YEAH, RIGHT.
SURE YOU'RE NOT TALKING ABOUT YOURSELF?
JUST LOOKING AT YOU MAKES ME WANNA PUSH YOU DOWN...
P-PUSH ME DOWN?
HERE?
*THEY'RE MARRIED

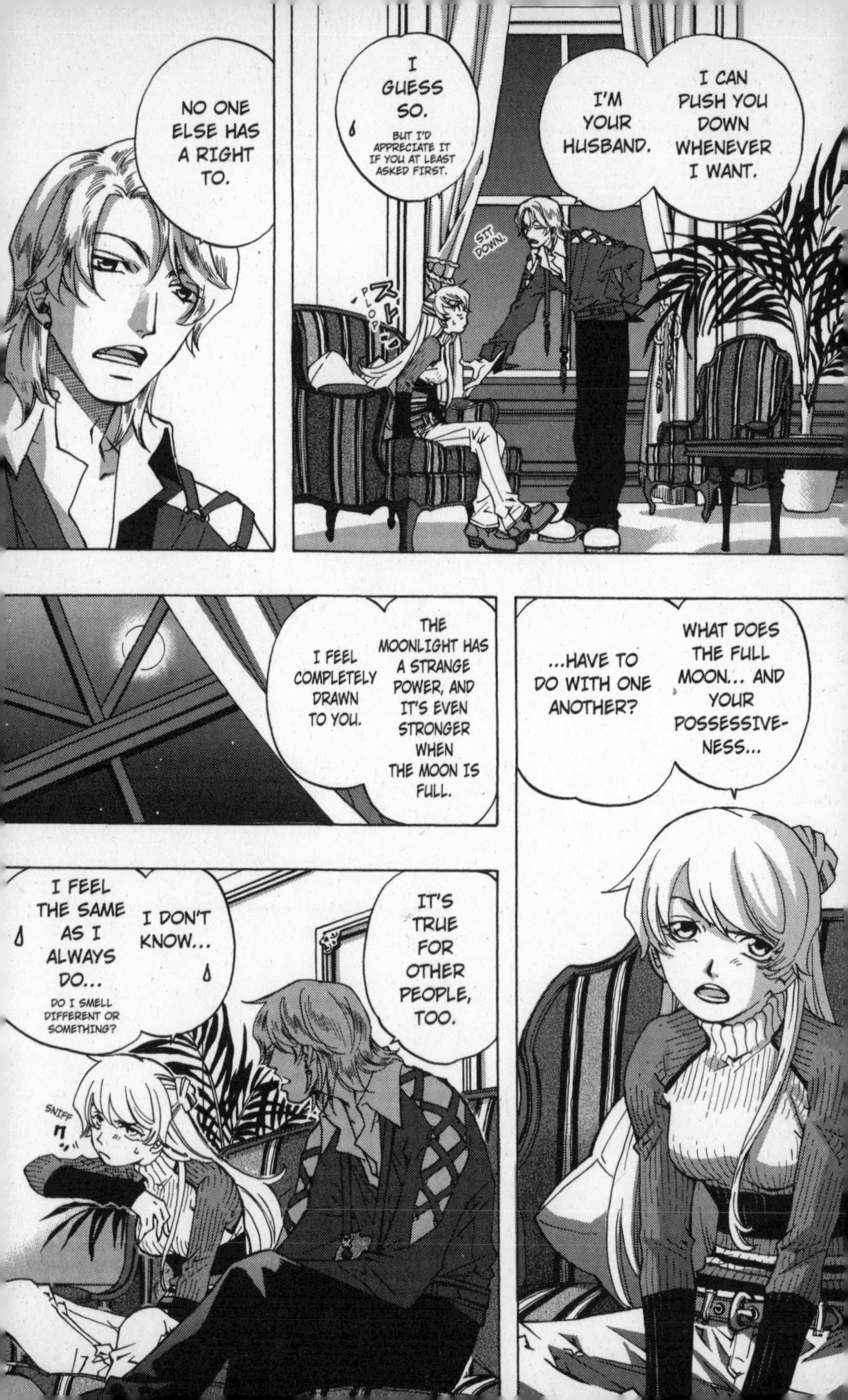
I CAN PUSH YOU DOWN WHENEVER I WANT.
I'M YOUR HUSBAND.
I GUESS SO.
BUT I'D APPRECIATE IT IF YOU AT LEAST ASKED FIRST.
SIT DOWN.
PLOP
NO ONE ELSE HAS A RIGHT TO.
WHAT DOES THE FULL MOON... AND YOUR POSSESSIVE-NESS...
...HAVE TO DO WITH ONE ANOTHER?
THE MOONLIGHT HAS A STRANGE POWER, AND IT'S EVEN STRONGER WHEN THE MOON IS FULL.
I FEEL COMPLETELY DRAWN TO YOU.
IT'S TRUE FOR OTHER PEOPLE, TOO.
I DON'T KNOW...
I FEEL THE SAME AS I ALWAYS DO...
DO I SMELL DIFFERENT OR SOMETHING?
SNIFF

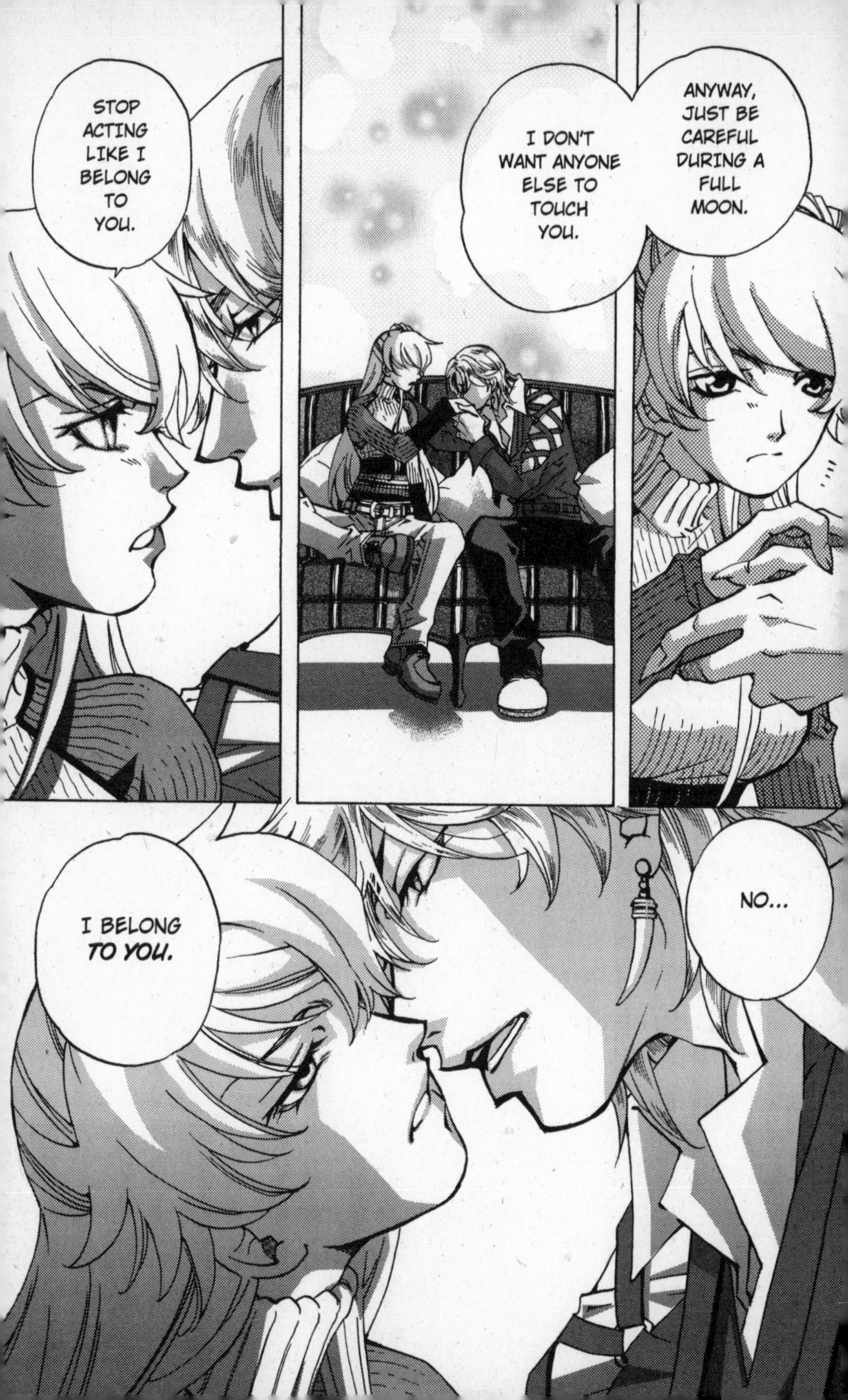
ANYWAY, JUST BE CAREFUL DURING A FULL MOON.
I DON'T WANT ANYONE ELSE TO TOUCH YOU.
STOP ACTING LIKE I BELONG TO YOU.
NO...
I BELONG *TO YOU.*

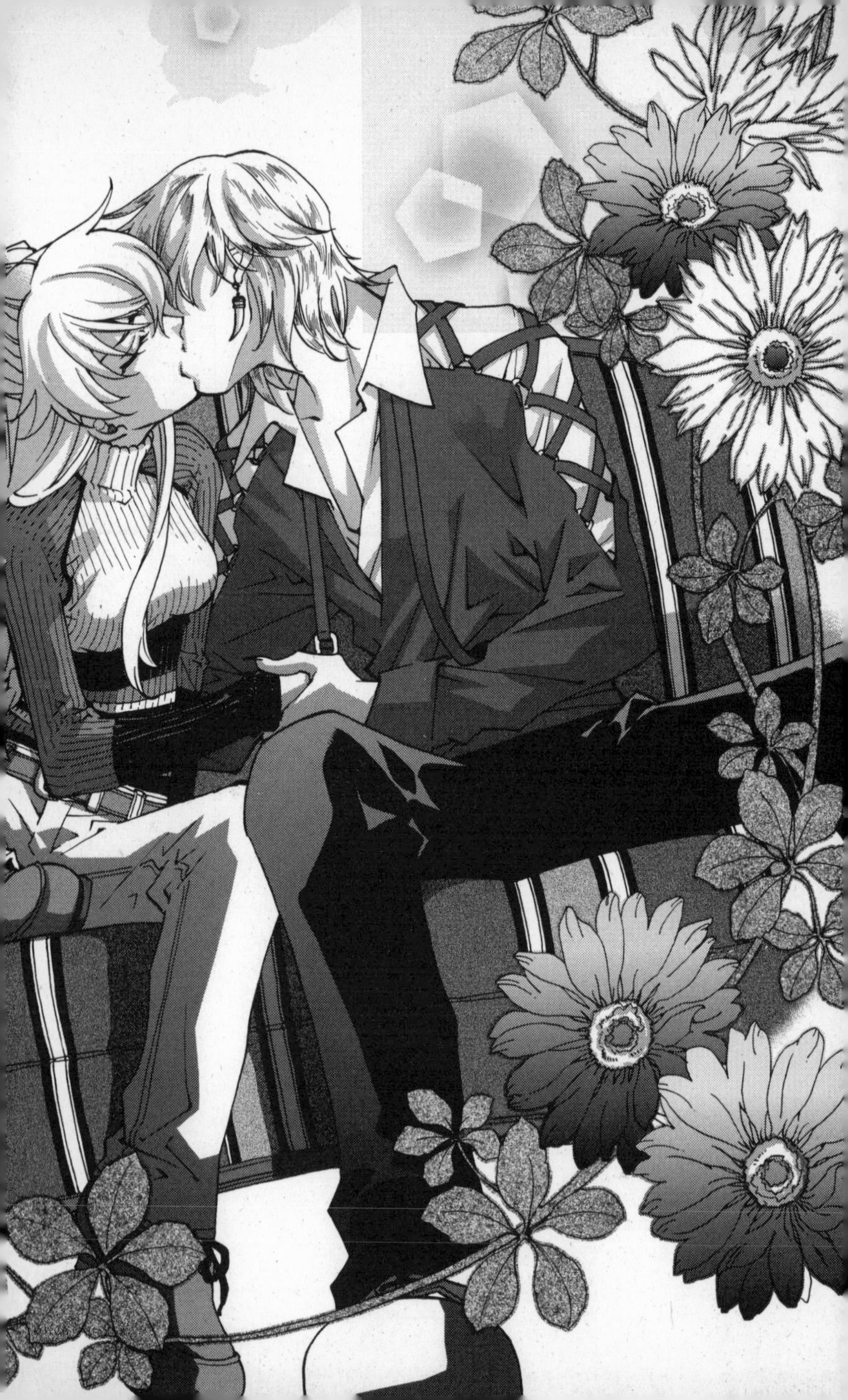

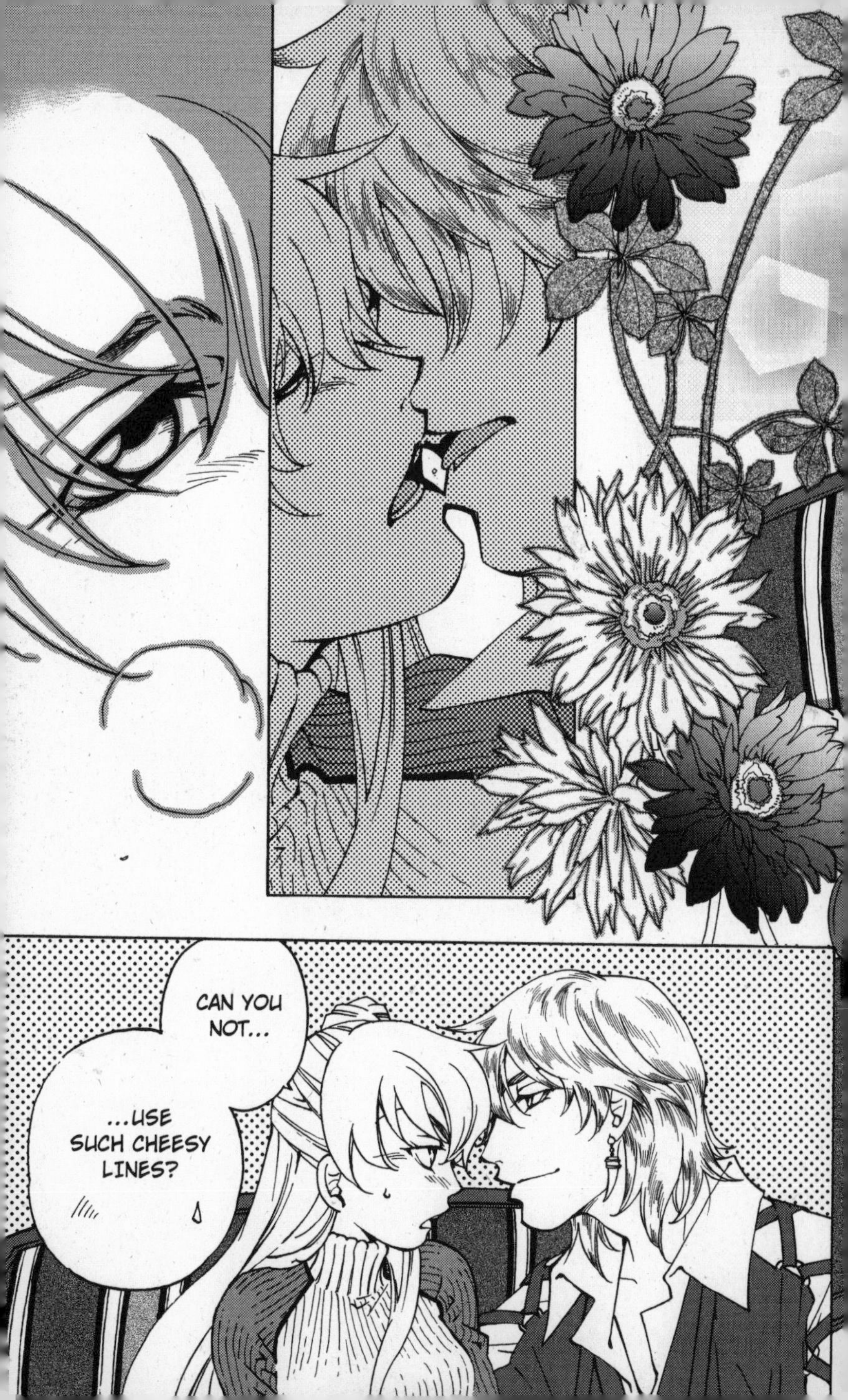
CAN YOU NOT...
...USE SUCH CHEESY LINES?

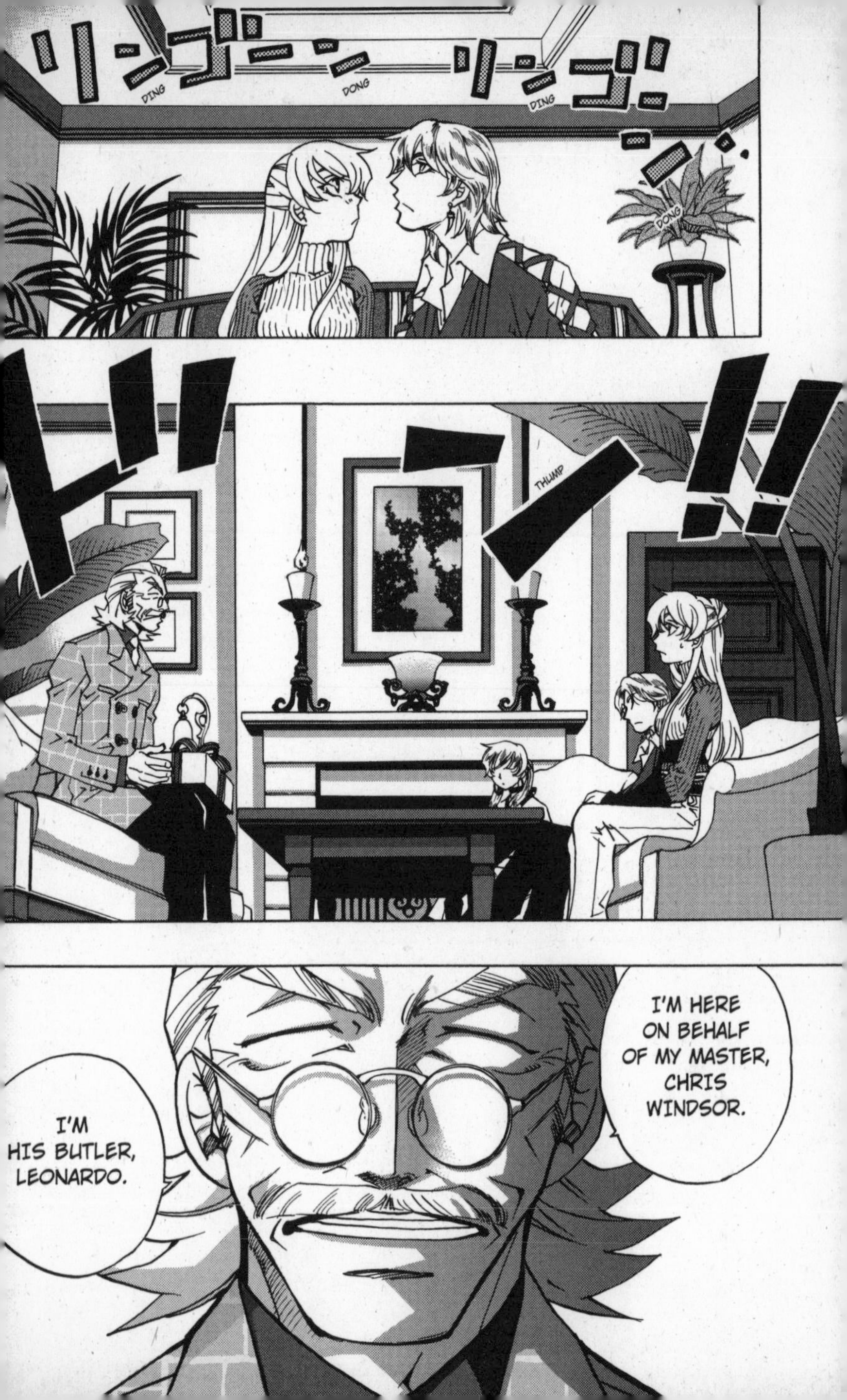

リンゴーン
DING
DONG
リンゴーン
DING
DONG
ドーン!!
THUMP
I'M HERE ON BEHALF OF MY MASTER, CHRIS WINDSOR.
I'M HIS BUTLER, LEONARDO.

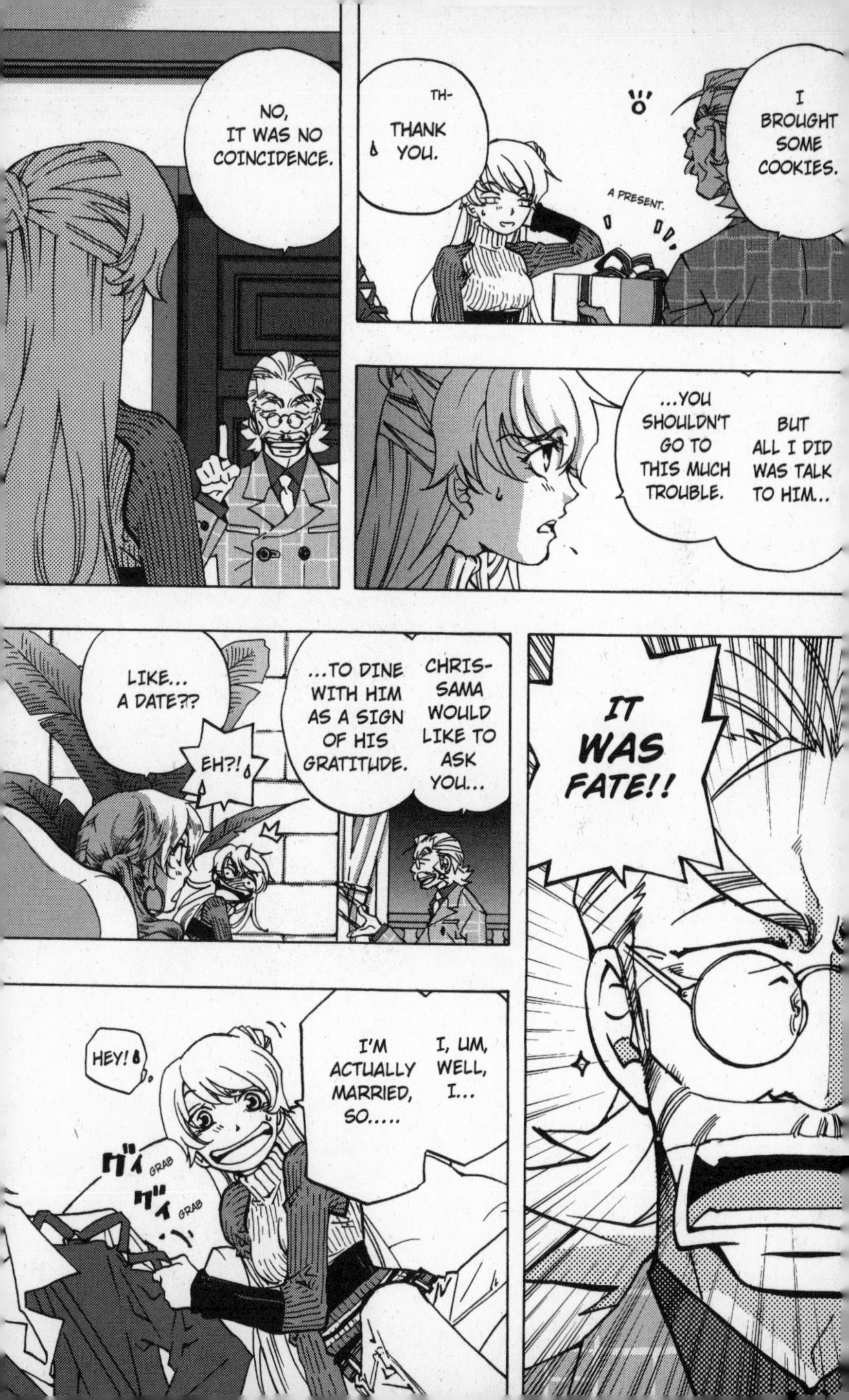
I BROUGHT SOME COOKIES.
A PRESENT.
TH-
THANK YOU.
BUT ALL I DID WAS TALK TO HIM...
...YOU SHOULDN'T GO TO THIS MUCH TROUBLE.
NO, IT WAS NO COINCIDENCE.
IT WAS FATE!!
CHRIS-SAMA WOULD LIKE TO ASK YOU...
...TO DINE WITH HIM AS A SIGN OF HIS GRATITUDE.
EH?!
LIKE... A DATE??
I, UM, WELL, I...
I'M ACTUALLY MARRIED, SO.....
HEY!
グイ GRAB
グイ GRAB

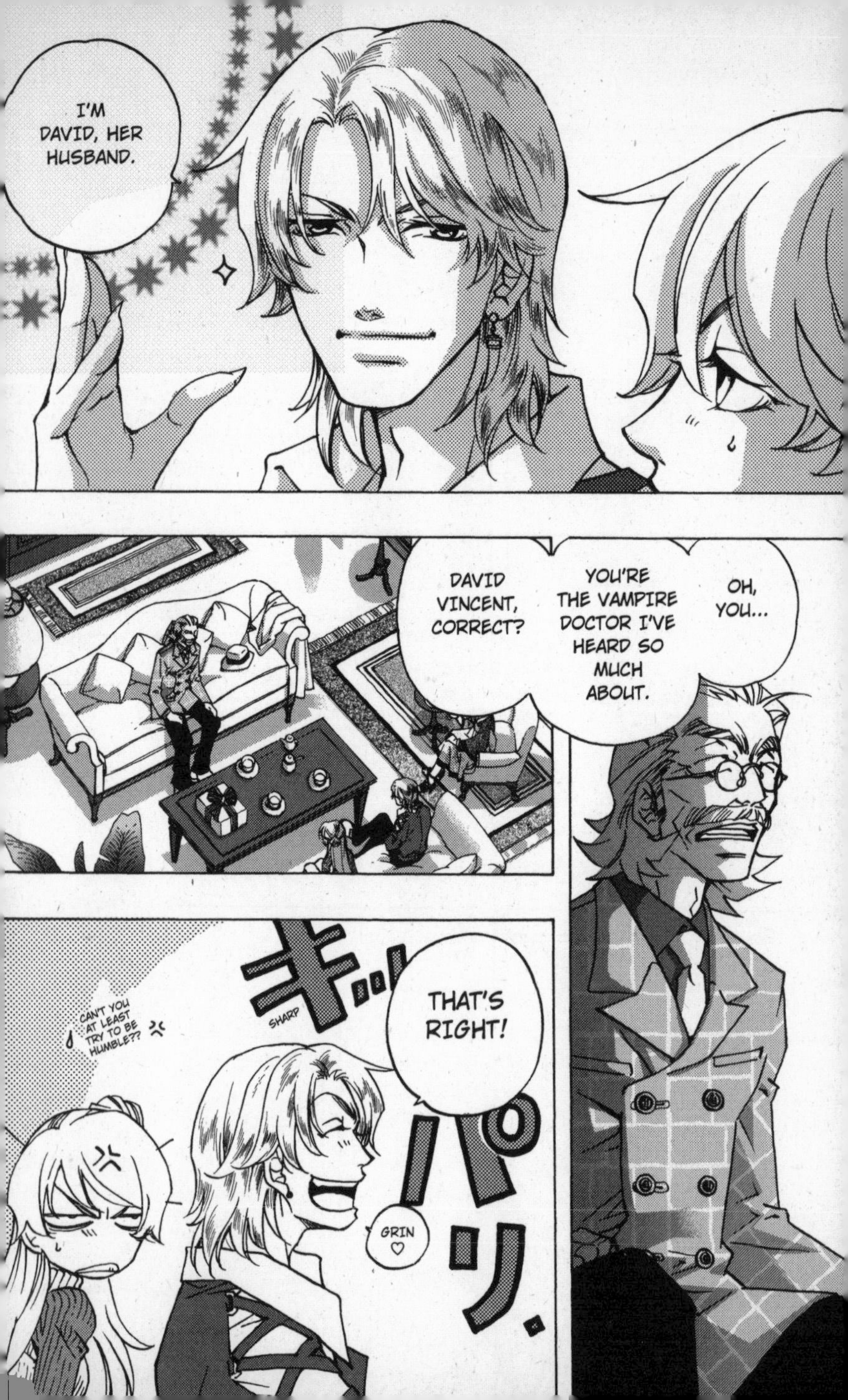
I'M DAVID, HER HUSBAND.
OH, YOU...
YOU'RE THE VAMPIRE DOCTOR I'VE HEARD SO MUCH ABOUT.
DAVID VINCENT, CORRECT?
SHARP
THAT'S RIGHT!
CAN'T YOU AT LEAST TRY TO BE HUMBLE??
GRIN ♡

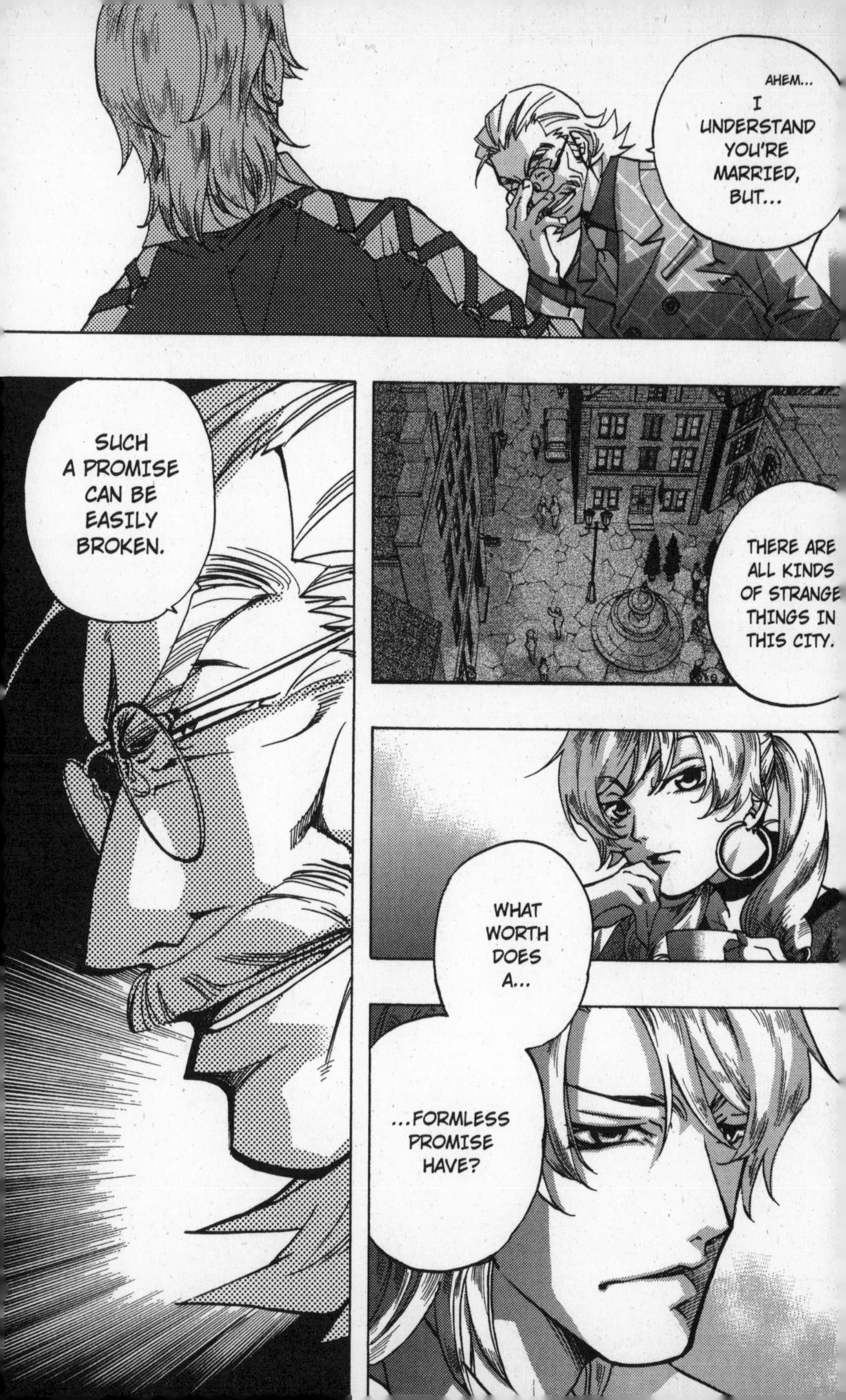
AHEM... I UNDERSTAND YOU'RE MARRIED, BUT...
SUCH A PROMISE CAN BE EASILY BROKEN.
THERE ARE ALL KINDS OF STRANGE THINGS IN THIS CITY.
WHAT WORTH DOES A...
...FORMLESS PROMISE HAVE?

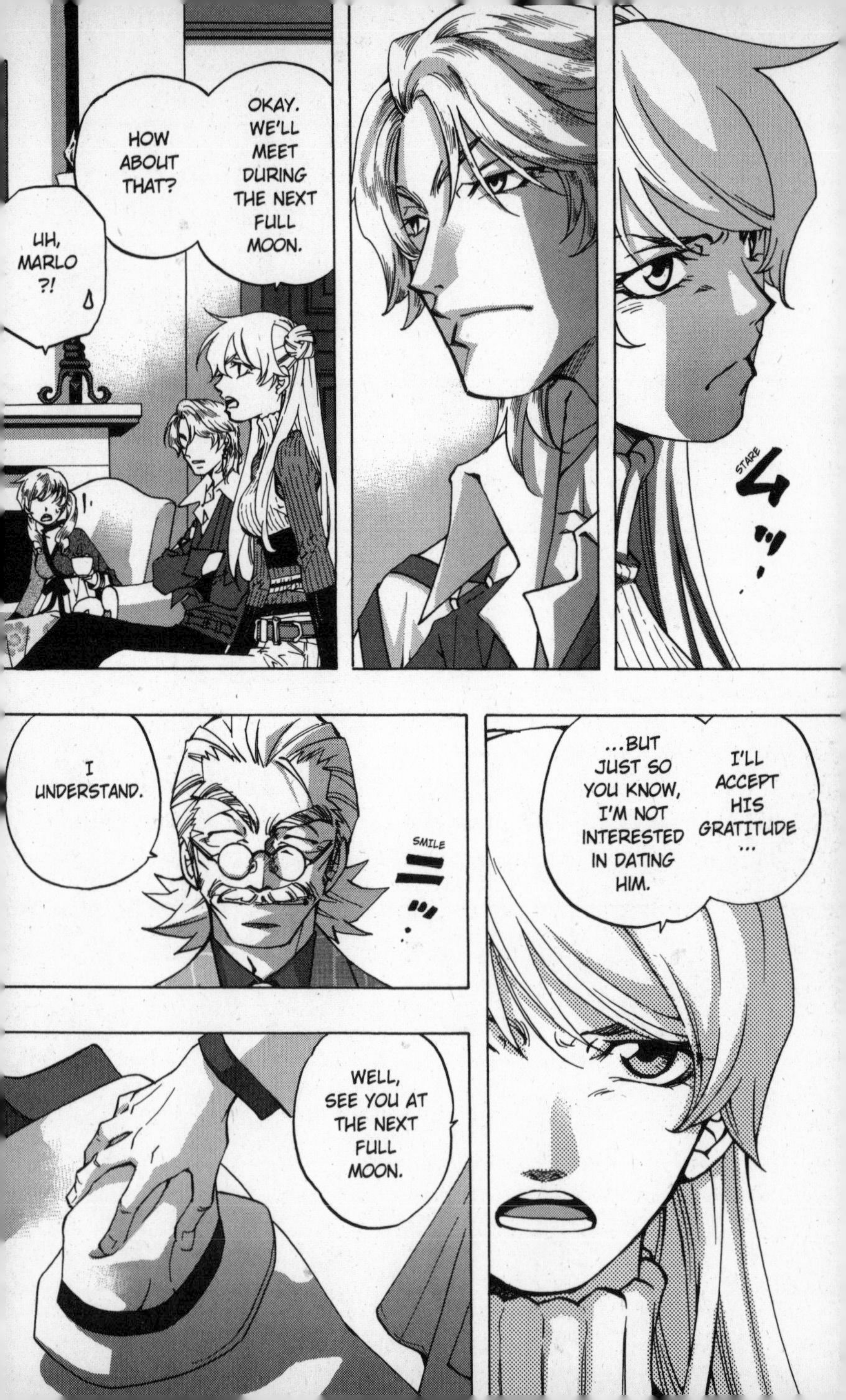
STARE
OKAY. WE'LL MEET DURING THE NEXT FULL MOON.
HOW ABOUT THAT?
UH, MARLO?!
I'LL ACCEPT HIS GRATITUDE...
...BUT JUST SO YOU KNOW, I'M NOT INTERESTED IN DATING HIM.
I UNDERSTAND.
SMILE
WELL, SEE YOU AT THE NEXT FULL MOON.

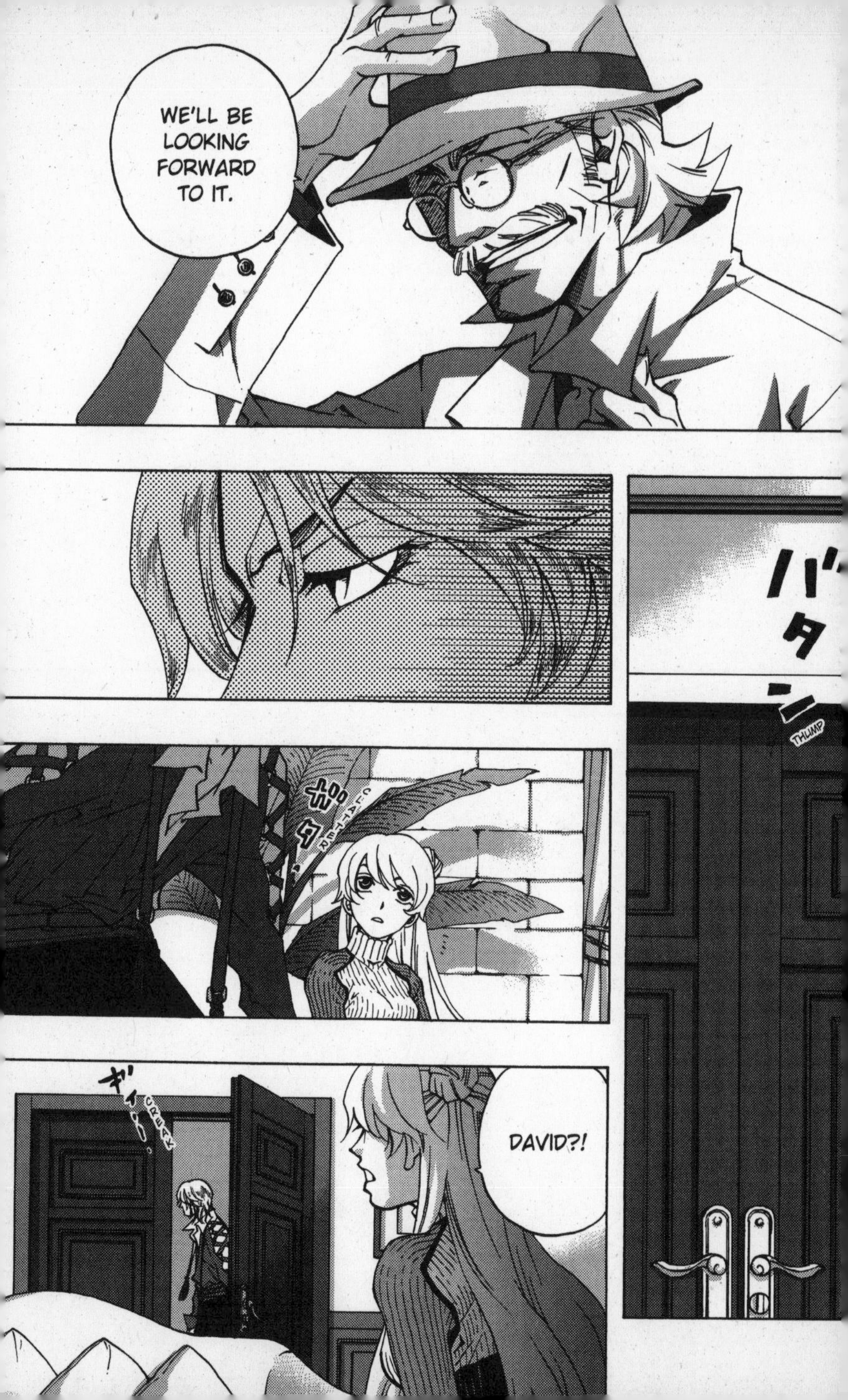
WE'LL BE LOOKING FORWARD TO IT.
バタン
THUMP
ガタ
CLATTER
ギィ…
CREAK
DAVID?!

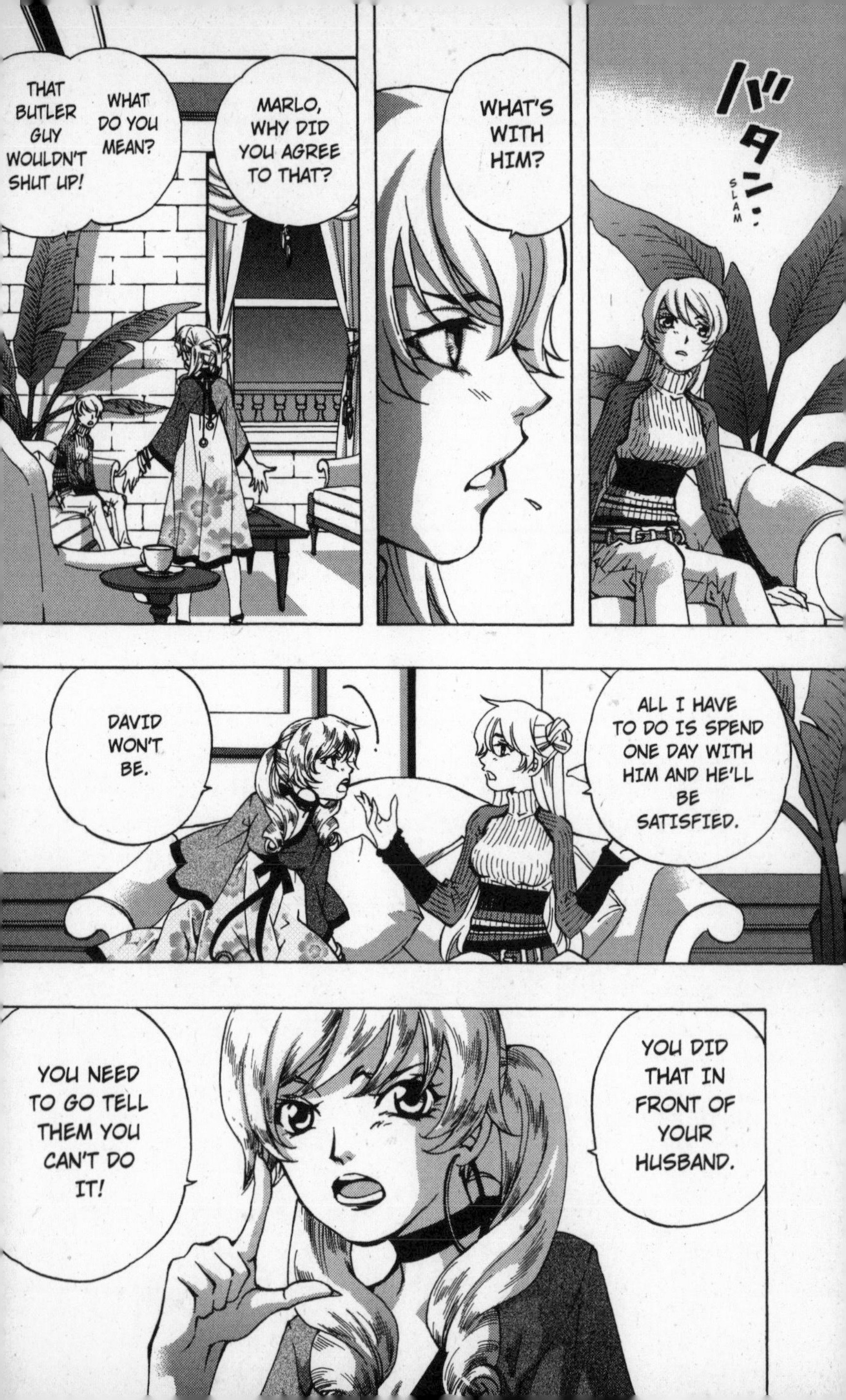
バタン
SLAM
WHAT'S WITH HIM?
MARLO, WHY DID YOU AGREE TO THAT?
WHAT DO YOU MEAN?
THAT BUTLER GUY WOULDN'T SHUT UP!
ALL I HAVE TO DO IS SPEND ONE DAY WITH HIM AND HE'LL BE SATISFIED.
DAVID WON'T BE.
YOU DID THAT IN FRONT OF YOUR HUSBAND.
YOU NEED TO GO TELL THEM YOU CAN'T DO IT!

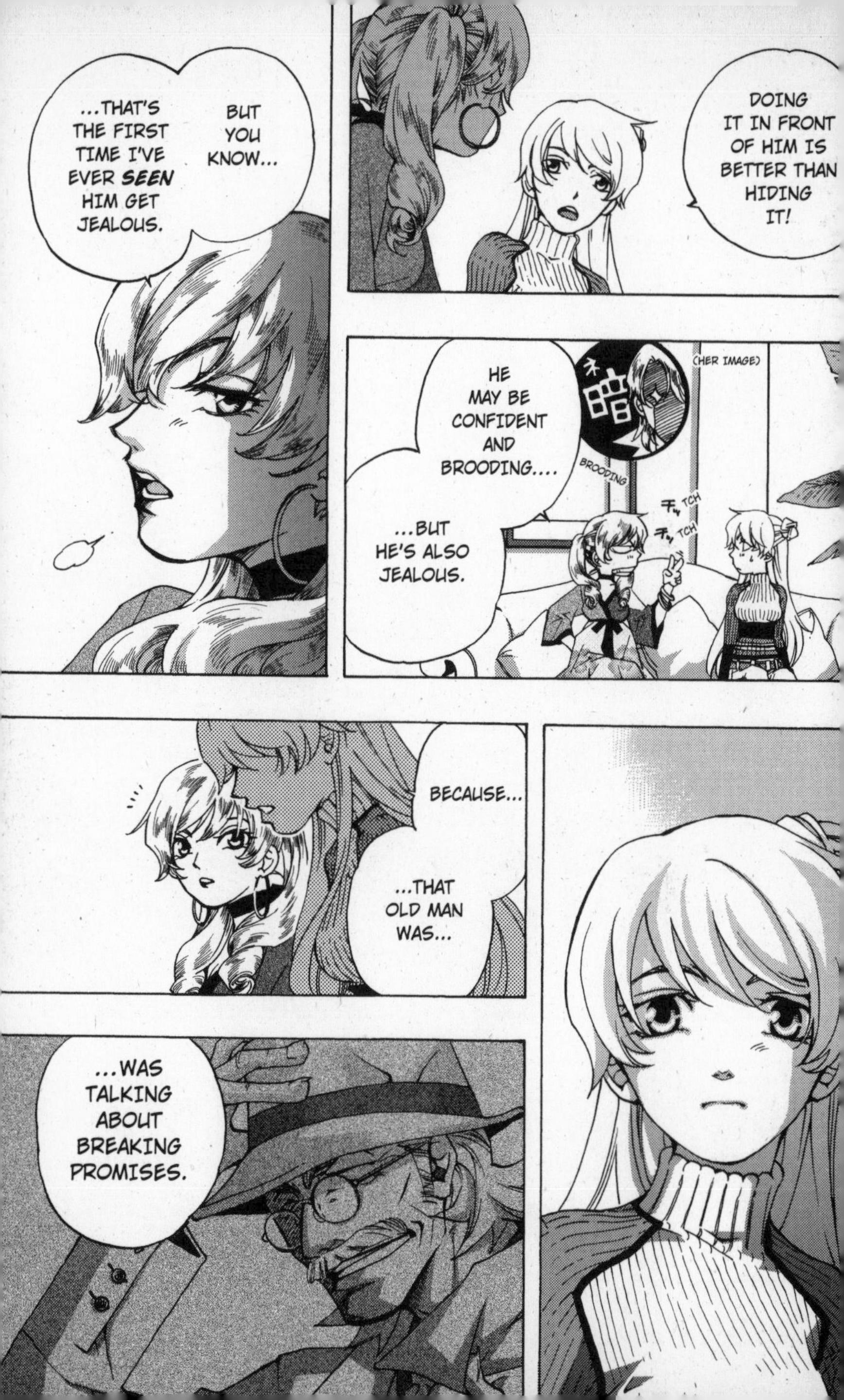
DOING IT IN FRONT OF HIM IS BETTER THAN HIDING IT!
HE MAY BE CONFIDENT AND BROODING....
(HER IMAGE)
ネ暗
BROODING
チッ TCH
チッ TCH
...BUT HE'S ALSO JEALOUS.
BUT YOU KNOW...
...THAT'S THE FIRST TIME I'VE EVER SEEN HIM GET JEALOUS.
BECAUSE...
...THAT OLD MAN WAS...
...WAS TALKING ABOUT BREAKING PROMISES.

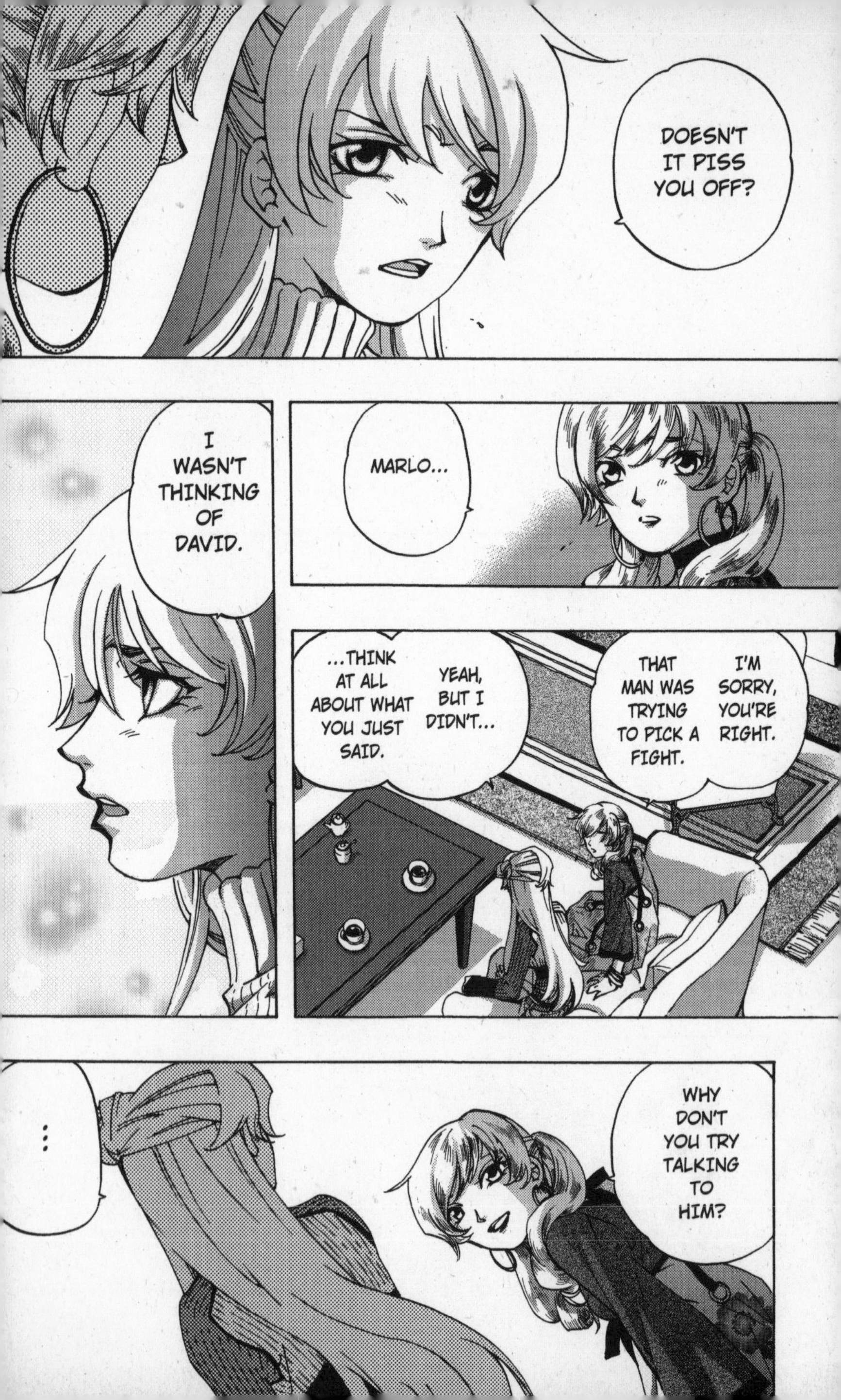
DOESN'T IT PISS YOU OFF?
MARLO...
I'M SORRY, YOU'RE RIGHT.
THAT MAN WAS TRYING TO PICK A FIGHT.
YEAH, BUT I DIDN'T...
...THINK AT ALL ABOUT WHAT YOU JUST SAID.
I WASN'T THINKING OF DAVID.
WHY DON'T YOU TRY TALKING TO HIM?
...

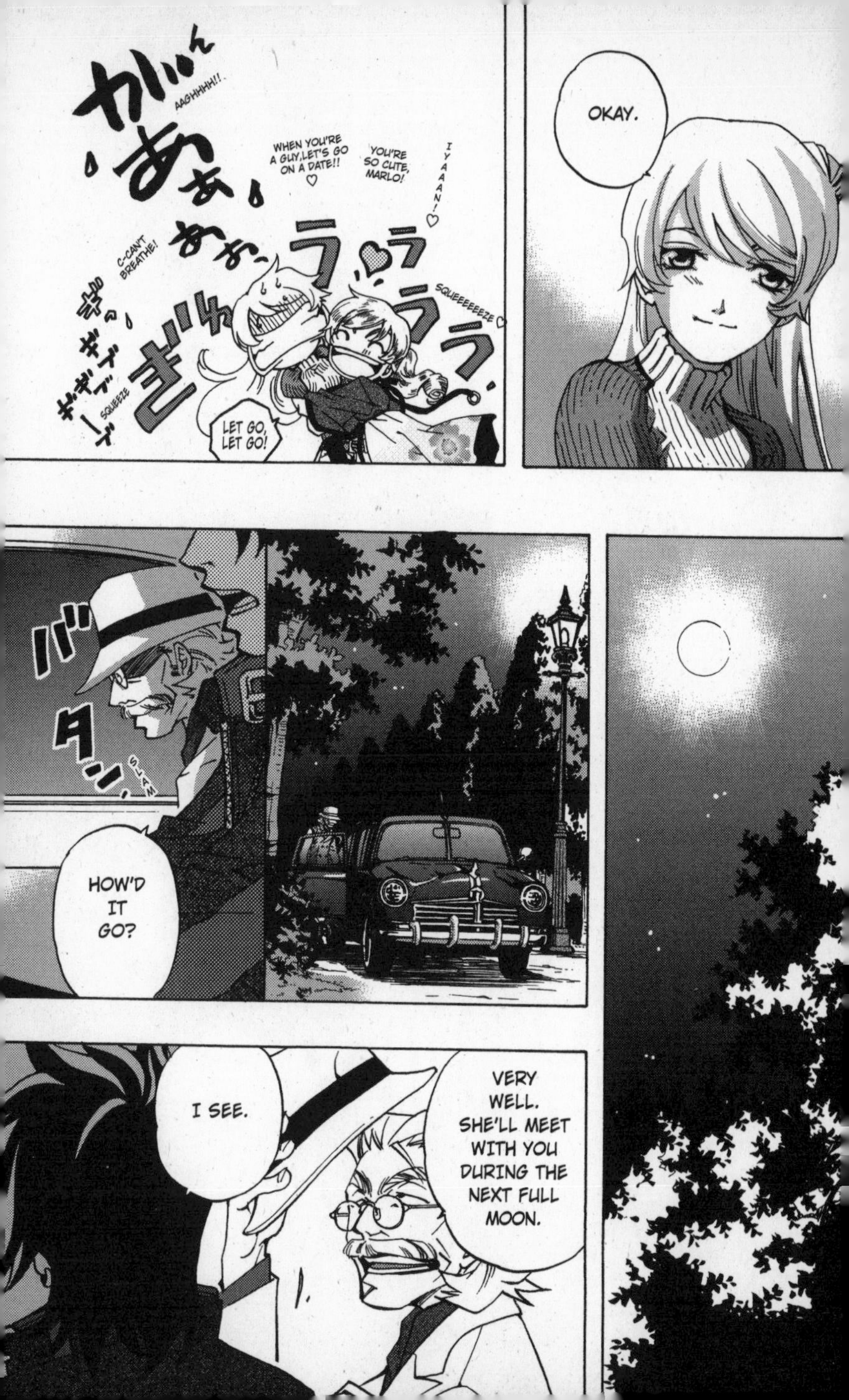
OKAY.
IYAAAAN! ♡
YOU'RE SO CUTE, MARLO!
WHEN YOU'RE A GUY,LET'S GO ON A DATE!! ♡
AAGHHHH!!
SQUEEEEEEZE ♡
C-CAN'T BREATHE!
SQUEEZE
LET GO, LET GO!
SLAM
HOW'D IT GO?
VERY WELL. SHE'LL MEET WITH YOU DURING THE NEXT FULL MOON.
I SEE.

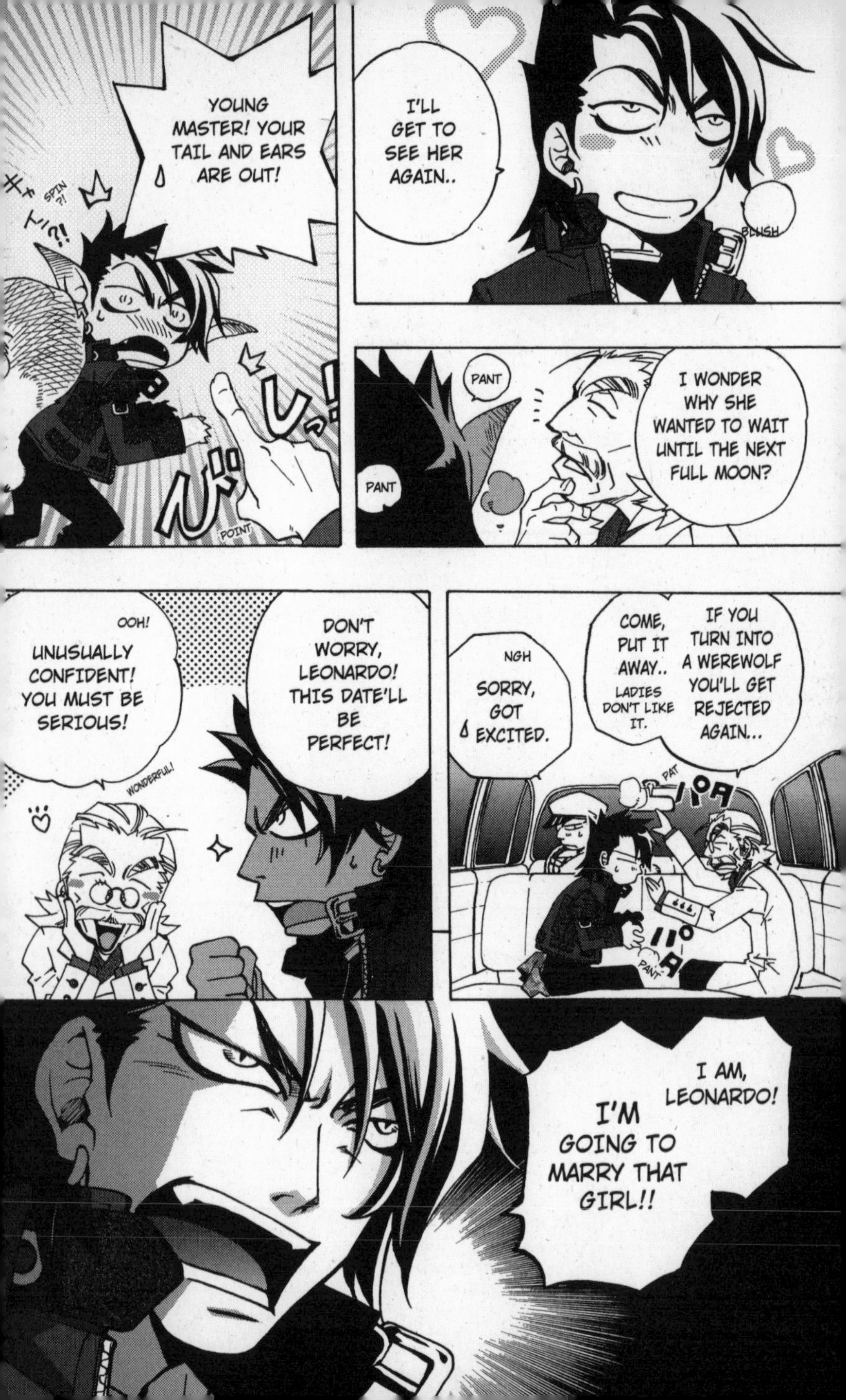
I'LL GET TO SEE HER AGAIN..
BLUSH
PANT
I WONDER WHY SHE WANTED TO WAIT UNTIL THE NEXT FULL MOON?
PANT
YOUNG MASTER! YOUR TAIL AND EARS ARE OUT!
SPIN ?!
POINT
IF YOU TURN INTO A WEREWOLF YOU'LL GET REJECTED AGAIN...
COME, PUT IT AWAY..
LADIES DON'T LIKE IT.
NGH
SORRY, GOT EXCITED.
PAT
PANT
DON'T WORRY, LEONARDO! THIS DATE'LL BE PERFECT!
OOH!
UNUSUALLY CONFIDENT! YOU MUST BE SERIOUS!
WONDERFUL!
I AM, LEONARDO!
I'M GOING TO MARRY THAT GIRL!!

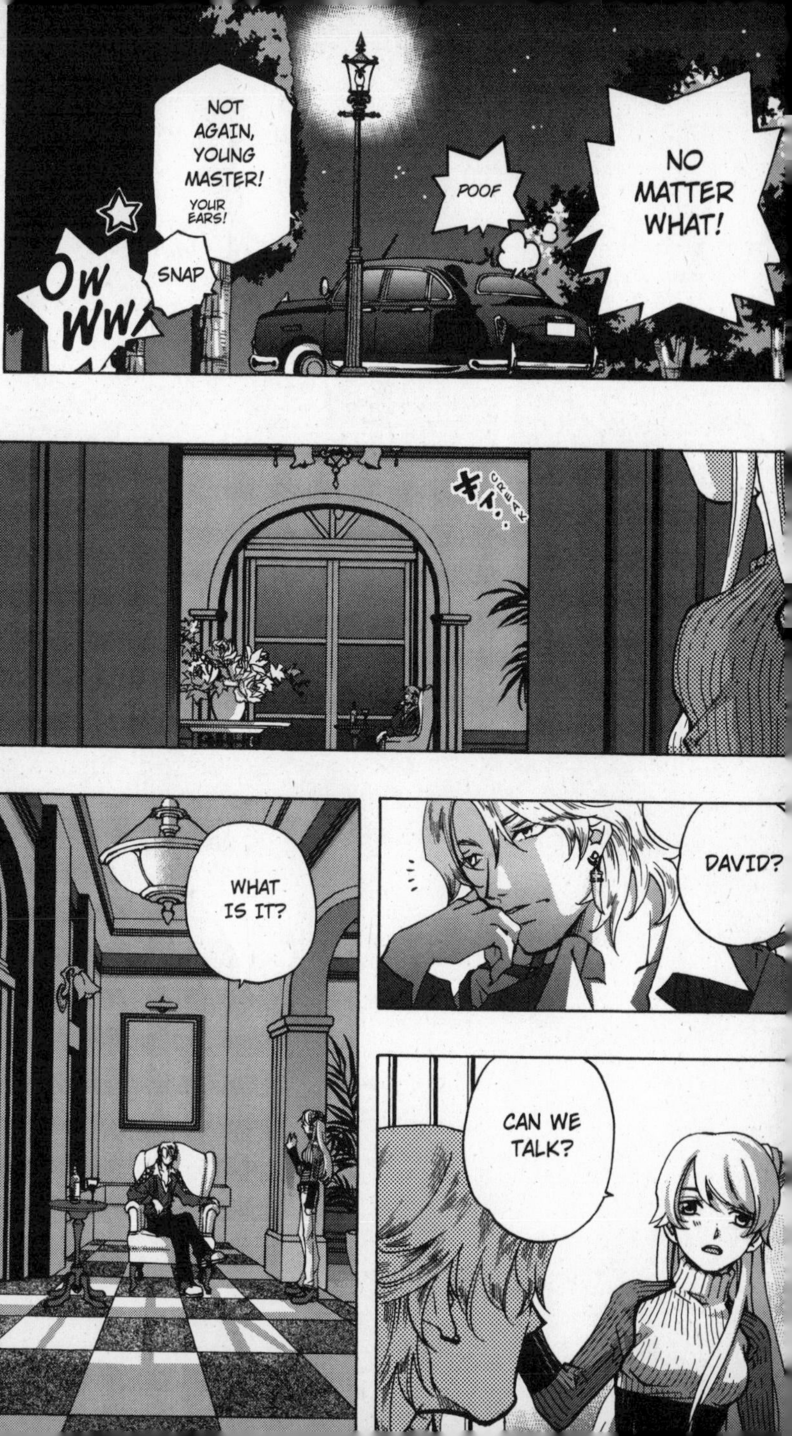
NO MATTER WHAT!
POOF
NOT AGAIN, YOUNG MASTER!
YOUR EARS!
SNAP
OWWW!
キィ・・
CREAK
DAVID?
CAN WE TALK?
WHAT IS IT?

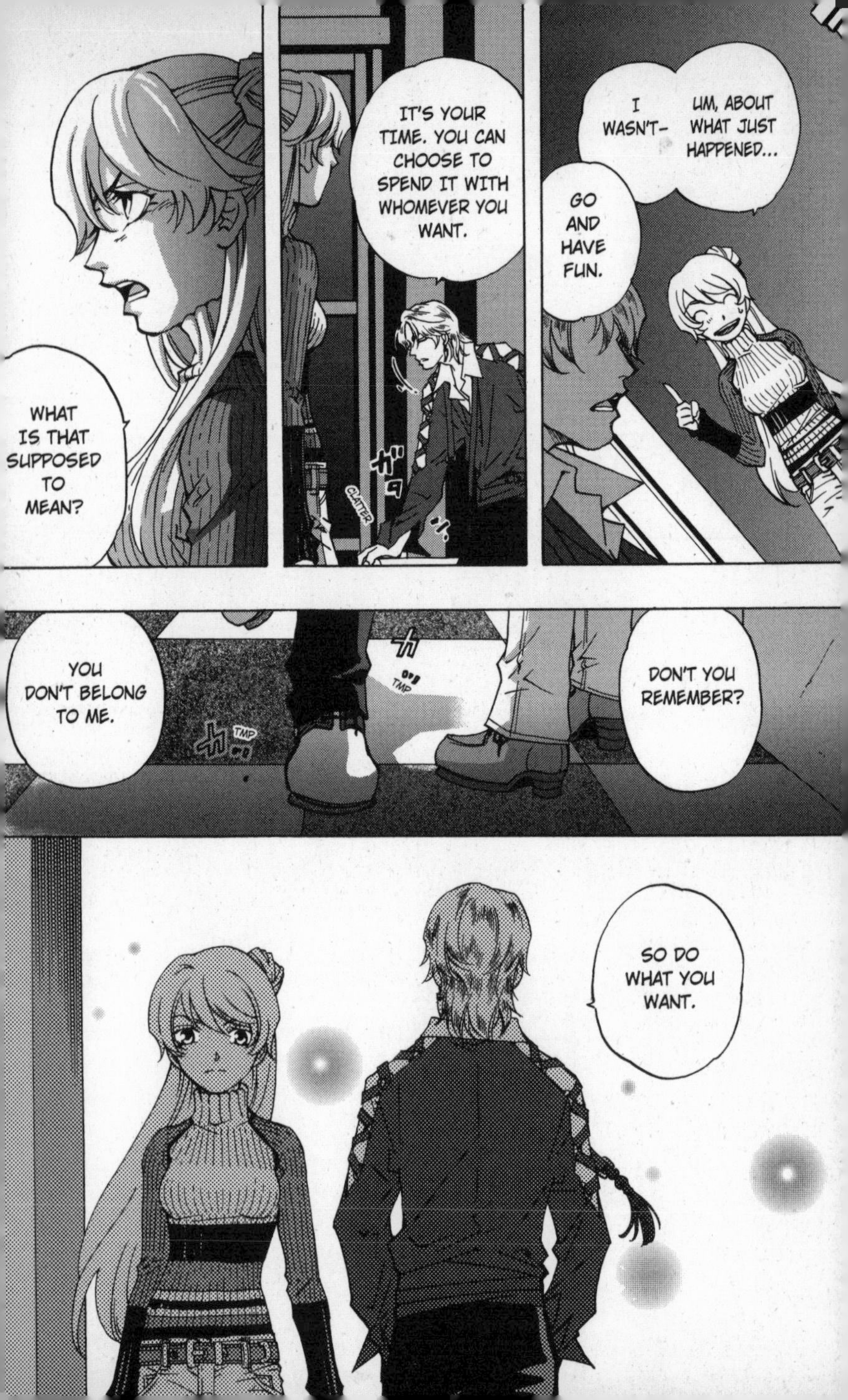
UM, ABOUT WHAT JUST HAPPENED...
I WASN'T-
GO AND HAVE FUN.
IT'S YOUR TIME. YOU CAN CHOOSE TO SPEND IT WITH WHOMEVER YOU WANT.
CLATTER
WHAT IS THAT SUPPOSED TO MEAN?
DON'T YOU REMEMBER?
TMP
TMP
YOU DON'T BELONG TO ME.
SO DO WHAT YOU WANT.

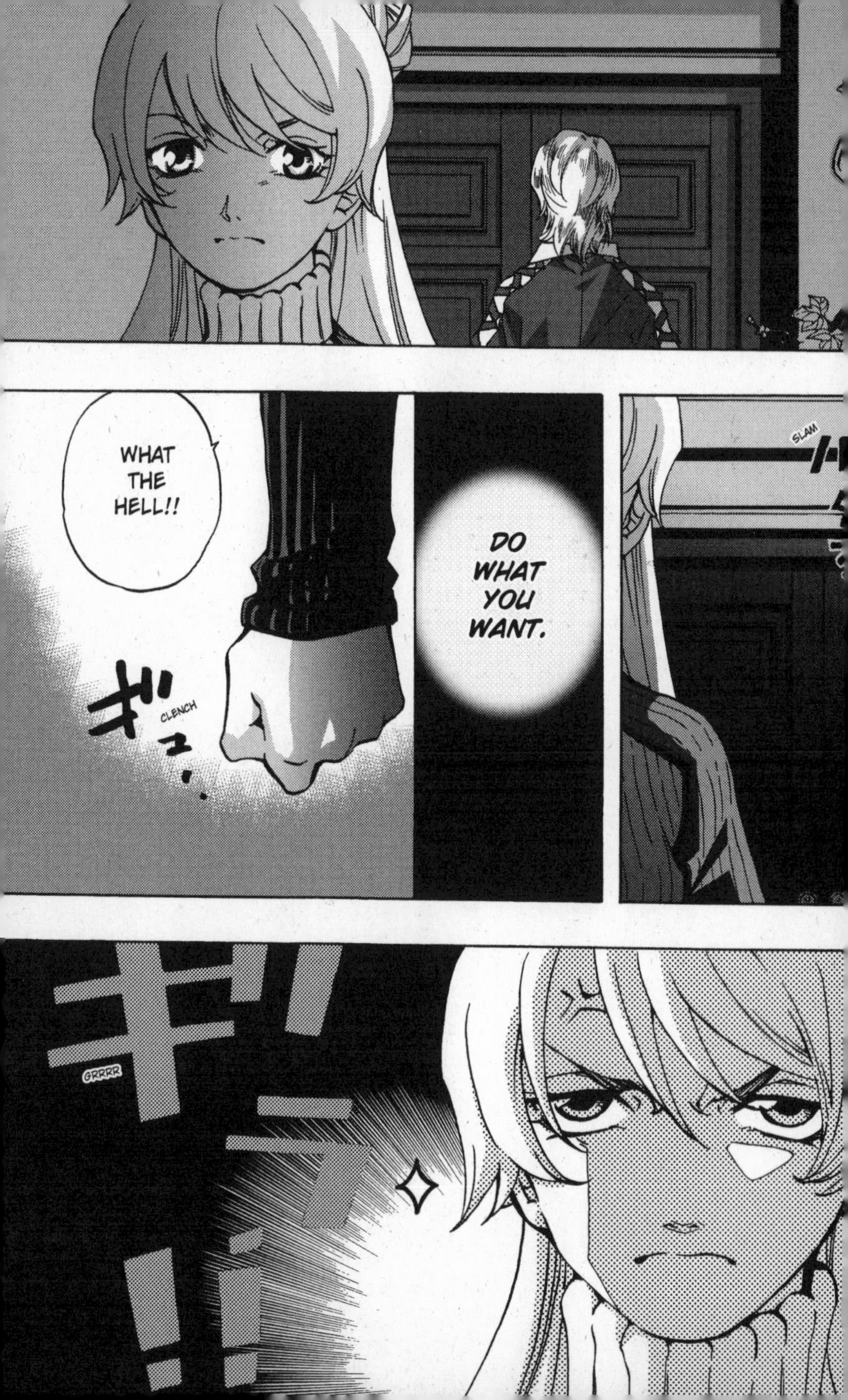
SLAM
DO WHAT YOU WANT.
WHAT THE HELL!!
CLENCH
GRRRR

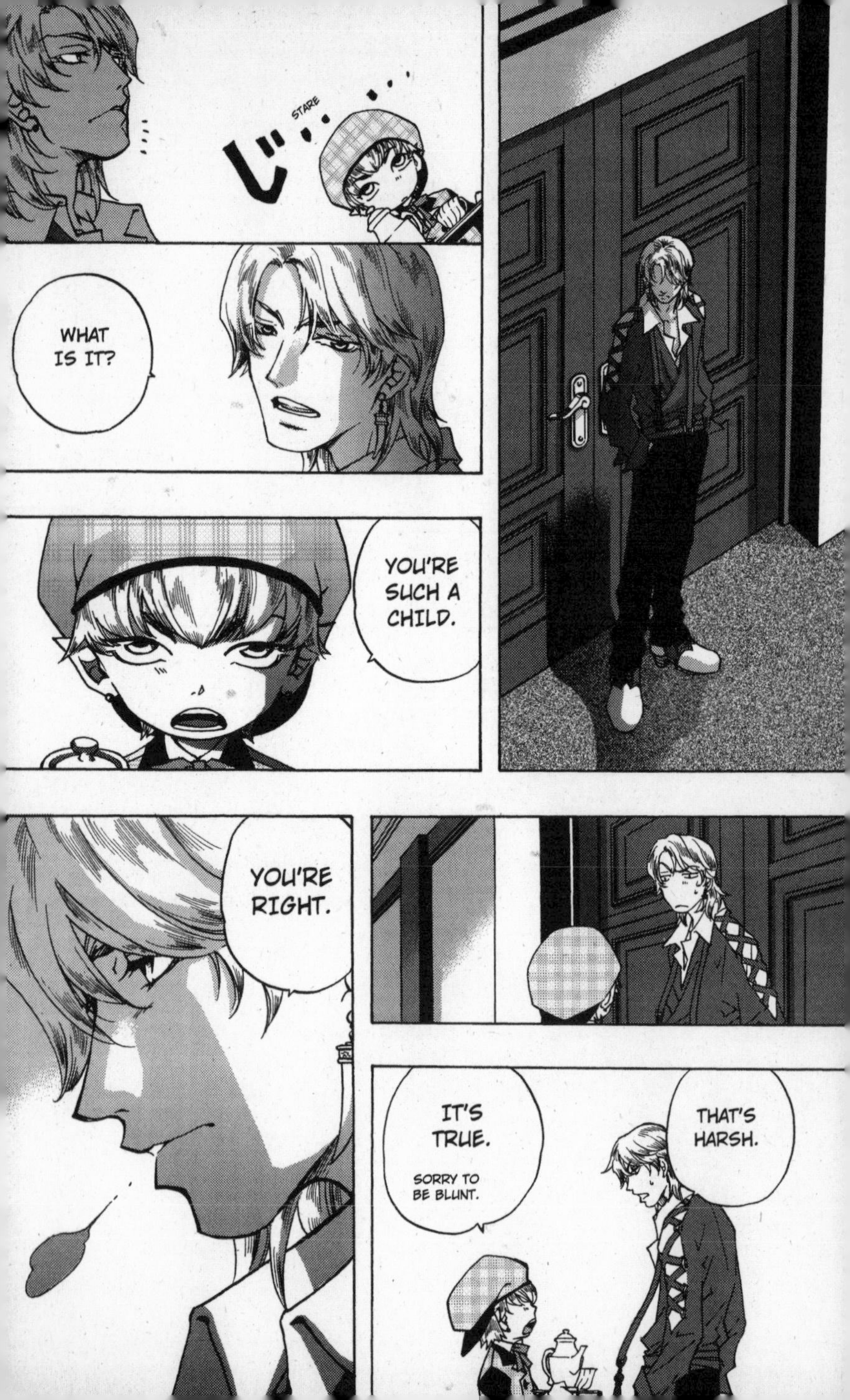
じ
STARE
WHAT IS IT?
YOU'RE SUCH A CHILD.
THAT'S HARSH.
IT'S TRUE.
SORRY TO BE BLUNT.
YOU'RE RIGHT.

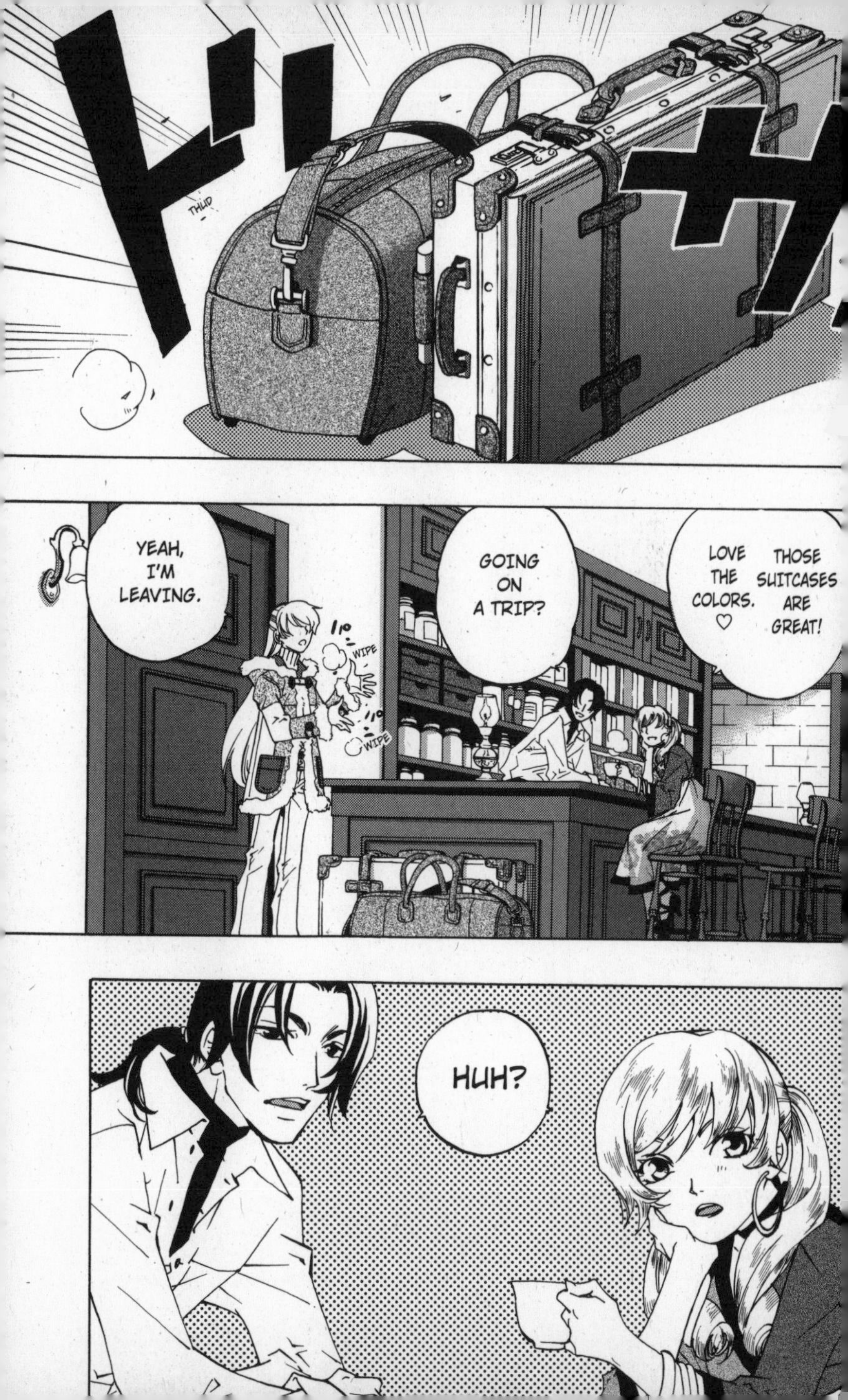
THUD
THOSE SUITCASES ARE GREAT!
LOVE THE COLORS. ♡
GOING ON A TRIP?
YEAH, I'M LEAVING.
WIPE
WIPE
HUH?

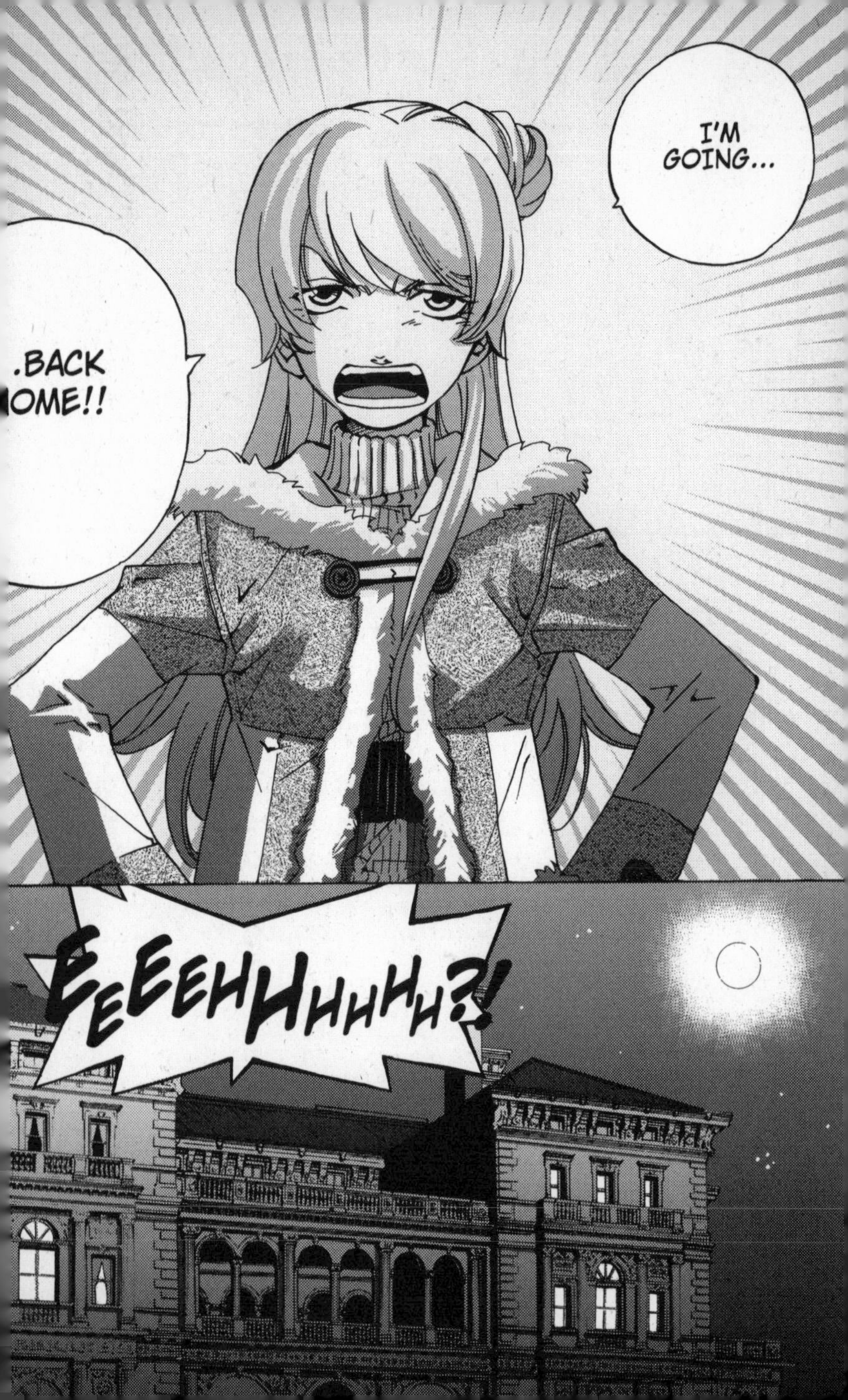
I'M GOING...
.BACK
OME!!
EEEEHHHHHH?!

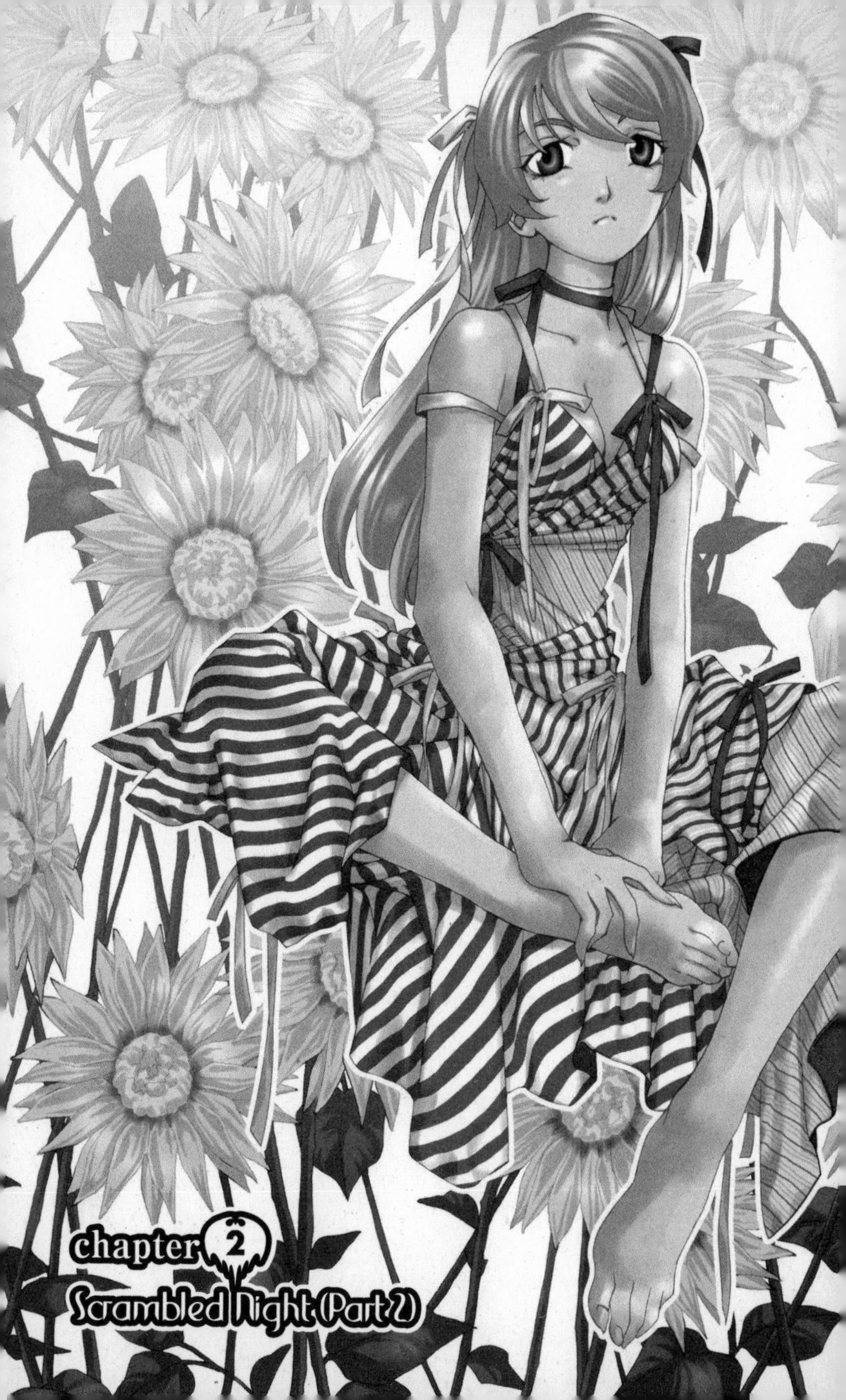
chapter 2
Scrambled Night (Part 2)

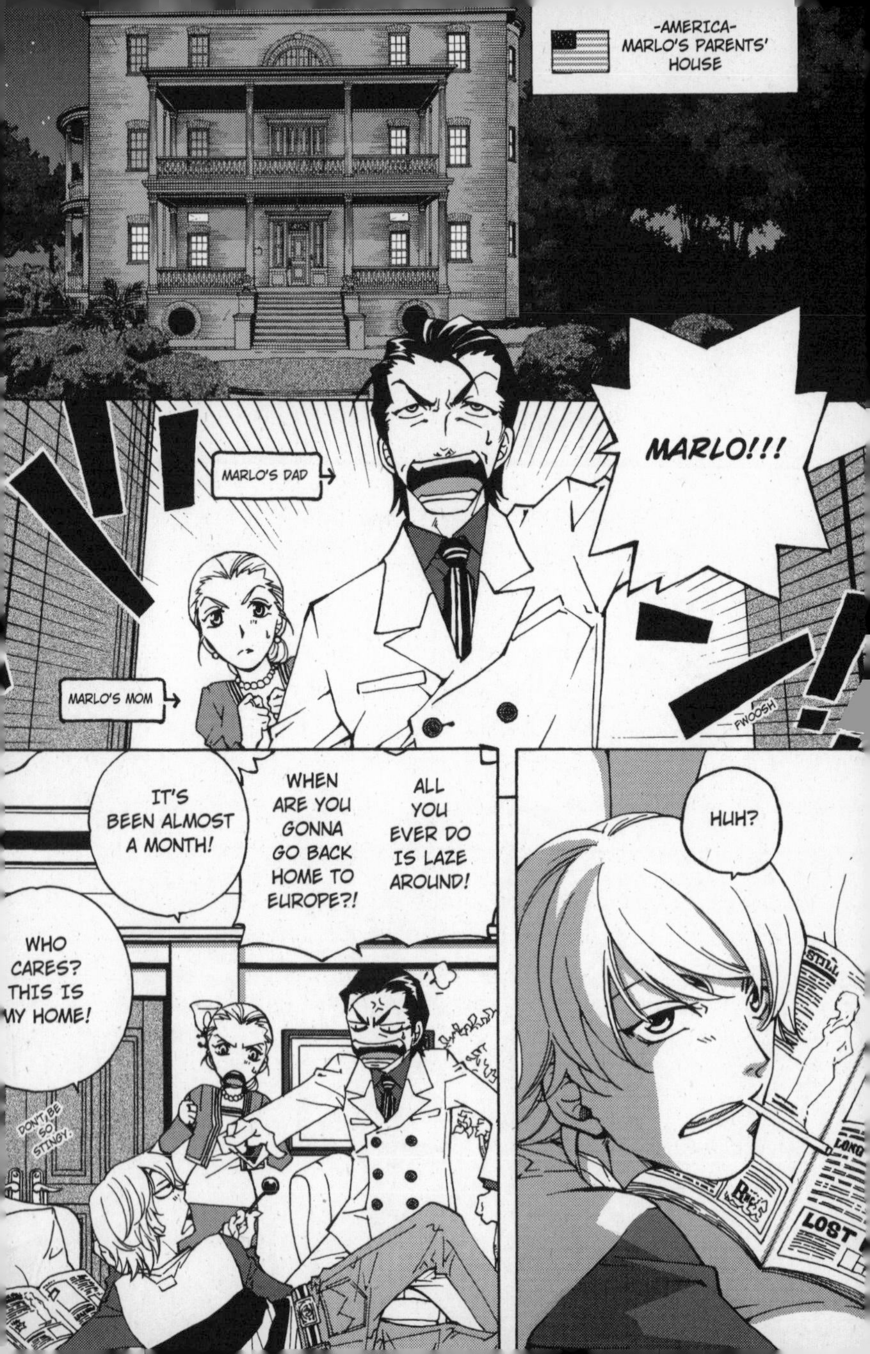
-AMERICA-
MARLO'S PARENTS' HOUSE
MARLO!!!
MARLO'S DAD
MARLO'S MOM
FWOOSH
HUH?
ALL YOU EVER DO IS LAZE AROUND!
WHEN ARE YOU GONNA GO BACK HOME TO EUROPE?!
IT'S BEEN ALMOST A MONTH!
WHO CARES? THIS IS MY HOME!
DON'T BE SO STINGY.

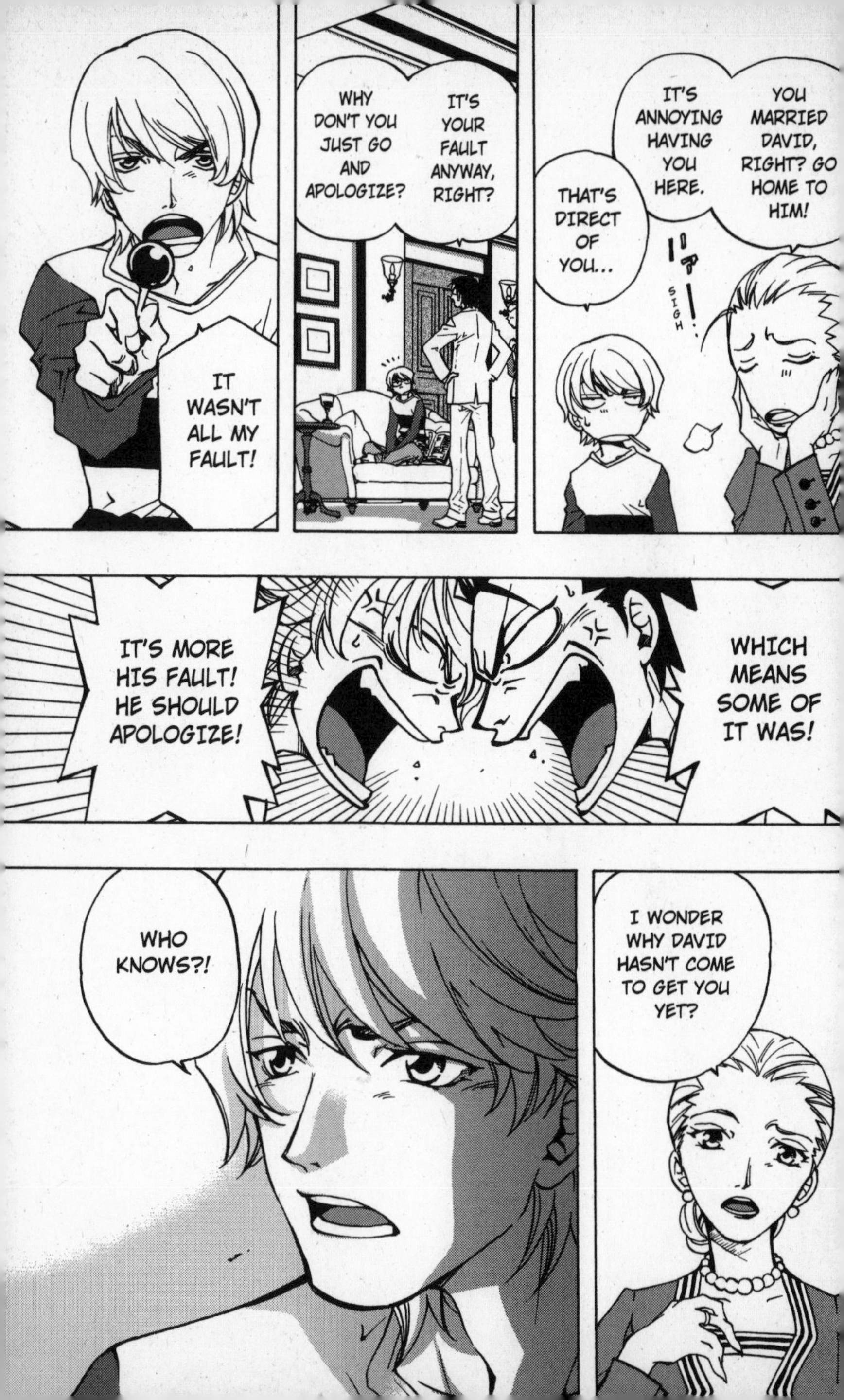
YOU MARRIED DAVID, RIGHT? GO HOME TO HIM!
IT'S ANNOYING HAVING YOU HERE.
SIGH
THAT'S DIRECT OF YOU...
IT'S YOUR FAULT ANYWAY, RIGHT?
WHY DON'T YOU JUST GO AND APOLOGIZE?
IT WASN'T ALL MY FAULT!
WHICH MEANS SOME OF IT WAS!
IT'S MORE HIS FAULT! HE SHOULD APOLOGIZE!
I WONDER WHY DAVID HASN'T COME TO GET YOU YET?
WHO KNOWS?!

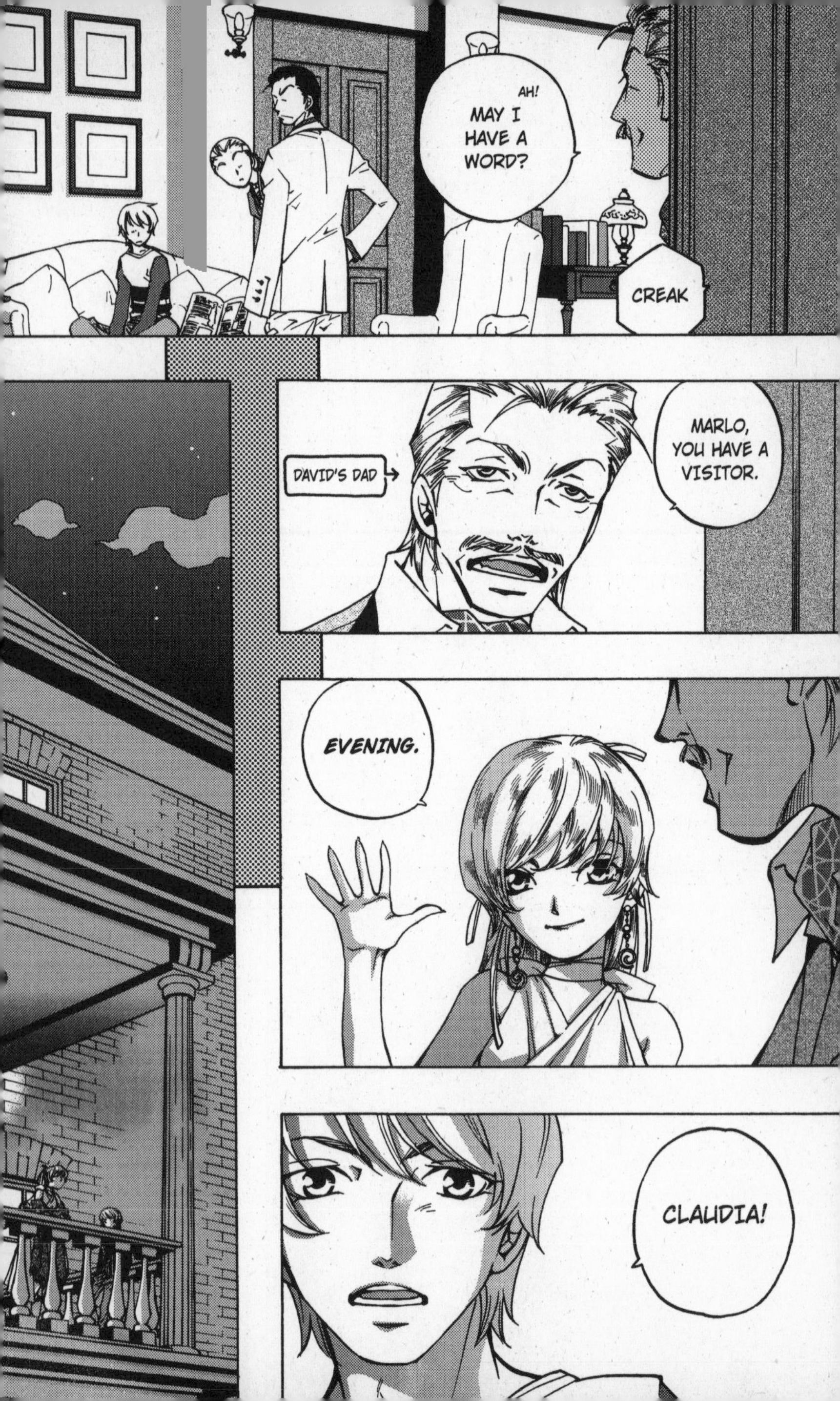
AH!
MAY I HAVE A WORD?
CREAK
MARLO, YOU HAVE A VISITOR.
DAVID'S DAD
EVENING.
CLAUDIA!

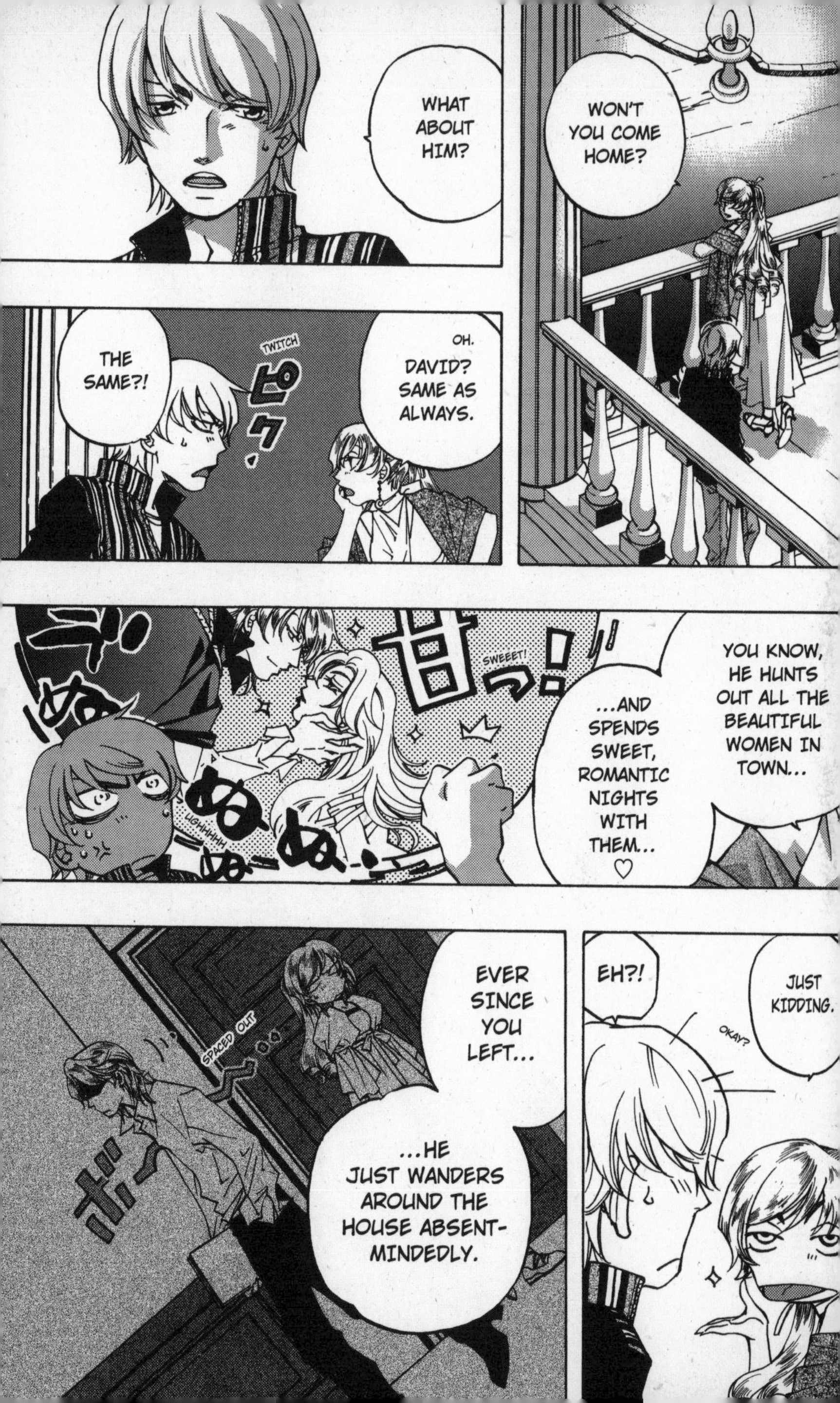
WON'T YOU COME HOME?
WHAT ABOUT HIM?
OH.
DAVID? SAME AS ALWAYS.
TWITCH
THE SAME?!
YOU KNOW, HE HUNTS OUT ALL THE BEAUTIFUL WOMEN IN TOWN...
...AND SPENDS SWEET, ROMANTIC NIGHTS WITH THEM... ♡
SWEEET!
UGHHHHH
JUST KIDDING.
OKAY?
EH?!
EVER SINCE YOU LEFT...
...HE JUST WANDERS AROUND THE HOUSE ABSENT-MINDEDLY.
SPACED OUT

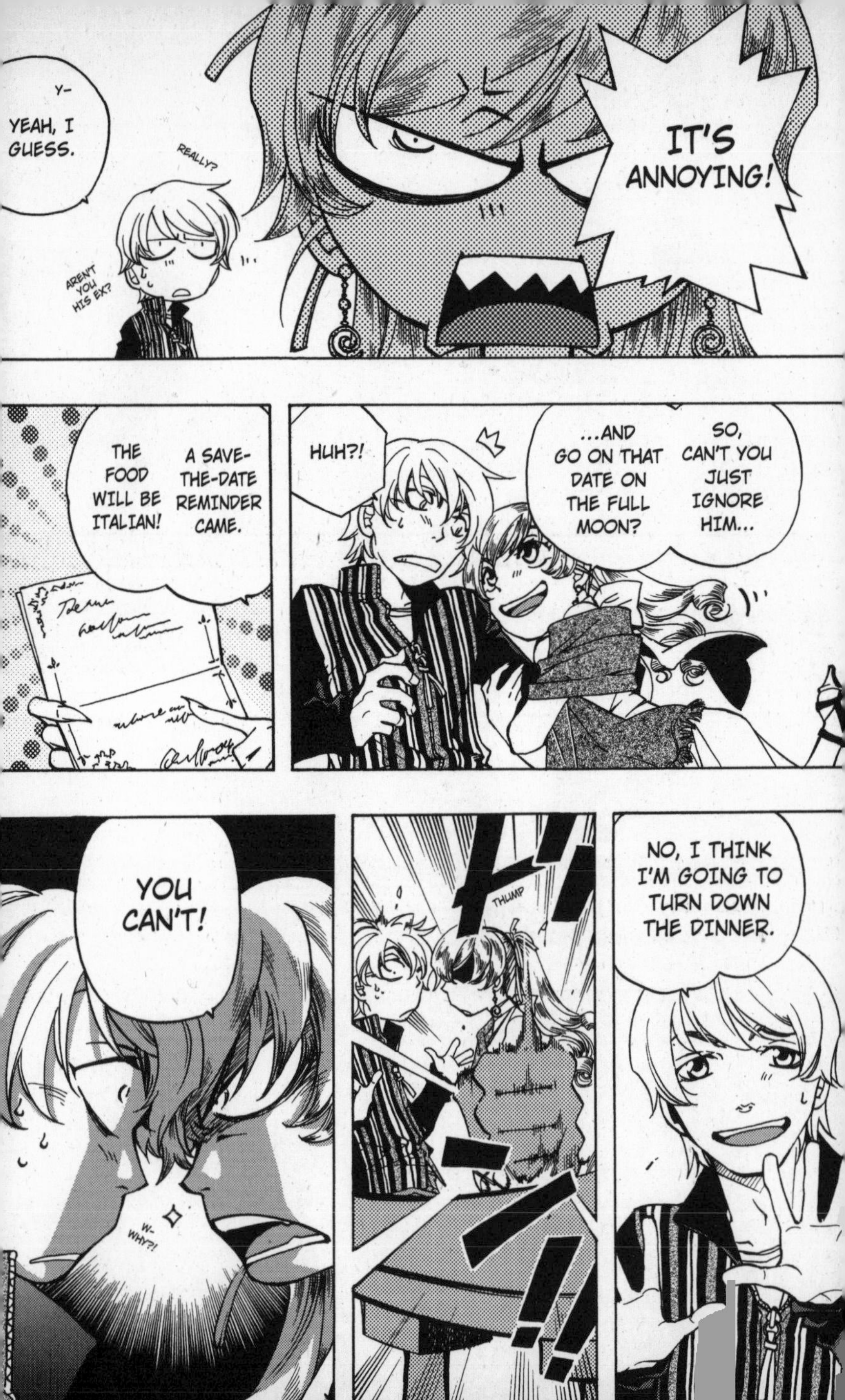
IT'S ANNOYING!
REALLY?
Y-
YEAH, I GUESS.
AREN'T YOU HIS EX?
SO, CAN'T YOU JUST IGNORE HIM...
...AND GO ON THAT DATE ON THE FULL MOON?
HUH?!
A SAVE-THE-DATE REMINDER CAME.
THE FOOD WILL BE ITALIAN!
NO, I THINK I'M GOING TO TURN DOWN THE DINNER.
THUMP
YOU CAN'T!
W-WHY?!

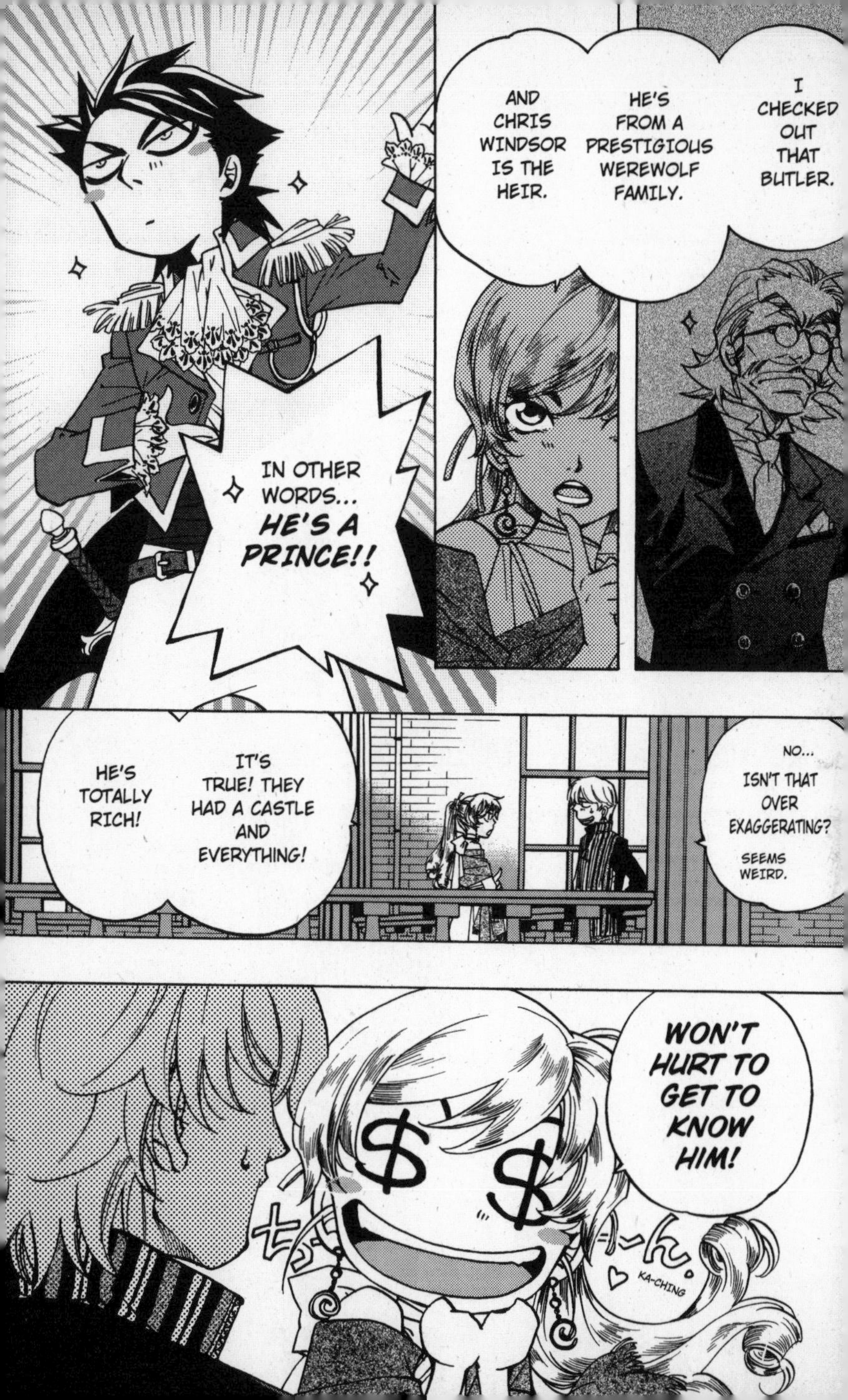
I CHECKED OUT THAT BUTLER.
HE'S FROM A PRESTIGIOUS WEREWOLF FAMILY.
AND CHRIS WINDSOR IS THE HEIR.
IN OTHER WORDS... ***HE'S A PRINCE!!***
NO... ISN'T THAT OVER EXAGGERATING?
SEEMS WEIRD.
IT'S TRUE! THEY HAD A CASTLE AND EVERYTHING!
HE'S TOTALLY RICH!
WON'T HURT TO GET TO KNOW HIM!
KA-CHING

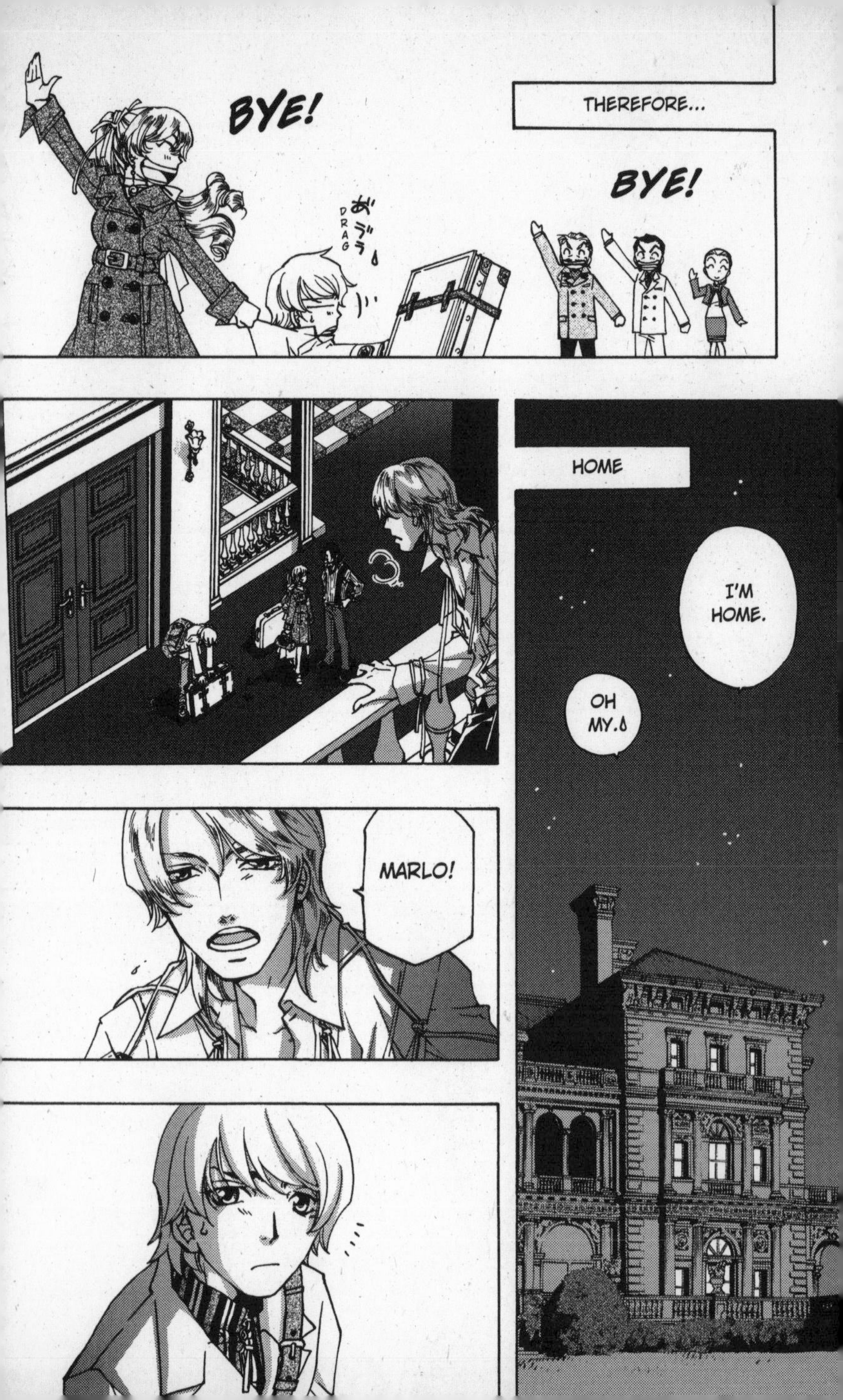
THEREFORE...
BYE!
BYE!
DRAG
HOME
I'M HOME.
OH MY.
MARLO!

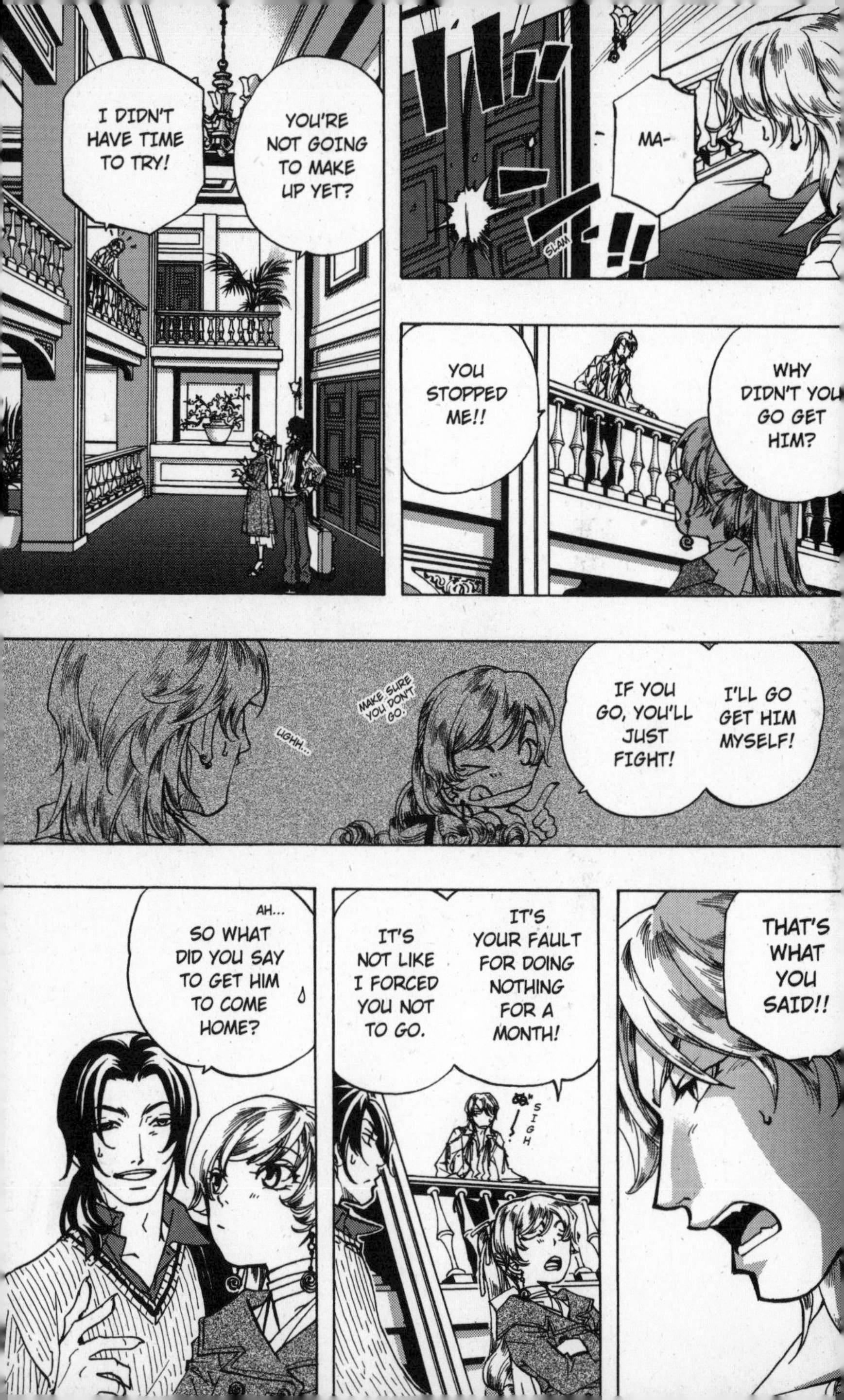
MA-
SLAM
WHY DIDN'T YOU GO GET HIM?
YOU STOPPED ME!!
YOU'RE NOT GOING TO MAKE UP YET?
I DIDN'T HAVE TIME TO TRY!
I'LL GO GET HIM MYSELF!
IF YOU GO, YOU'LL JUST FIGHT!
MAKE SURE YOU DON'T GO.
UGHH...
THAT'S WHAT YOU SAID!!
IT'S YOUR FAULT FOR DOING NOTHING FOR A MONTH!
IT'S NOT LIKE I FORCED YOU NOT TO GO.
SIGH
AH...
SO WHAT DID YOU SAY TO GET HIM TO COME HOME?

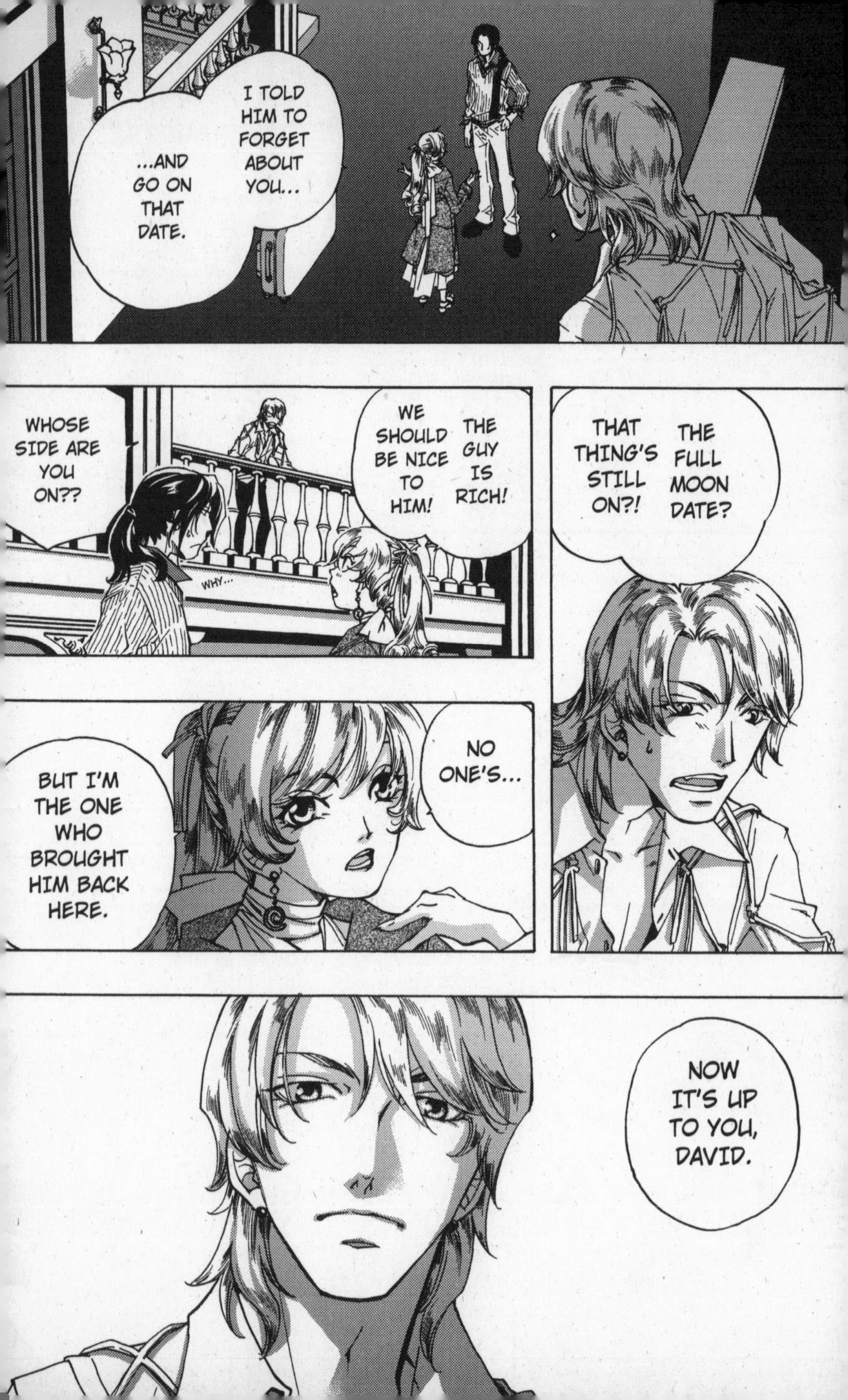
I TOLD HIM TO FORGET ABOUT YOU...
...AND GO ON THAT DATE.
THE FULL MOON DATE?
THAT THING'S STILL ON?!
THE GUY IS RICH!
WE SHOULD BE NICE TO HIM!
WHOSE SIDE ARE YOU ON??
WHY...
NO ONE'S...
BUT I'M THE ONE WHO BROUGHT HIM BACK HERE.
NOW IT'S UP TO YOU, DAVID.

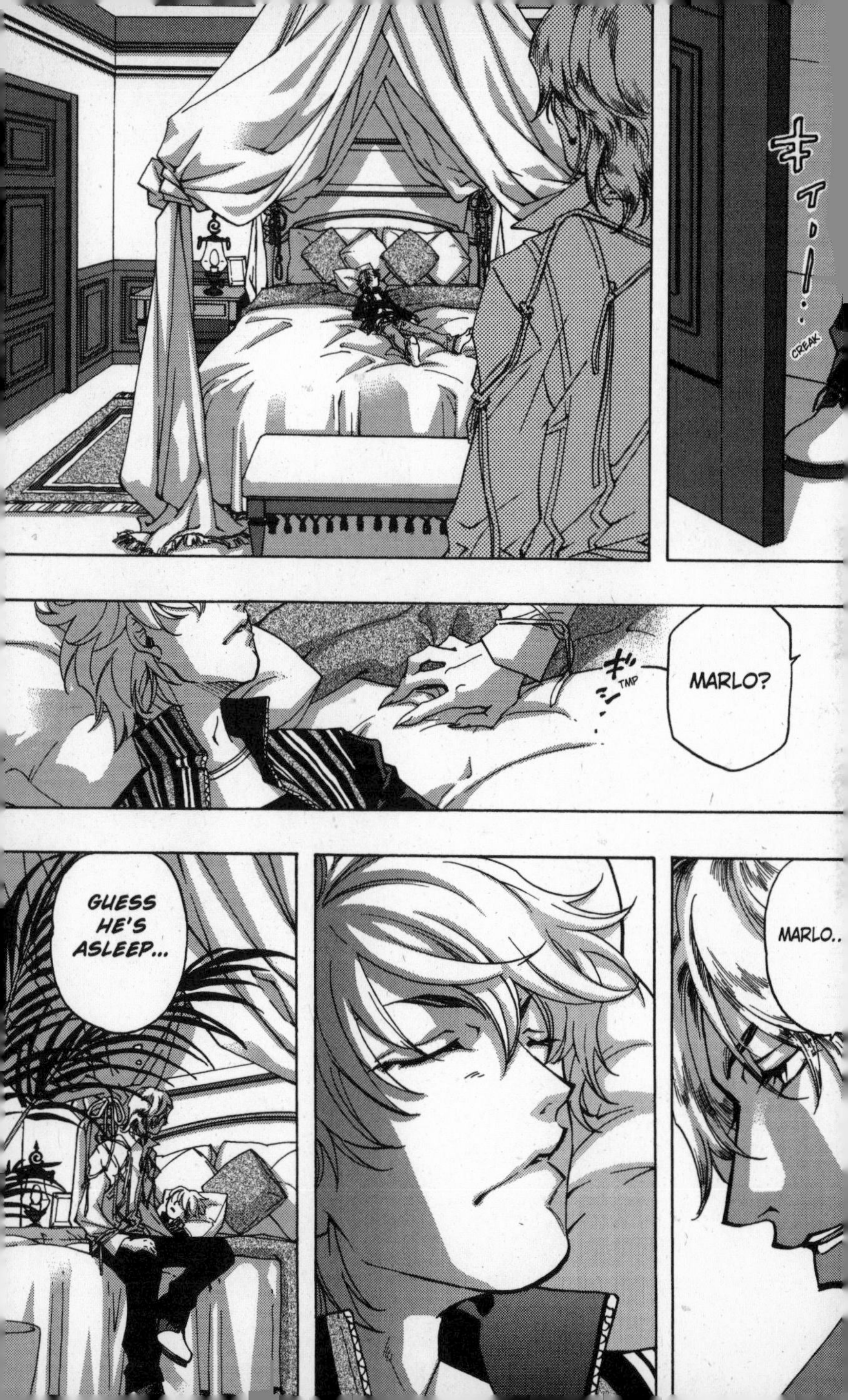
CREAK
TMP
MARLO?
MARLO..
GUESS HE'S ASLEEP...

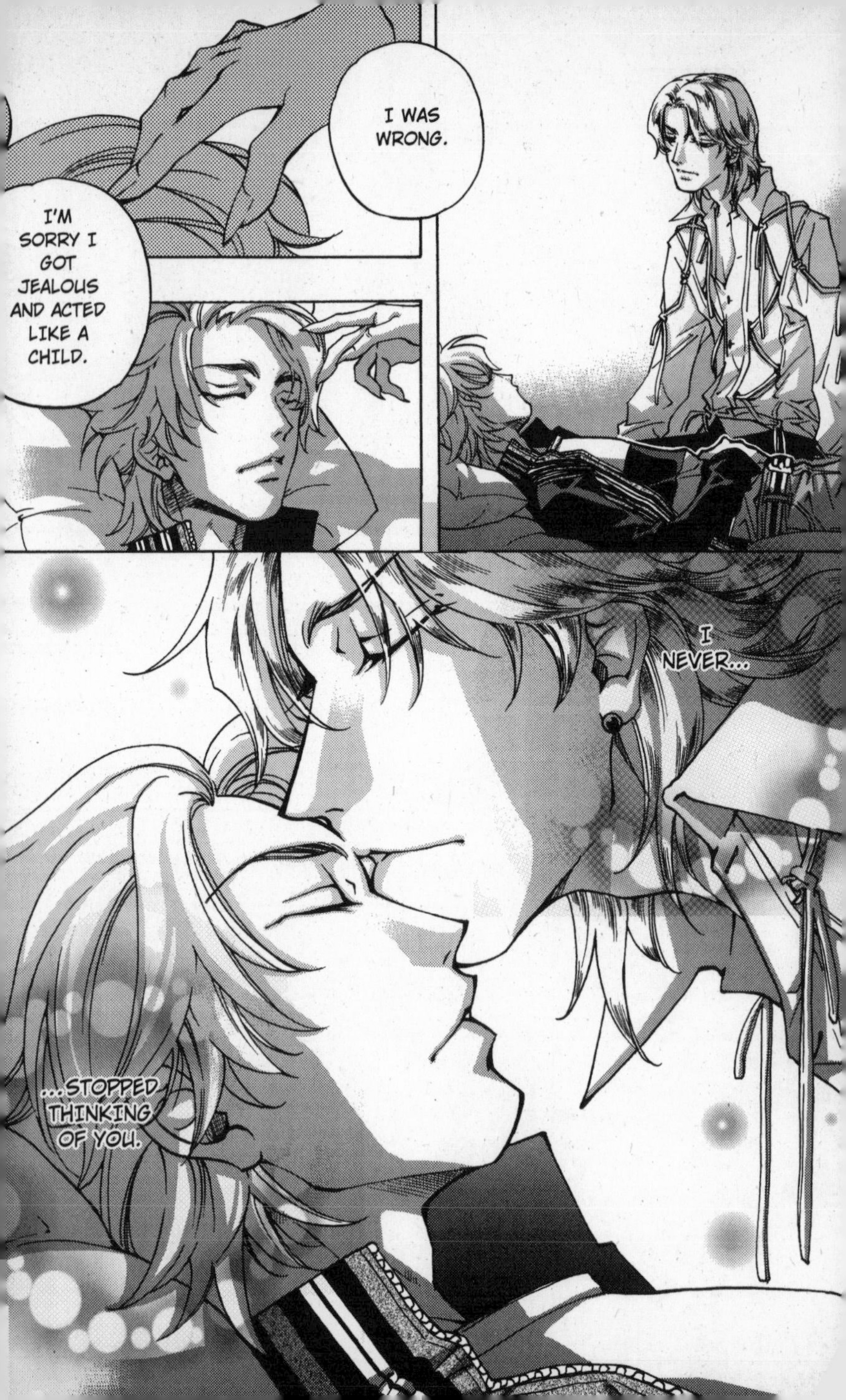
I WAS WRONG.
I'M SORRY I GOT JEALOUS AND ACTED LIKE A CHILD.
I NEVER...
...STOPPED THINKING OF YOU.

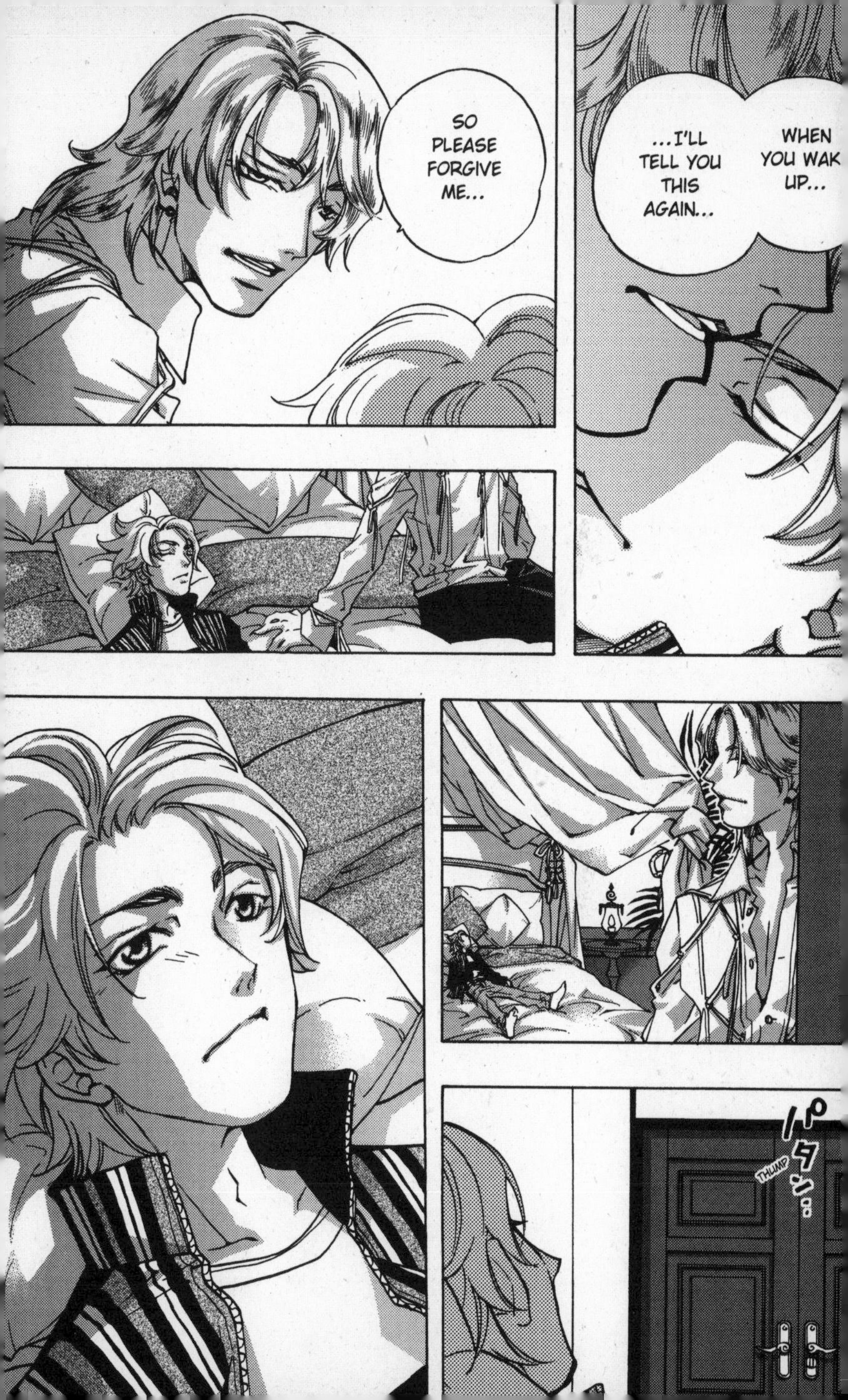
WHEN YOU WAK UP...
...I'LL TELL YOU THIS AGAIN...
SO PLEASE FORGIVE ME...
THUMP

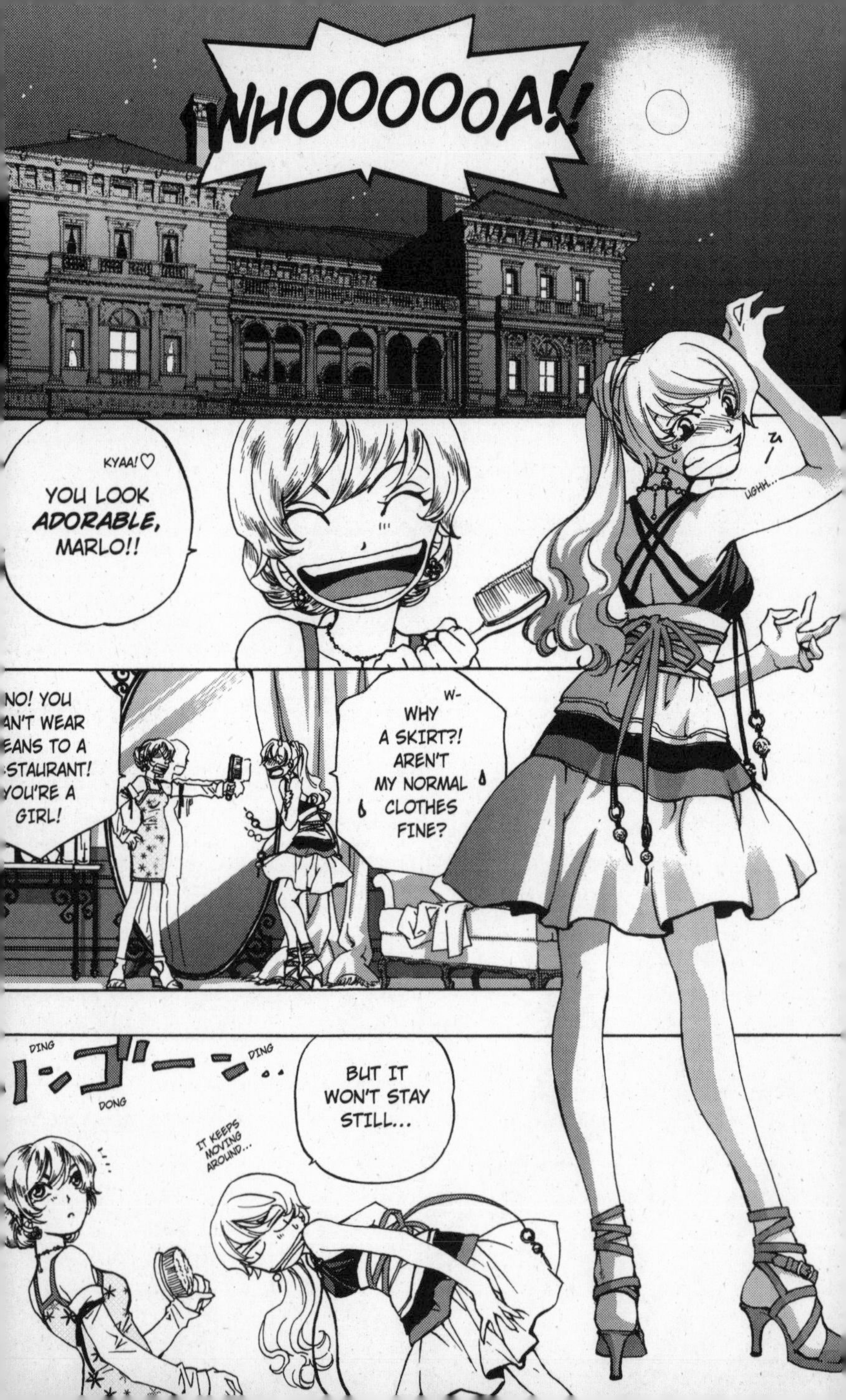

WHOOOOOA!!
UGHH...
KYAA!♡ YOU LOOK ADORABLE, MARLO!!
W- WHY A SKIRT?! AREN'T MY NORMAL CLOTHES FINE?
NO! YOU AN'T WEAR EANS TO A STAURANT! YOU'RE A GIRL!
DING DING DONG
BUT IT WON'T STAY STILL...
IT KEEPS MOVING AROUND...

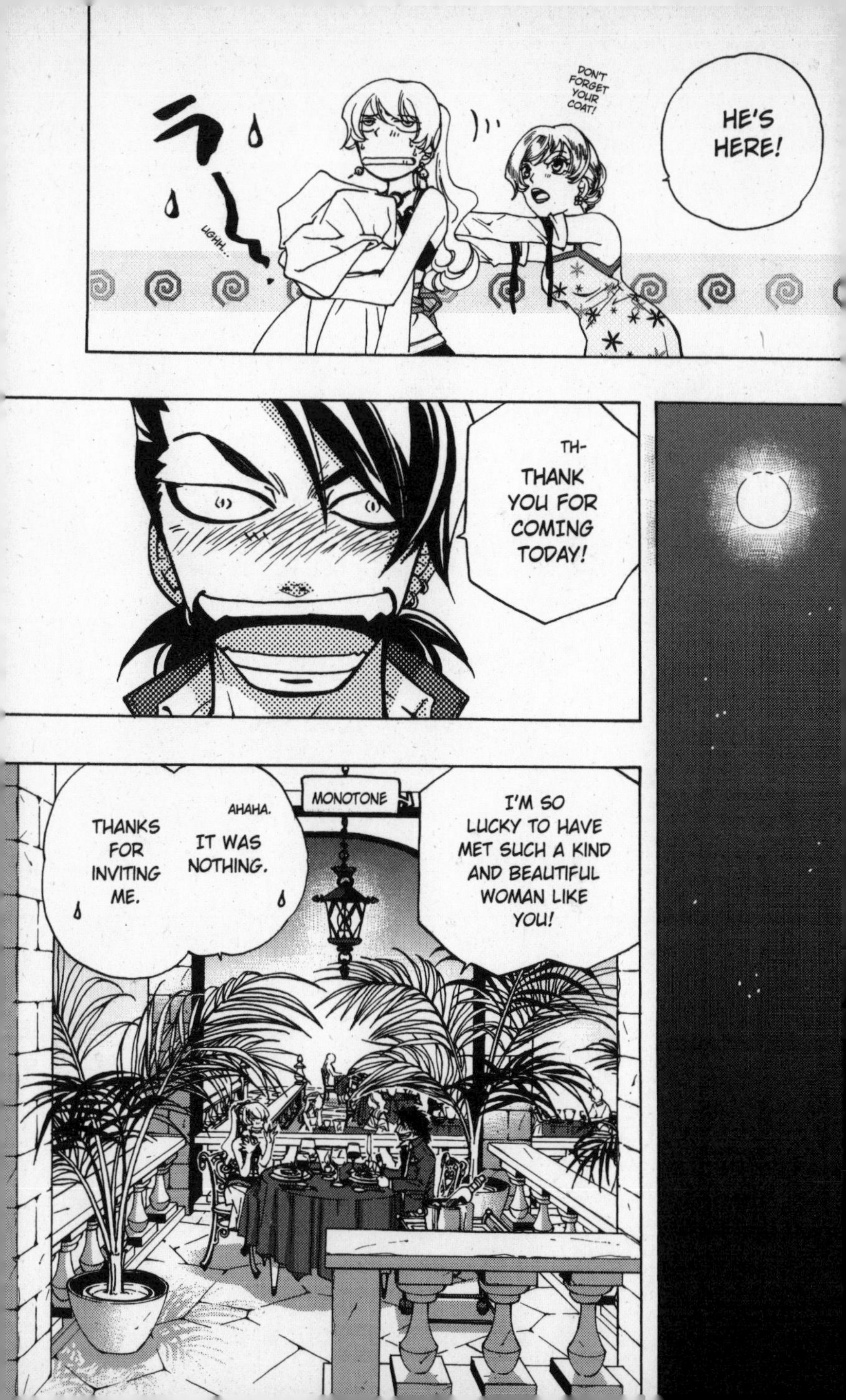
HE'S HERE!
DON'T FORGET YOUR COAT!
UGHH...
TH- THANK YOU FOR COMING TODAY!
I'M SO LUCKY TO HAVE MET SUCH A KIND AND BEAUTIFUL WOMAN LIKE YOU!
MONOTONE
AHAHA. IT WAS NOTHING.
THANKS FOR INVITING ME.

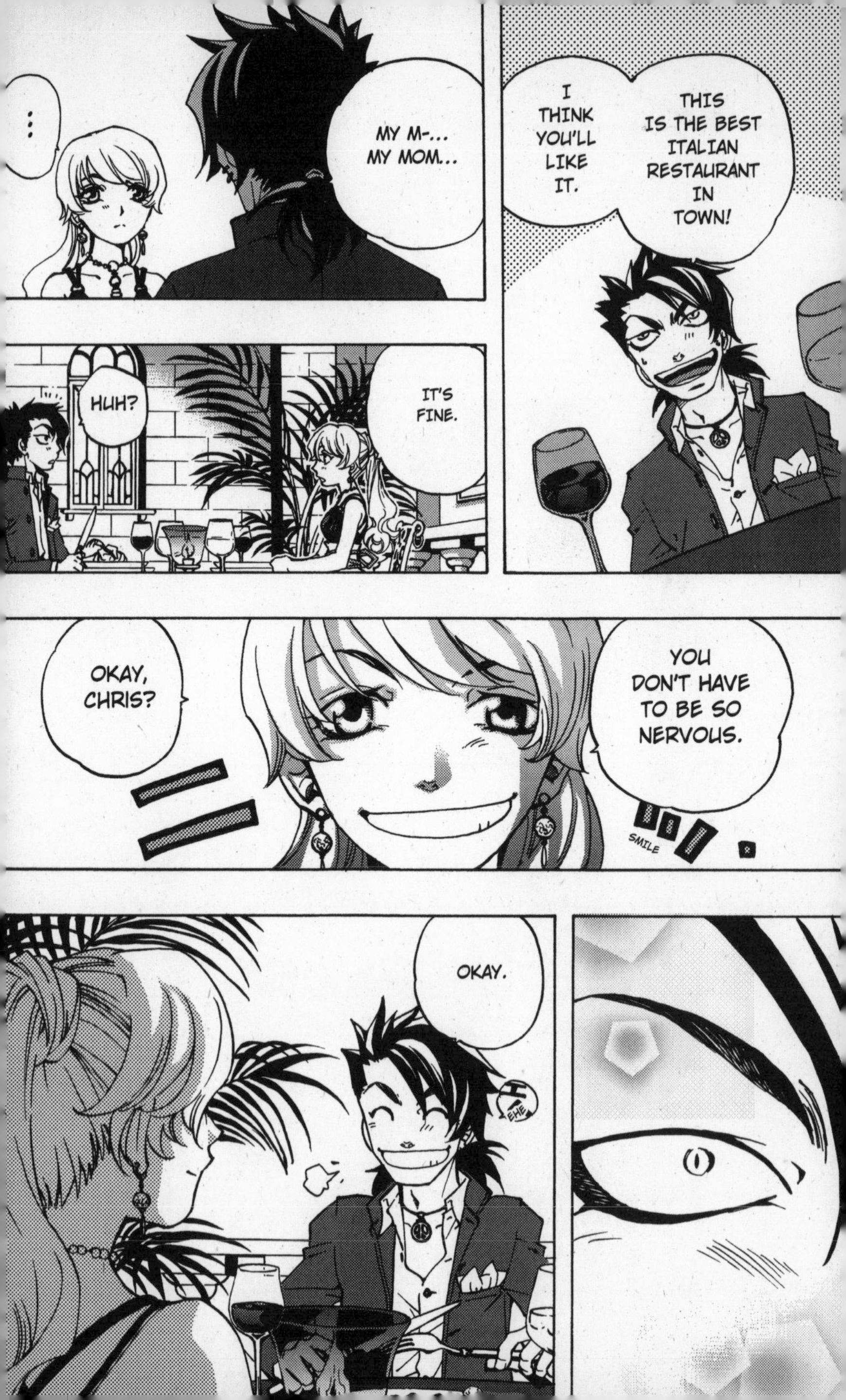
THIS IS THE BEST ITALIAN RESTAURANT IN TOWN!
I THINK YOU'LL LIKE IT.
MY M-... MY MOM...
...
IT'S FINE.
HUH?
YOU DON'T HAVE TO BE SO NERVOUS.
SMILE
OKAY, CHRIS?
OKAY.
EHE

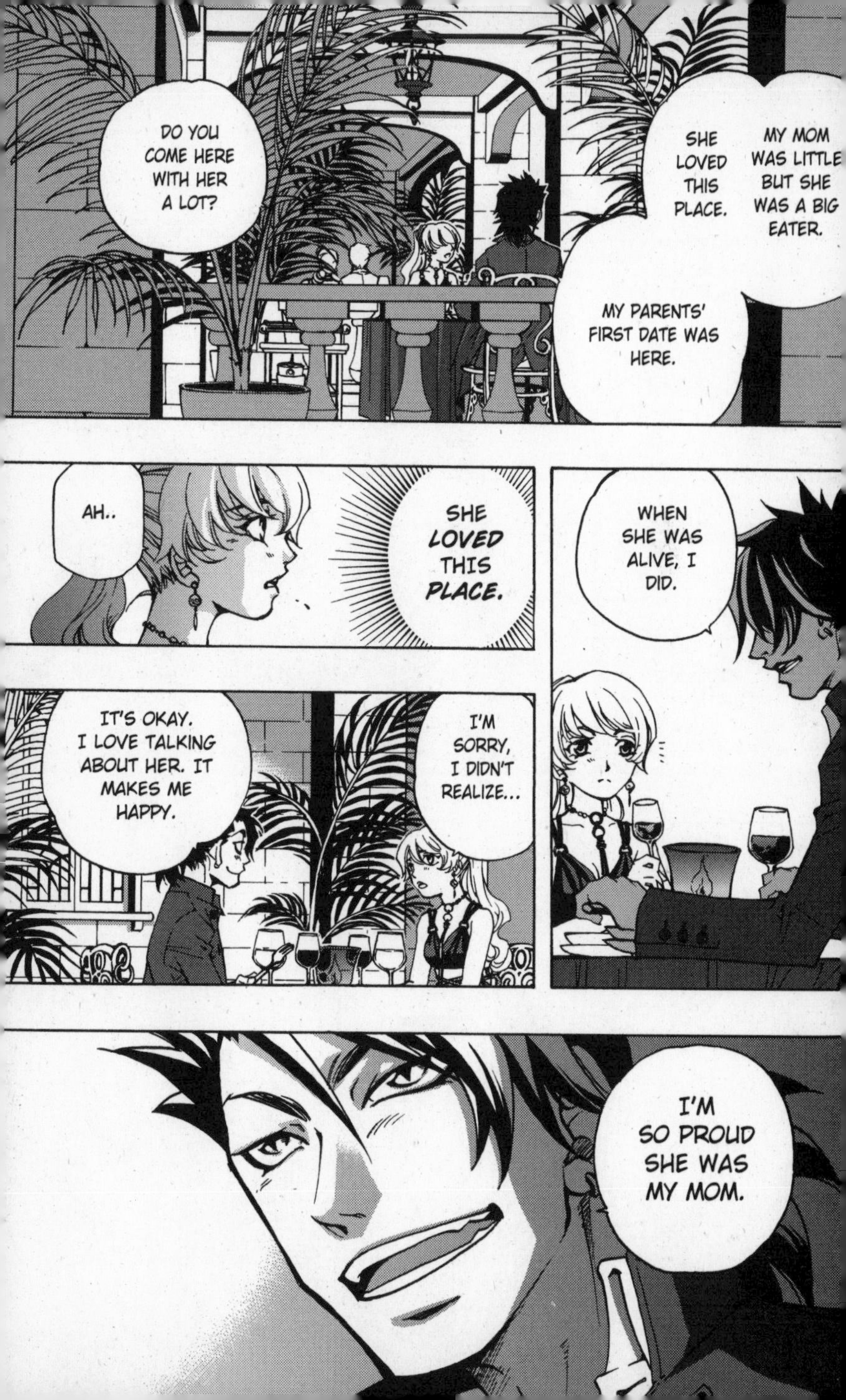

MY MOM WAS LITTLE BUT SHE WAS A BIG EATER.
SHE LOVED THIS PLACE.
DO YOU COME HERE WITH HER A LOT?
MY PARENTS' FIRST DATE WAS HERE.
WHEN SHE WAS ALIVE, I DID.
SHE *LOVED* THIS *PLACE.*
AH..
I'M SORRY, I DIDN'T REALIZE...
IT'S OKAY. I LOVE TALKING ABOUT HER. IT MAKES ME HAPPY.
I'M SO PROUD SHE WAS MY MOM.

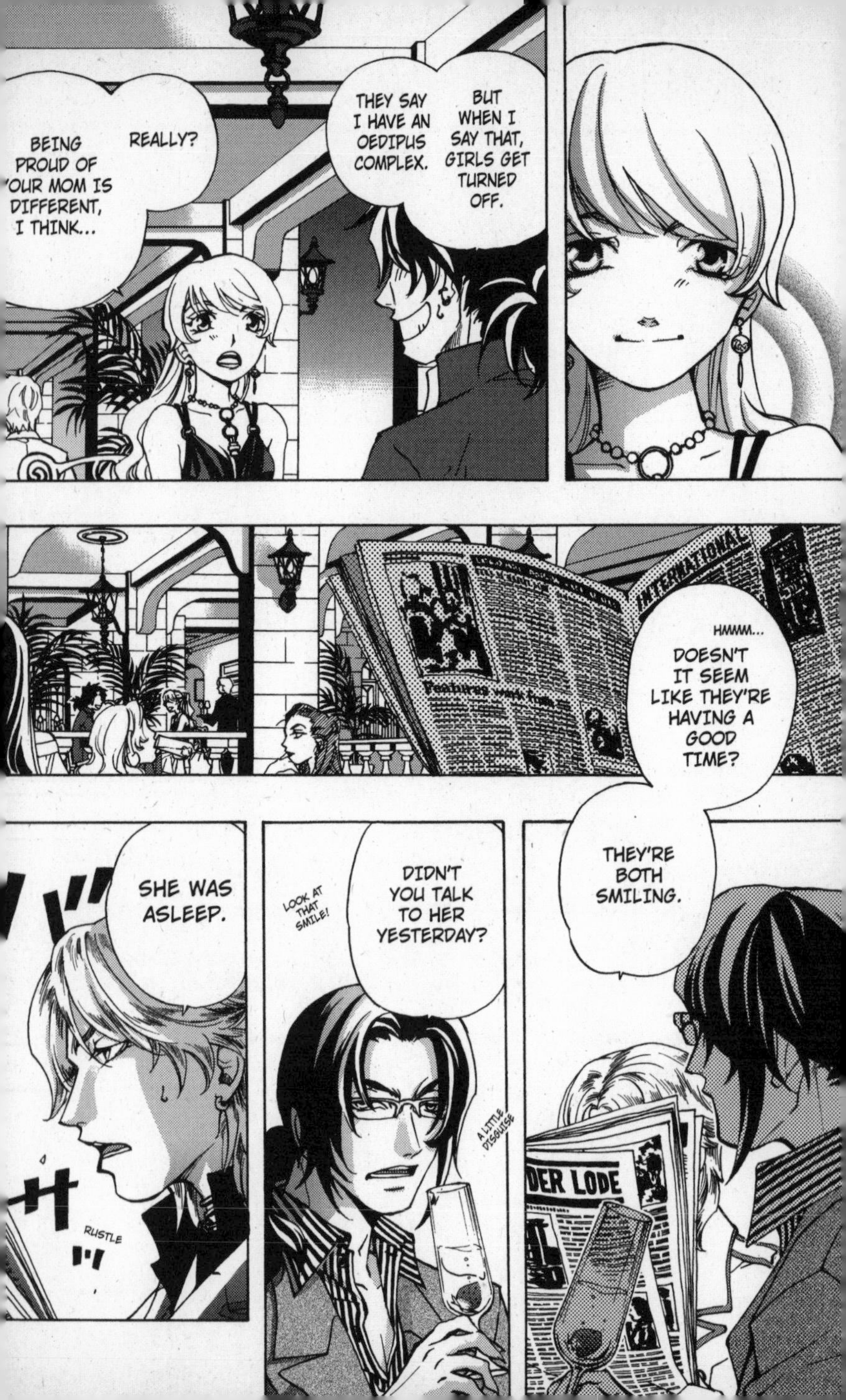
BUT WHEN I SAY THAT, GIRLS GET TURNED OFF.
THEY SAY I HAVE AN OEDIPUS COMPLEX.
REALLY?
BEING PROUD OF YOUR MOM IS DIFFERENT, I THINK...
INTERNATIONAL
HMMM...
DOESN'T IT SEEM LIKE THEY'RE HAVING A GOOD TIME?
THEY'RE BOTH SMILING.
DER LODE
A LITTLE DISGUISE
DIDN'T YOU TALK TO HER YESTERDAY?
LOOK AT THAT SMILE!
SHE WAS ASLEEP.
RUSTLE

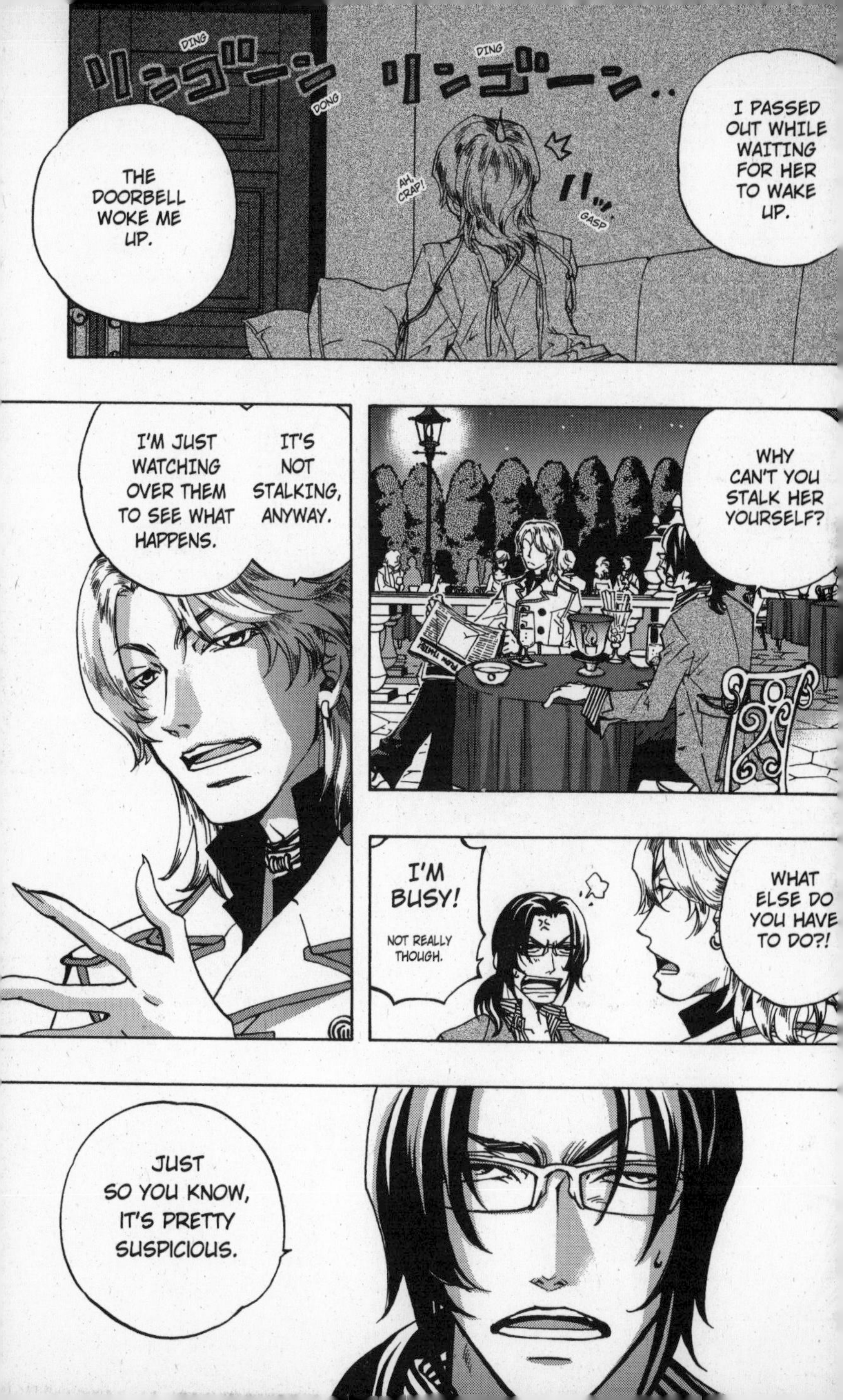
I PASSED OUT WHILE WAITING FOR HER TO WAKE UP.
リンゴーン..
DING
リンゴーン
DING
DONG
AH, CRAP!
GASP
THE DOORBELL WOKE ME UP.
WHY CAN'T YOU STALK HER YOURSELF?
WHAT ELSE DO YOU HAVE TO DO?!
I'M BUSY!
NOT REALLY THOUGH.
IT'S NOT STALKING, ANYWAY.
I'M JUST WATCHING OVER THEM TO SEE WHAT HAPPENS.
JUST SO YOU KNOW, IT'S PRETTY SUSPICIOUS.

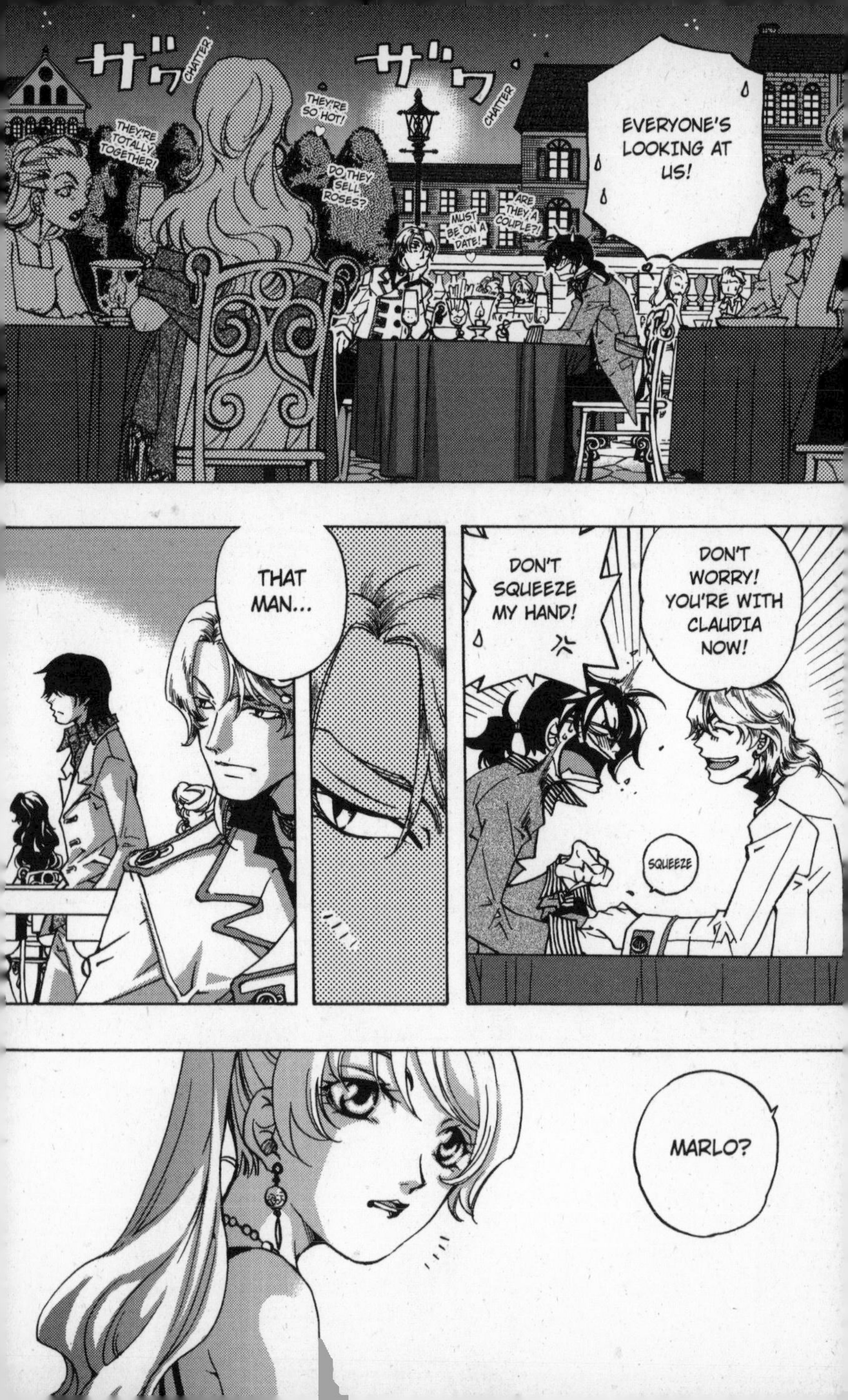
EVERYONE'S LOOKING AT US!
ザワ CHATTER
ARE THEY A COUPLE?!
MUST BE ON A DATE!
DO THEY SELL ROSES?
THEY'RE SO HOT!
ザワ CHATTER
THEY'RE TOTALLY TOGETHER!
DON'T WORRY! YOU'RE WITH CLAUDIA NOW!
DON'T SQUEEZE MY HAND!
SQUEEZE
THAT MAN...
MARLO?

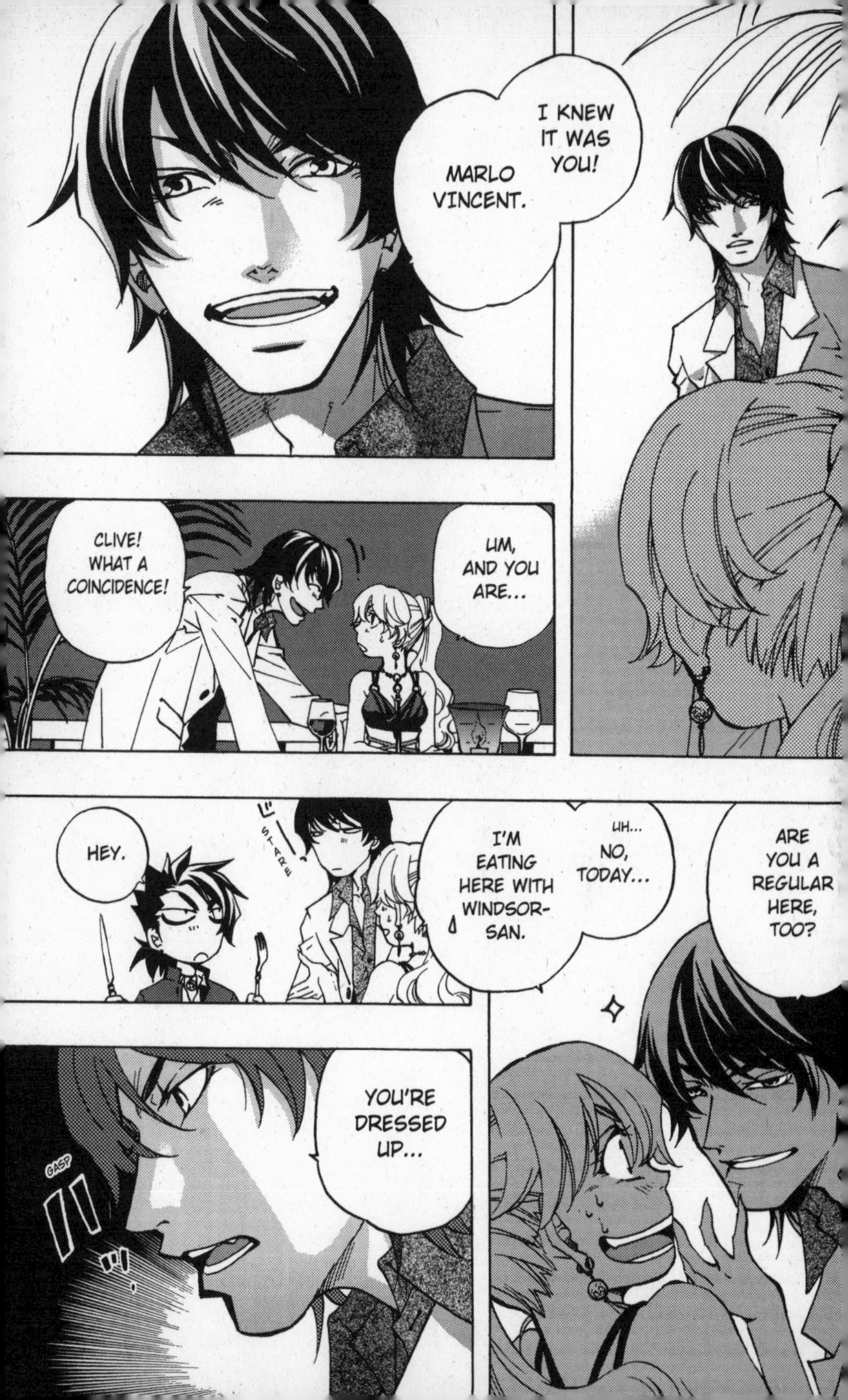
I KNEW IT WAS YOU!
MARLO VINCENT.
UM, AND YOU ARE...
CLIVE! WHAT A COINCIDENCE!
ARE YOU A REGULAR HERE, TOO?
UH... NO, TODAY...
I'M EATING HERE WITH WINDSOR-SAN.
ジ
STARE
HEY.
YOU'RE DRESSED UP...
GASP

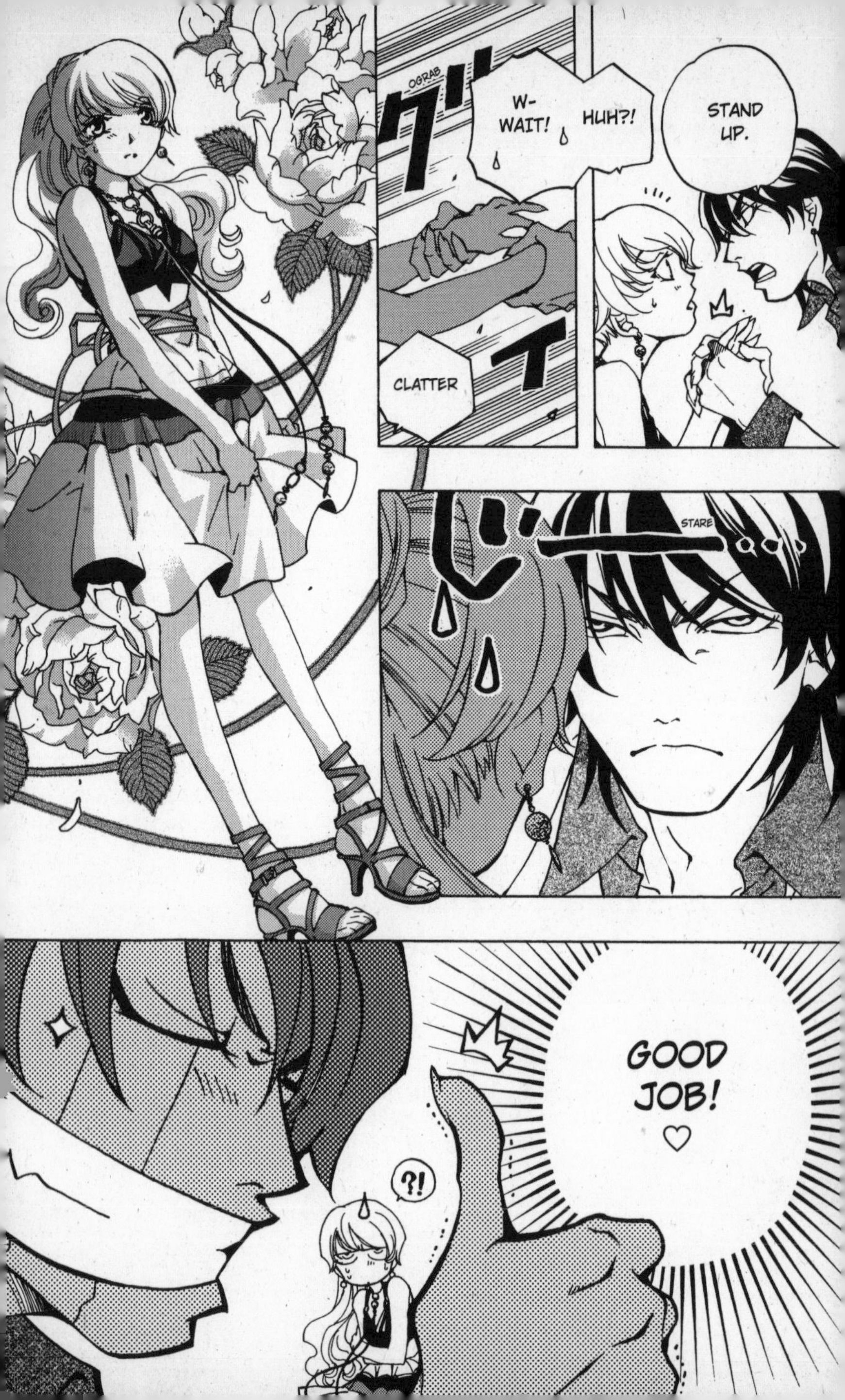

STAND UP.
HUH?!
W-WAIT!
GRAB
CLATTER
STARE
GOOD JOB! ♡
?!

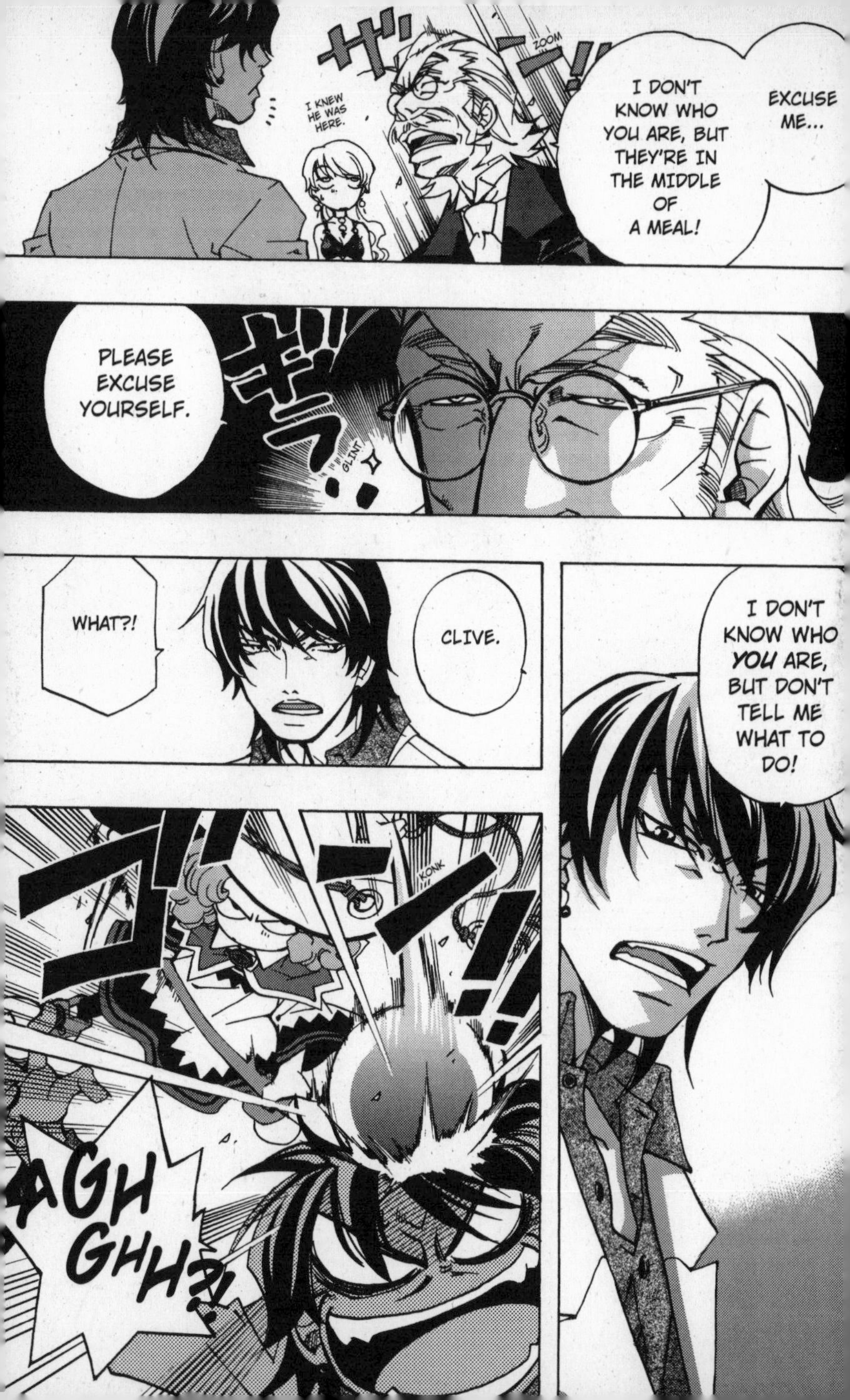
EXCUSE ME...
I DON'T KNOW WHO YOU ARE, BUT THEY'RE IN THE MIDDLE OF A MEAL!
ZOOM
I KNEW HE WAS HERE.
PLEASE EXCUSE YOURSELF.
GLINT
I DON'T KNOW WHO *YOU* ARE, BUT DON'T TELL ME WHAT TO DO!
CLIVE.
WHAT?!
KONK
AGH GHH?!

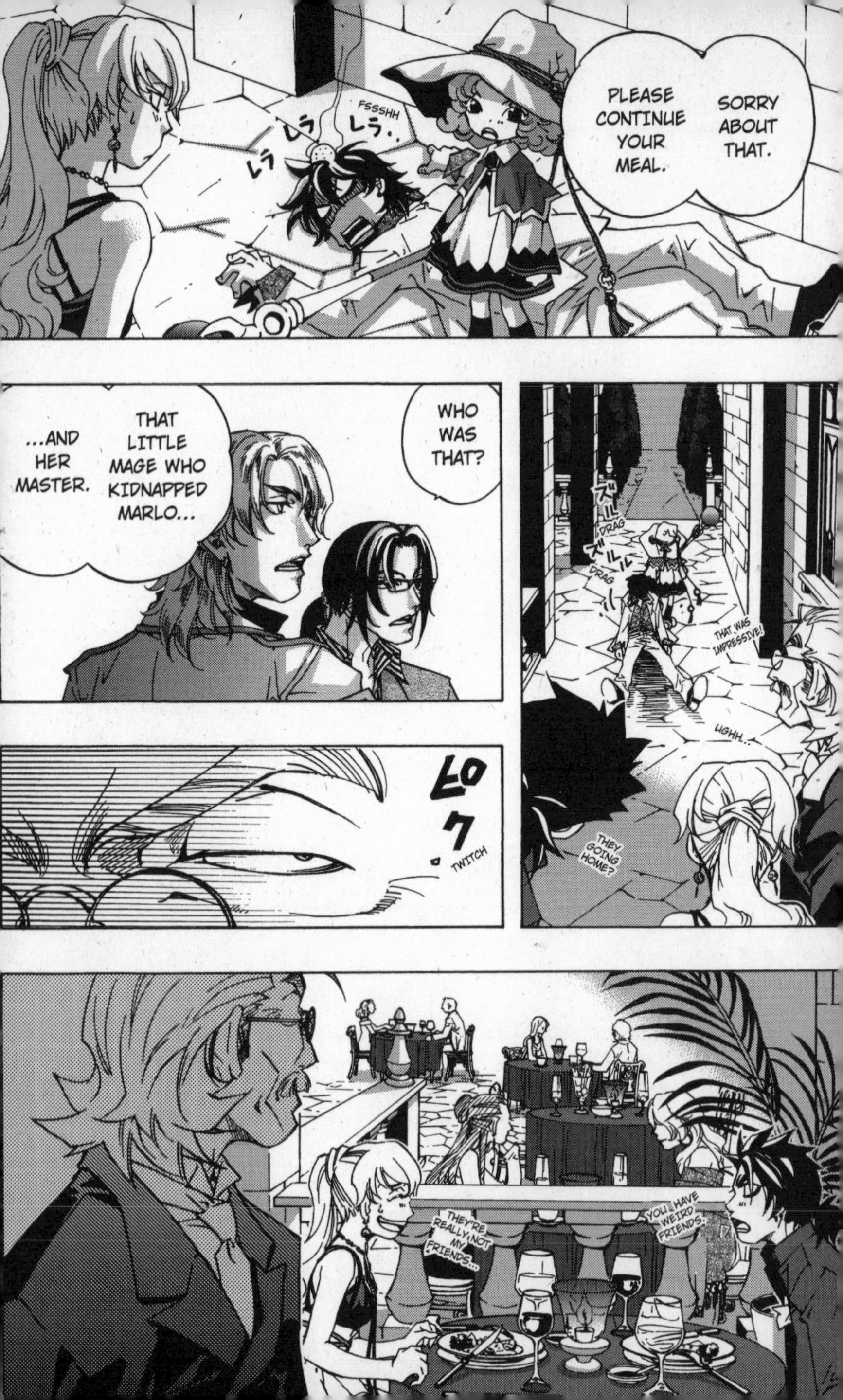
SORRY ABOUT THAT.
PLEASE CONTINUE YOUR MEAL.
FSSSHH
DRAG
DRAG
THAT WAS IMPRESSIVE!
UGHH..
THEY GOING HOME?
WHO WAS THAT?
THAT LITTLE MAGE WHO KIDNAPPED MARLO...
...AND HER MASTER.
TWITCH
YOU HAVE WEIRD FRIENDS.
THEY'RE REALLY NOT MY FRIENDS...

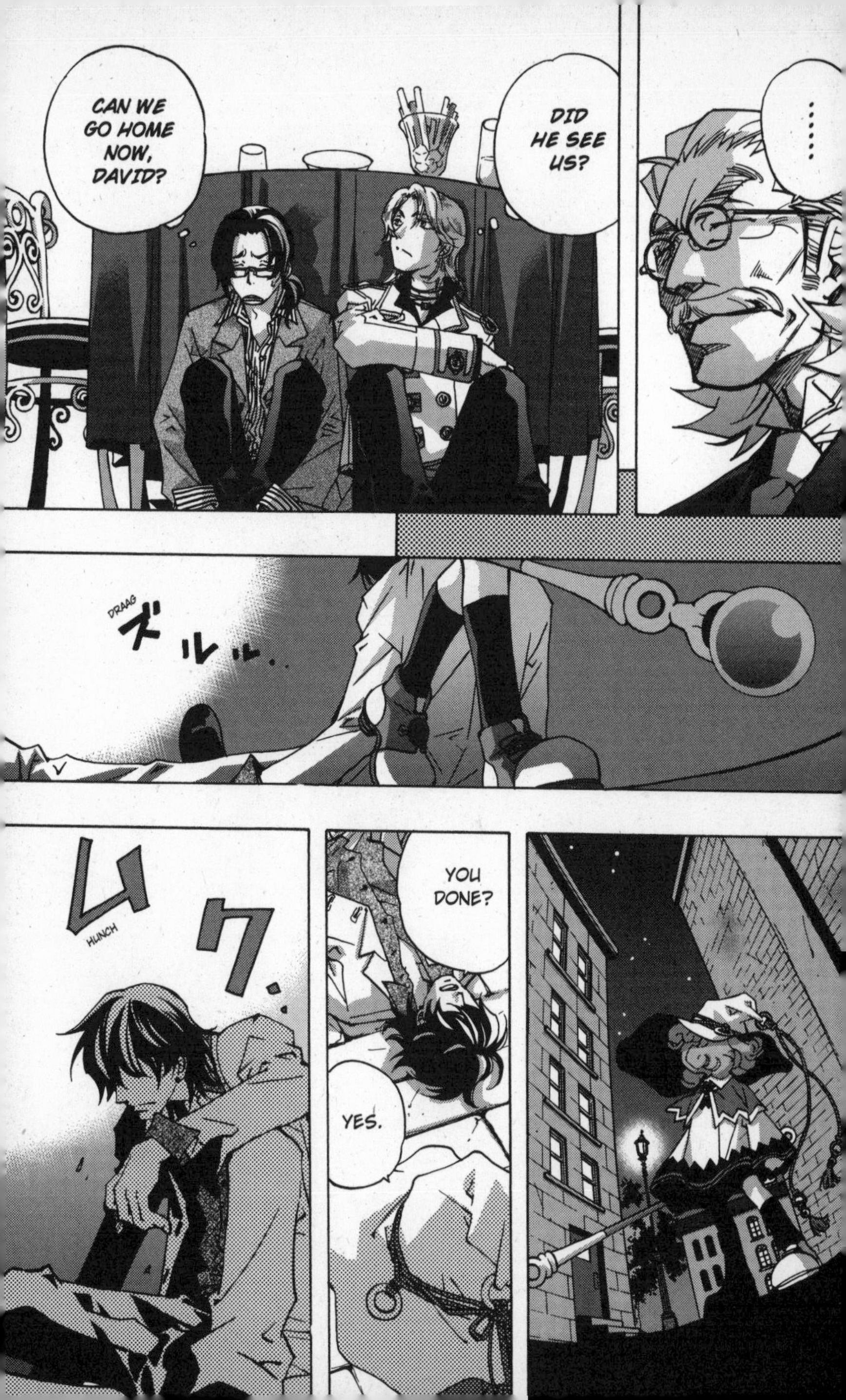
......
DID HE SEE US?
CAN WE GO HOME NOW, DAVID?
DRAAG
ズルル..
YOU DONE?
YES.
ムク.
HUNCH

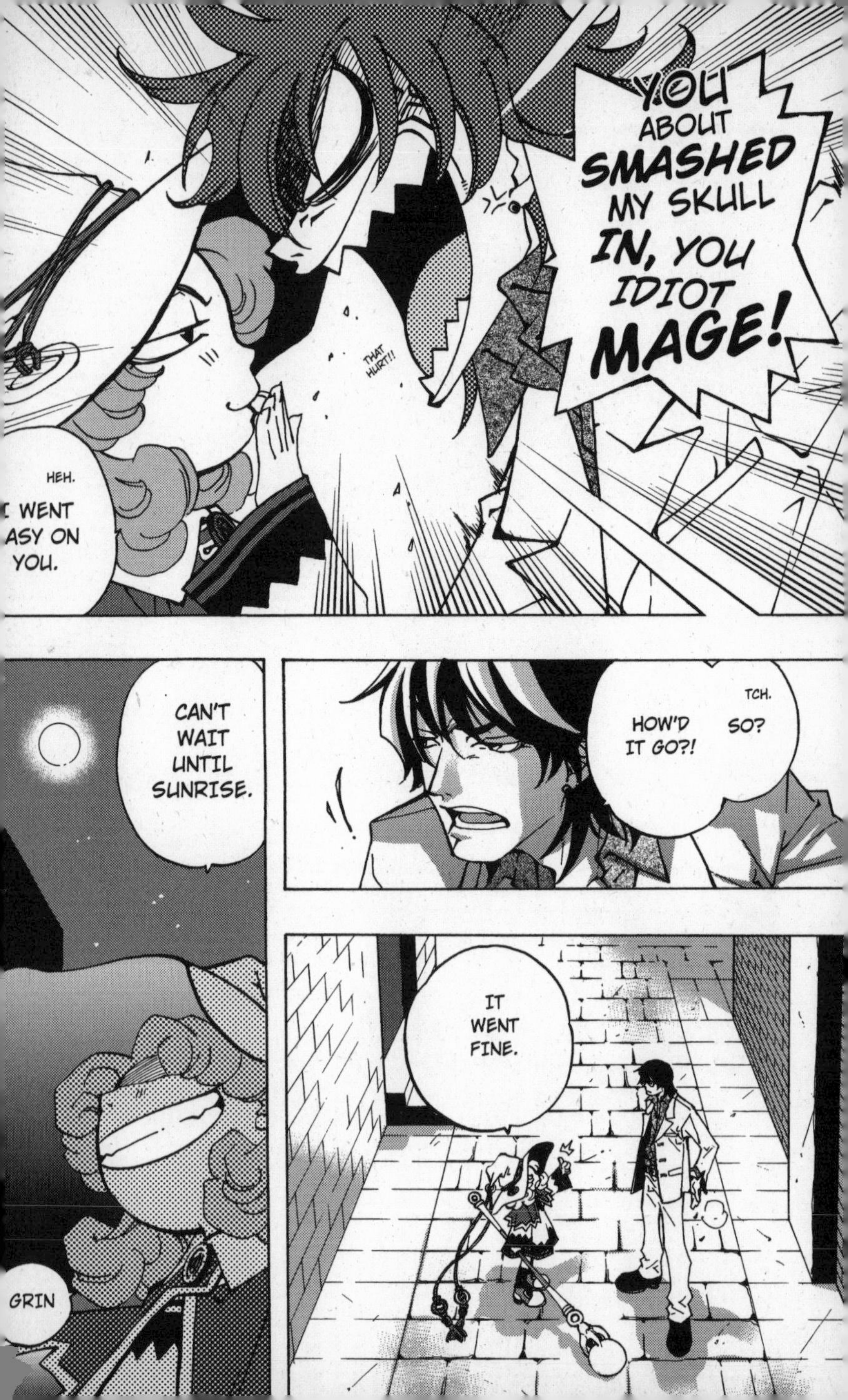
YOU ABOUT SMASHED MY SKULL IN, YOU IDIOT MAGE!
THAT HURT!!
HEH.
I WENT ASY ON YOU.
TCH. SO?
HOW'D IT GO?!
IT WENT FINE.
CAN'T WAIT UNTIL SUNRISE.
GRIN

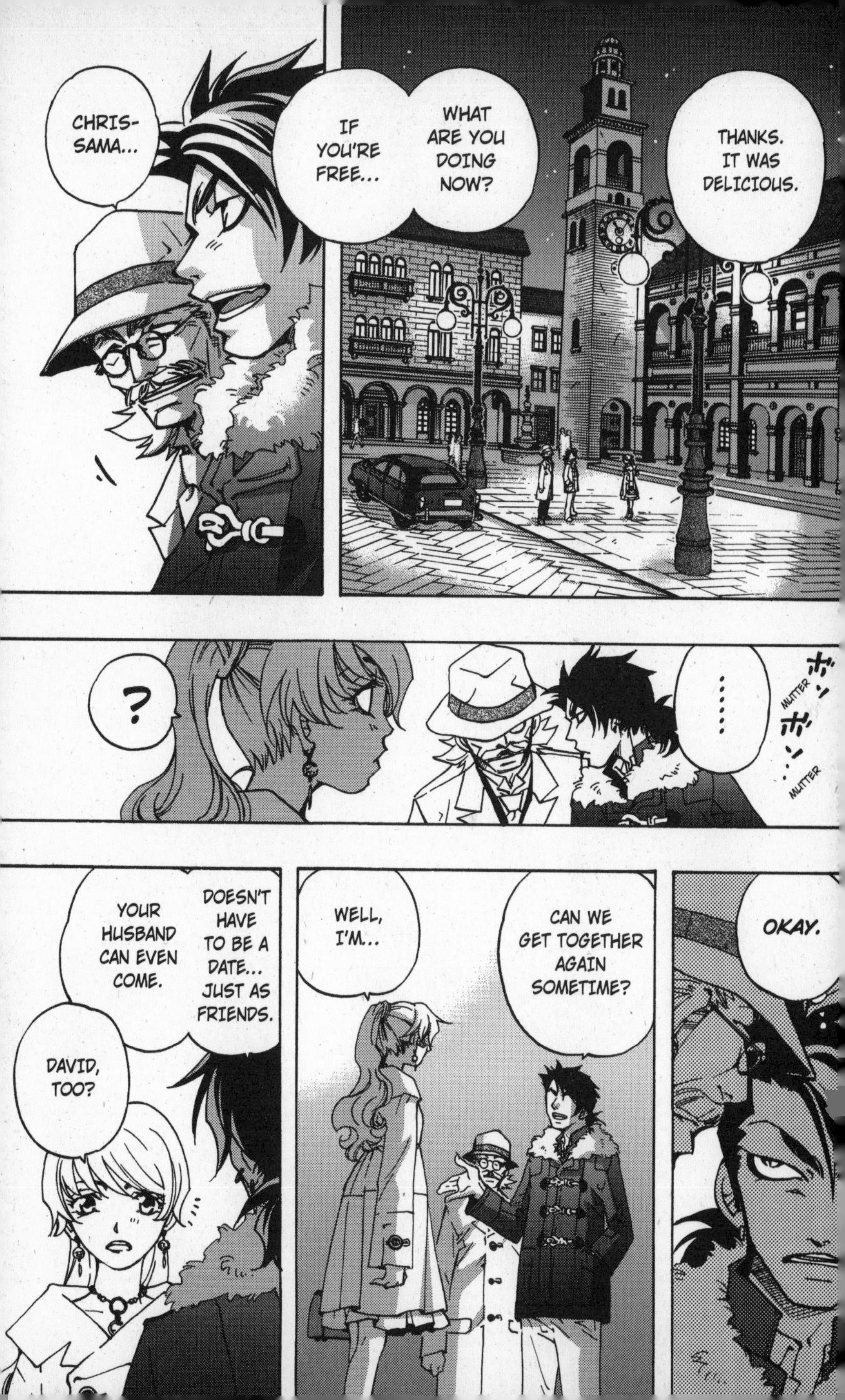
THANKS. IT WAS DELICIOUS.
WHAT ARE YOU DOING NOW?
IF YOU'RE FREE...
CHRIS-SAMA...
......
MUTTER
MUTTER
?
OKAY.
CAN WE GET TOGETHER AGAIN SOMETIME?
WELL, I'M...
DOESN'T HAVE TO BE A DATE... JUST AS FRIENDS.
YOUR HUSBAND CAN EVEN COME.
DAVID, TOO?

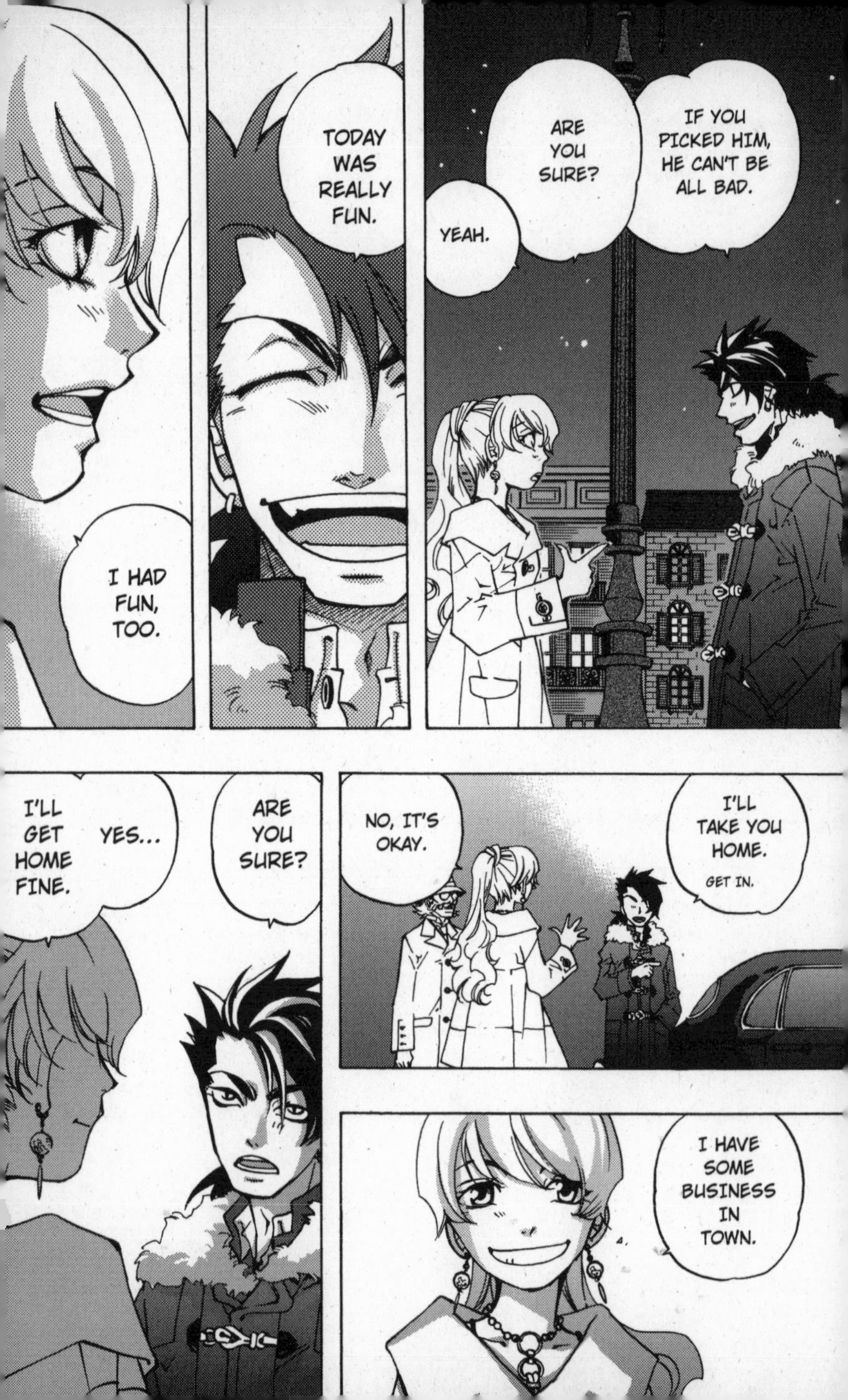
IF YOU PICKED HIM, HE CAN'T BE ALL BAD.
ARE YOU SURE?
YEAH.
TODAY WAS REALLY FUN.
I HAD FUN, TOO.
I'LL TAKE YOU HOME.
GET IN.
NO, IT'S OKAY.
I HAVE SOME BUSINESS IN TOWN.
ARE YOU SURE?
YES...
I'LL GET HOME FINE.

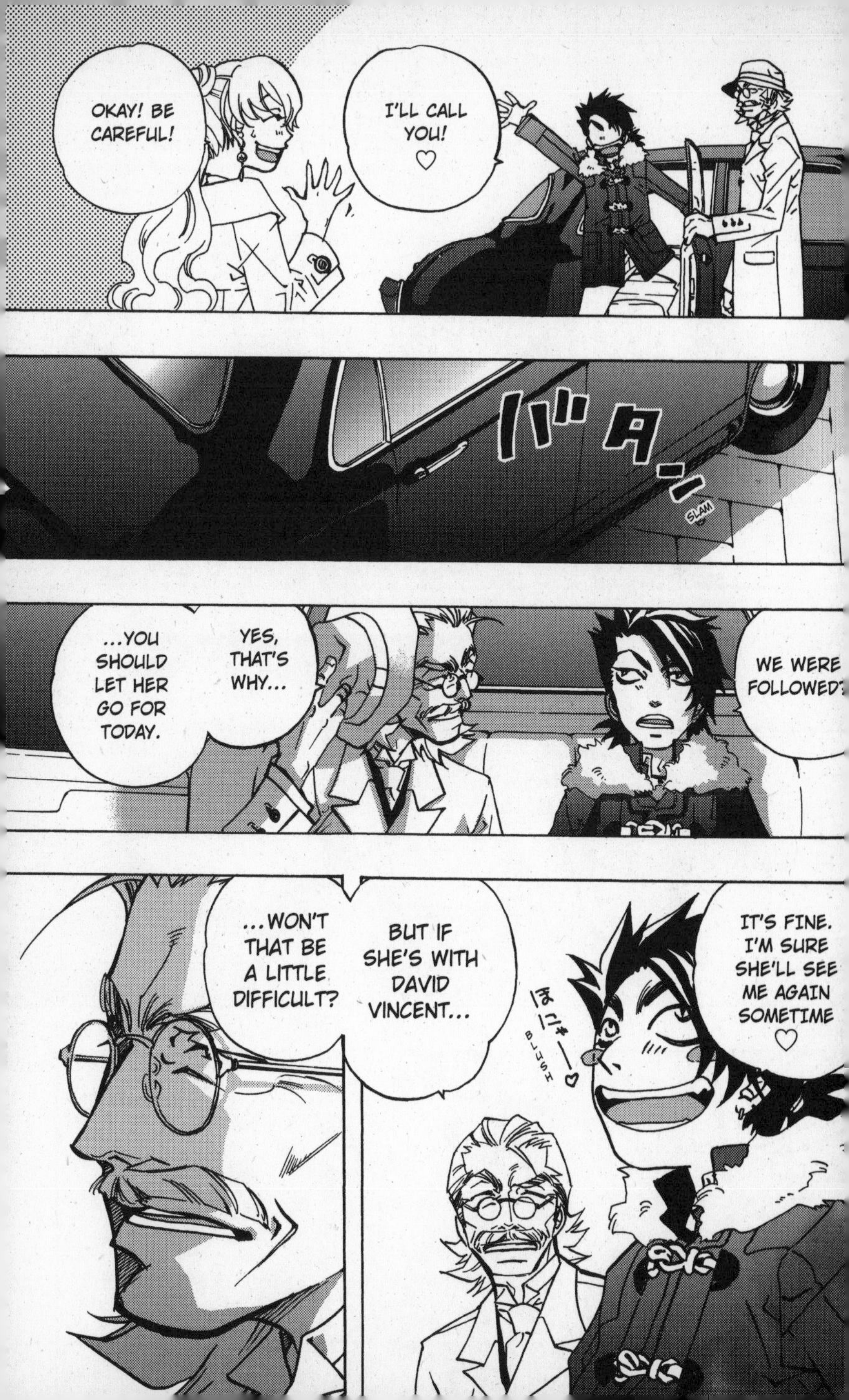
I'LL CALL YOU! ♡
OKAY! BE CAREFUL!
SLAM
WE WERE FOLLOWED?
YES, THAT'S WHY...
...YOU SHOULD LET HER GO FOR TODAY.
IT'S FINE. I'M SURE SHE'LL SEE ME AGAIN SOMETIME ♡
ほにゃー♡
BLUSH
BUT IF SHE'S WITH DAVID VINCENT...
...WON'T THAT BE A LITTLE DIFFICULT?

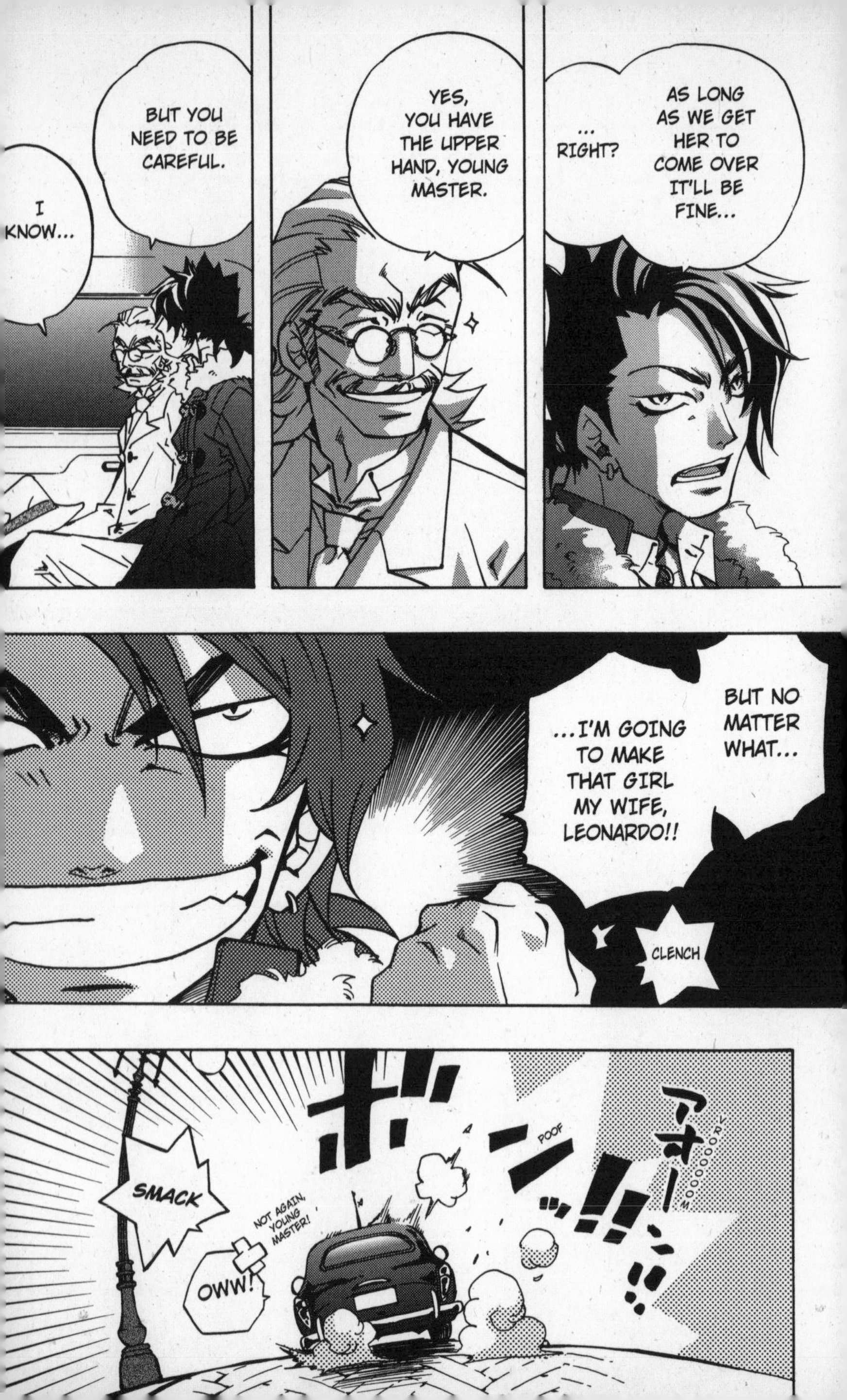
AS LONG AS WE GET HER TO COME OVER IT'LL BE FINE...
...RIGHT?
YES, YOU HAVE THE UPPER HAND, YOUNG MASTER.
BUT YOU NEED TO BE CAREFUL.
I KNOW...
BUT NO MATTER WHAT...
...I'M GOING TO MAKE THAT GIRL MY WIFE, LEONARDO!!
CLENCH
VROOOOOOOOM
POOF
NOT AGAIN, YOUNG MASTER!
SMACK
OWW!

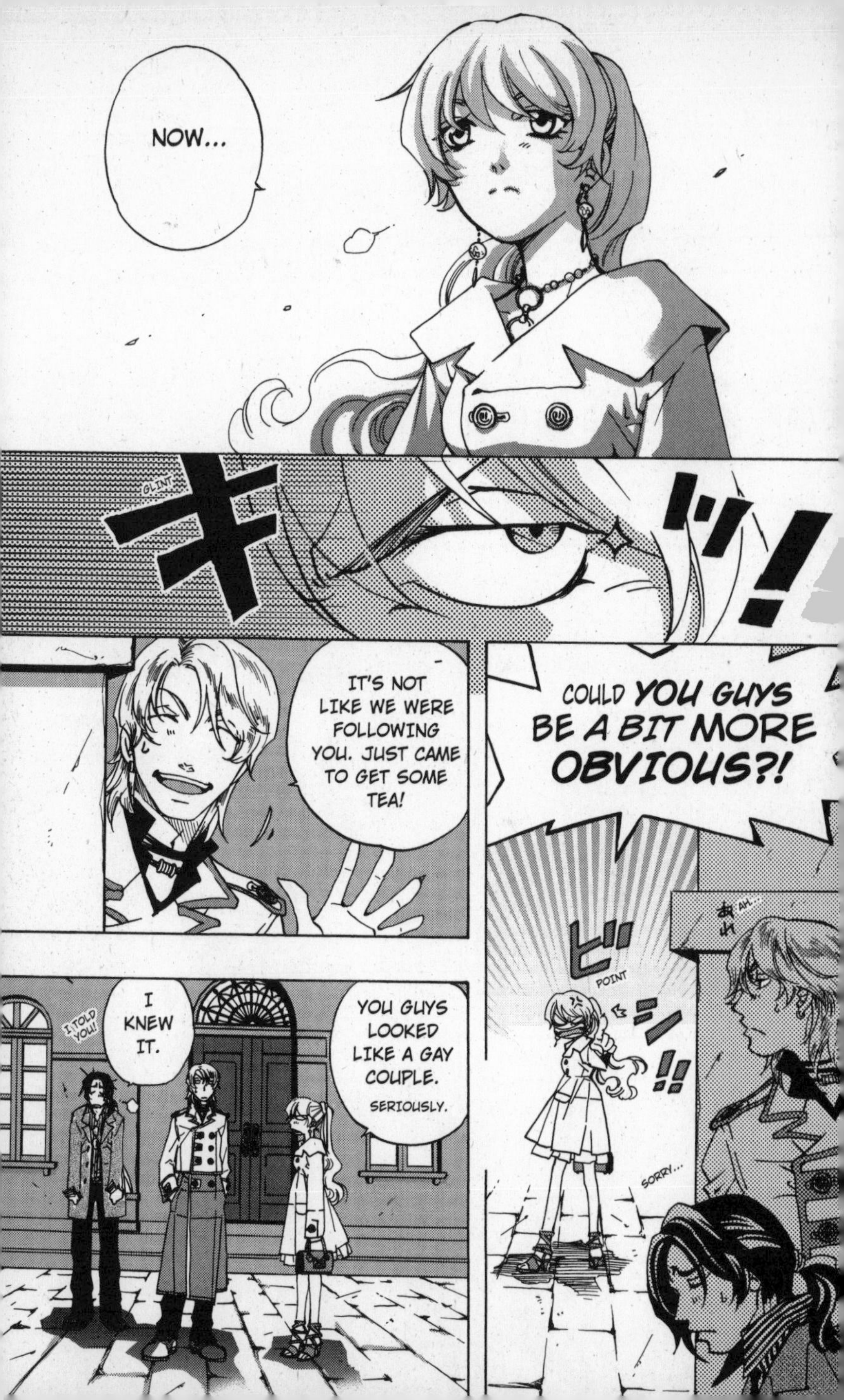

NOW...
キッ!
GLINT
COULD YOU GUYS BE A BIT MORE OBVIOUS?!
あれ
AH...
ビシッ!!
POINT
SORRY...
IT'S NOT LIKE WE WERE FOLLOWING YOU. JUST CAME TO GET SOME TEA!
YOU GUYS LOOKED LIKE A GAY COUPLE.
SERIOUSLY.
I KNEW IT.
I TOLD YOU!

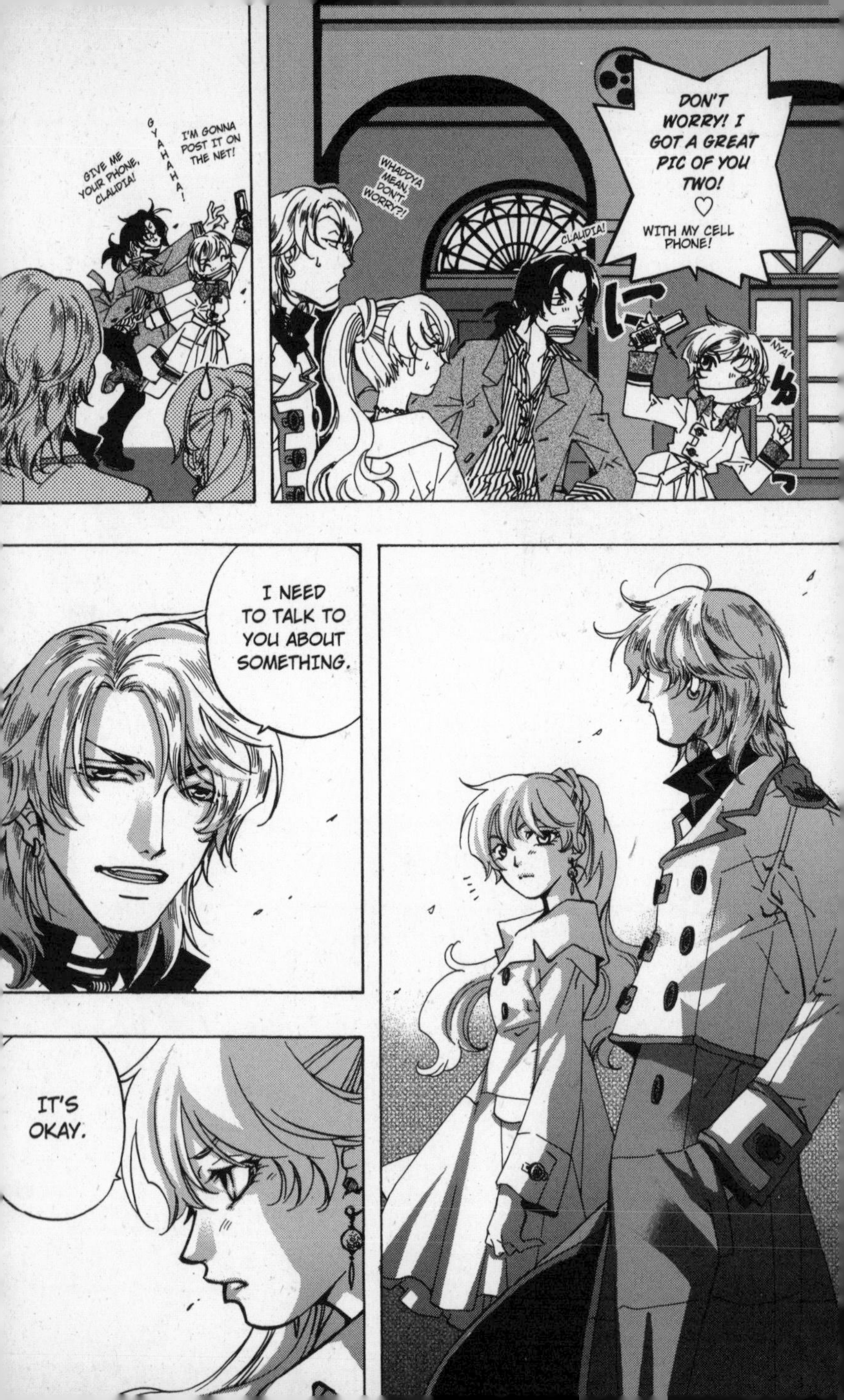
DON'T WORRY! I GOT A GREAT PIC OF YOU TWO! ♡
WITH MY CELL PHONE!
NYA!
CLAUDIA!
WHADDYA MEAN, DON'T WORRY?!
I'M GONNA POST IT ON THE NET!
GYAHAHA!
GIVE ME YOUR PHONE, CLAUDIA!
I NEED TO TALK TO YOU ABOUT SOMETHING.
IT'S OKAY.

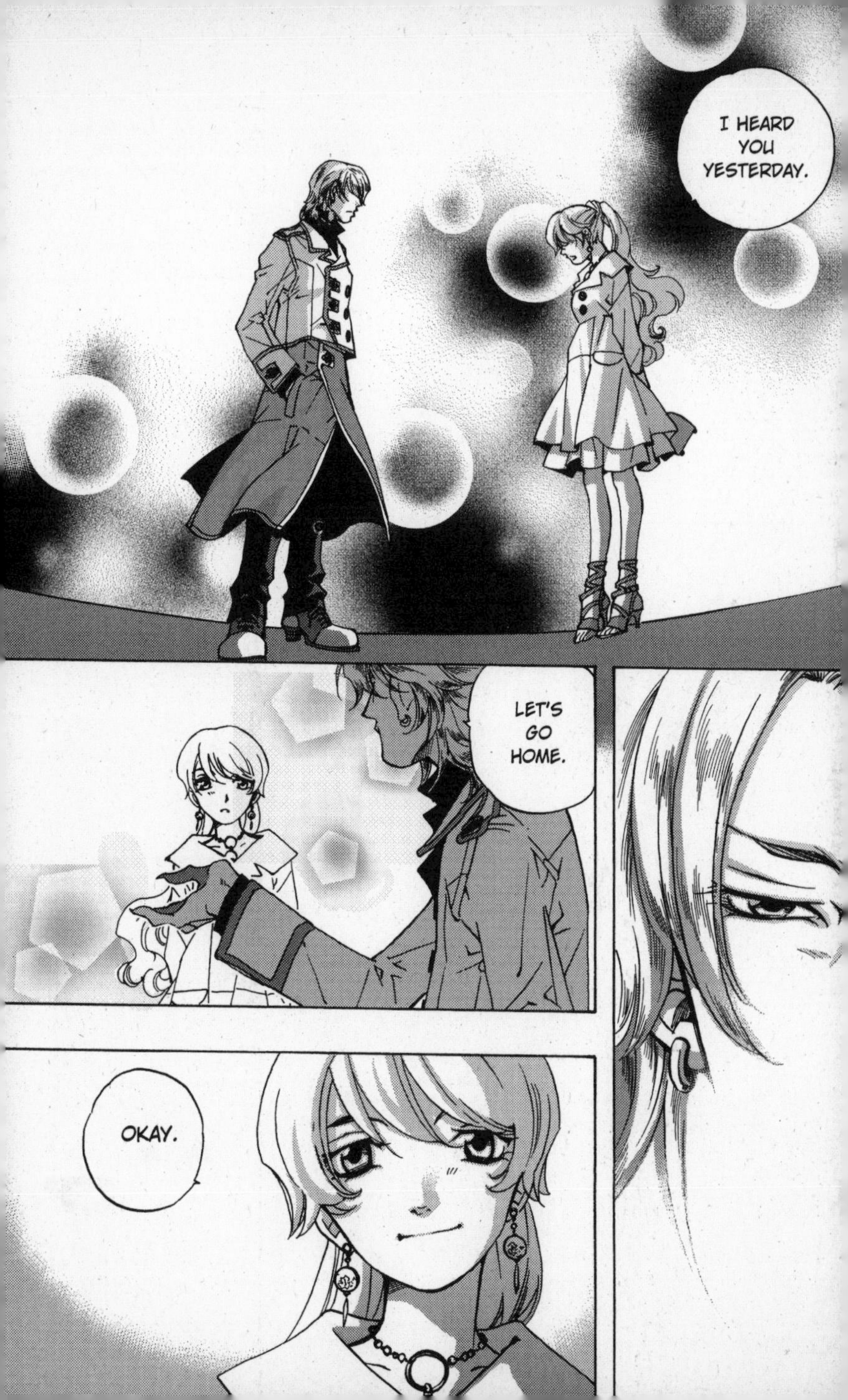
I HEARD YOU YESTERDAY.
LET'S GO HOME.
OKAY.

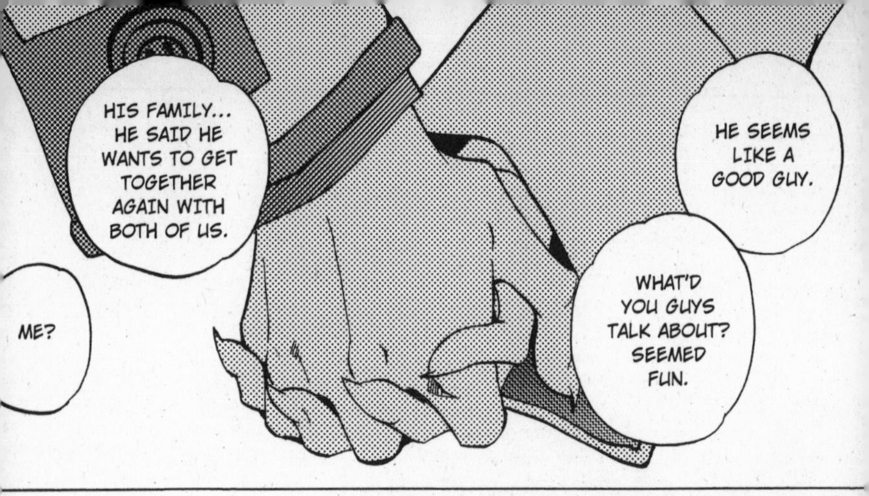
HE SEEMS LIKE A GOOD GUY.
WHAT'D YOU GUYS TALK ABOUT? SEEMED FUN.
HIS FAMILY... HE SAID HE WANTS TO GET TOGETHER AGAIN WITH BOTH OF US.
ME?

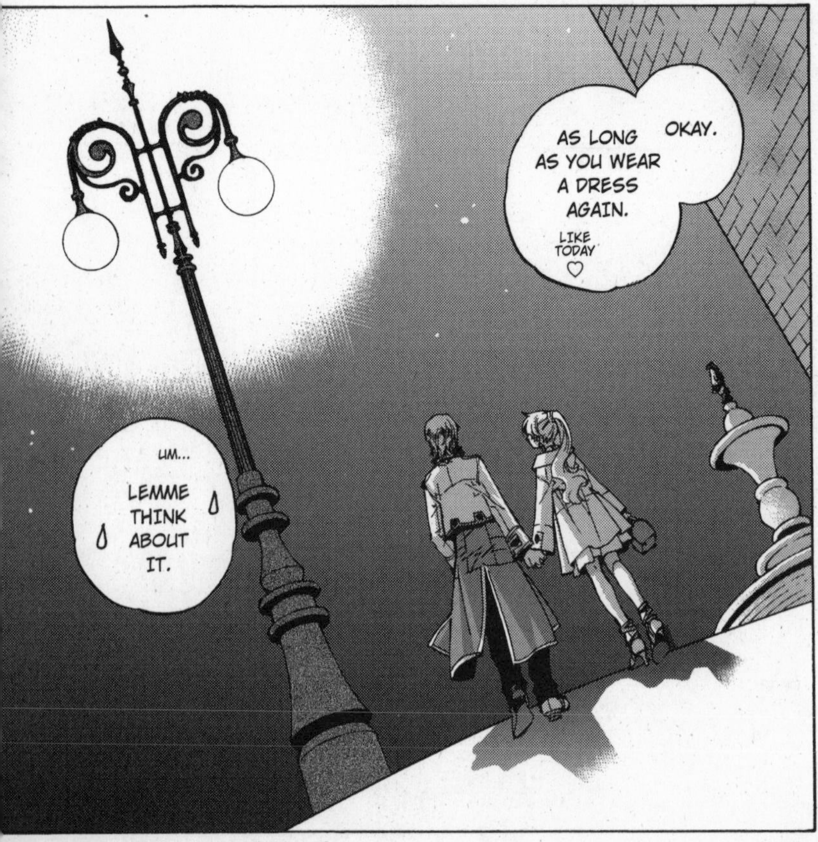
OKAY.
AS LONG AS YOU WEAR A DRESS AGAIN.
LIKE TODAY ♡
UM... LEMME THINK ABOUT IT.

CHAPTER 2 / END

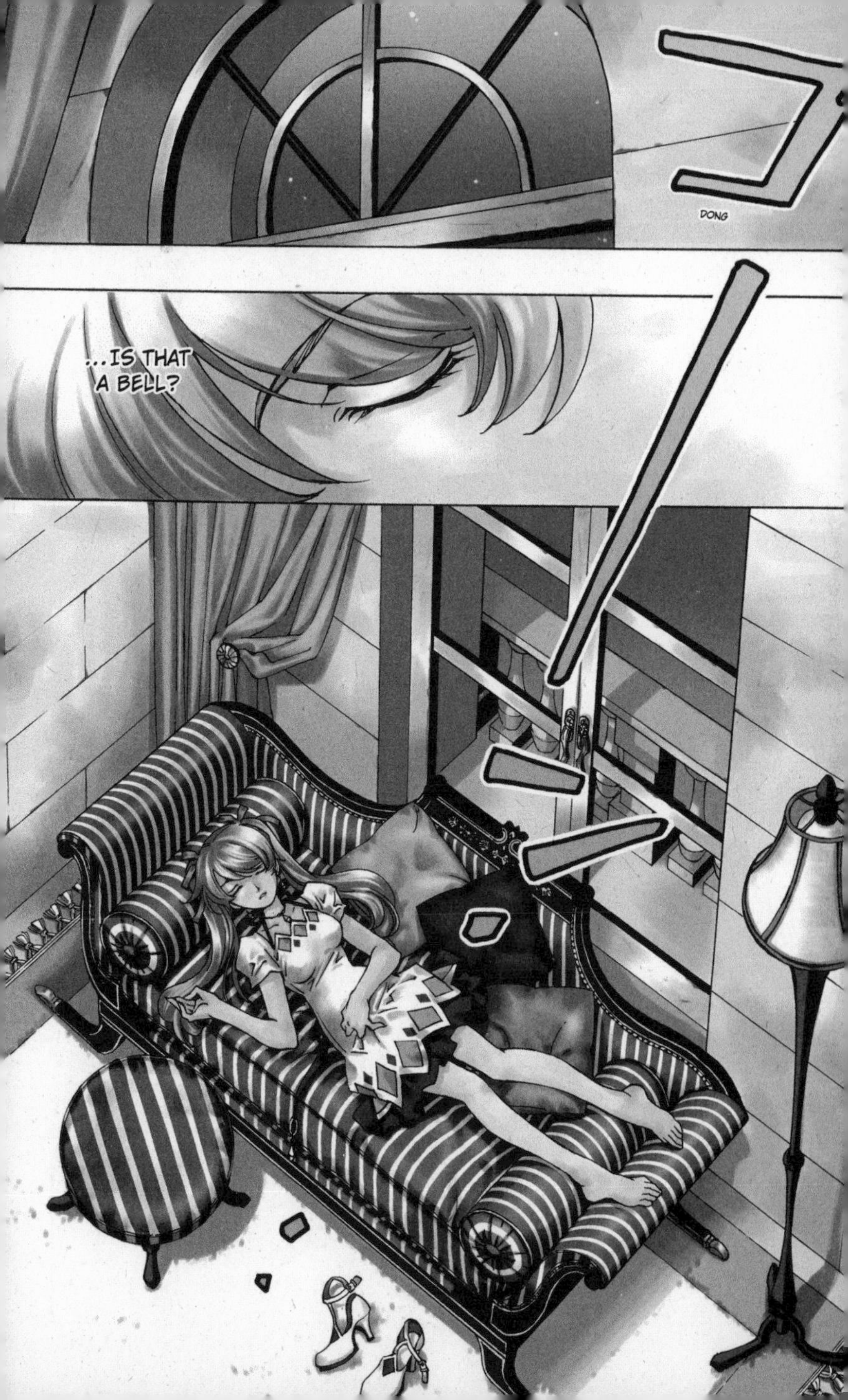
DONG
...IS THAT A BELL?

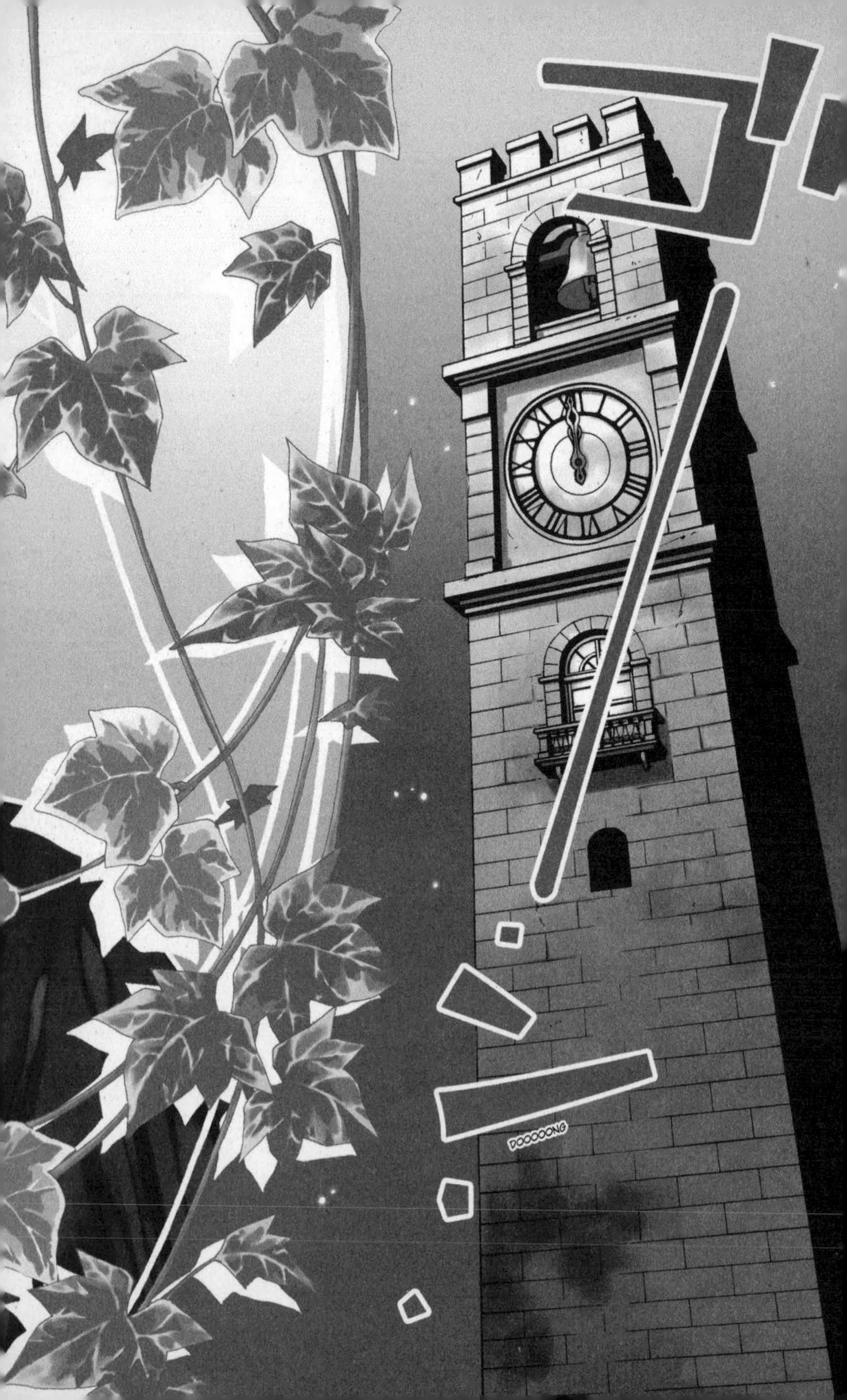
DOOOOONG

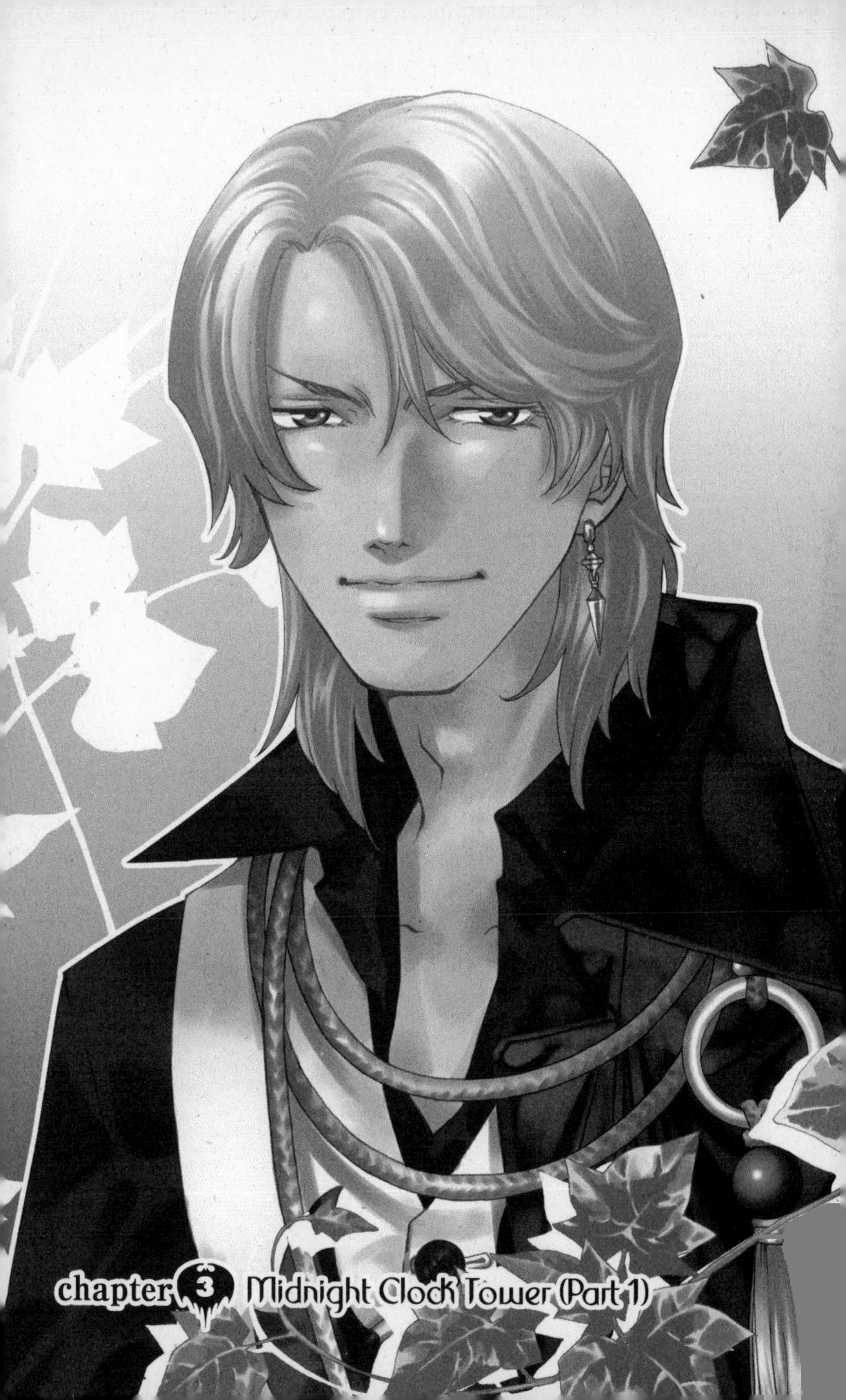

chapter 3 Midnight Clock Tower (Part 1)

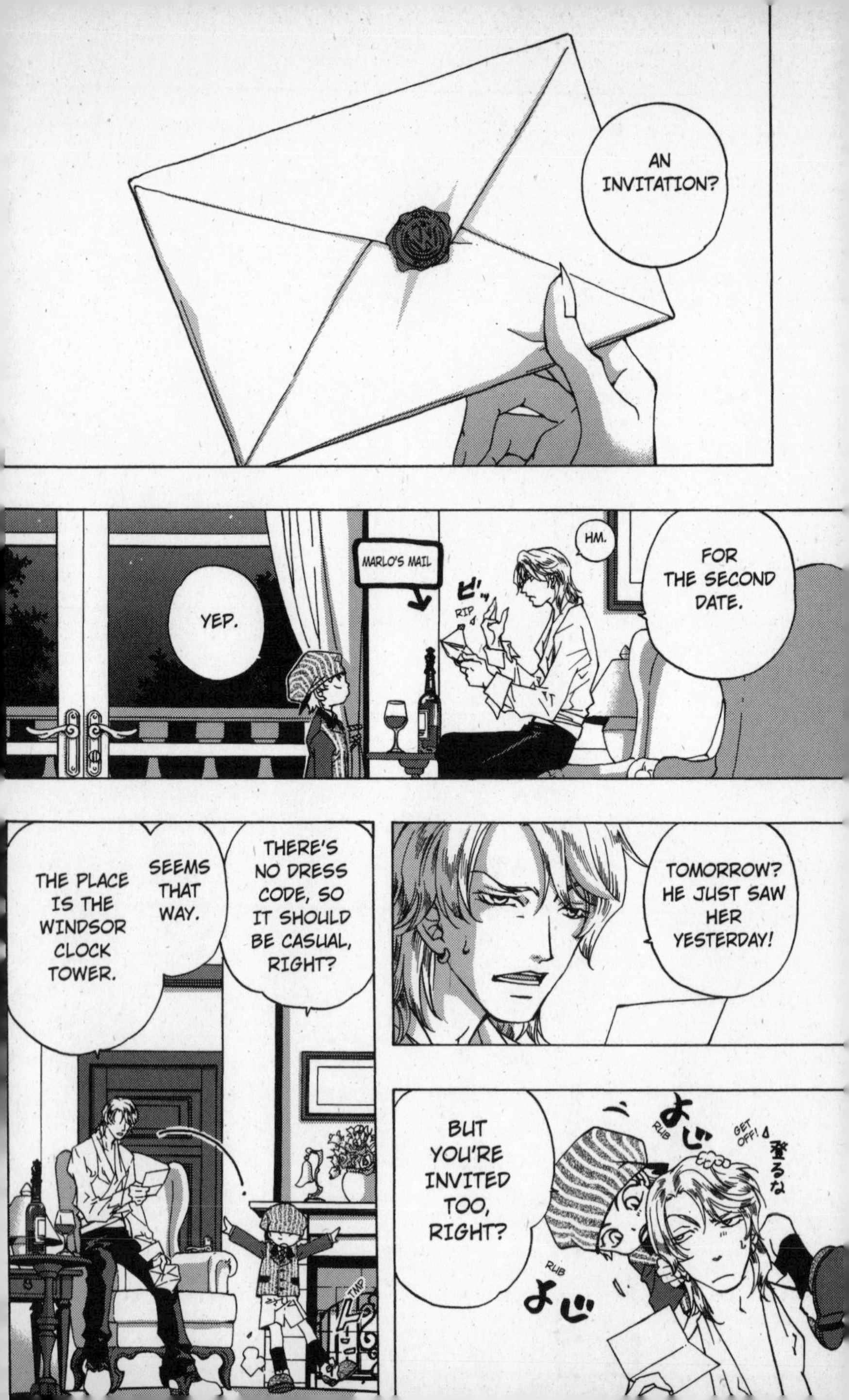
AN INVITATION?
FOR THE SECOND DATE.
HM.
MARLO'S MAIL
ビッ RIP
YEP.
TOMORROW? HE JUST SAW HER YESTERDAY!
BUT YOU'RE INVITED TOO, RIGHT?
よじ RUB
GET OFF! 登るな
RUB よじ
THERE'S NO DRESS CODE, SO IT SHOULD BE CASUAL, RIGHT?
SEEMS THAT WAY.
THE PLACE IS THE WINDSOR CLOCK TOWER.
TMP

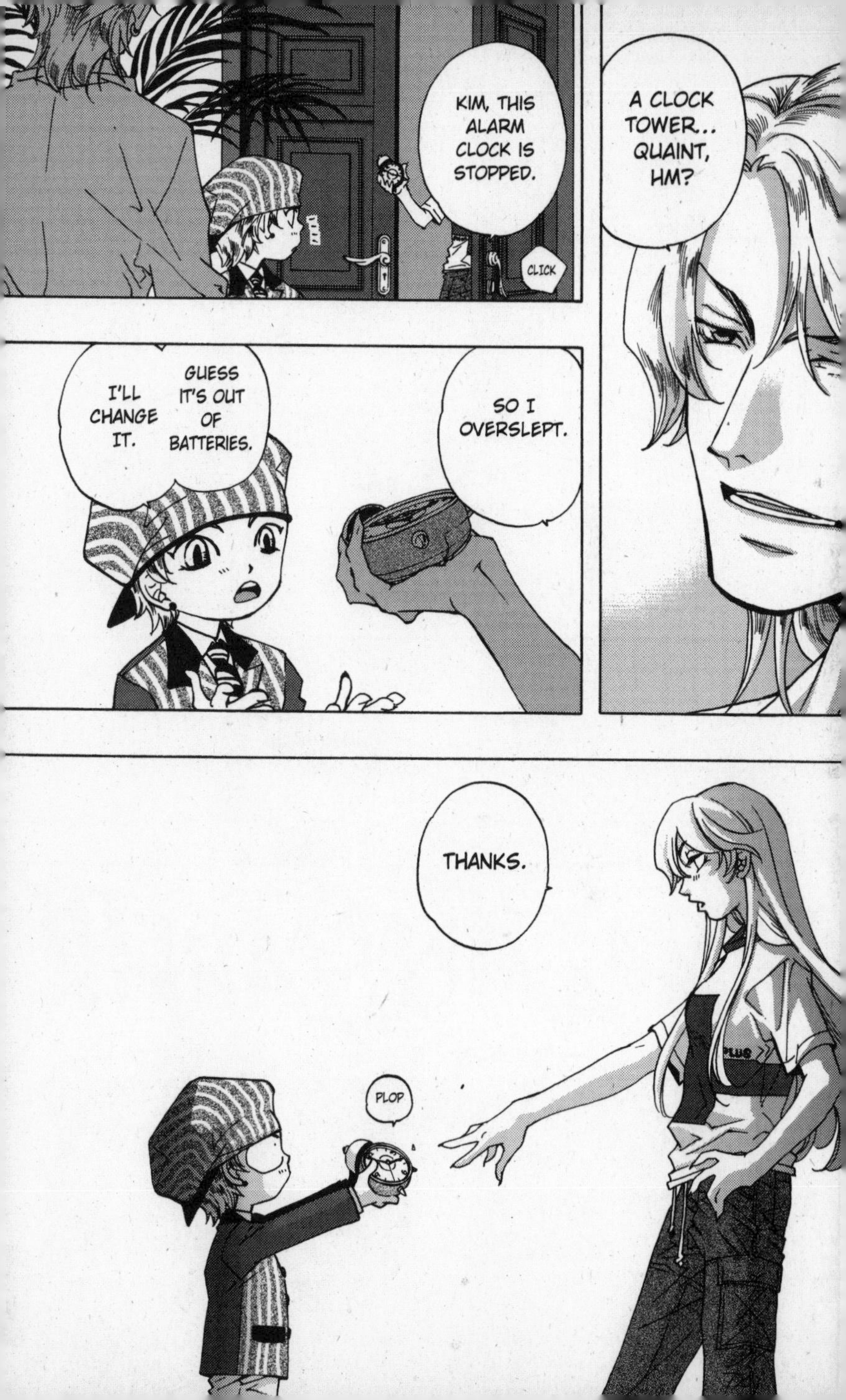
A CLOCK TOWER... QUAINT, HM?
KIM, THIS ALARM CLOCK IS STOPPED.
CLICK
SO I OVERSLEPT.
GUESS IT'S OUT OF BATTERIES.
I'LL CHANGE IT.
THANKS.
PLOP

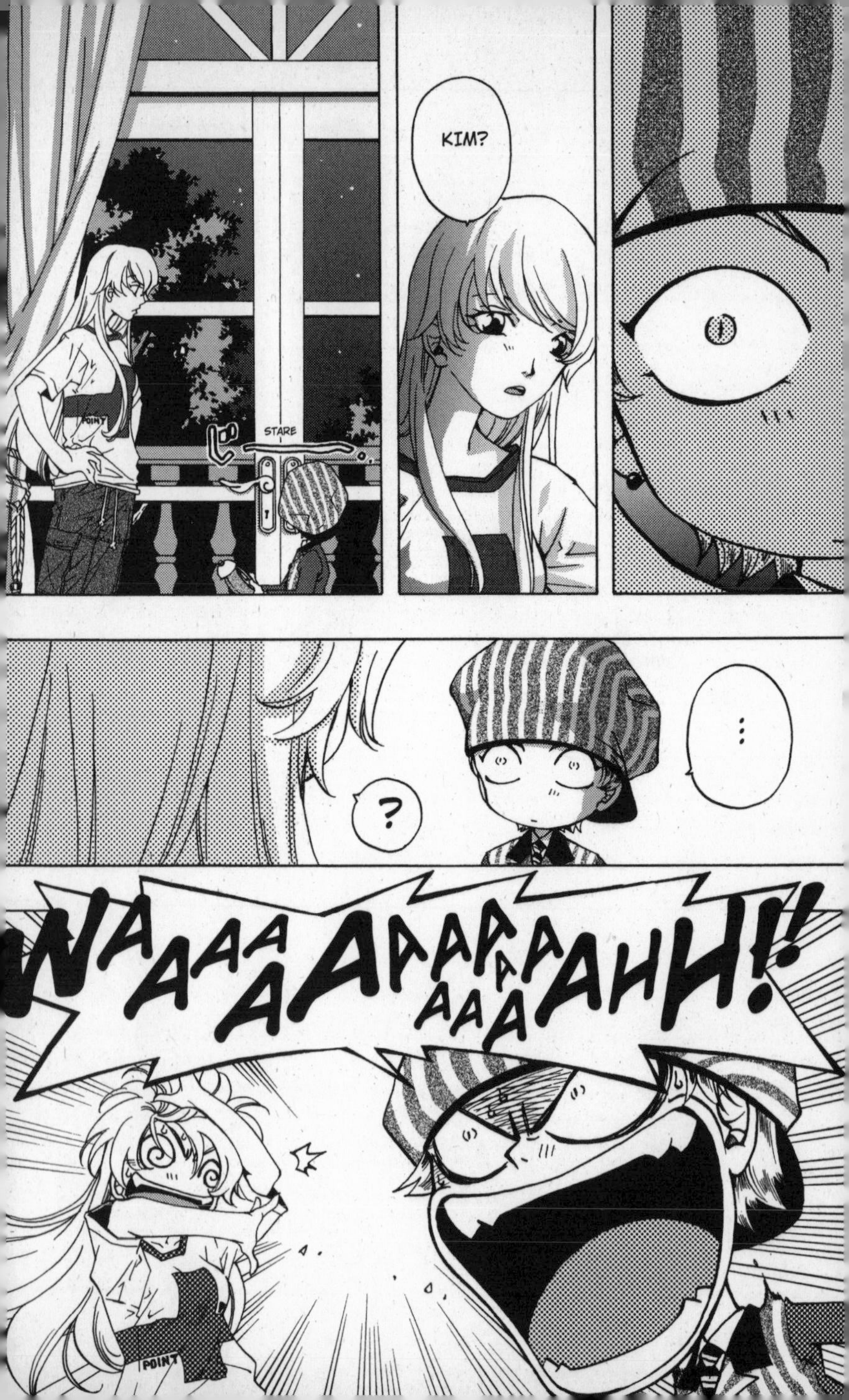
KIM?
STARE
...
?
WAAAAAAAAAAAAAAHH!!

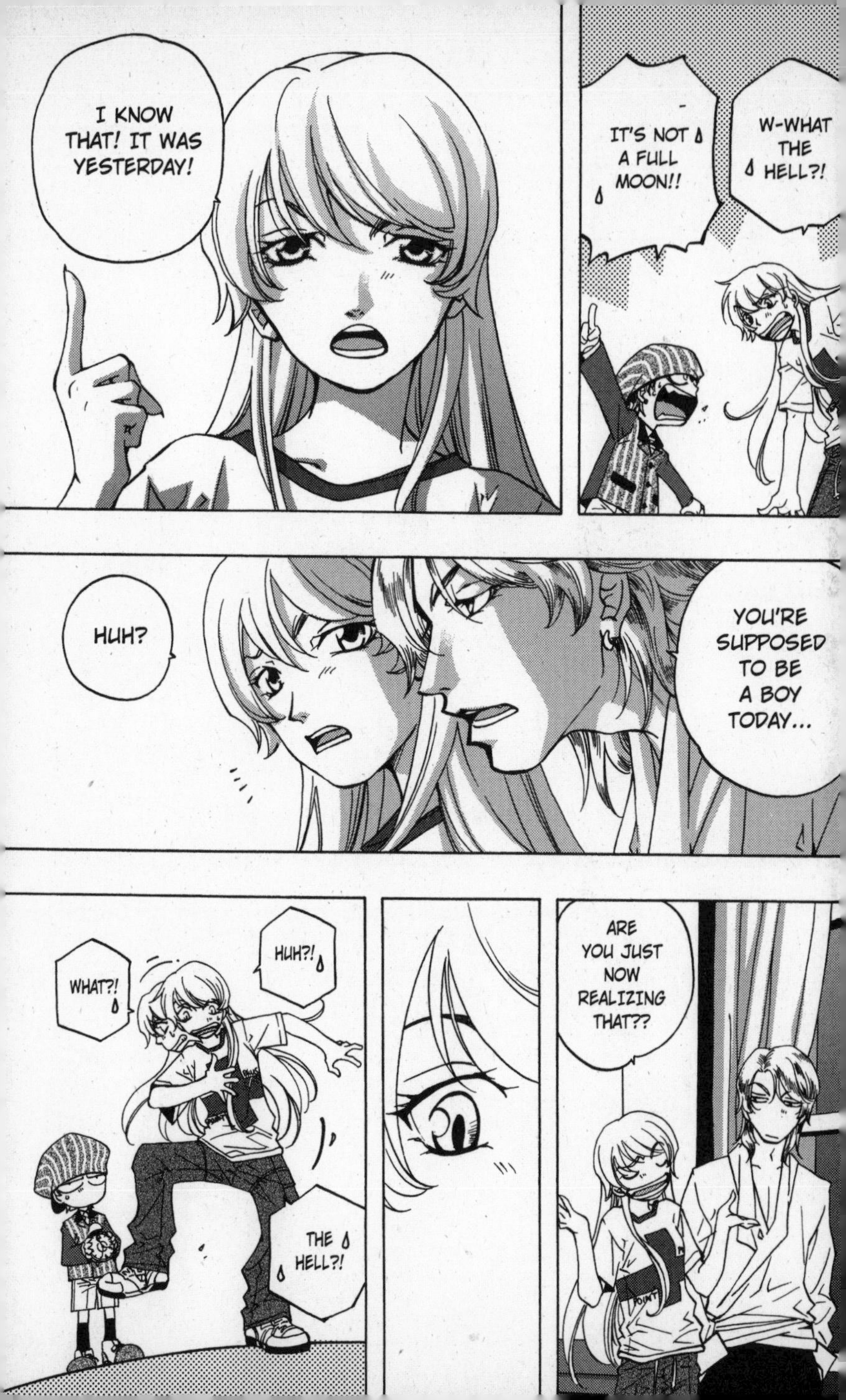
W-WHAT THE HELL?!
IT'S NOT A FULL MOON!!
I KNOW THAT! IT WAS YESTERDAY!
YOU'RE SUPPOSED TO BE A BOY TODAY...
HUH?
ARE YOU JUST NOW REALIZING THAT??
HUH?!
WHAT?!
THE HELL?!

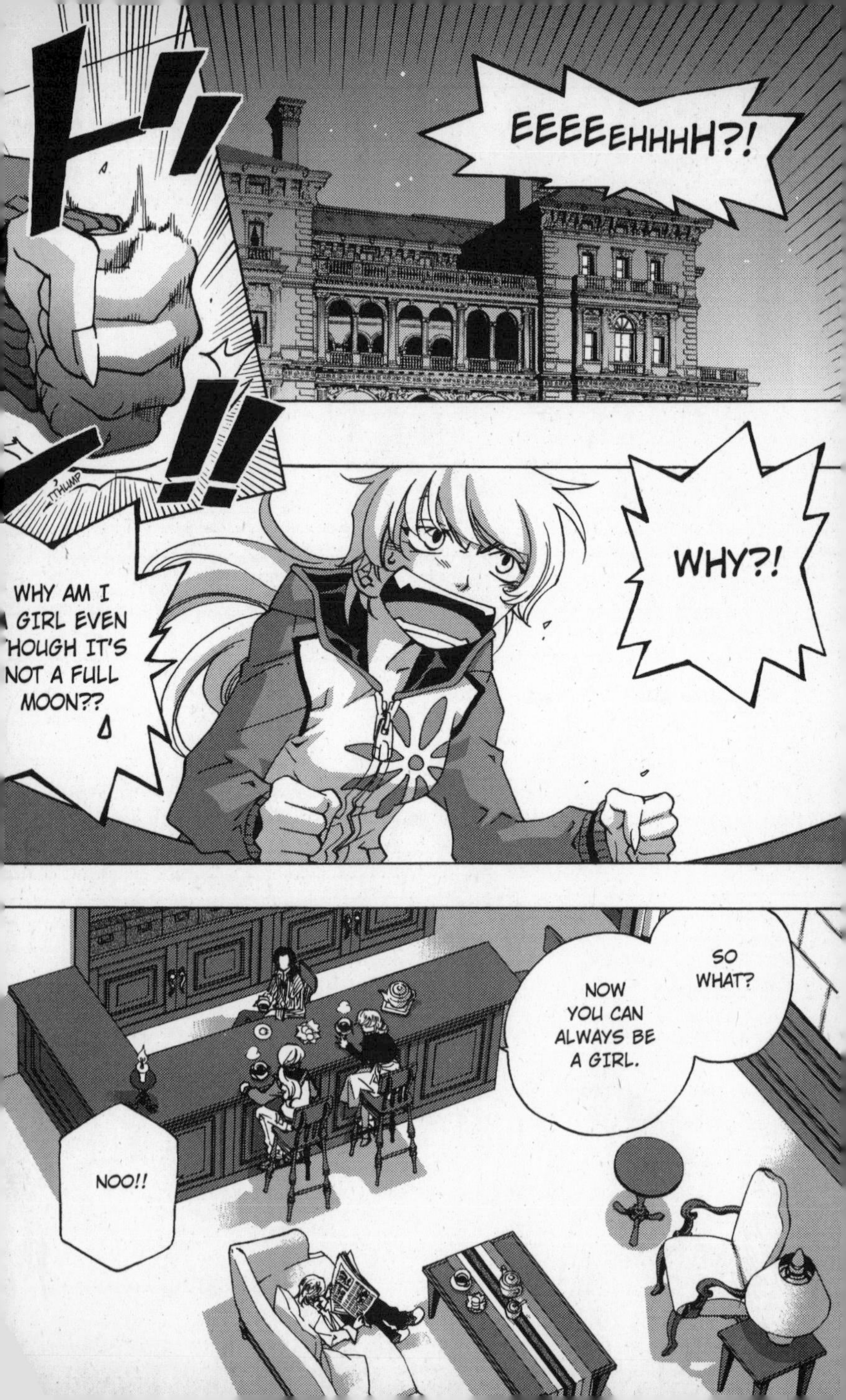
EEEEEHHHH?!
TTHUMP
WHY?!
WHY AM I GIRL EVEN HOUGH IT'S NOT A FULL MOON??
SO WHAT?
NOW YOU CAN ALWAYS BE A GIRL.
NOO!!

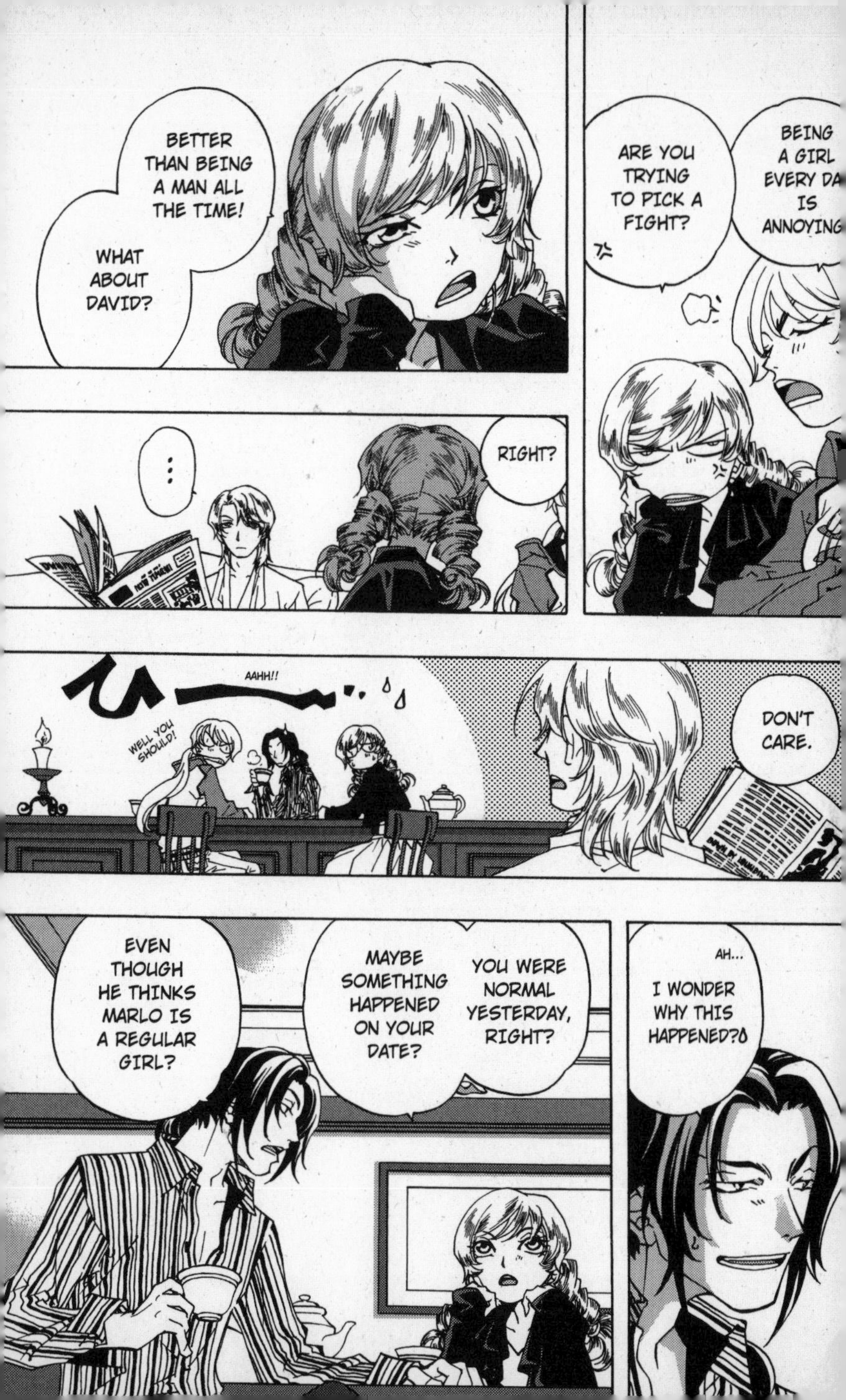
BEING A GIRL EVERY DA IS ANNOYING
ARE YOU TRYING TO PICK A FIGHT?
BETTER THAN BEING A MAN ALL THE TIME!
WHAT ABOUT DAVID?
RIGHT?
...
DON'T CARE.
AAHH!!
WELL YOU SHOULD!
AH...
I WONDER WHY THIS HAPPENED?
YOU WERE NORMAL YESTERDAY, RIGHT?
MAYBE SOMETHING HAPPENED ON YOUR DATE?
EVEN THOUGH HE THINKS MARLO IS A REGULAR GIRL?

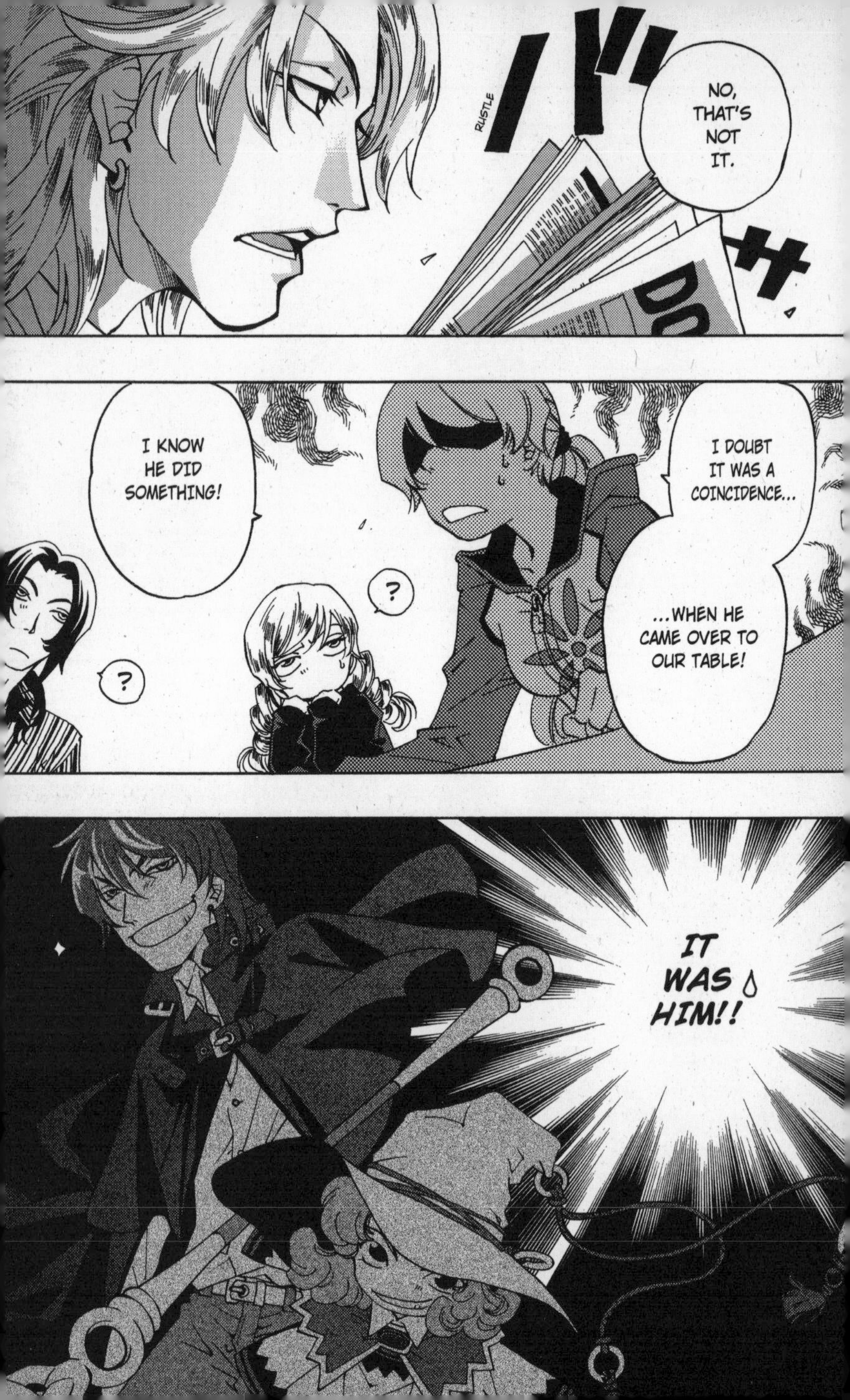
NO, THAT'S NOT IT.
RUSTLE
I DOUBT IT WAS A COINCIDENCE...
...WHEN HE CAME OVER TO OUR TABLE!
I KNOW HE DID SOMETHING!
?
?
IT WAS HIM!!

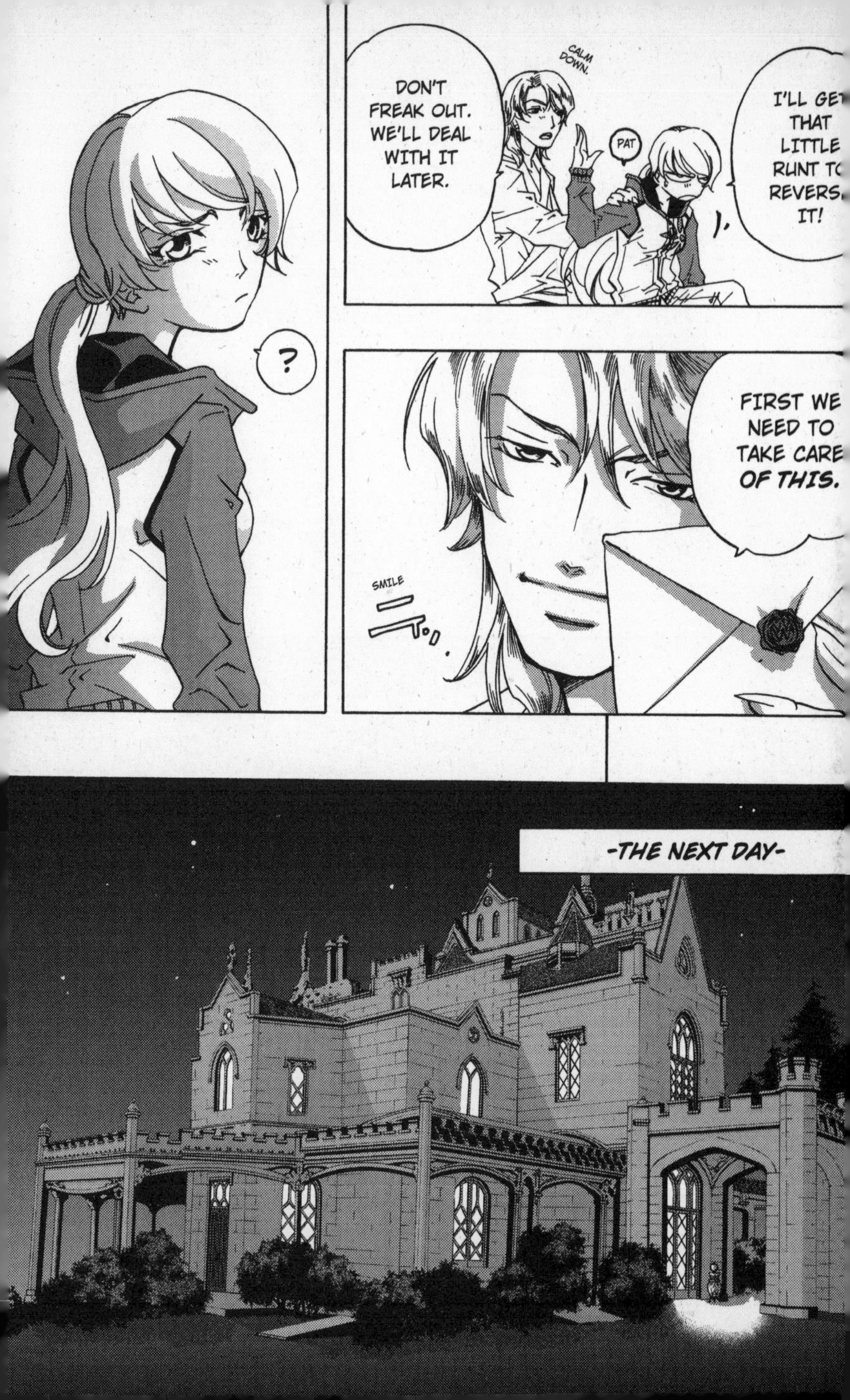
I'LL GET THAT LITTLE RUNT TO REVERSE IT!
CALM DOWN.
PAT
DON'T FREAK OUT. WE'LL DEAL WITH IT LATER.
FIRST WE NEED TO TAKE CARE OF THIS.
SMILE
?
-THE NEXT DAY-

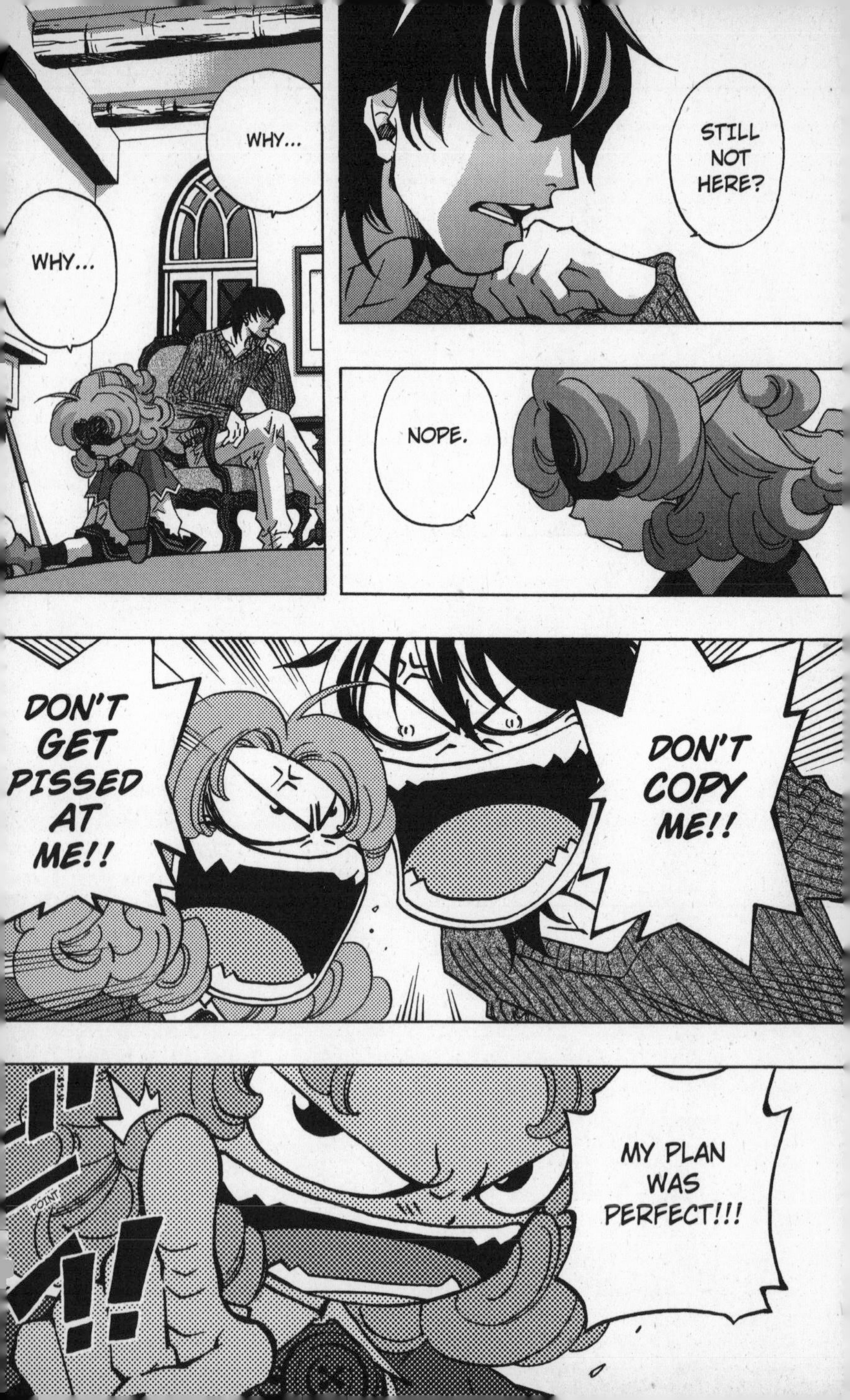
STILL NOT HERE?
NOPE.
WHY...
WHY...
DON'T COPY ME!!
DON'T GET PISSED AT ME!!
MY PLAN WAS PERFECT!!!
POINT

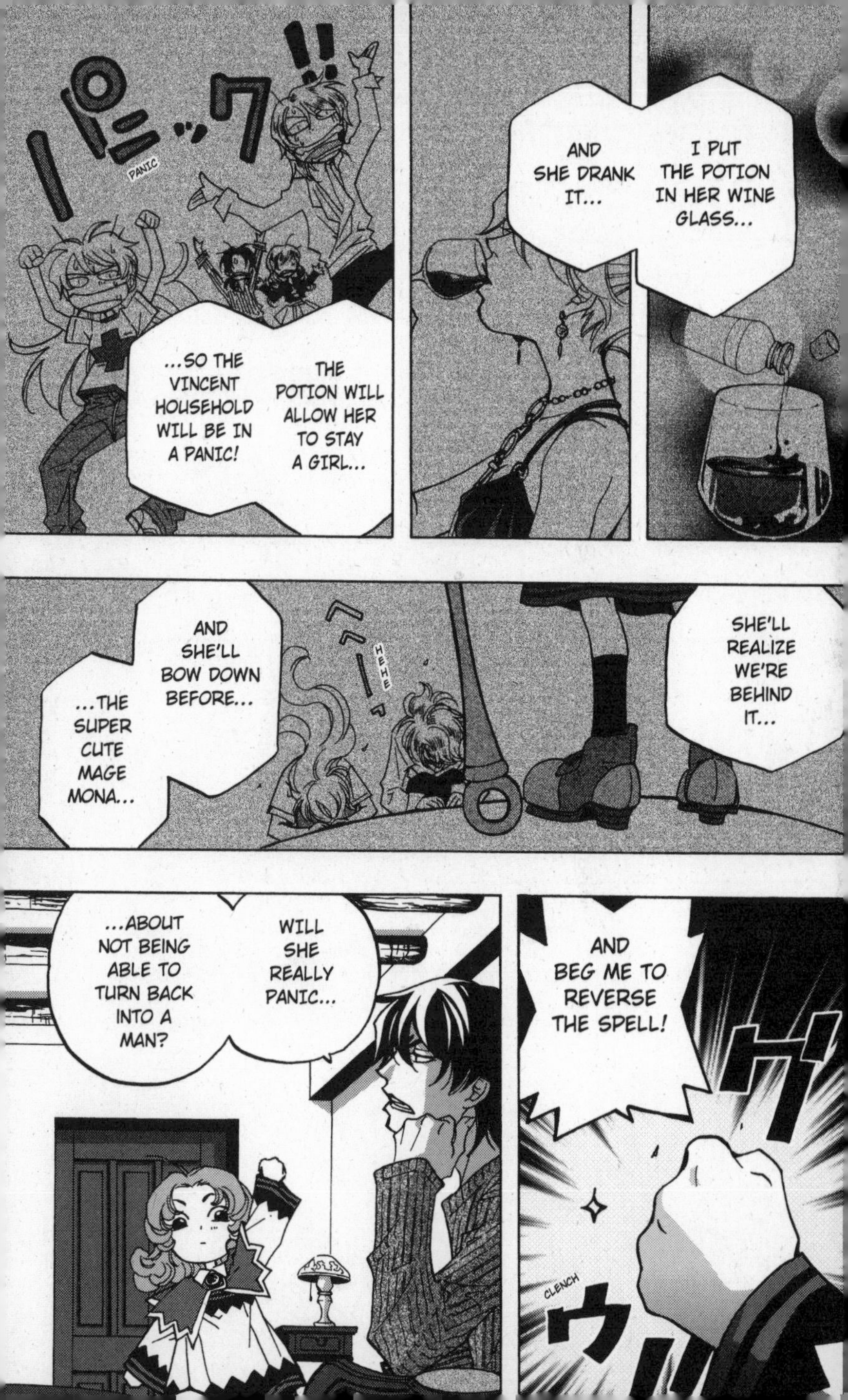
I PUT THE POTION IN HER WINE GLASS...
AND SHE DRANK IT...
THE POTION WILL ALLOW HER TO STAY A GIRL...
...SO THE VINCENT HOUSEHOLD WILL BE IN A PANIC!
PANIC
SHE'LL REALIZE WE'RE BEHIND IT...
AND SHE'LL BOW DOWN BEFORE...
...THE SUPER CUTE MAGE MONA...
HEHE
AND BEG ME TO REVERSE THE SPELL!
CLENCH
WILL SHE REALLY PANIC...
...ABOUT NOT BEING ABLE TO TURN BACK INTO A MAN?

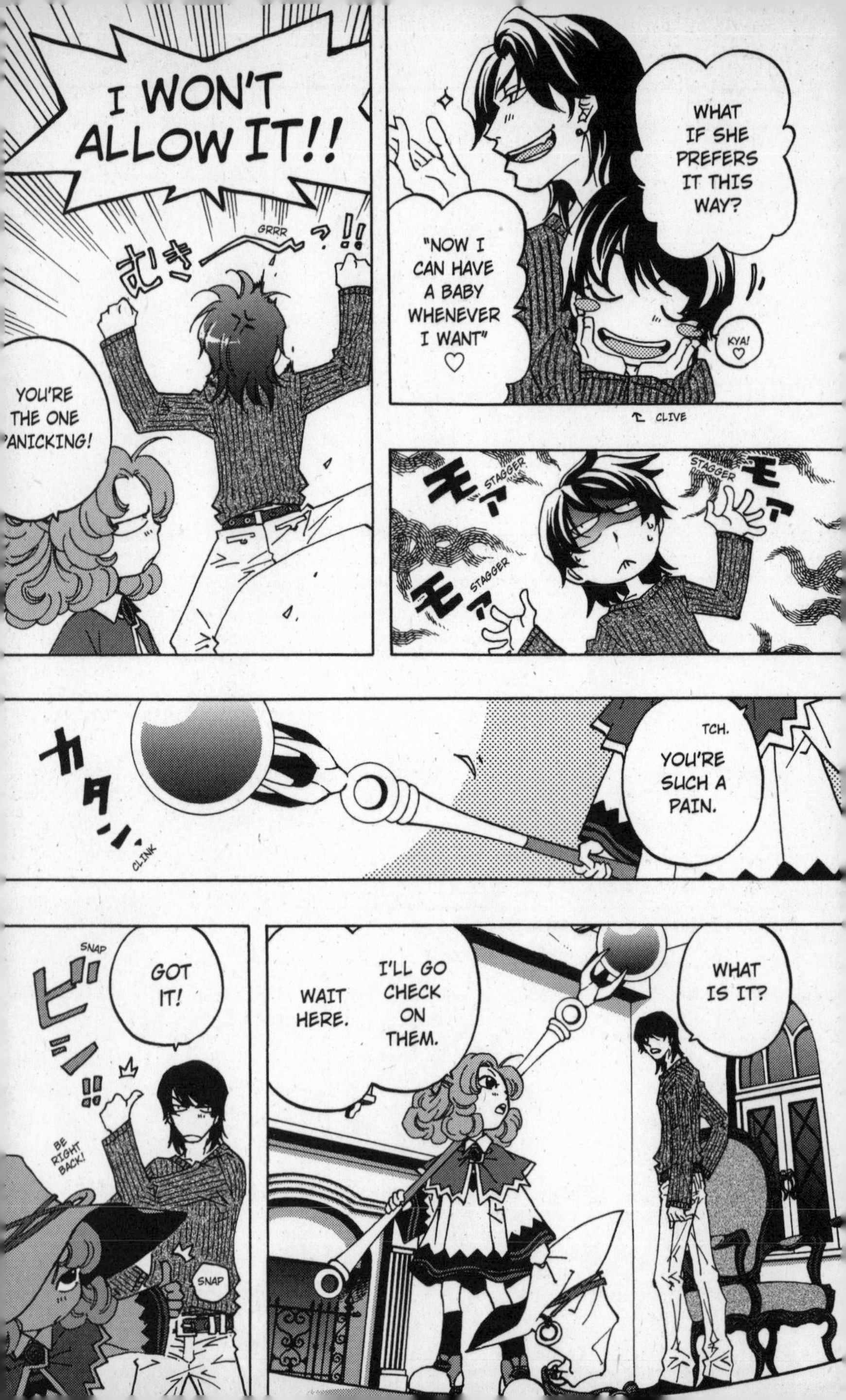
WHAT IF SHE PREFERS IT THIS WAY?
"NOW I CAN HAVE A BABY WHENEVER I WANT" ♡
KYA! ♡
CLIVE
STAGGER
STAGGER
STAGGER
I WON'T ALLOW IT!!
GRRR
むき
YOU'RE THE ONE PANICKING!
TCH. YOU'RE SUCH A PAIN.
CLINK
WHAT IS IT?
I'LL GO CHECK ON THEM.
WAIT HERE.
GOT IT!
SNAP
BE RIGHT BACK!
SNAP

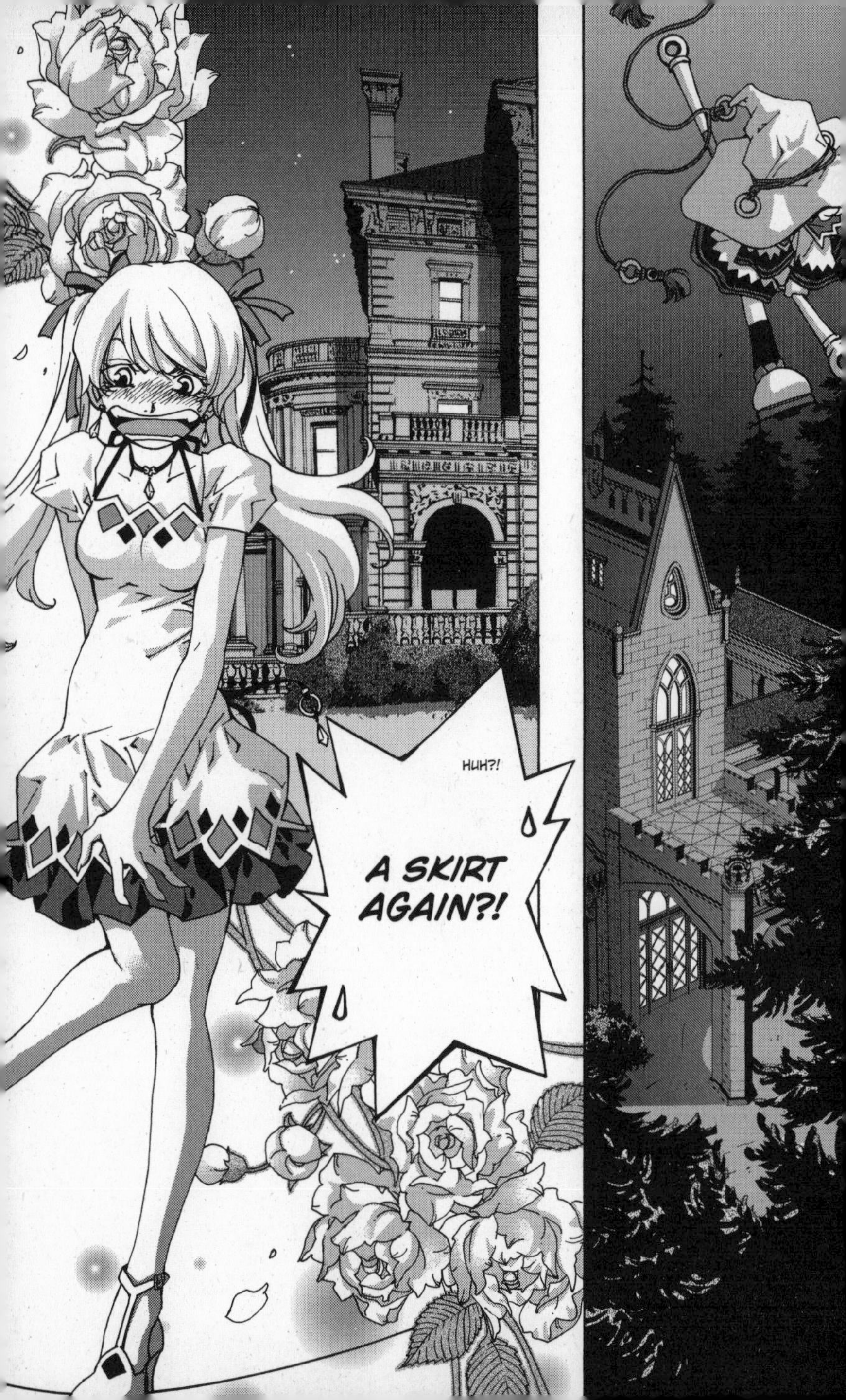
HUH?!
A SKIRT AGAIN?!

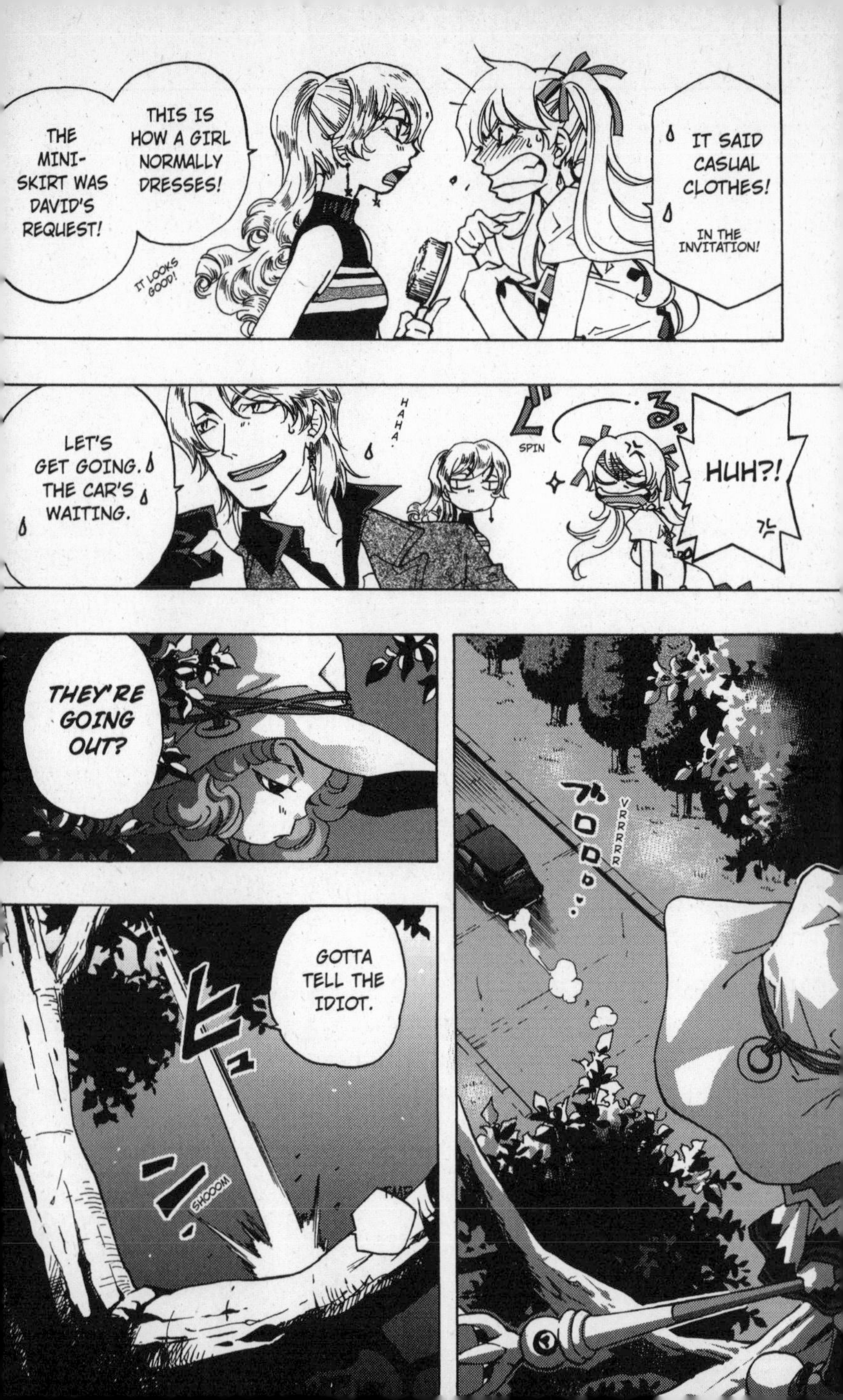

IT SAID CASUAL CLOTHES!
IN THE INVITATION!
THIS IS HOW A GIRL NORMALLY DRESSES!
THE MINI-SKIRT WAS DAVID'S REQUEST!
IT LOOKS GOOD!
HUH?!
SPIN
HAHA
LET'S GET GOING. THE CAR'S WAITING.
VRRRRR
THEY'RE GOING OUT?
GOTTA TELL THE IDIOT.
SHOOOM

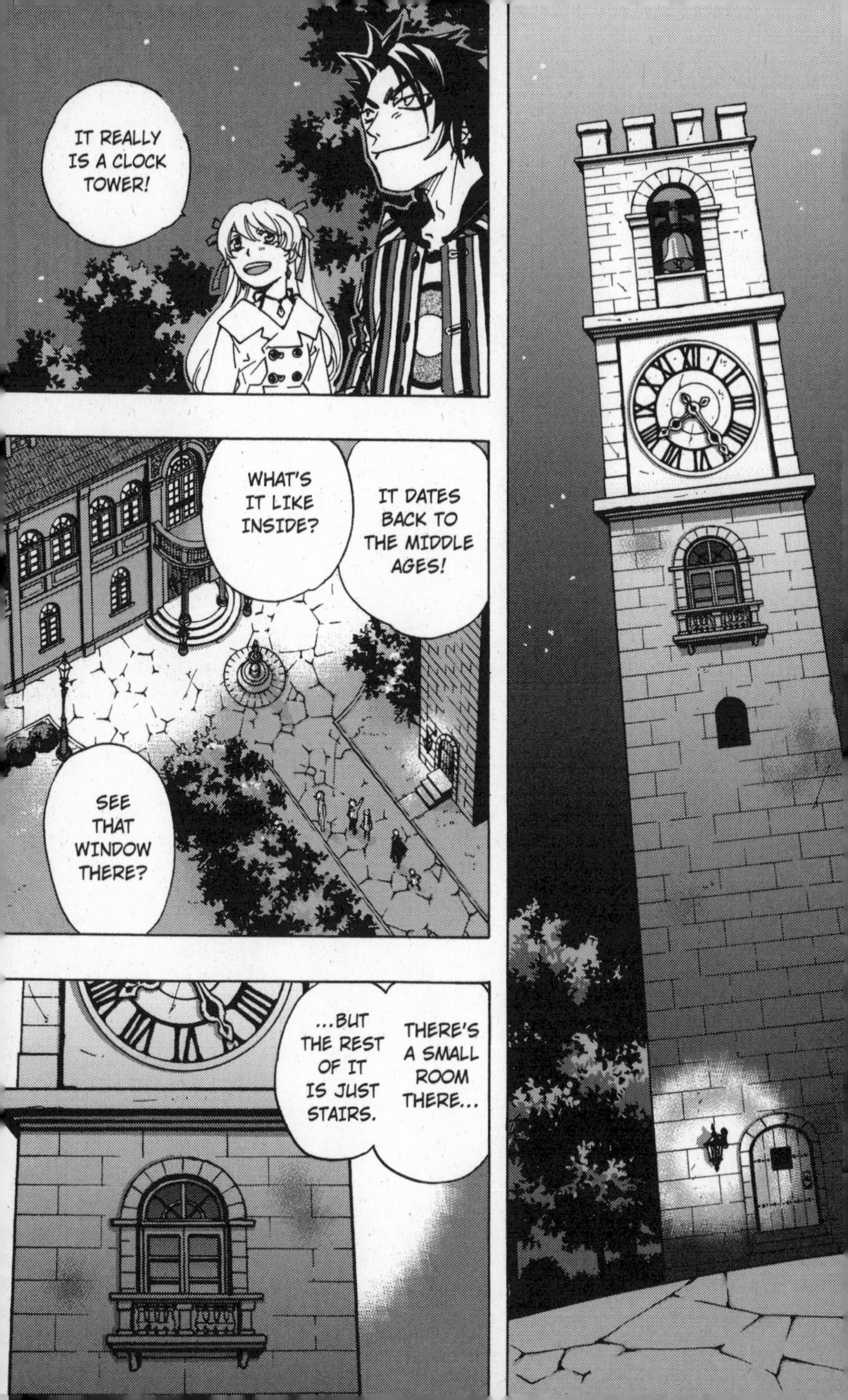
IT REALLY IS A CLOCK TOWER!
IT DATES BACK TO THE MIDDLE AGES!
WHAT'S IT LIKE INSIDE?
SEE THAT WINDOW THERE?
THERE'S A SMALL ROOM THERE...
...BUT THE REST OF IT IS JUST STAIRS.

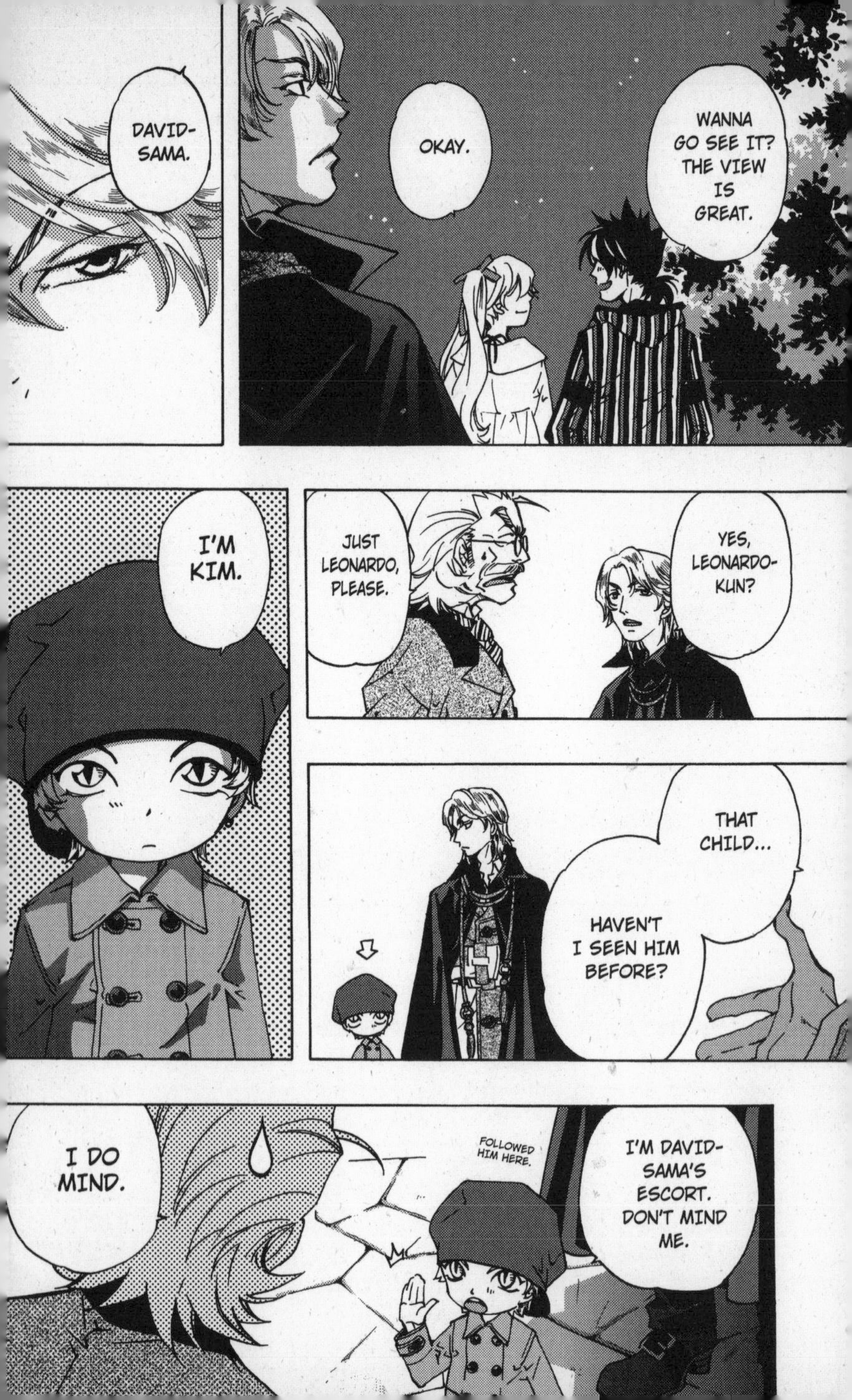
WANNA GO SEE IT? THE VIEW IS GREAT.
OKAY.
DAVID-SAMA.
YES, LEONARDO-KUN?
JUST LEONARDO, PLEASE.
THAT CHILD...
HAVEN'T I SEEN HIM BEFORE?
I'M KIM.
I'M DAVID-SAMA'S ESCORT. DON'T MIND ME.
FOLLOWED HIM HERE.
I DO MIND.

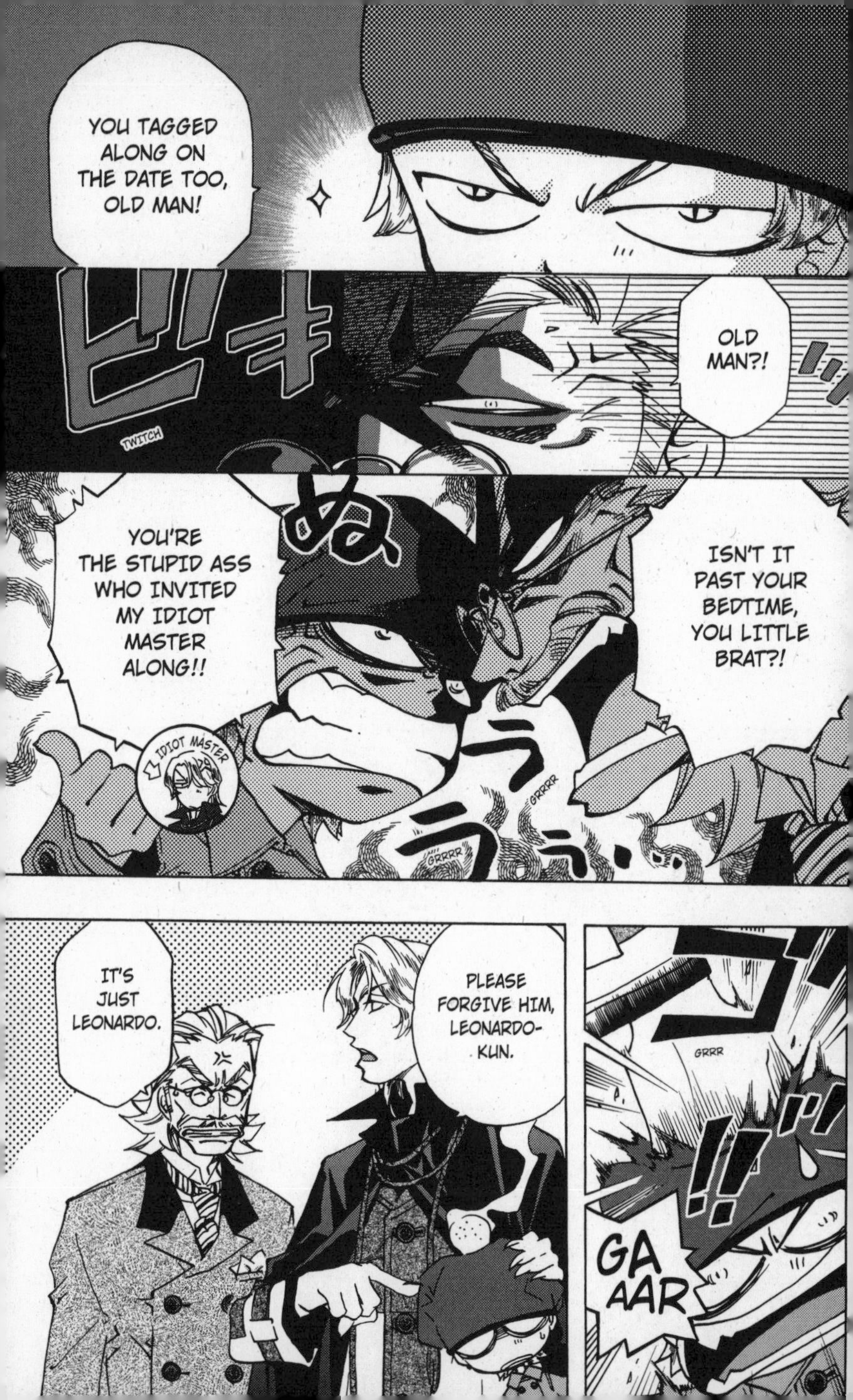
YOU TAGGED ALONG ON THE DATE TOO, OLD MAN!
OLD MAN?!
TWITCH
ISN'T IT PAST YOUR BEDTIME, YOU LITTLE BRAT?!
YOU'RE THE STUPID ASS WHO INVITED MY IDIOT MASTER ALONG!!
IDIOT MASTER
GRRRR
GRRRR
GRRR
GA AAR
PLEASE FORGIVE HIM, LEONARDO-KUN.
IT'S JUST LEONARDO.

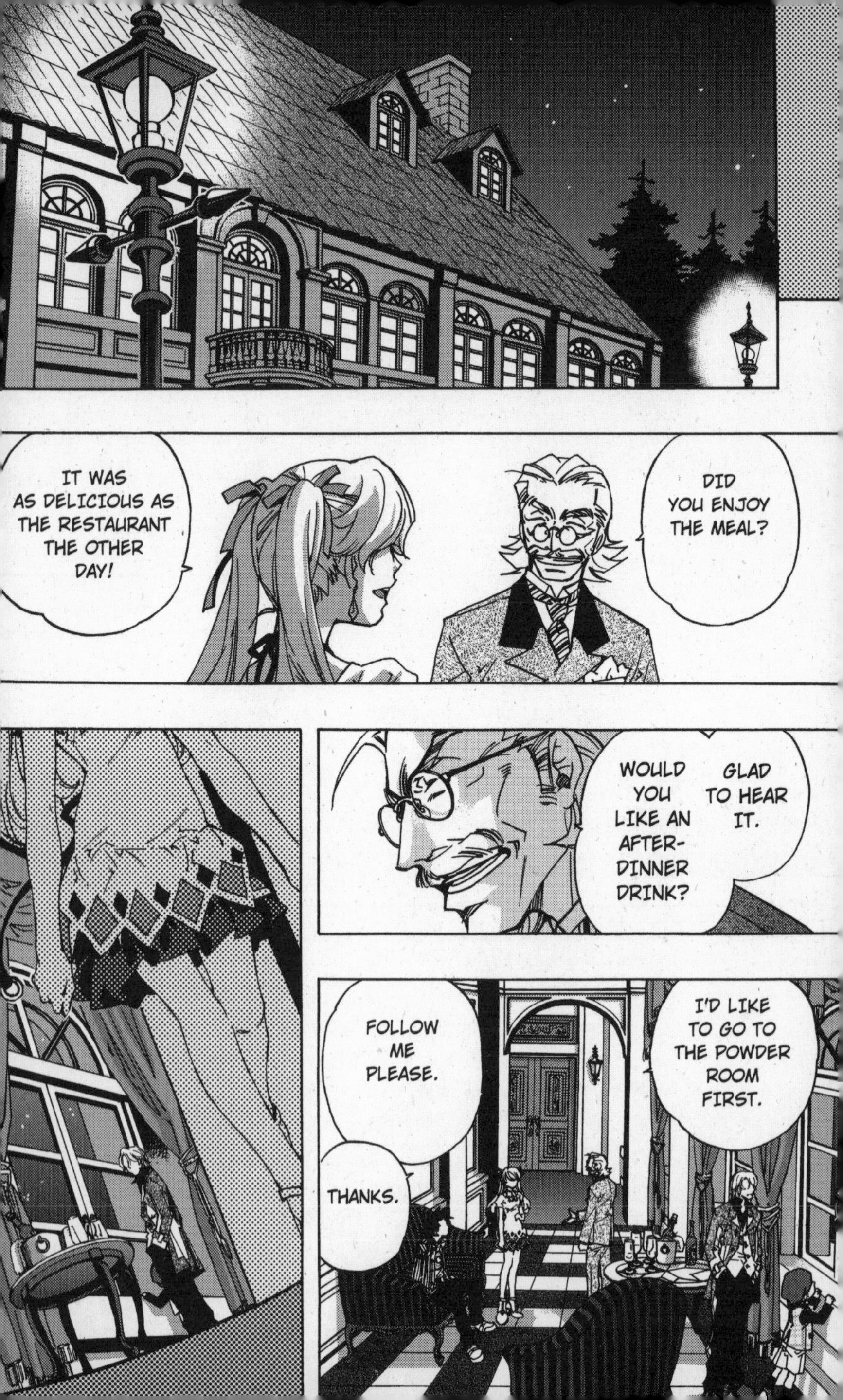
DID YOU ENJOY THE MEAL?
IT WAS AS DELICIOUS AS THE RESTAURANT THE OTHER DAY!
GLAD TO HEAR IT.
WOULD YOU LIKE AN AFTER-DINNER DRINK?
I'D LIKE TO GO TO THE POWDER ROOM FIRST.
FOLLOW ME PLEASE.
THANKS.

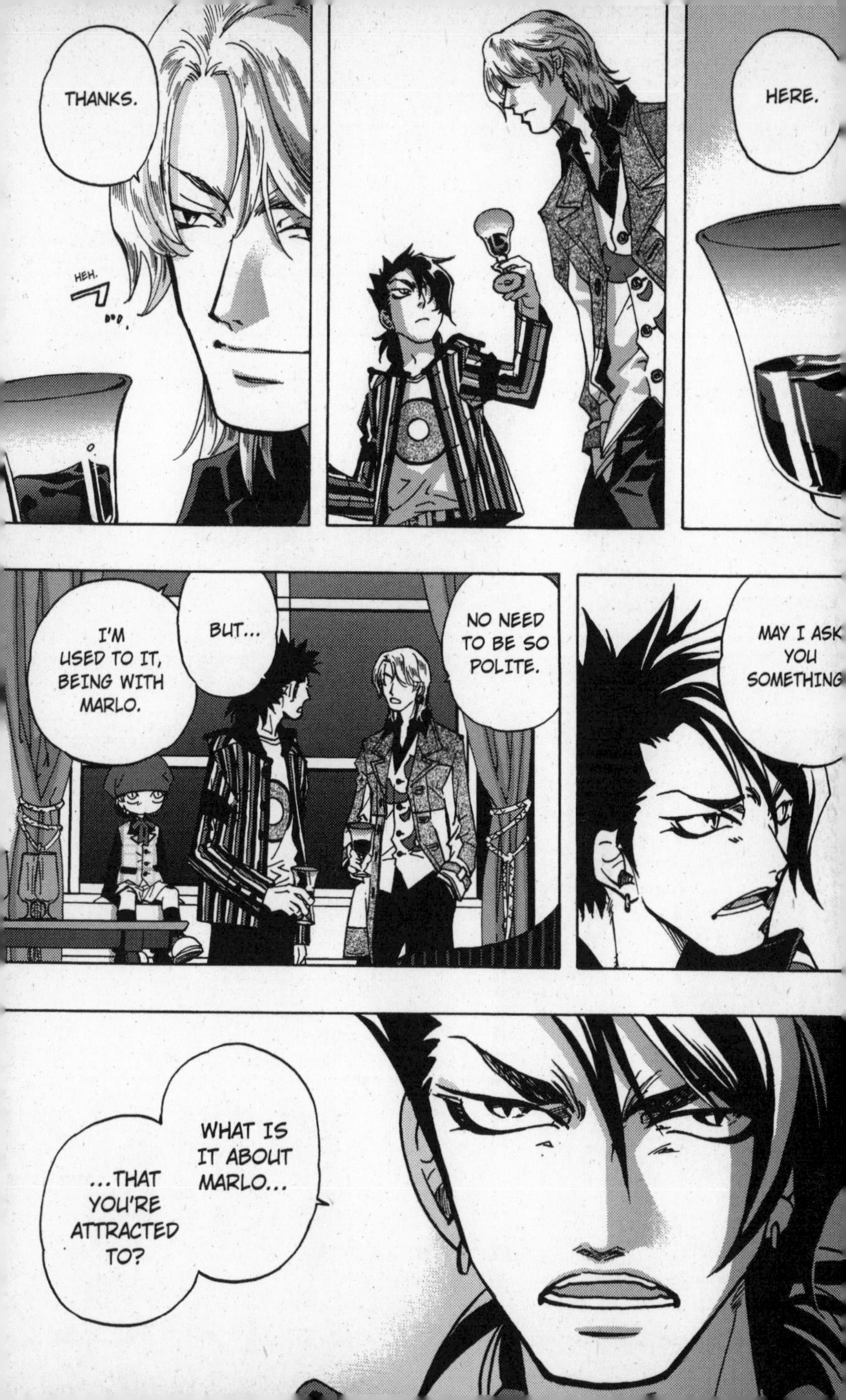
HERE.
THANKS.
HEH.
MAY I ASK YOU SOMETHING
NO NEED TO BE SO POLITE.
BUT...
I'M USED TO IT, BEING WITH MARLO.
WHAT IS IT ABOUT MARLO...
...THAT YOU'RE ATTRACTED TO?

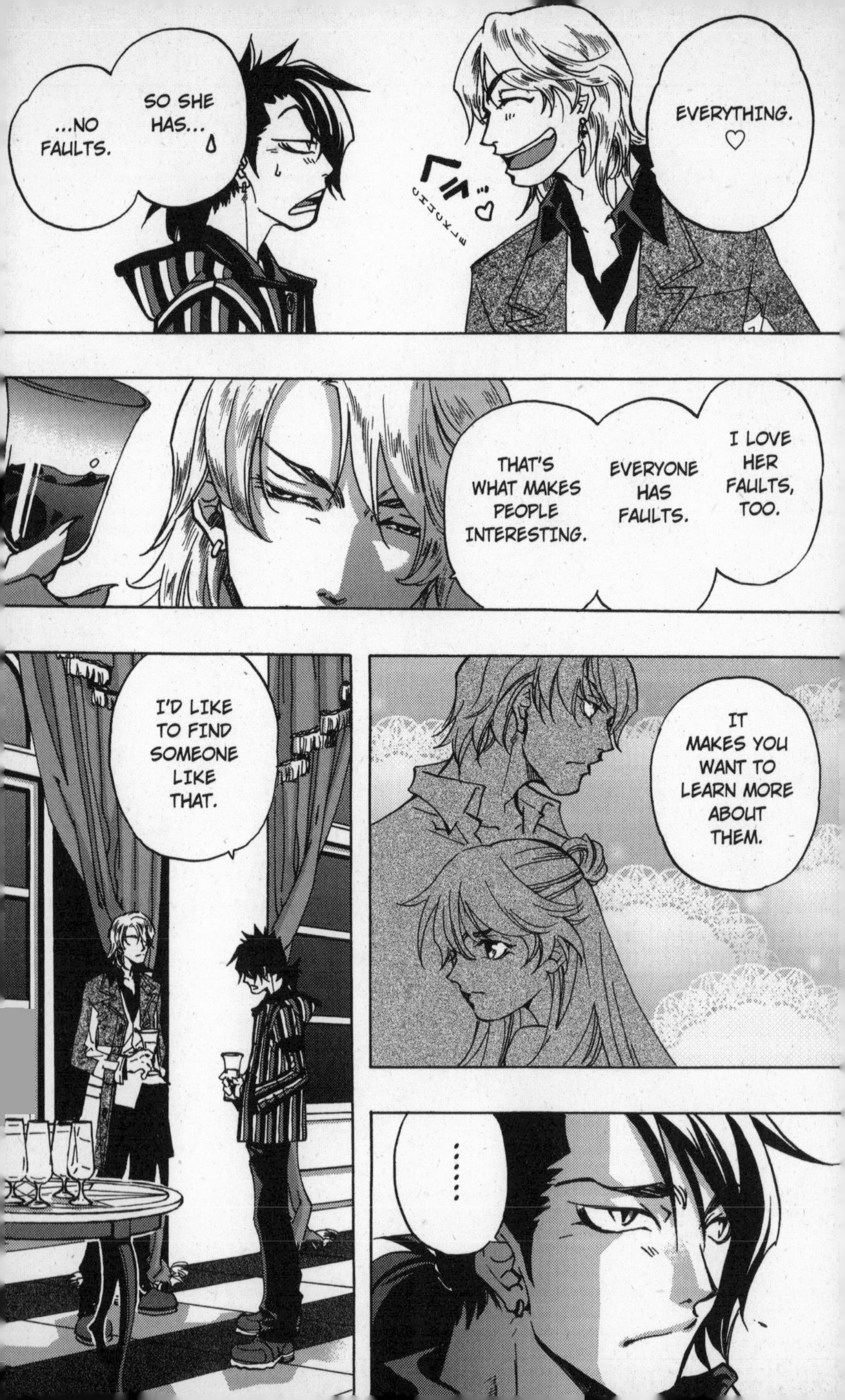
EVERYTHING. ♡
SO SHE HAS...
...NO FAULTS.
I LOVE HER FAULTS, TOO.
EVERYONE HAS FAULTS.
THAT'S WHAT MAKES PEOPLE INTERESTING.
IT MAKES YOU WANT TO LEARN MORE ABOUT THEM.
......
I'D LIKE TO FIND SOMEONE LIKE THAT.

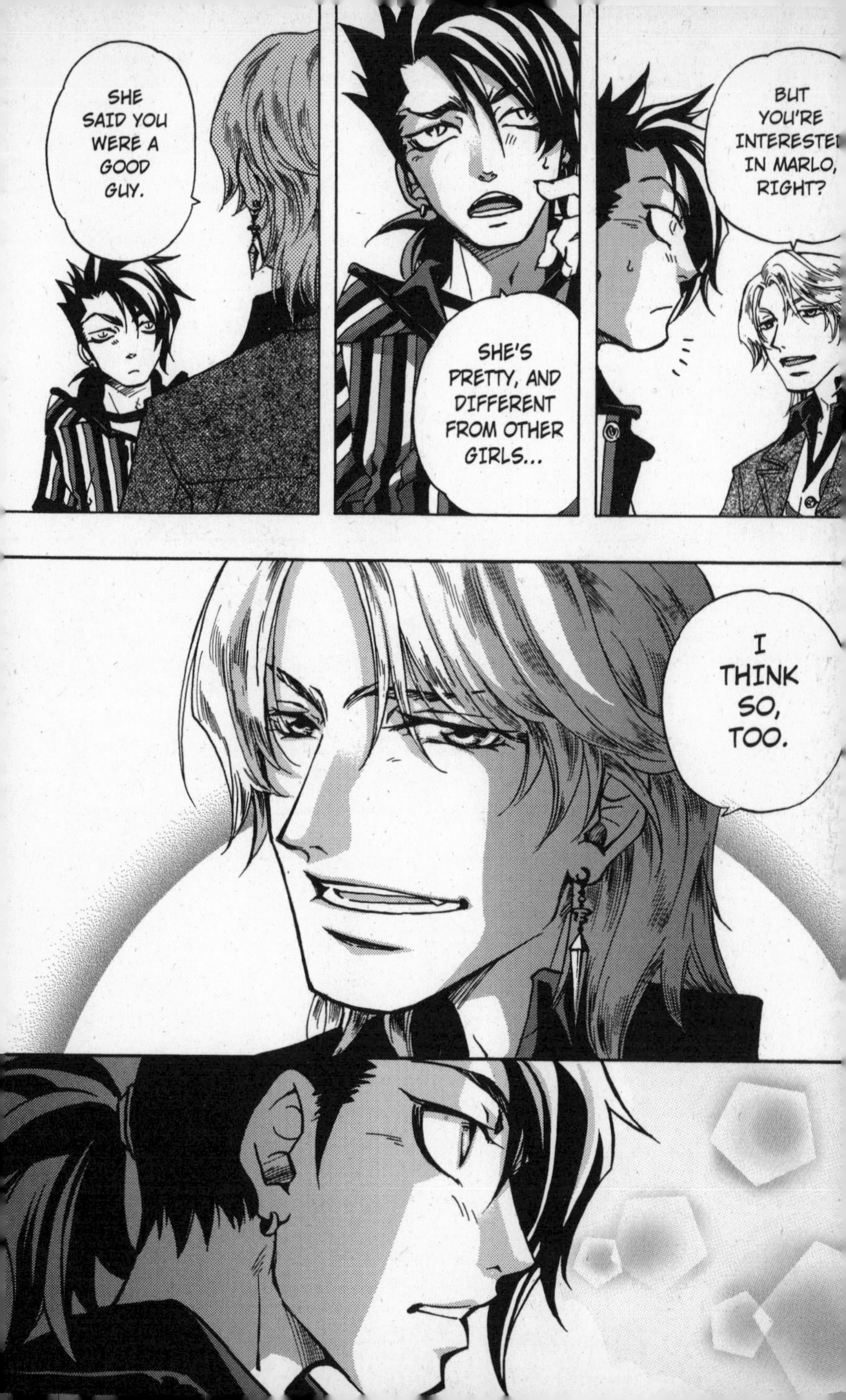
BUT YOU'RE INTERESTED IN MARLO, RIGHT?
SHE'S PRETTY, AND DIFFERENT FROM OTHER GIRLS...
SHE SAID YOU WERE A GOOD GUY.
I THINK SO, TOO.

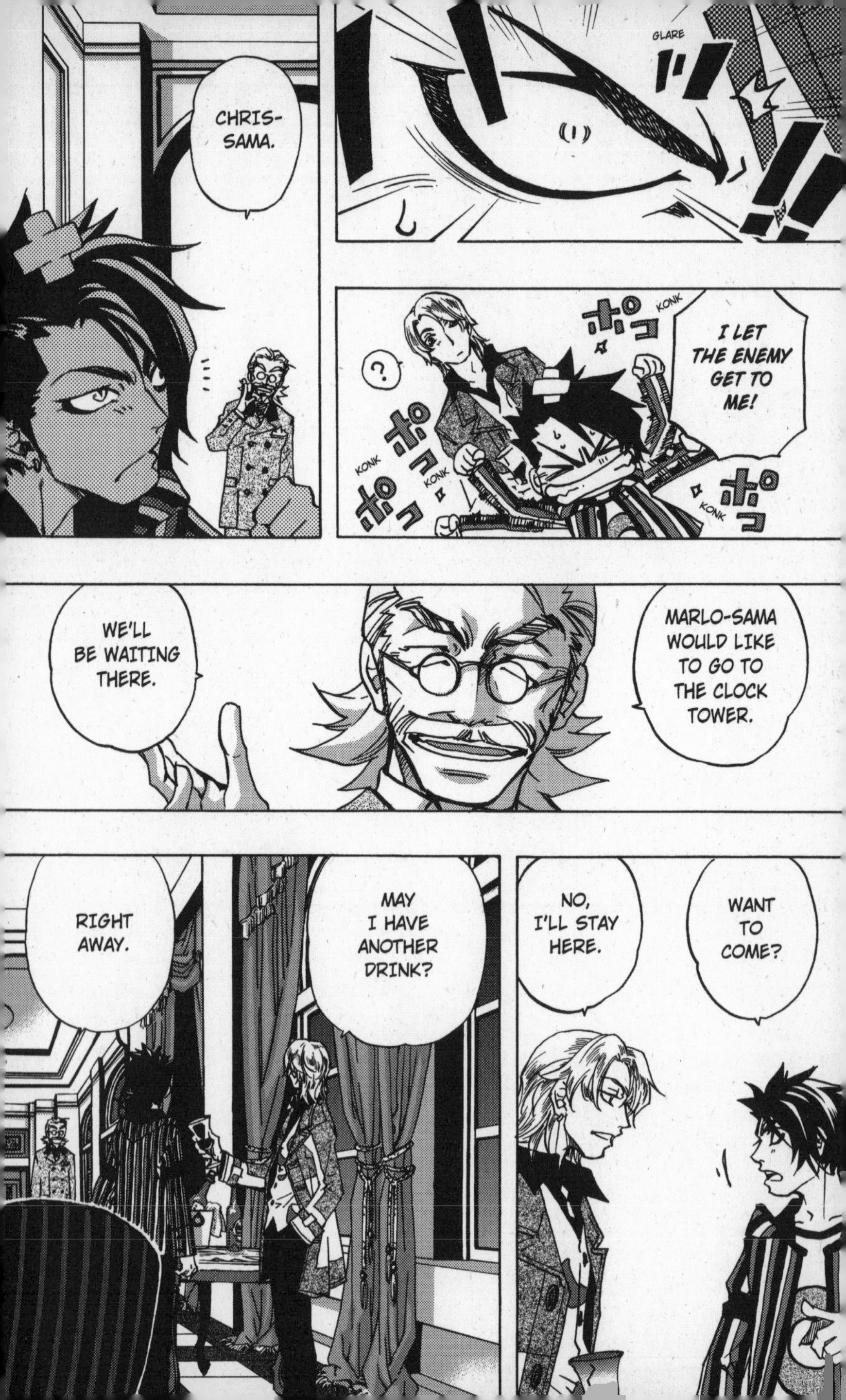
GLARE
I LET THE ENEMY GET TO ME!
KONK
?
KONK
KONK
KONK
CHRIS-SAMA.
MARLO-SAMA WOULD LIKE TO GO TO THE CLOCK TOWER.
WE'LL BE WAITING THERE.
WANT TO COME?
NO, I'LL STAY HERE.
MAY I HAVE ANOTHER DRINK?
RIGHT AWAY.

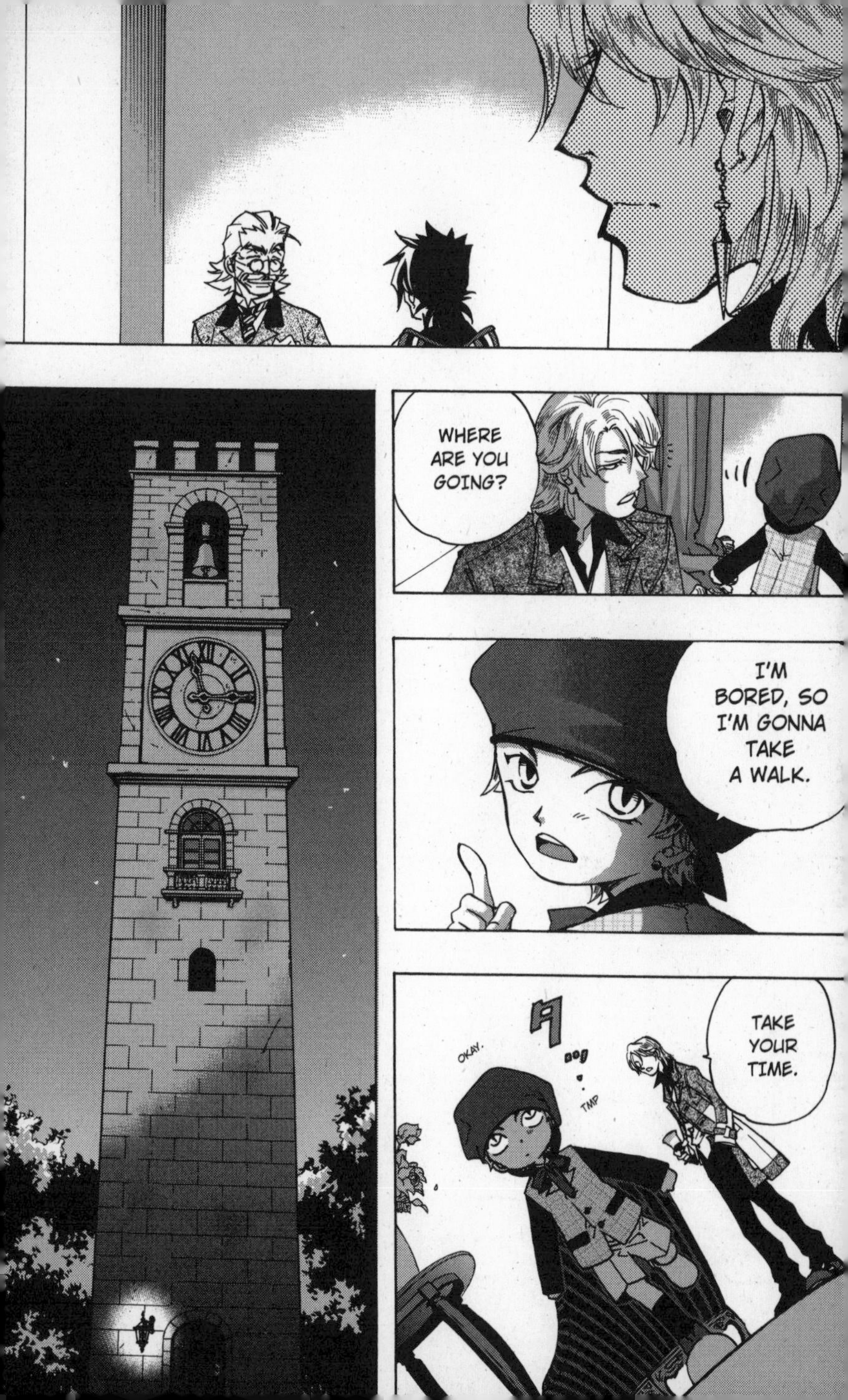
WHERE ARE YOU GOING?
I'M BORED, SO I'M GONNA TAKE A WALK.
TAKE YOUR TIME.
OKAY.
TMP

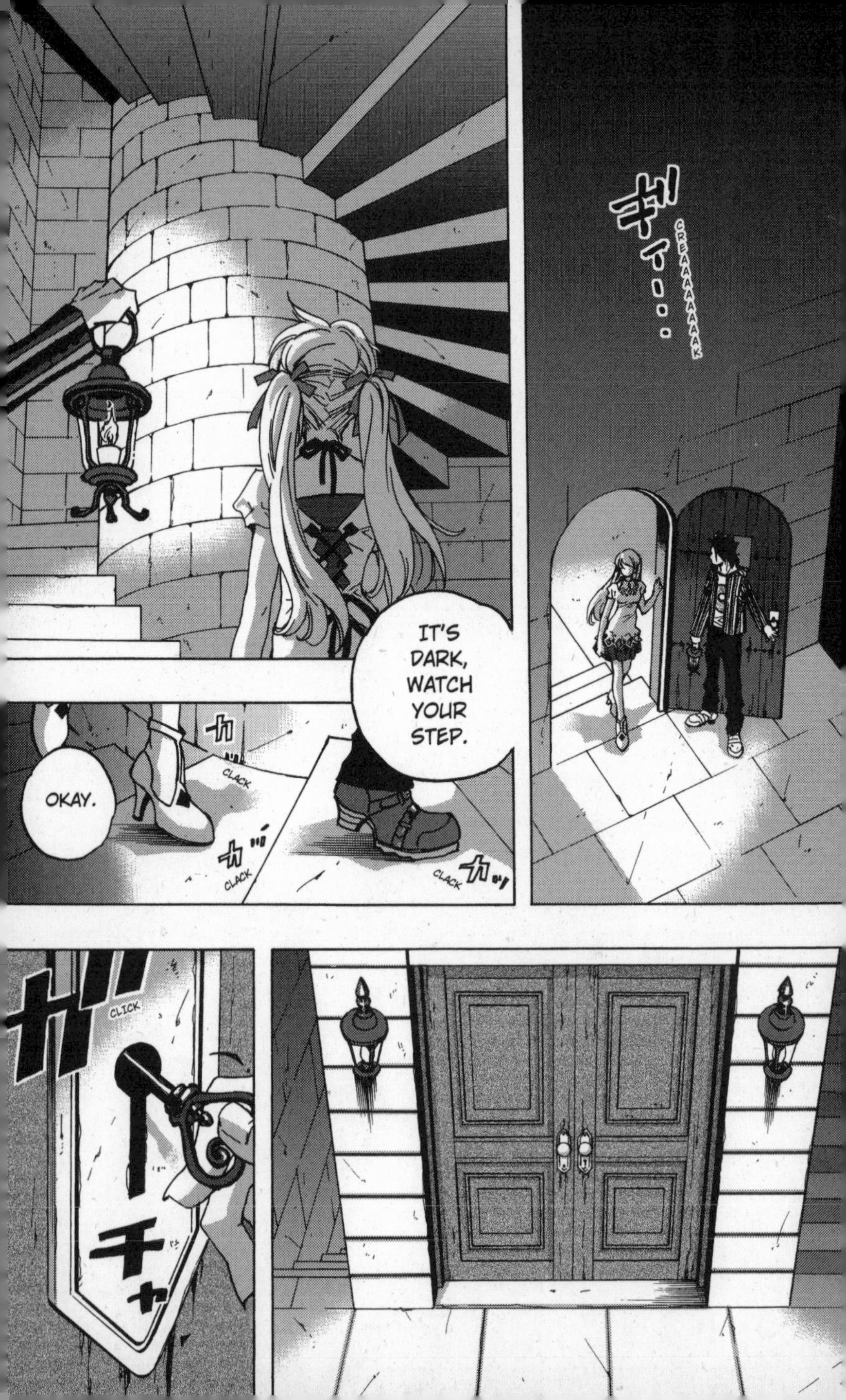
CREAAAAAAK
IT'S DARK, WATCH YOUR STEP.
CLACK
CLACK
OKAY.
CLACK
CLICK

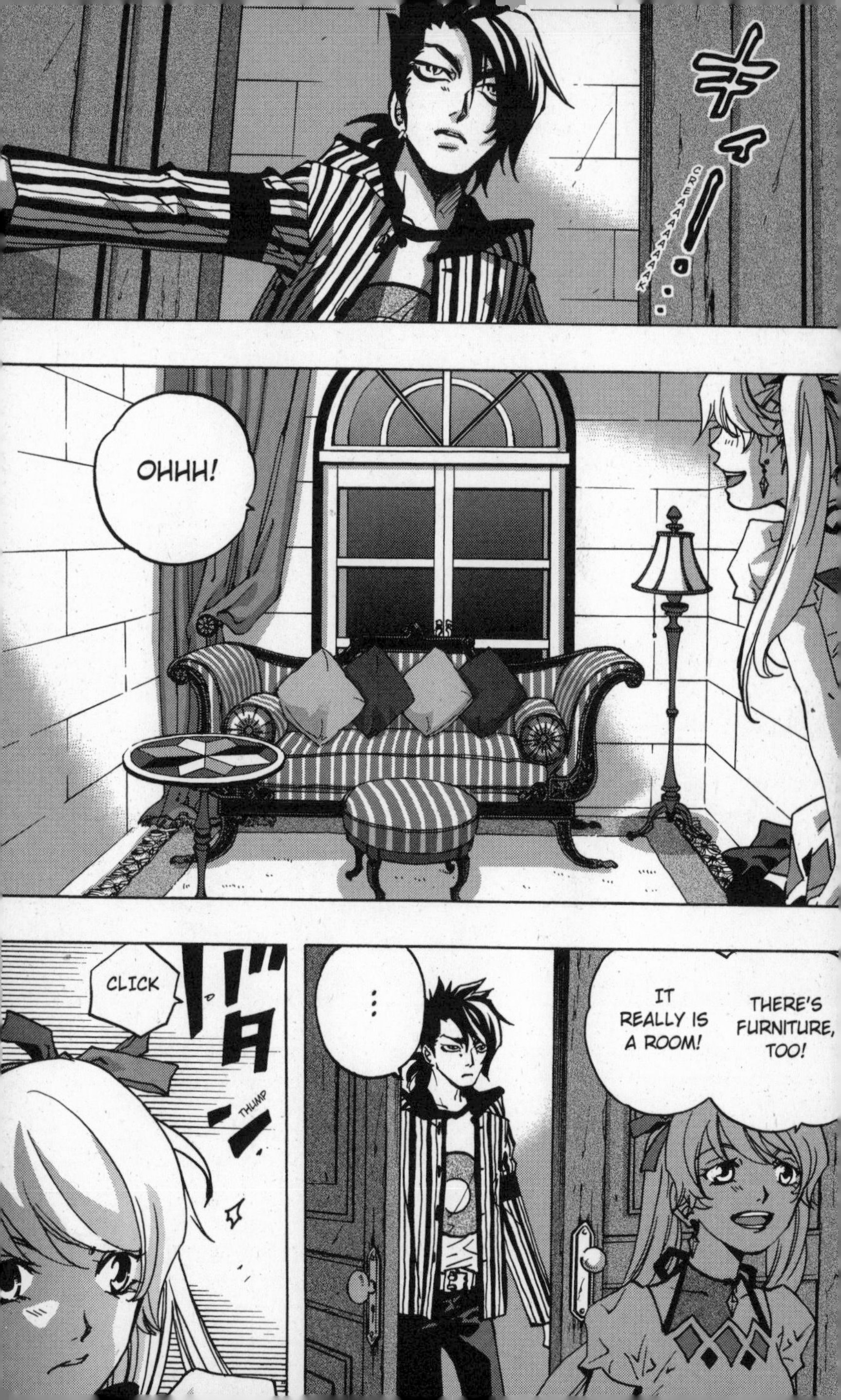
CREAAAAAAAAK
OHHH!
IT REALLY IS A ROOM!
THERE'S FURNITURE, TOO!
...
CLICK
THUMP

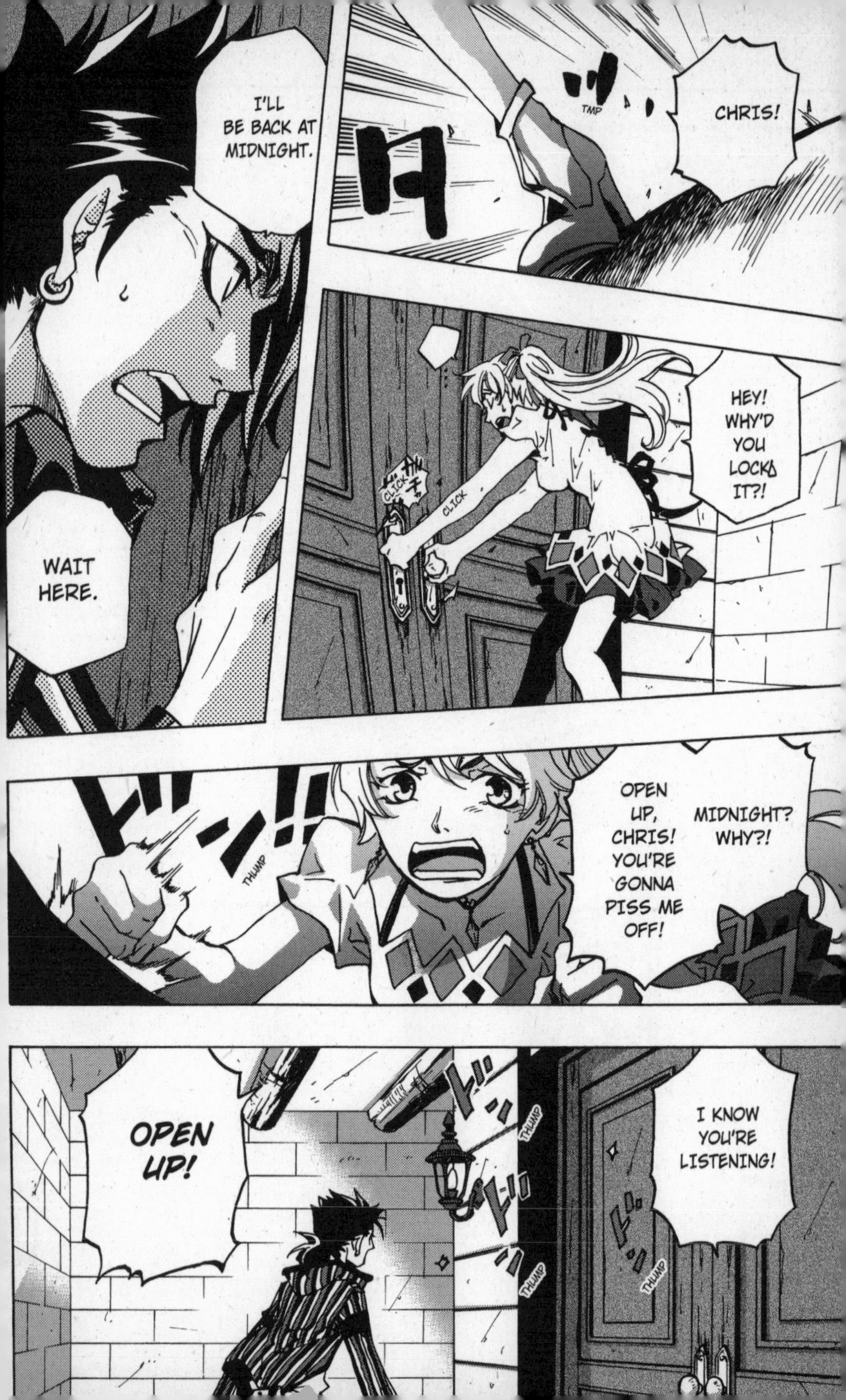
CHRIS!
TMP
HEY! WHY'D YOU LOCK IT?!
CLICK
CLICK
I'LL BE BACK AT MIDNIGHT.
WAIT HERE.
MIDNIGHT? WHY?!
OPEN UP, CHRIS! YOU'RE GONNA PISS ME OFF!
THUMP
I KNOW YOU'RE LISTENING!
THUMP
THUMP
THUMP
OPEN UP!

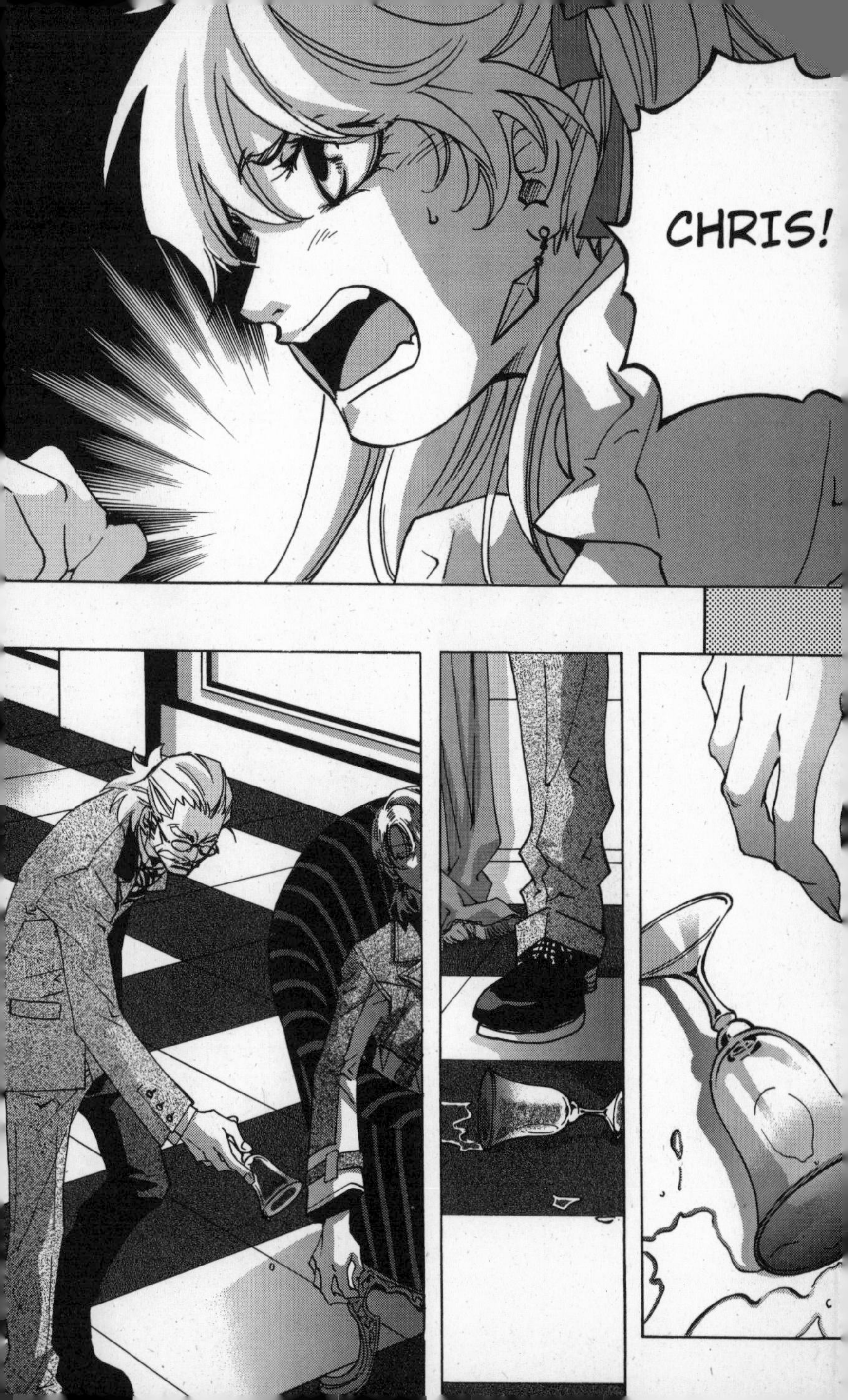
CHRIS!

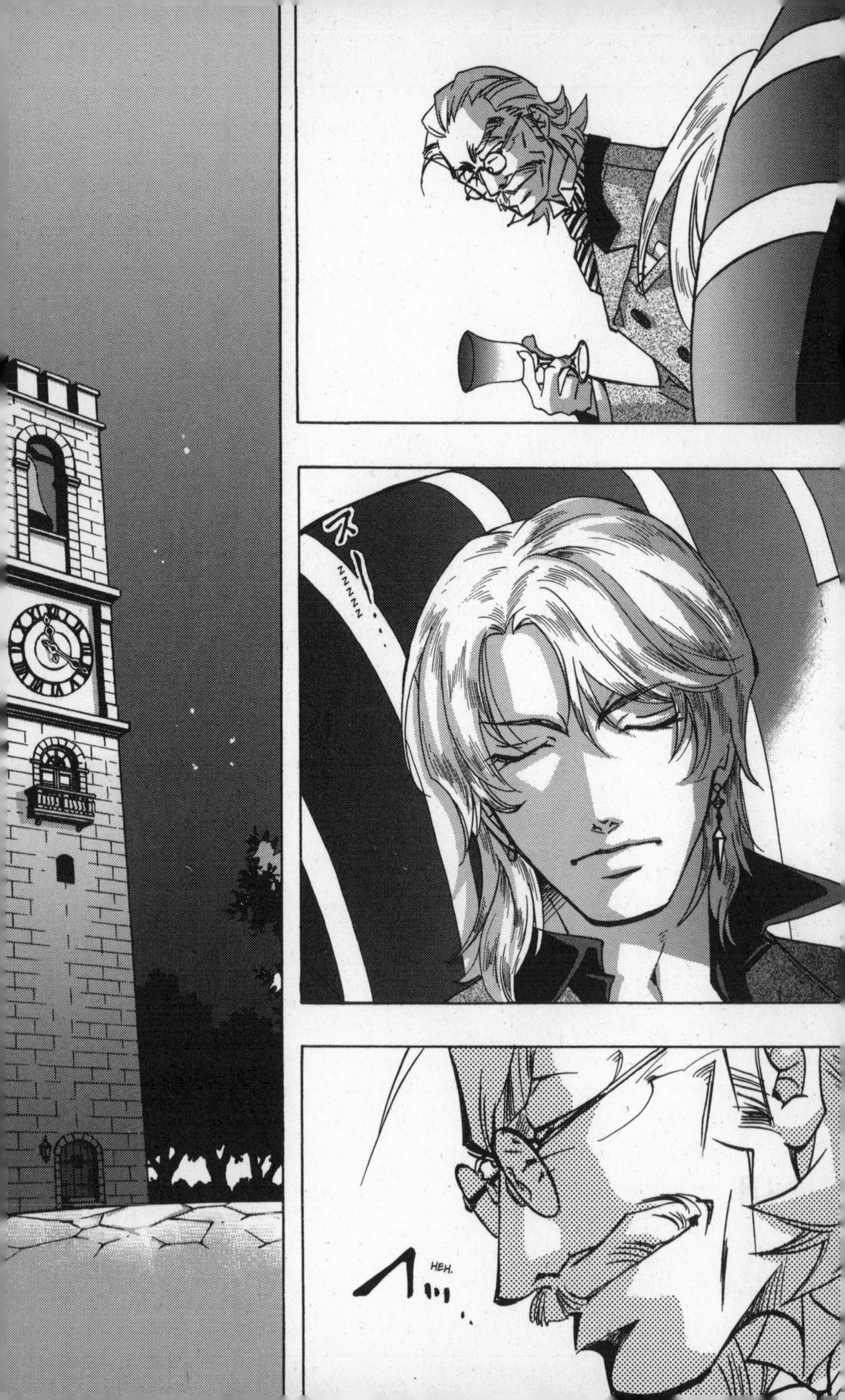
スー
ZZZZZ...
ヘ...
HEH.

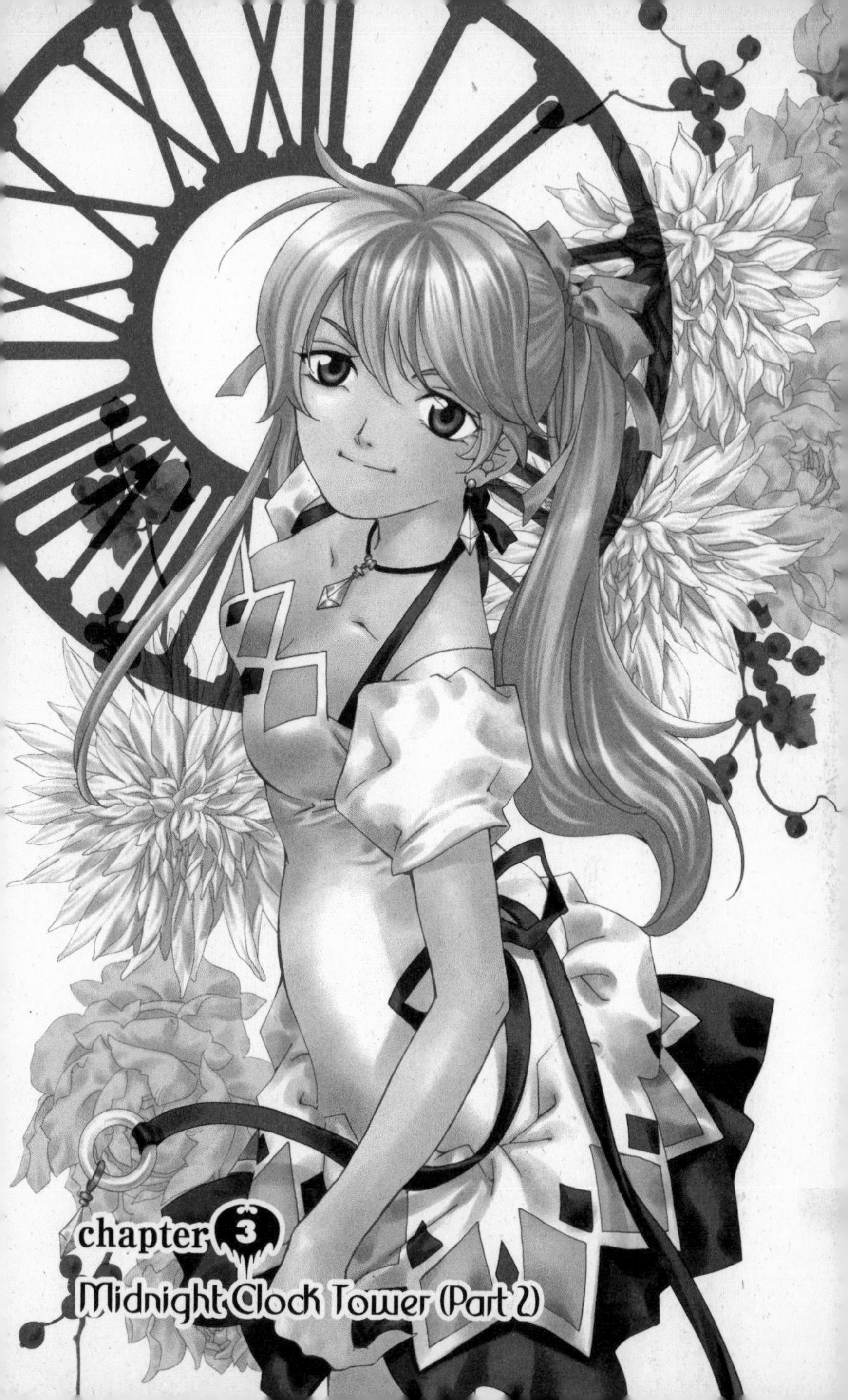

chapter 3
Midnight Clock Tower (Part 2)

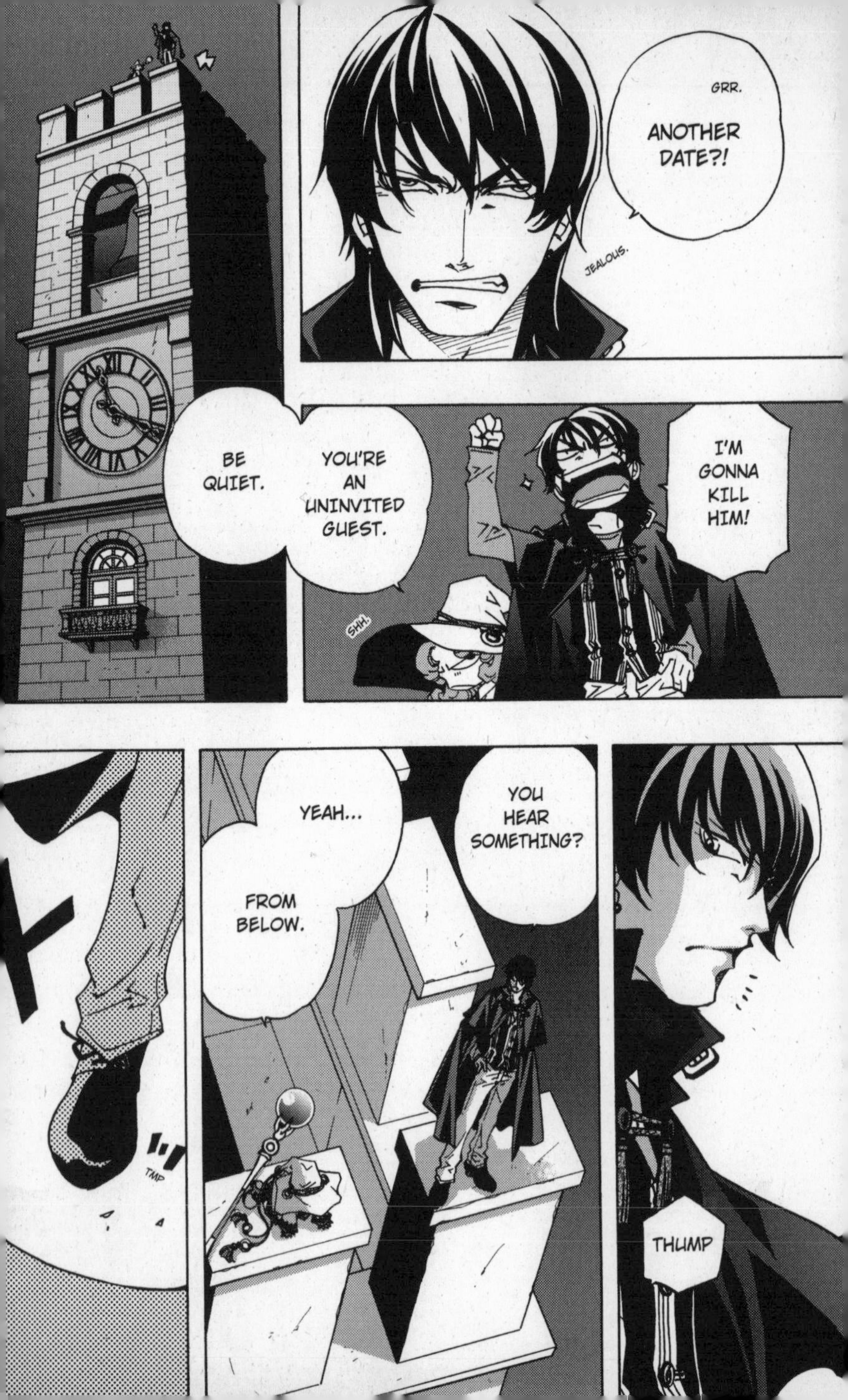
GRR.
ANOTHER DATE?!
JEALOUS.
I'M GONNA KILL HIM!
BE QUIET. YOU'RE AN UNINVITED GUEST.
SHH.
THUMP
YOU HEAR SOMETHING?
YEAH... FROM BELOW.
TMP

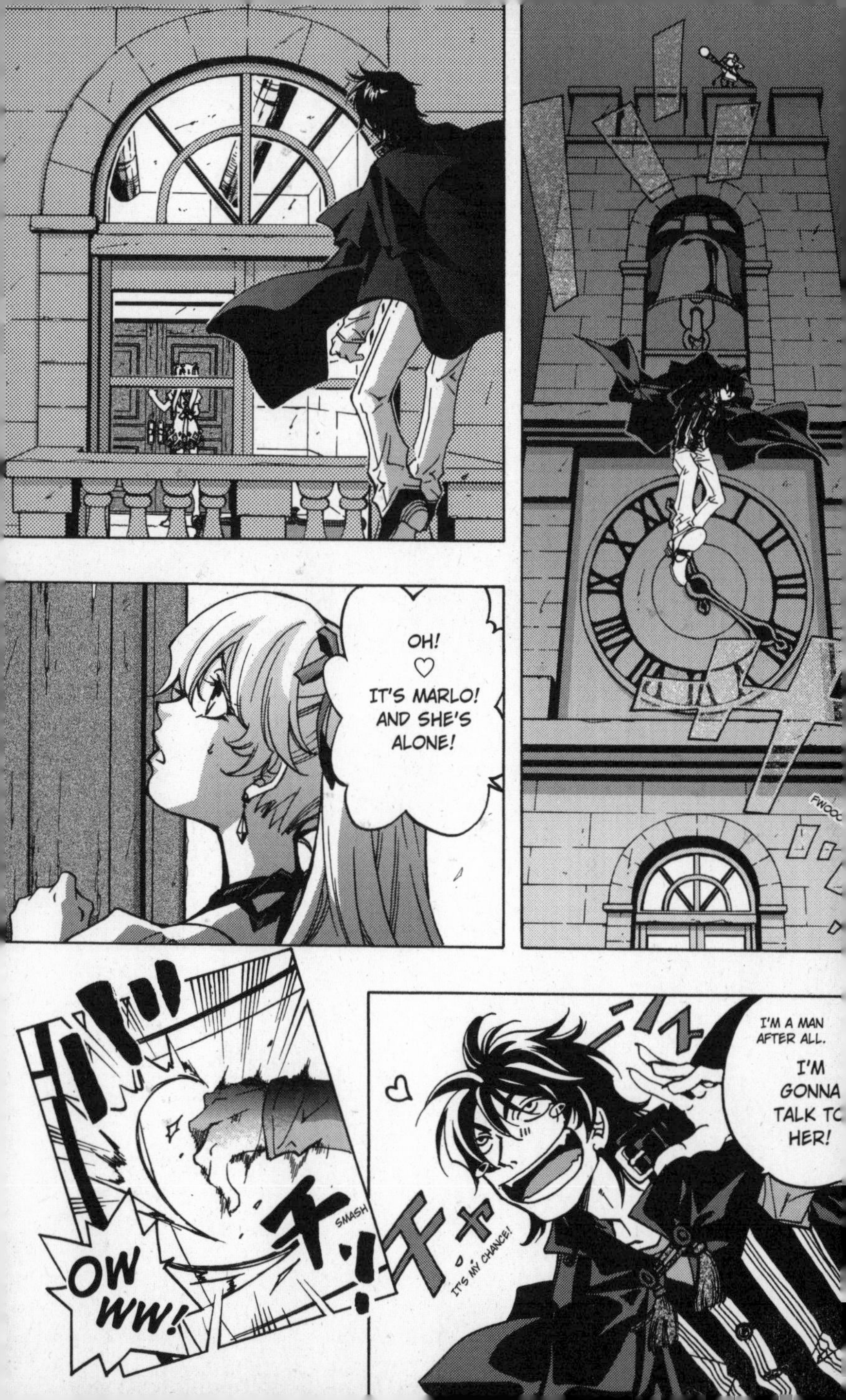
FWOOO
OH! ♡ IT'S MARLO! AND SHE'S ALONE!
I'M A MAN AFTER ALL.
I'M GONNA TALK TO HER!
IT'S MY CHANCE!
SMASH
OWWW!

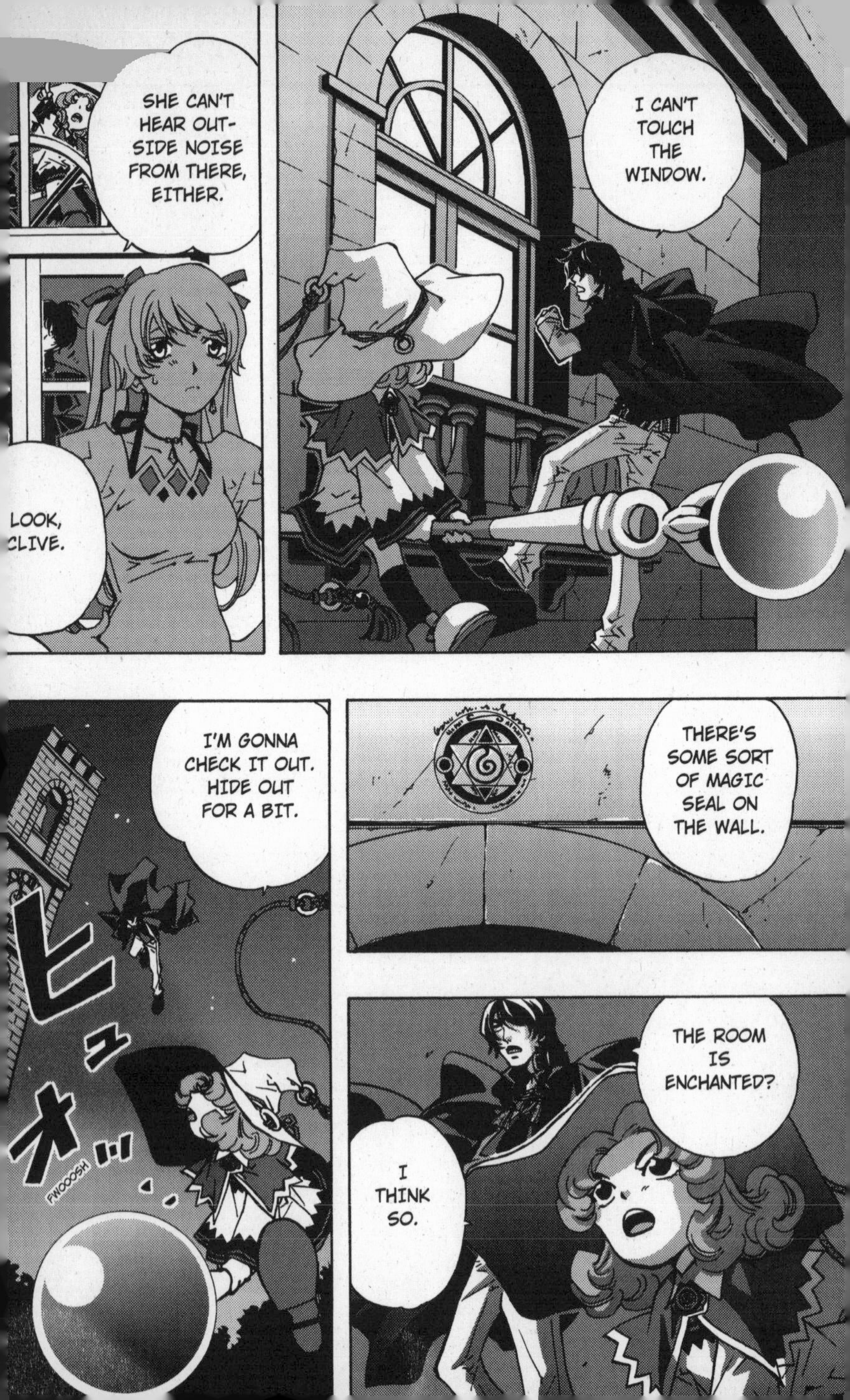
I CAN'T TOUCH THE WINDOW.
SHE CAN'T HEAR OUT-SIDE NOISE FROM THERE, EITHER.
LOOK, CLIVE.
THERE'S SOME SORT OF MAGIC SEAL ON THE WALL.
THE ROOM IS ENCHANTED?
I THINK SO.
I'M GONNA CHECK IT OUT. HIDE OUT FOR A BIT.
FWOOOSH

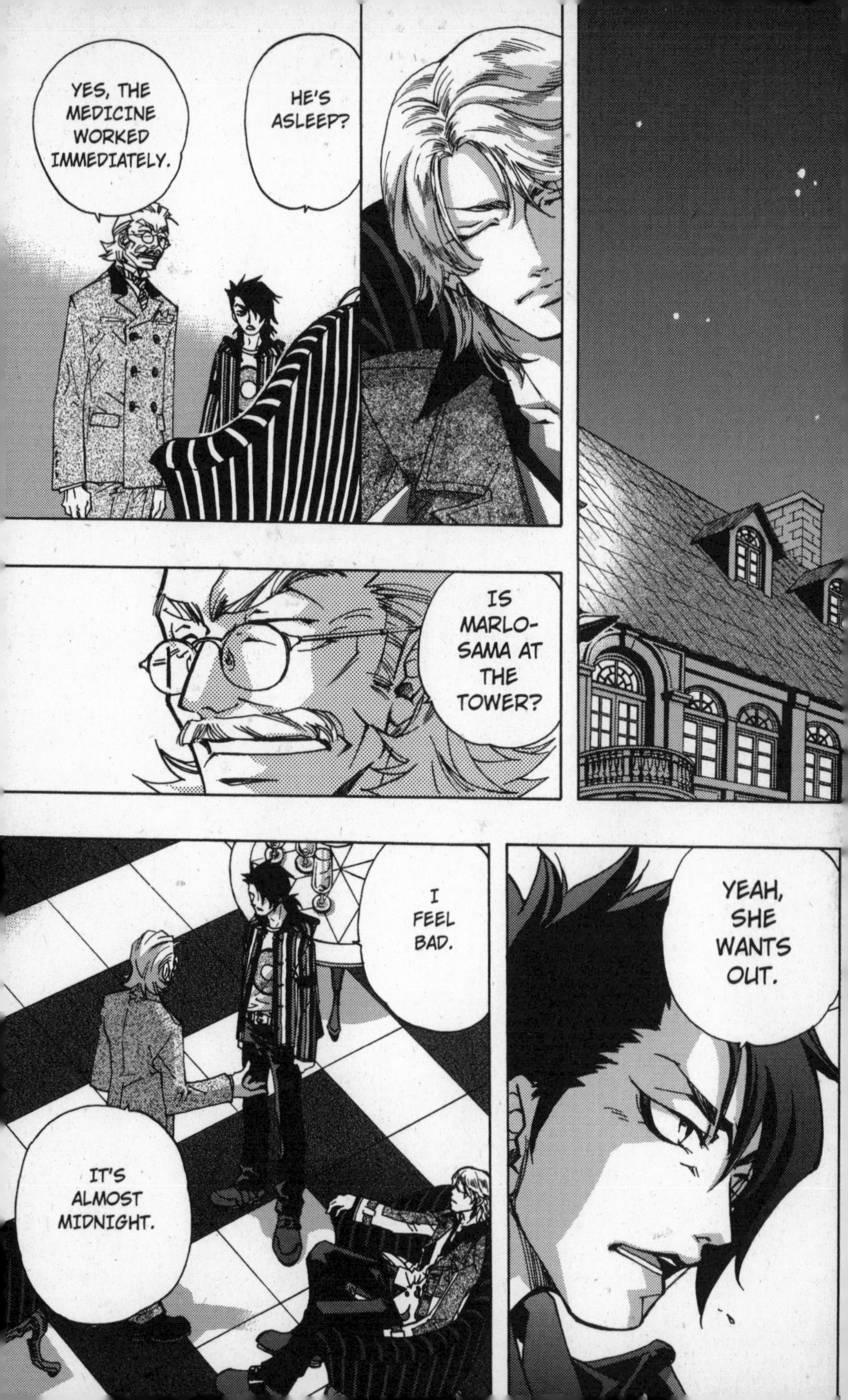
HE'S ASLEEP?
YES, THE MEDICINE WORKED IMMEDIATELY.
IS MARLO-SAMA AT THE TOWER?
YEAH, SHE WANTS OUT.
I FEEL BAD.
IT'S ALMOST MIDNIGHT.

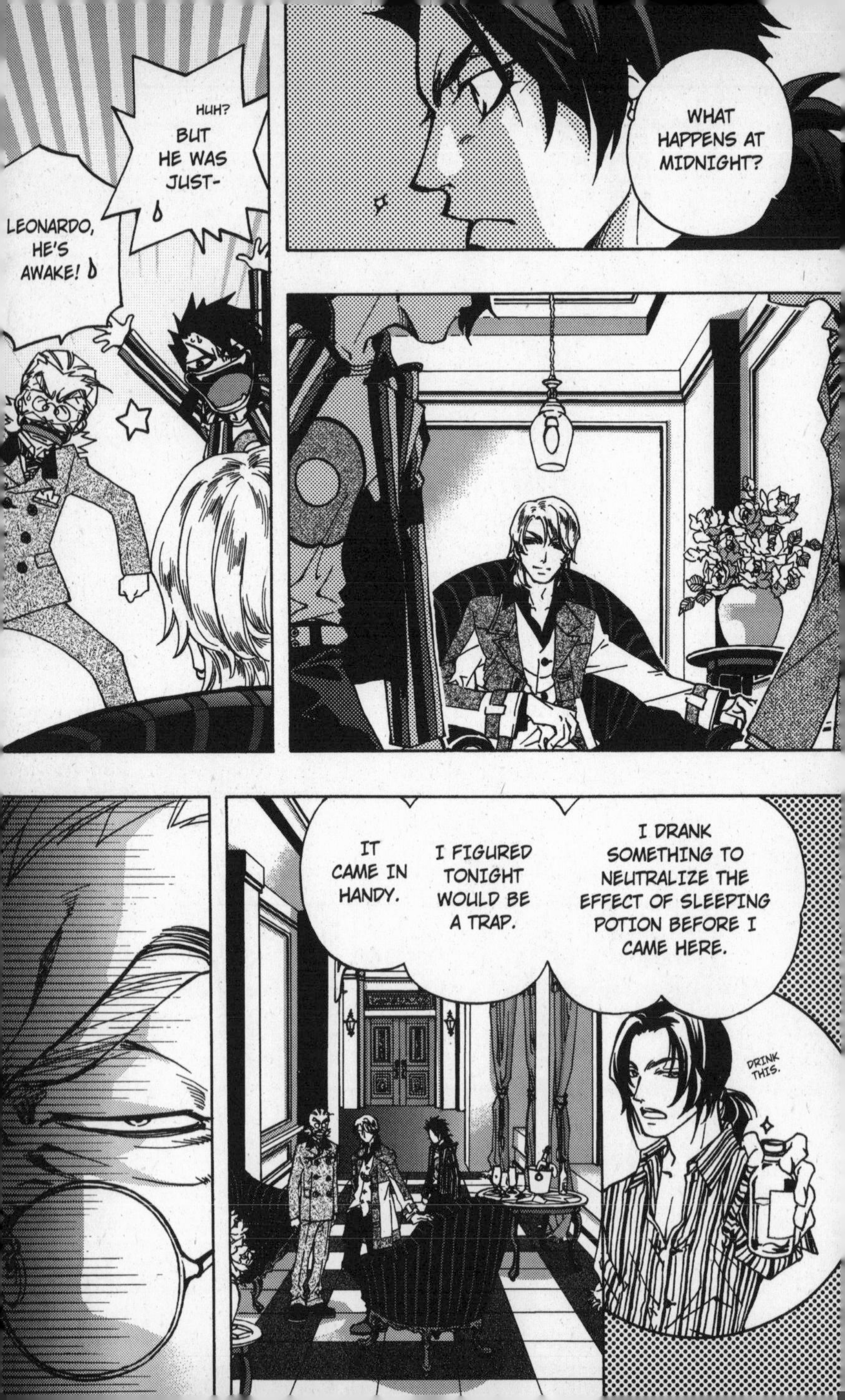
WHAT HAPPENS AT MIDNIGHT?
HUH? BUT HE WAS JUST-
LEONARDO, HE'S AWAKE!
I DRANK SOMETHING TO NEUTRALIZE THE EFFECT OF SLEEPING POTION BEFORE I CAME HERE.
I FIGURED TONIGHT WOULD BE A TRAP.
IT CAME IN HANDY.
DRINK THIS.

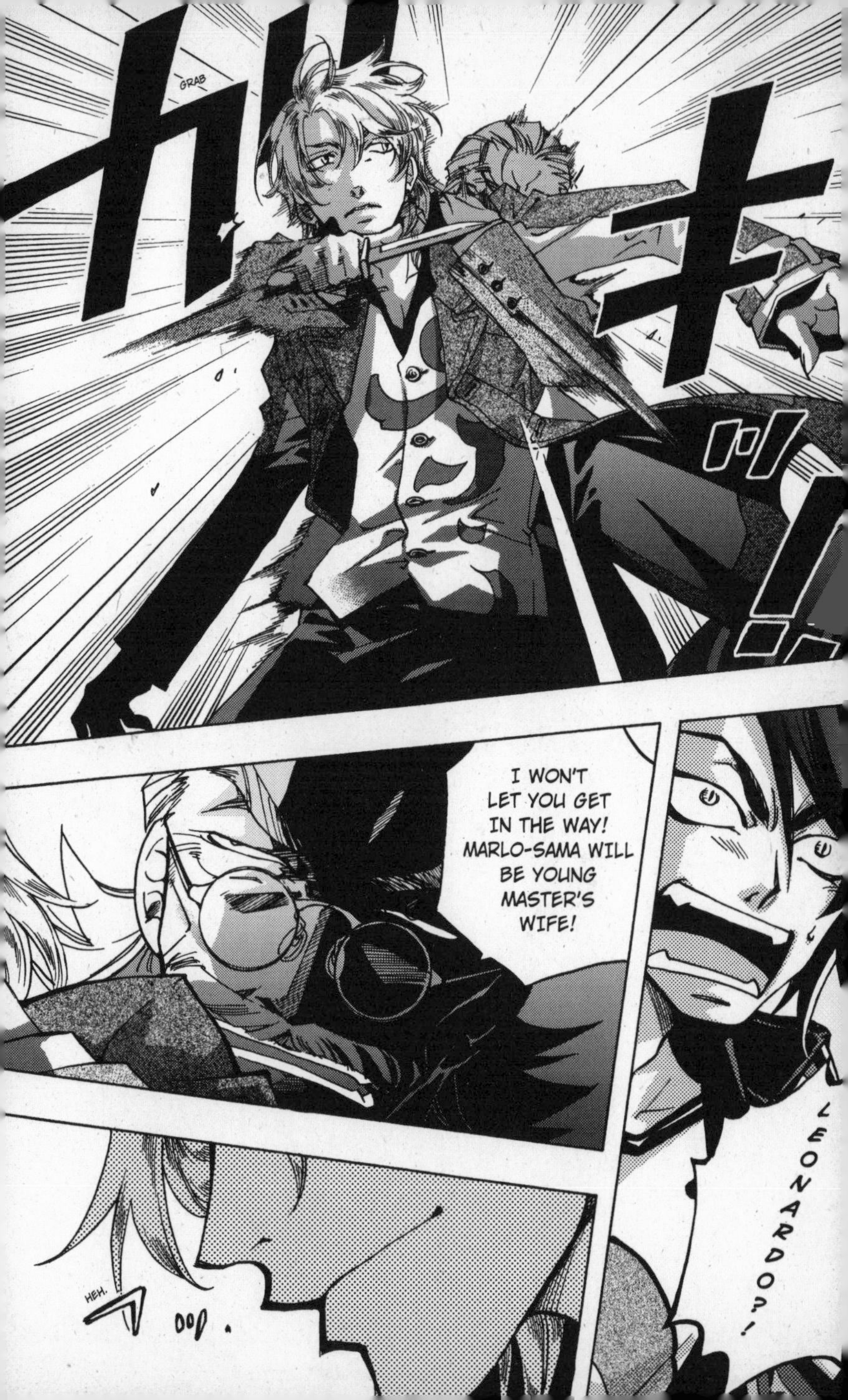
GRAB
I WON'T LET YOU GET IN THE WAY! MARLO-SAMA WILL BE YOUNG MASTER'S WIFE!
LEONARDO?!
HEH.

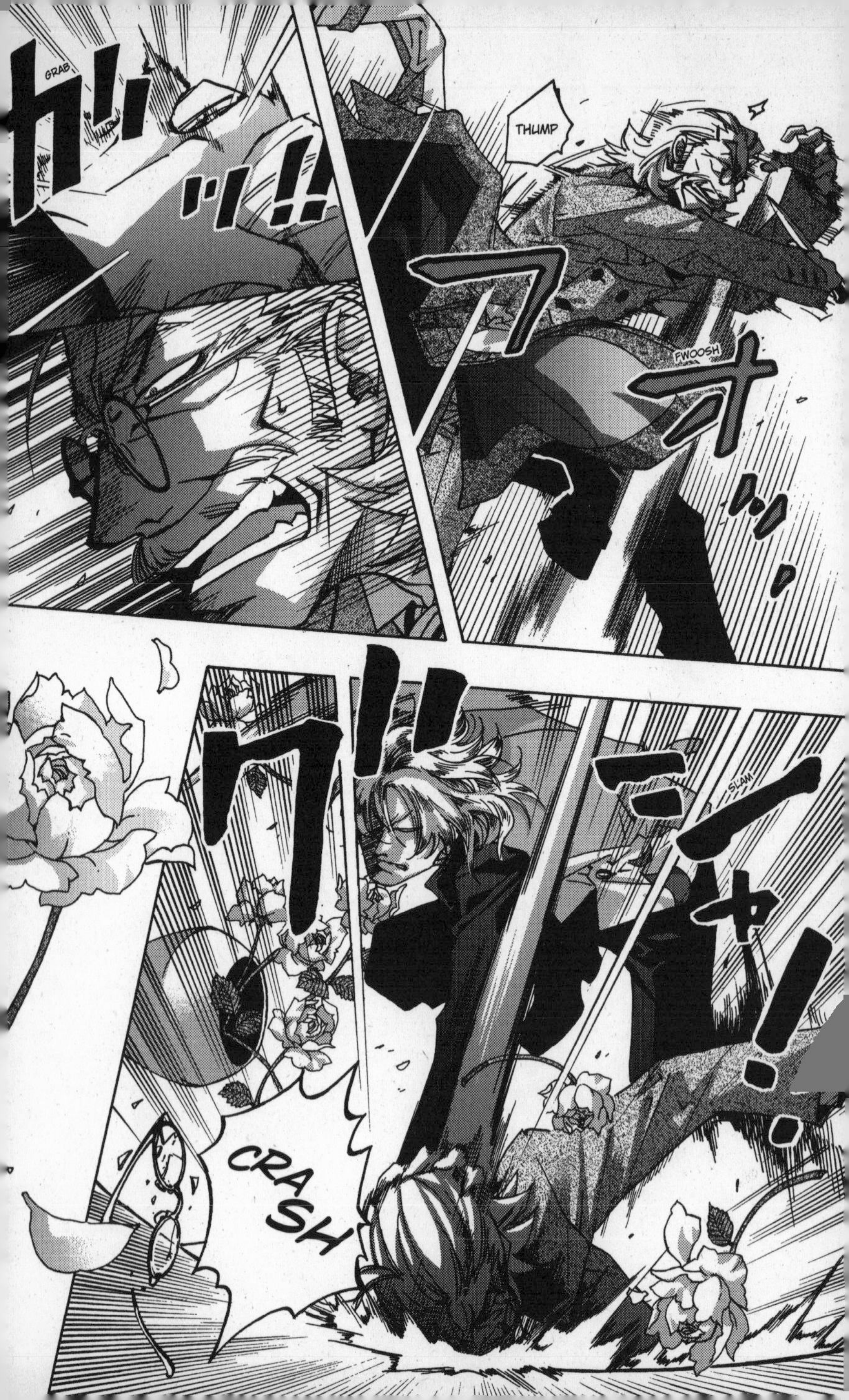
THUMP
FWOOSH
GRAB
SLAM
CRASH

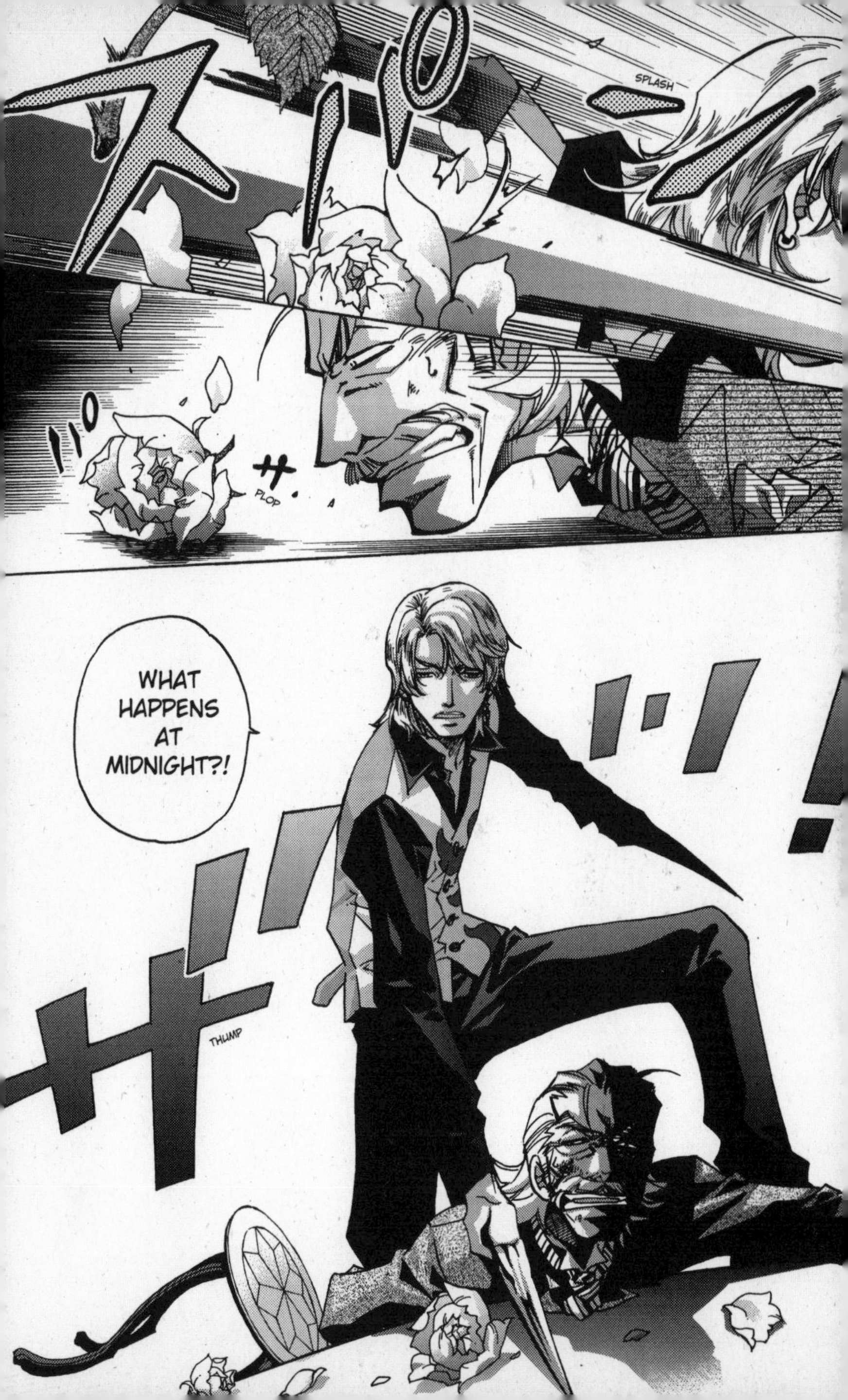
SPLASH
PLOP
WHAT HAPPENS AT MIDNIGHT?!
THUMP

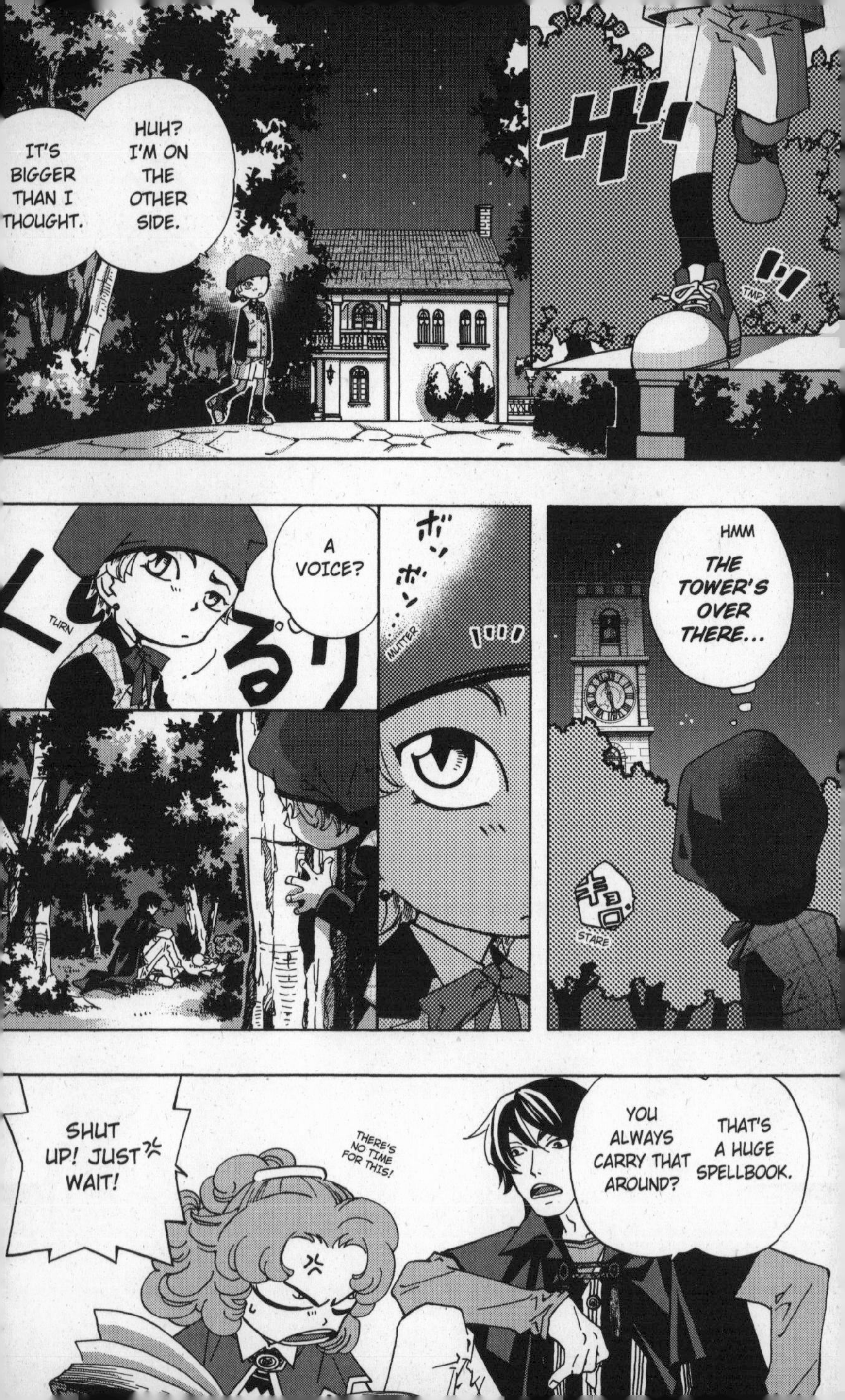
TMP
HUH? I'M ON THE OTHER SIDE.
IT'S BIGGER THAN I THOUGHT.
HMM
THE TOWER'S OVER THERE...
STARE
MUTTER
A VOICE?
TURN
THAT'S A HUGE SPELLBOOK.
YOU ALWAYS CARRY THAT AROUND?
THERE'S NO TIME FOR THIS!
SHUT UP! JUST WAIT!

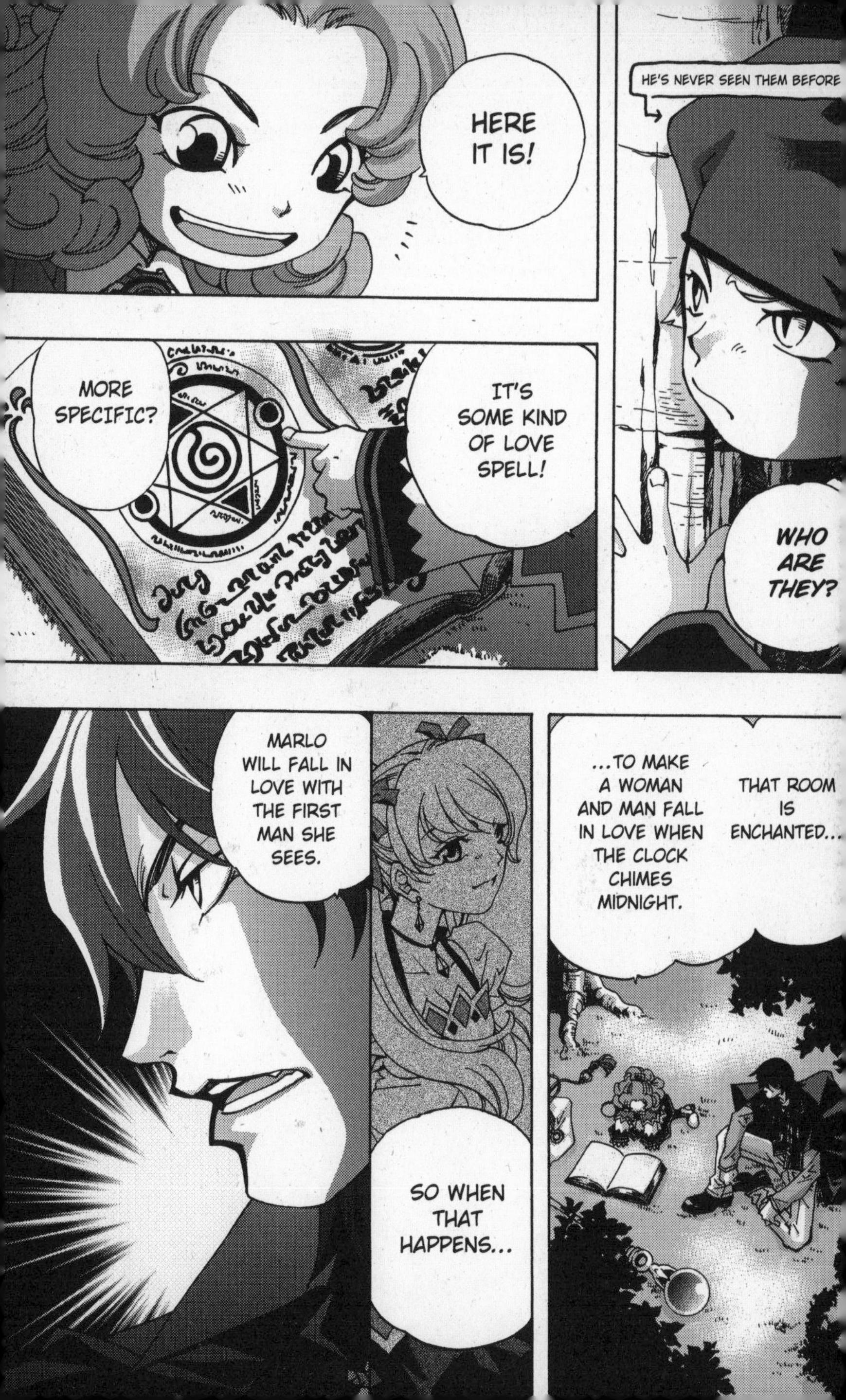
HE'S NEVER SEEN THEM BEFORE
WHO ARE THEY?
HERE IT IS!
IT'S SOME KIND OF LOVE SPELL!
MORE SPECIFIC?
THAT ROOM IS ENCHANTED...
...TO MAKE A WOMAN AND MAN FALL IN LOVE WHEN THE CLOCK CHIMES MIDNIGHT.
MARLO WILL FALL IN LOVE WITH THE FIRST MAN SHE SEES.
SO WHEN THAT HAPPENS...

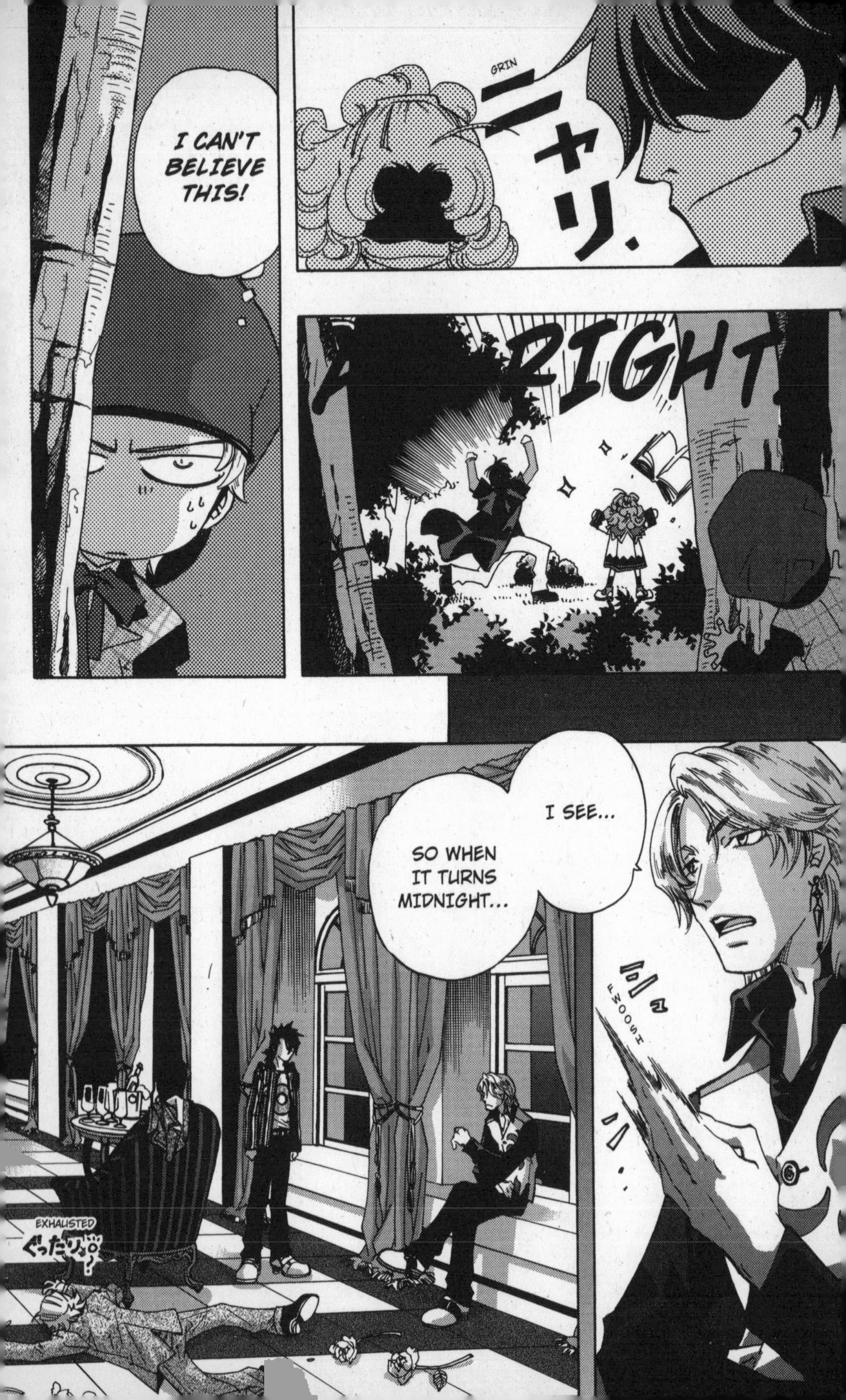
GRIN
ニヤリ.
RIGHT
I CAN'T BELIEVE THIS!
I SEE...
SO WHEN IT TURNS MIDNIGHT...
FWOOSH
EXHAUSTED
ぐったり

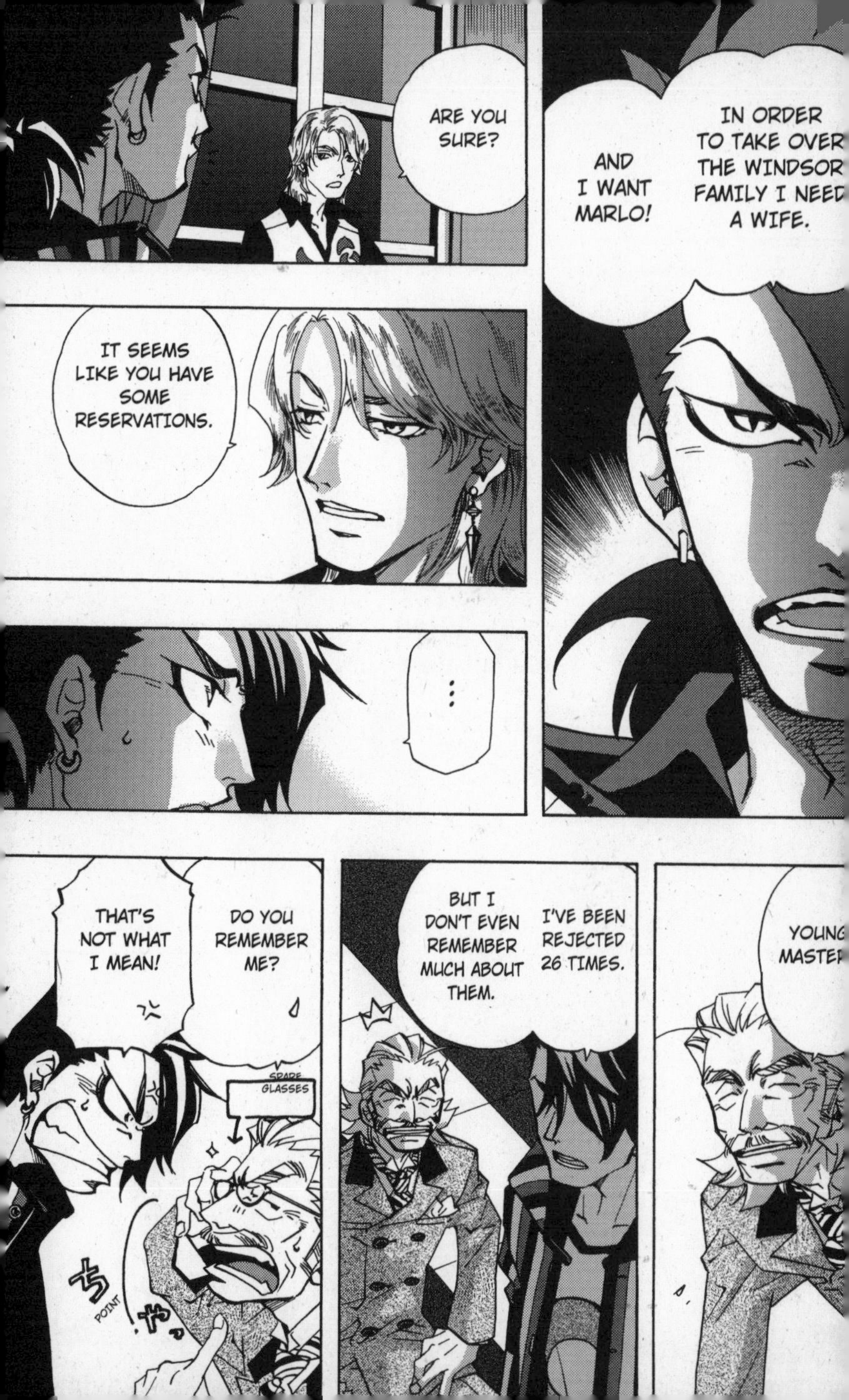
IN ORDER TO TAKE OVER THE WINDSOR FAMILY I NEED A WIFE.
AND I WANT MARLO!
ARE YOU SURE?
IT SEEMS LIKE YOU HAVE SOME RESERVATIONS.
...
YOUNG MASTE
I'VE BEEN REJECTED 26 TIMES.
BUT I DON'T EVEN REMEMBER MUCH ABOUT THEM.
DO YOU REMEMBER ME?
THAT'S NOT WHAT I MEAN!
SPARE GLASSES
POINT

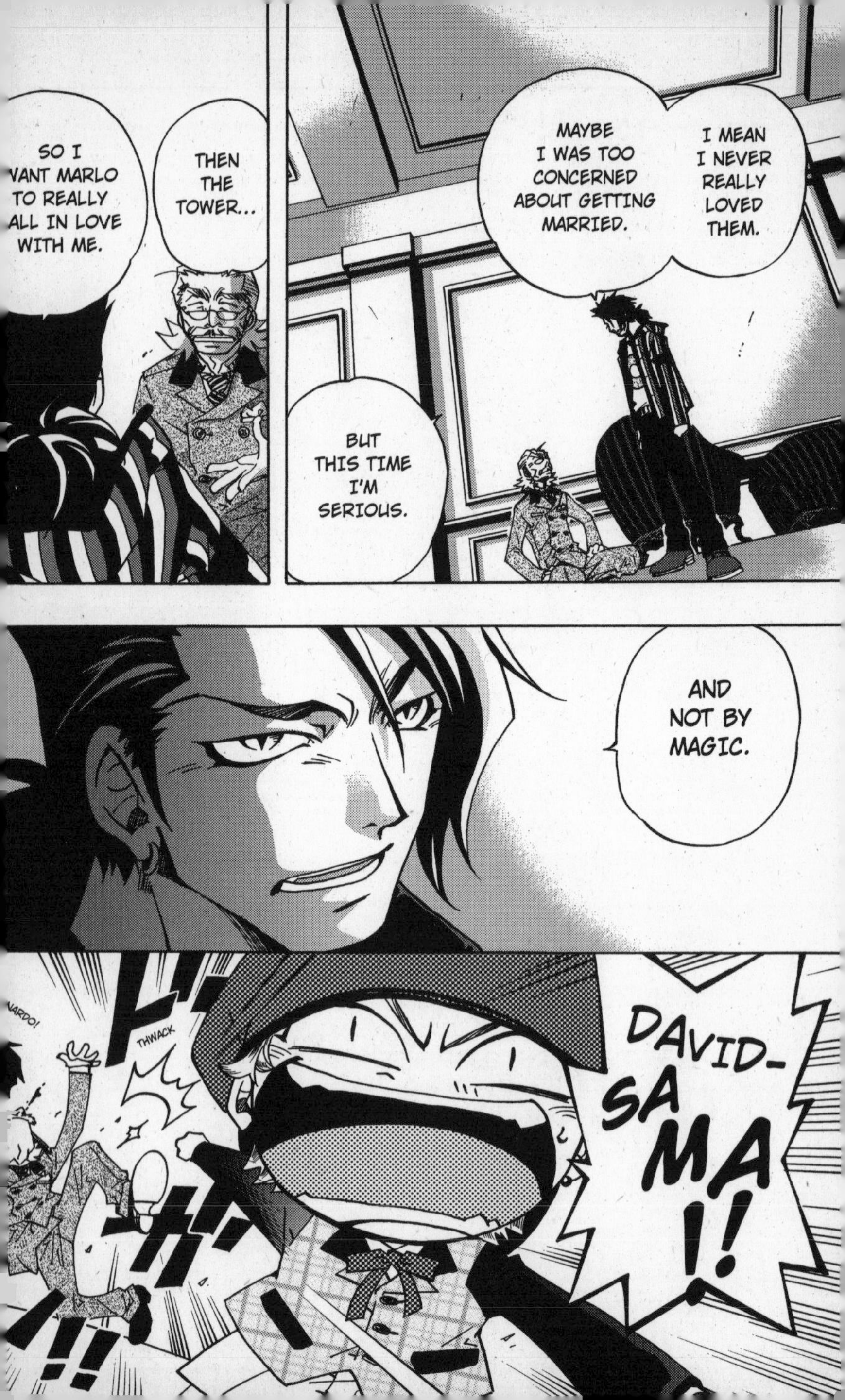

I MEAN I NEVER REALLY LOVED THEM.
MAYBE I WAS TOO CONCERNED ABOUT GETTING MARRIED.
BUT THIS TIME I'M SERIOUS.
THEN THE TOWER...
SO I VANT MARLO TO REALLY ALL IN LOVE WITH ME.
AND NOT BY MAGIC.
DAVID-SAMA!
THWACK
NARDO!

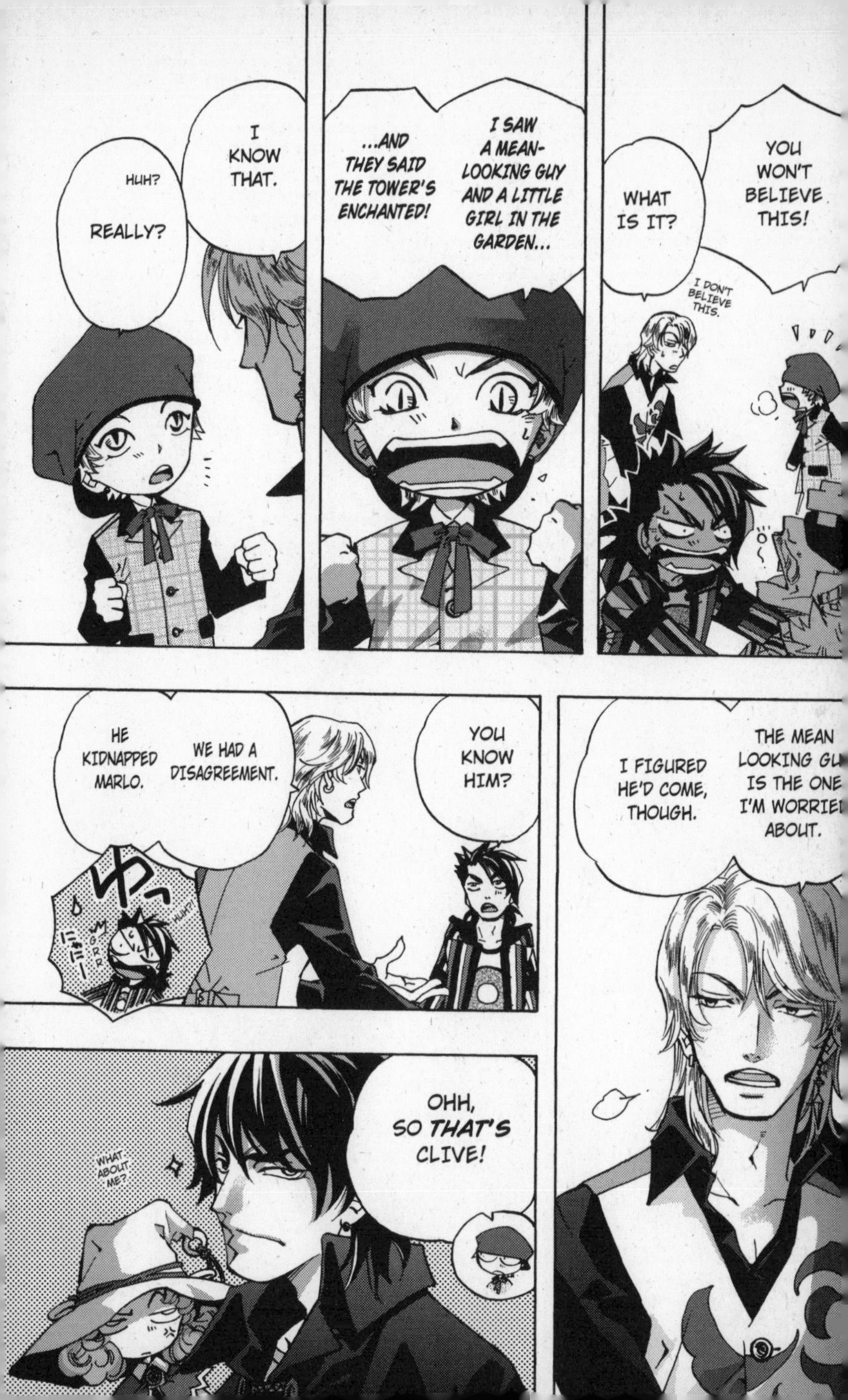
YOU WON'T BELIEVE THIS!
WHAT IS IT?
I DON'T BELIEVE THIS.
I SAW A MEAN-LOOKING GUY AND A LITTLE GIRL IN THE GARDEN...
...AND THEY SAID THE TOWER'S ENCHANTED!
I KNOW THAT.
HUH?
REALLY?
THE MEAN LOOKING GU IS THE ONE I'M WORRIE ABOUT.
I FIGURED HE'D COME, THOUGH.
YOU KNOW HIM?
WE HAD A DISAGREEMENT.
HE KIDNAPPED MARLO.
HUH?!
GRR
OHH, SO THAT'S CLIVE!
WHAT ABOUT ME?

HUH?!

I'M SORRY, YOUNG MASTER.

HE'S GONNA SHOW UP AT MIDNIGHT, ISN'T HE?

THE GIRL IS A MAGE, SO SHE PICKED UP ON THE MAGIC.

THWACK!

UGHHH

SHOOM

TMP

OOHHH!!

おぉーっ!!

HEY!

THUMP

I'M GOING TO MAKE YOUNG MASTER'S WISH COME TRUE!

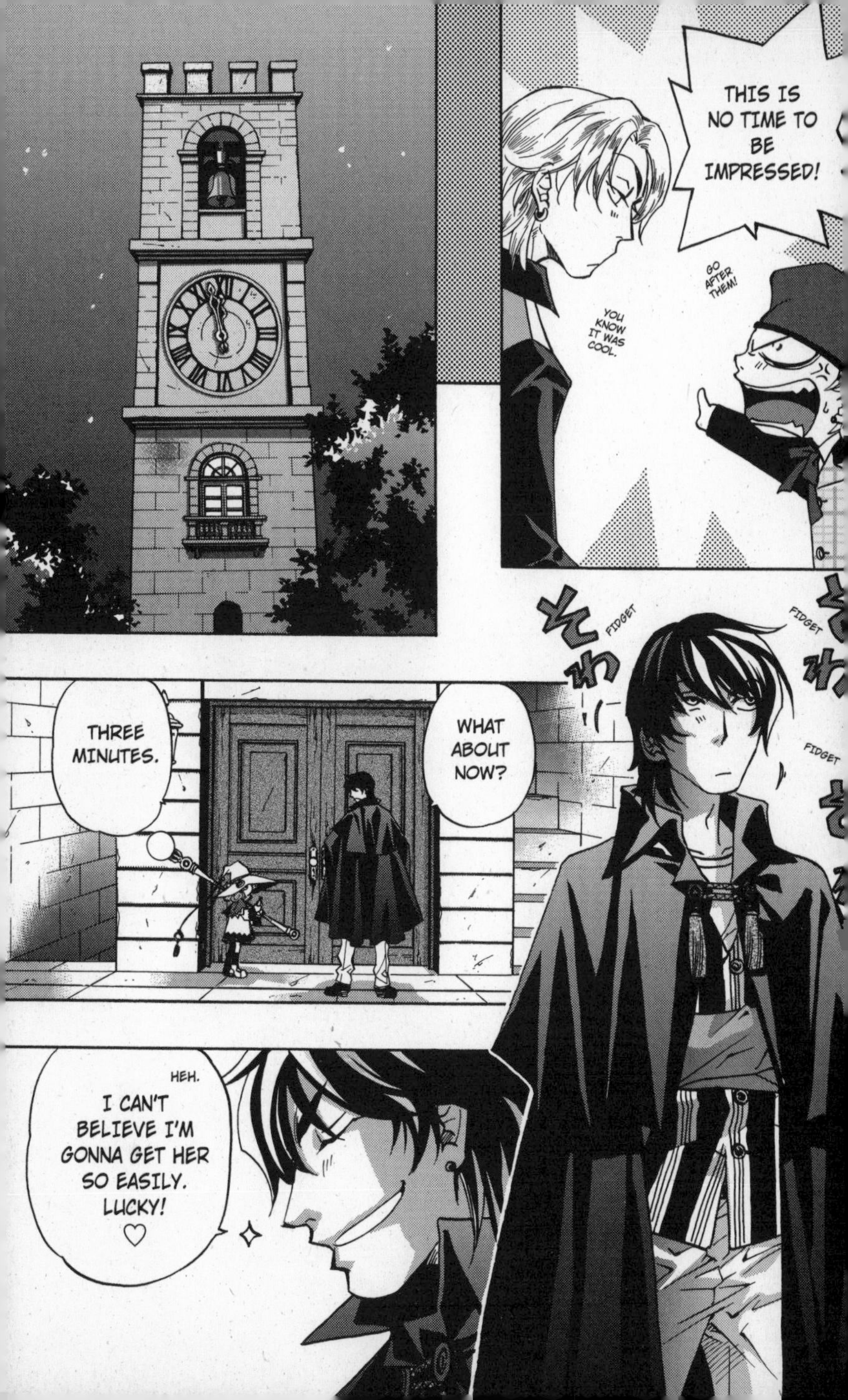
THIS IS NO TIME TO BE IMPRESSED!
GO AFTER THEM!
YOU KNOW IT WAS COOL.
FIDGET
FIDGET
FIDGET
WHAT ABOUT NOW?
THREE MINUTES.
HEH.
I CAN'T BELIEVE I'M GONNA GET HER SO EASILY. LUCKY! ♡

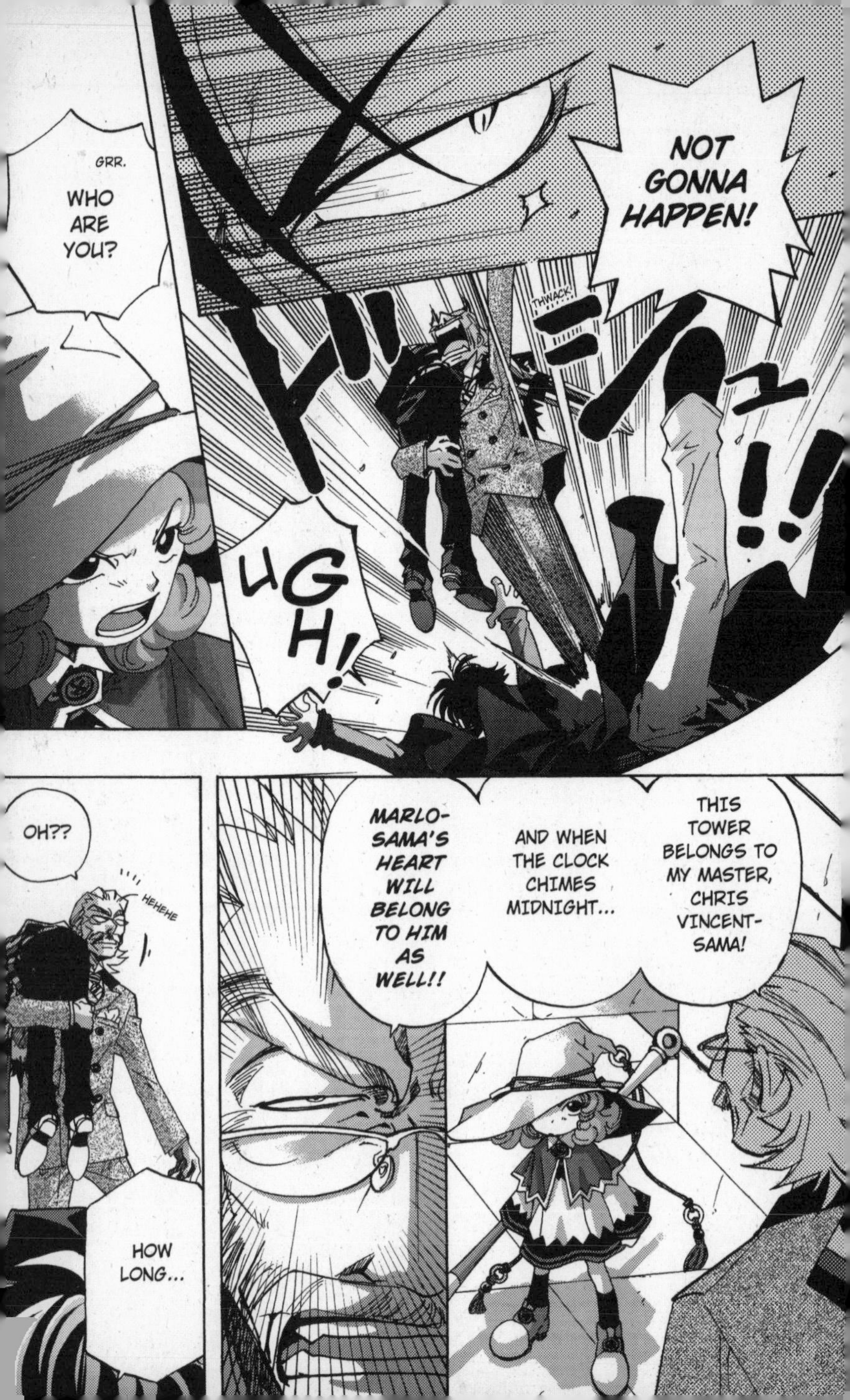
NOT GONNA HAPPEN!
THWACK
UGH!
GRR.
WHO ARE YOU?
THIS TOWER BELONGS TO MY MASTER, CHRIS VINCENT-SAMA!
AND WHEN THE CLOCK CHIMES MIDNIGHT...
MARLO-SAMA'S HEART WILL BELONG TO HIM AS WELL!!
OH??
HEHEHE
HOW LONG...

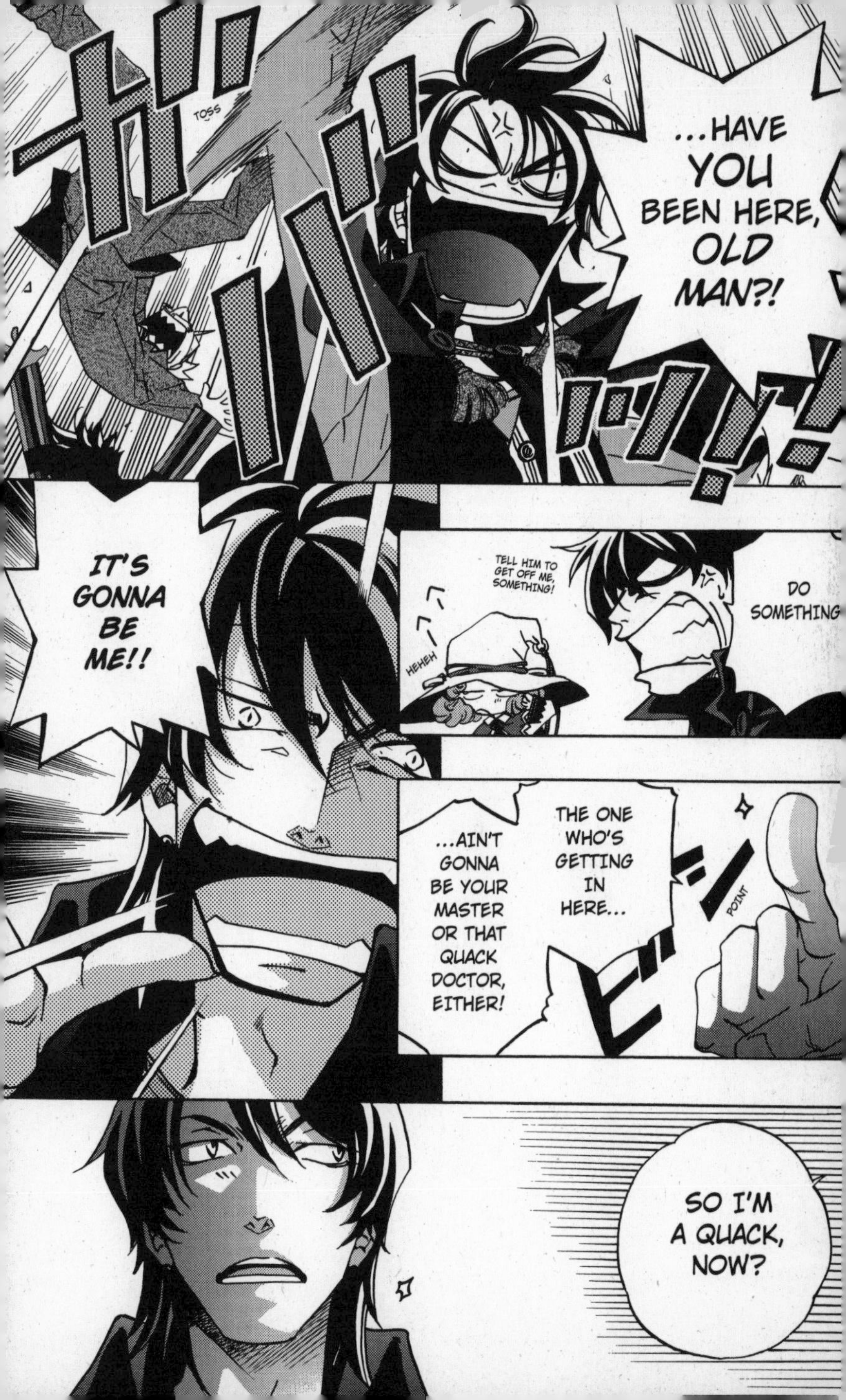
...HAVE YOU BEEN HERE, OLD MAN?!
TOSS
DO SOMETHING
TELL HIM TO GET OFF ME, SOMETHING!
HEHEH
THE ONE WHO'S GETTING IN HERE...
...AIN'T GONNA BE YOUR MASTER OR THAT QUACK DOCTOR, EITHER!
POINT
IT'S GONNA BE ME!!
SO I'M A QUACK, NOW?

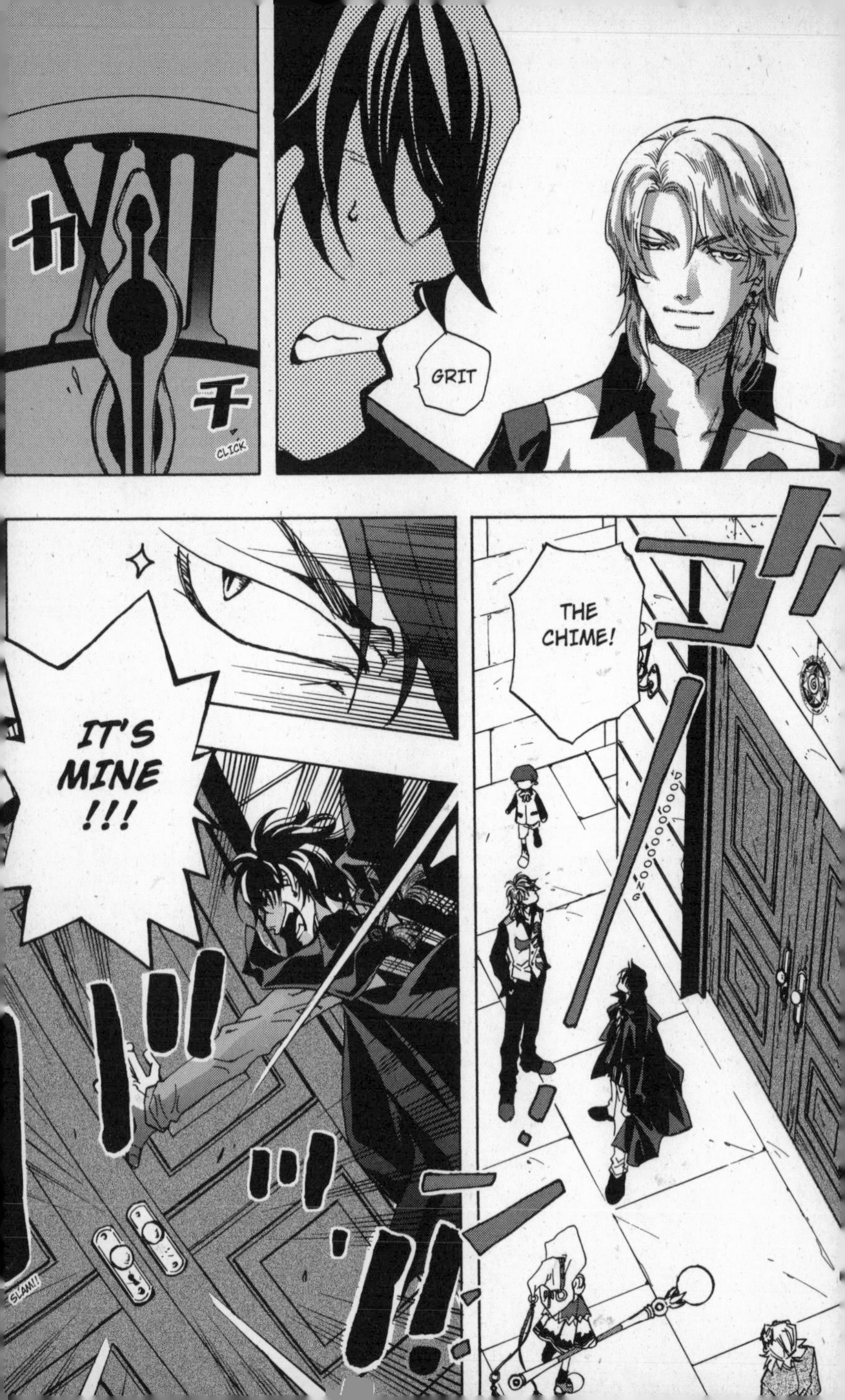
GRIT
カチ
CLICK
THE CHIME!
DOOOOOOOOONG
IT'S MINE!!!
SLAM!!

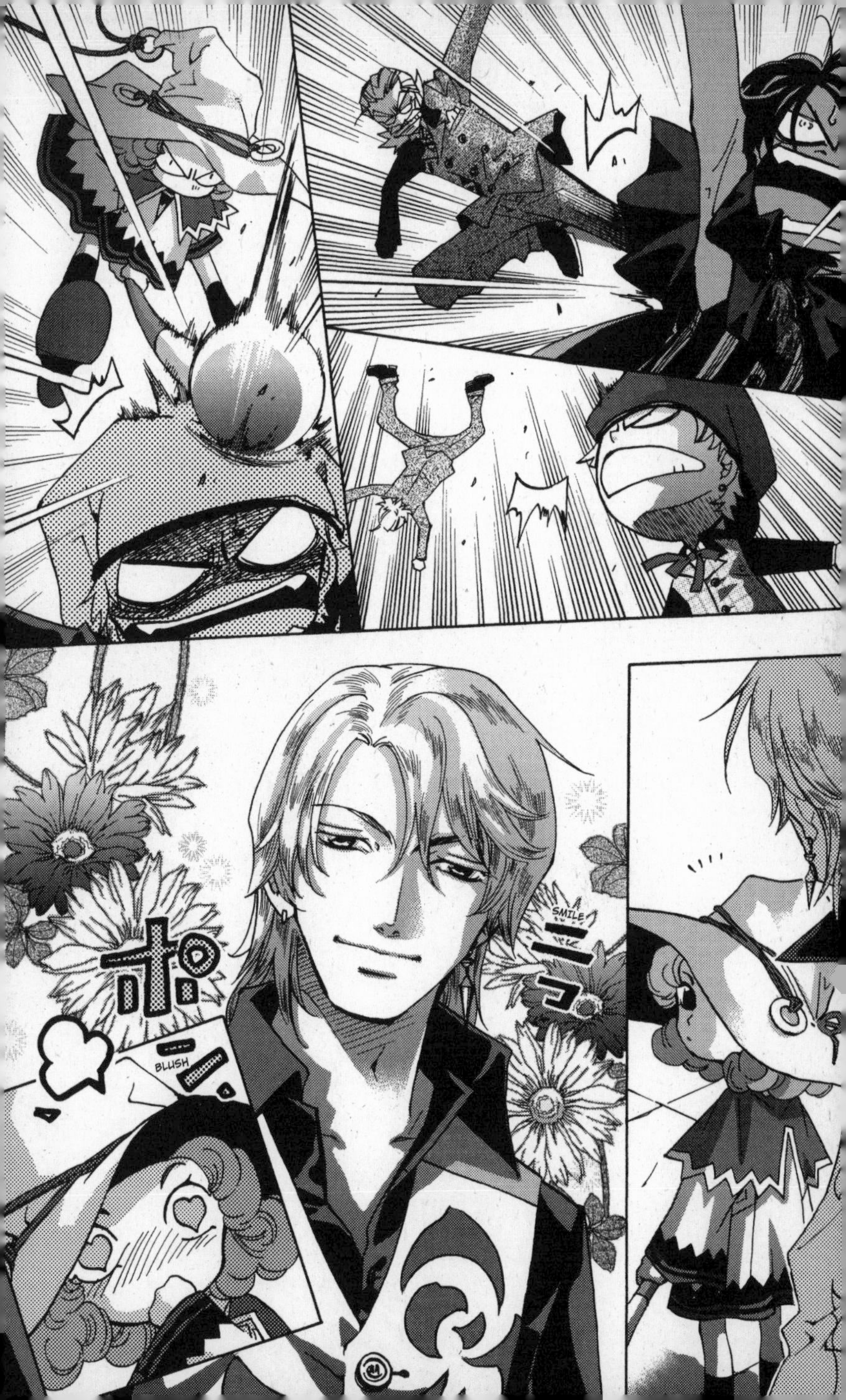
SMILE
BLUSH

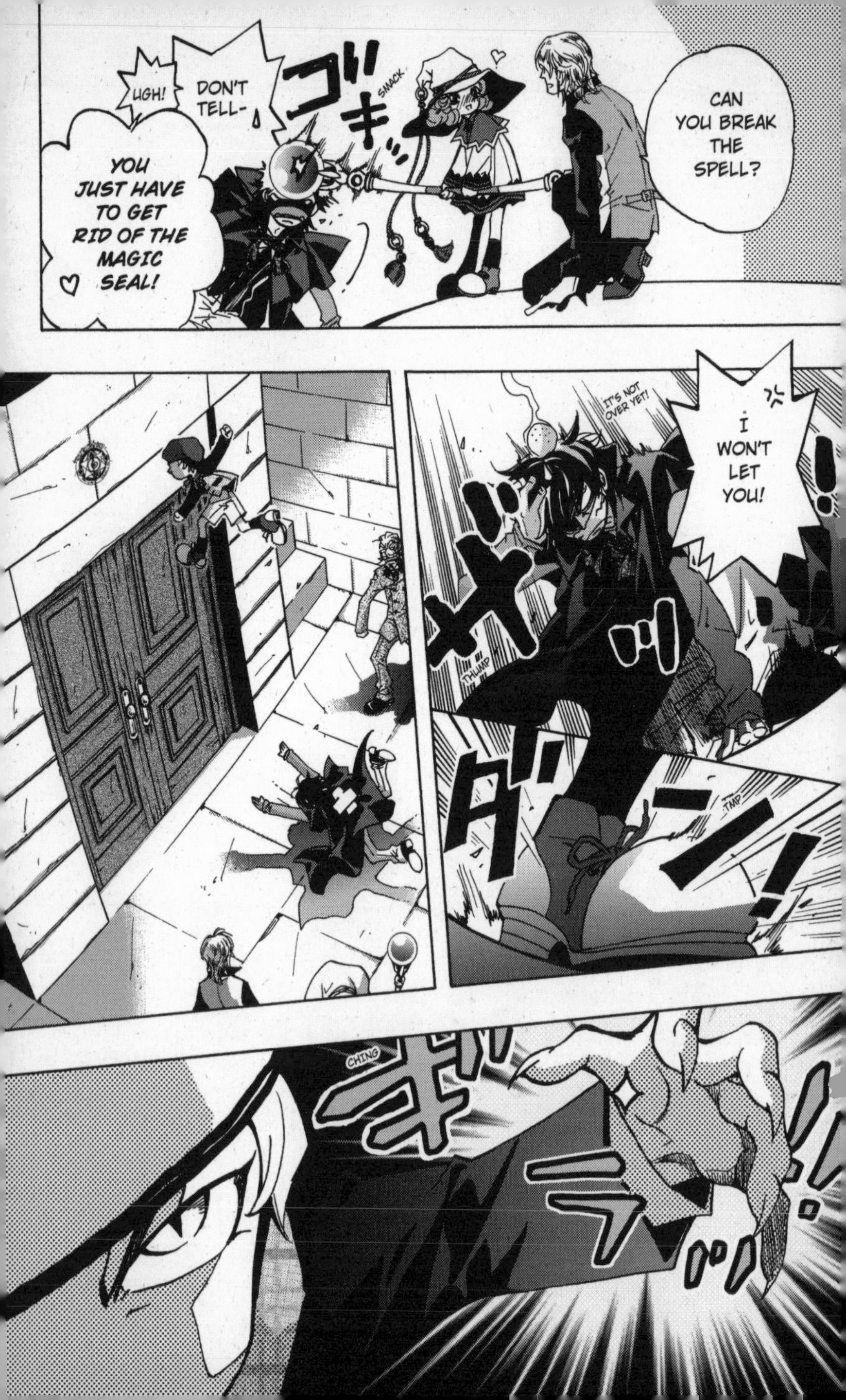
CAN YOU BREAK THE SPELL?
SMACK
DON'T TELL-
UGH!
YOU JUST HAVE TO GET RID OF THE MAGIC SEAL!
I WON'T LET YOU!
IT'S NOT OVER YET!
THUMP
TMP
CHING

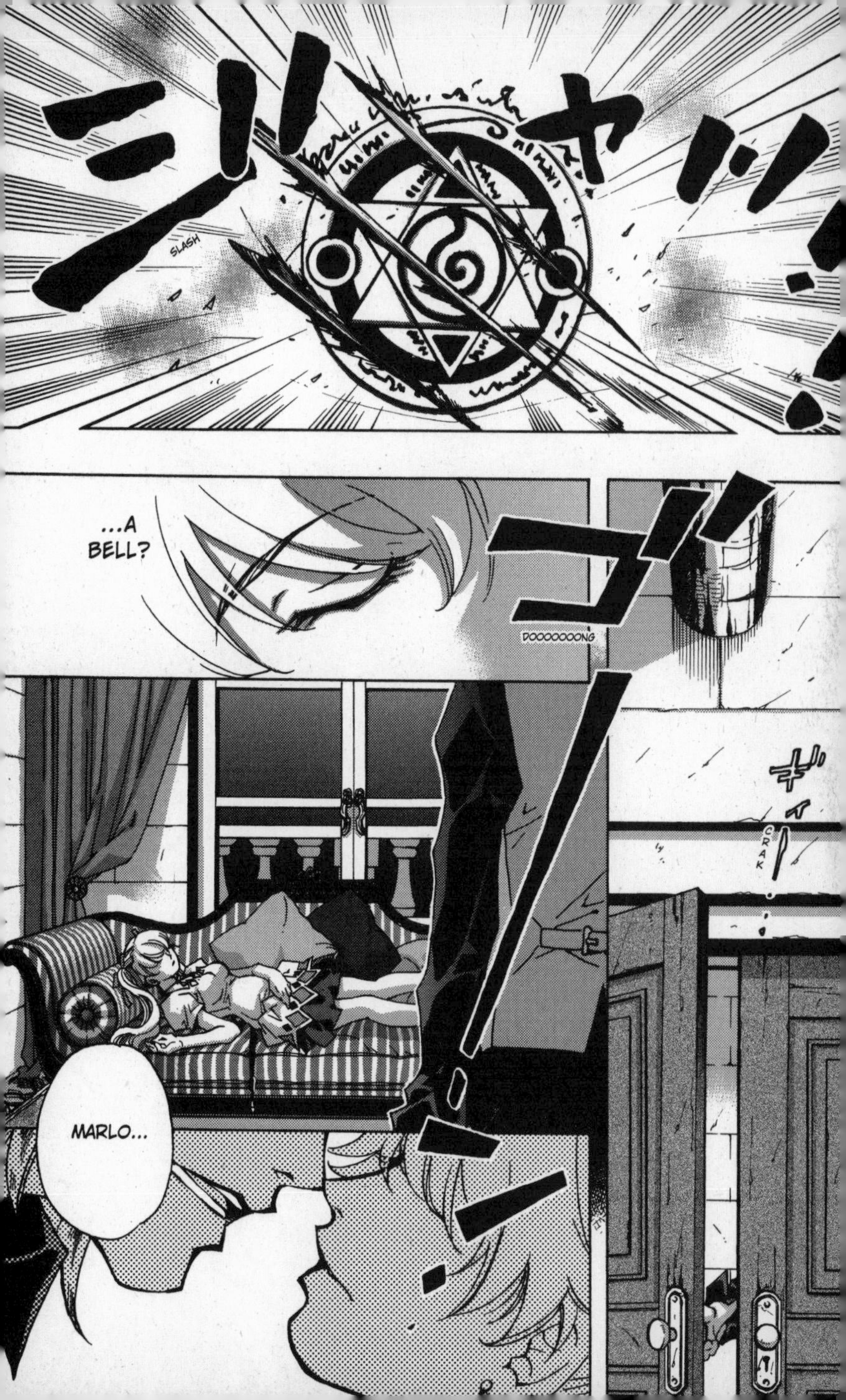
SLASH
DOOOOOOONG
...A BELL?
CRAK
MARLO...

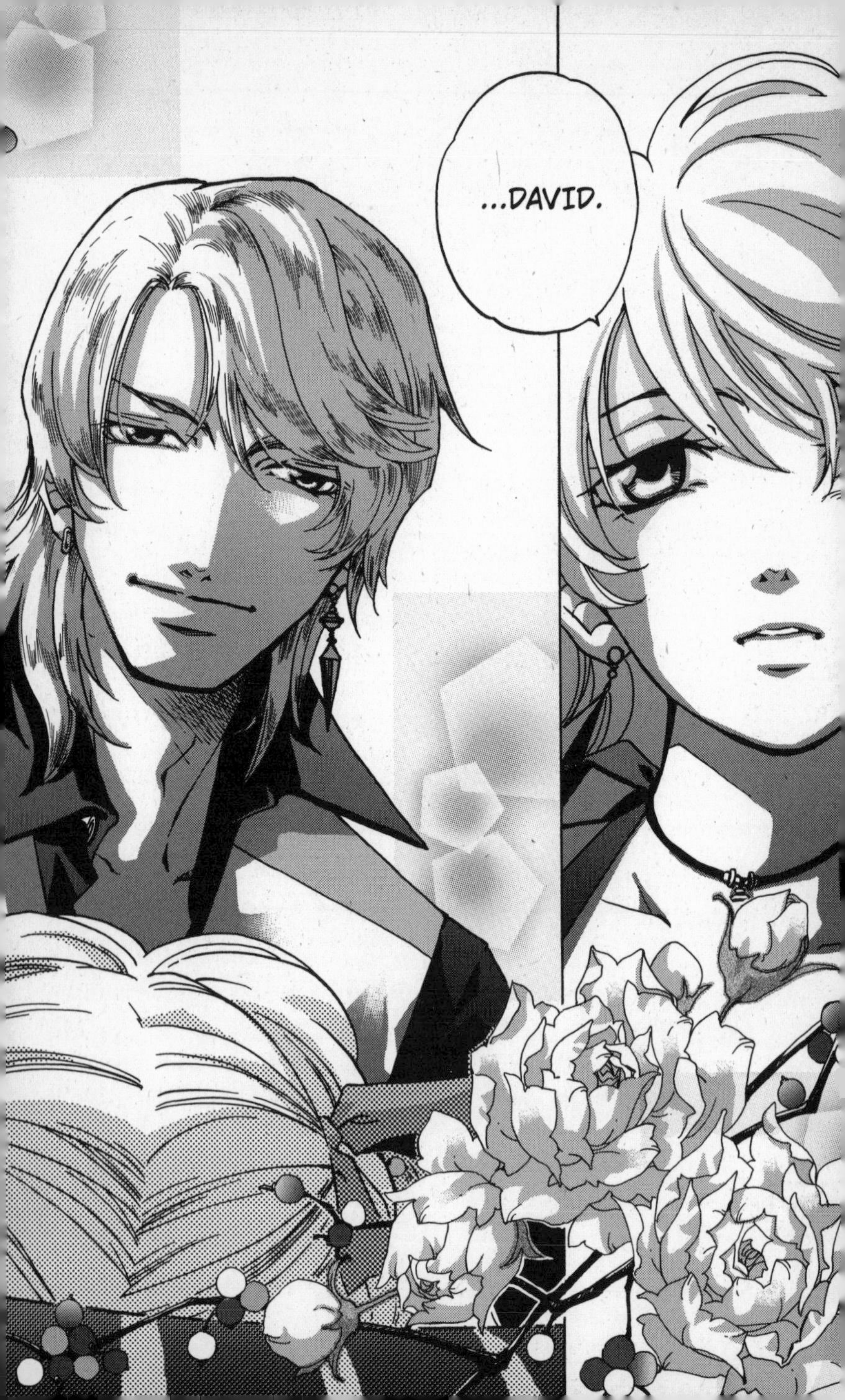
...DAVID.

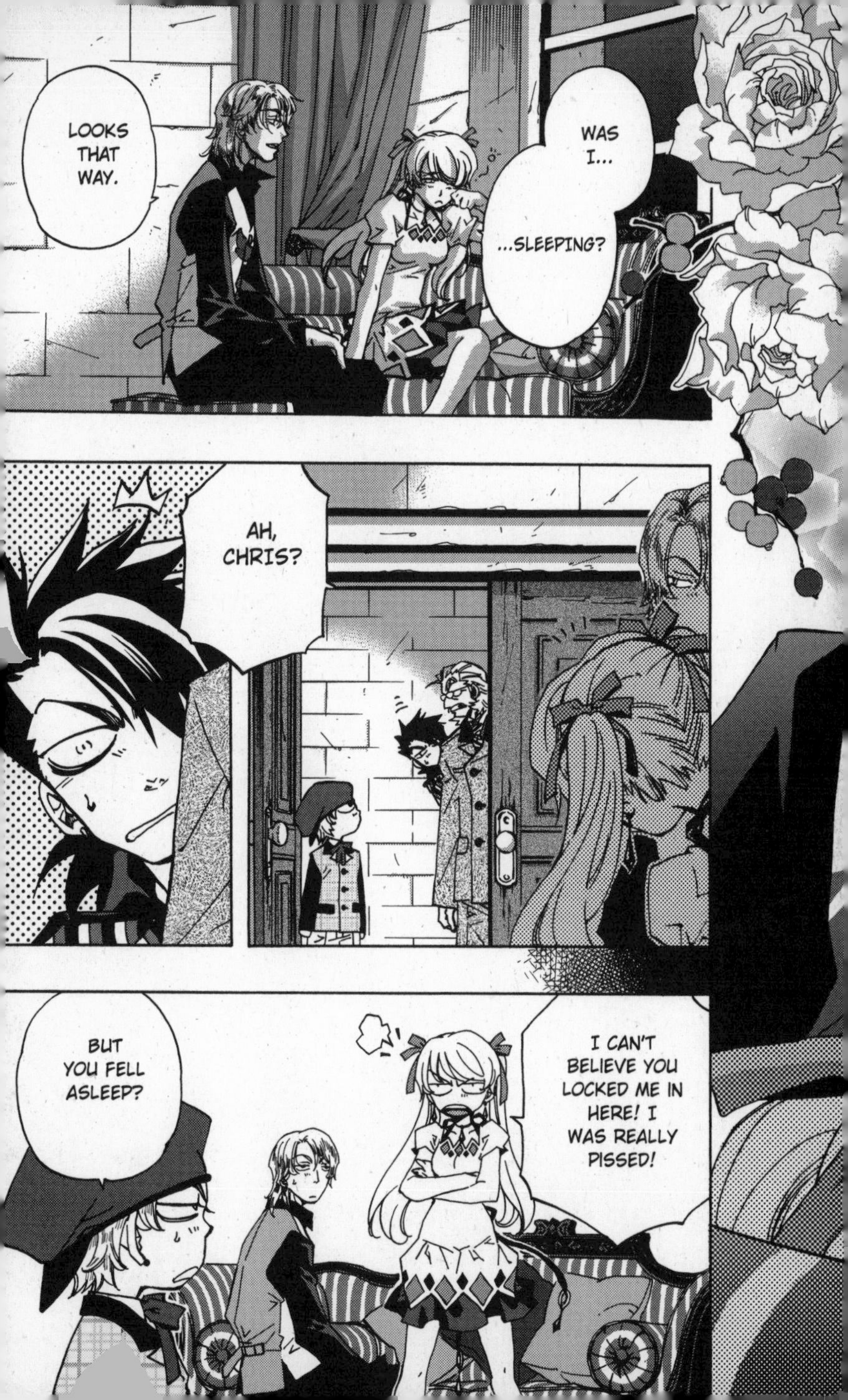
WAS I... ...SLEEPING?
LOOKS THAT WAY.
AH, CHRIS?
I CAN'T BELIEVE YOU LOCKED ME IN HERE! I WAS REALLY PISSED!
BUT YOU FELL ASLEEP?

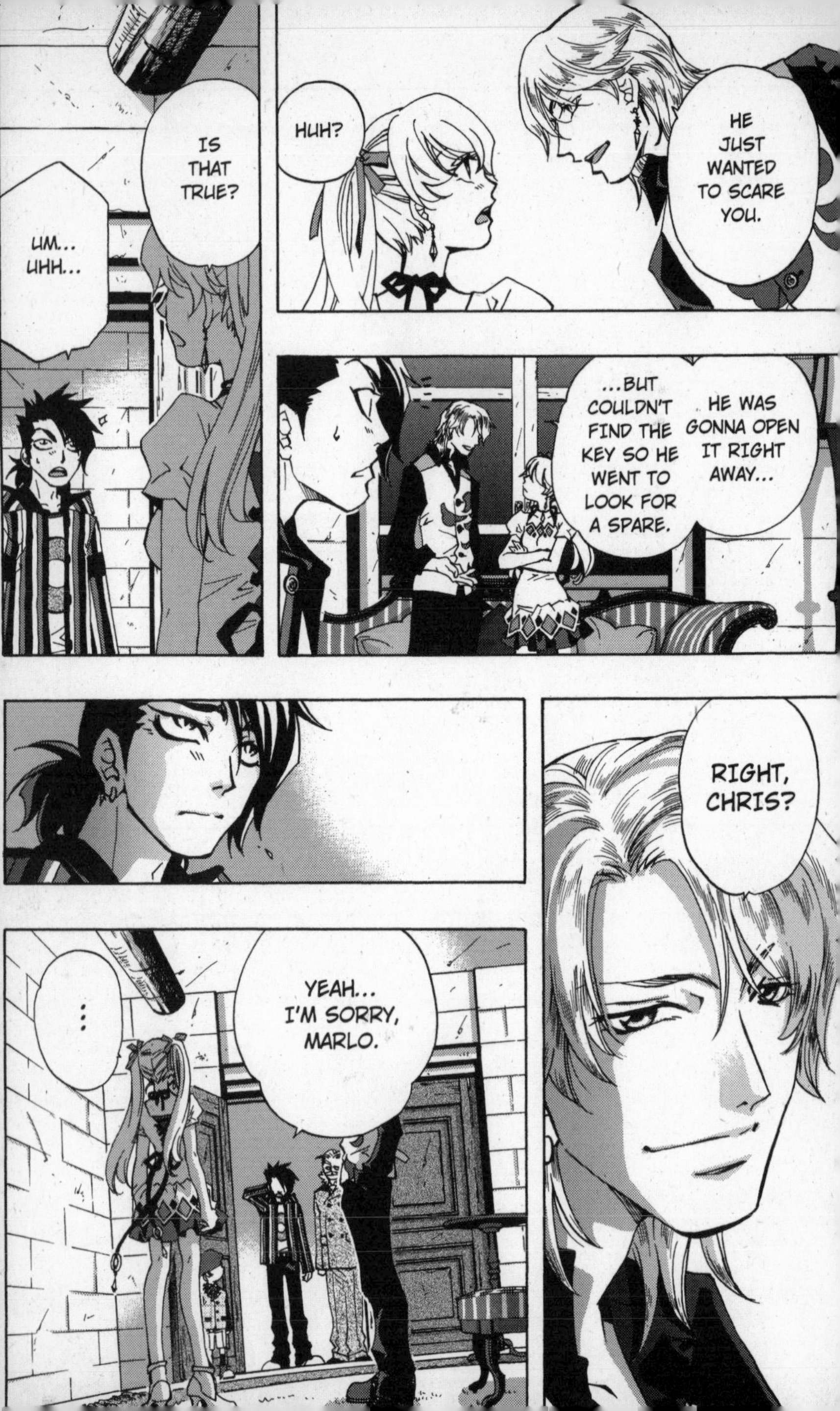
HE JUST WANTED TO SCARE YOU.
HUH?
HE WAS GONNA OPEN IT RIGHT AWAY...
...BUT COULDN'T FIND THE KEY SO HE WENT TO LOOK FOR A SPARE.
IS THAT TRUE?
UM... UHH...
RIGHT, CHRIS?
YEAH... I'M SORRY, MARLO.
...

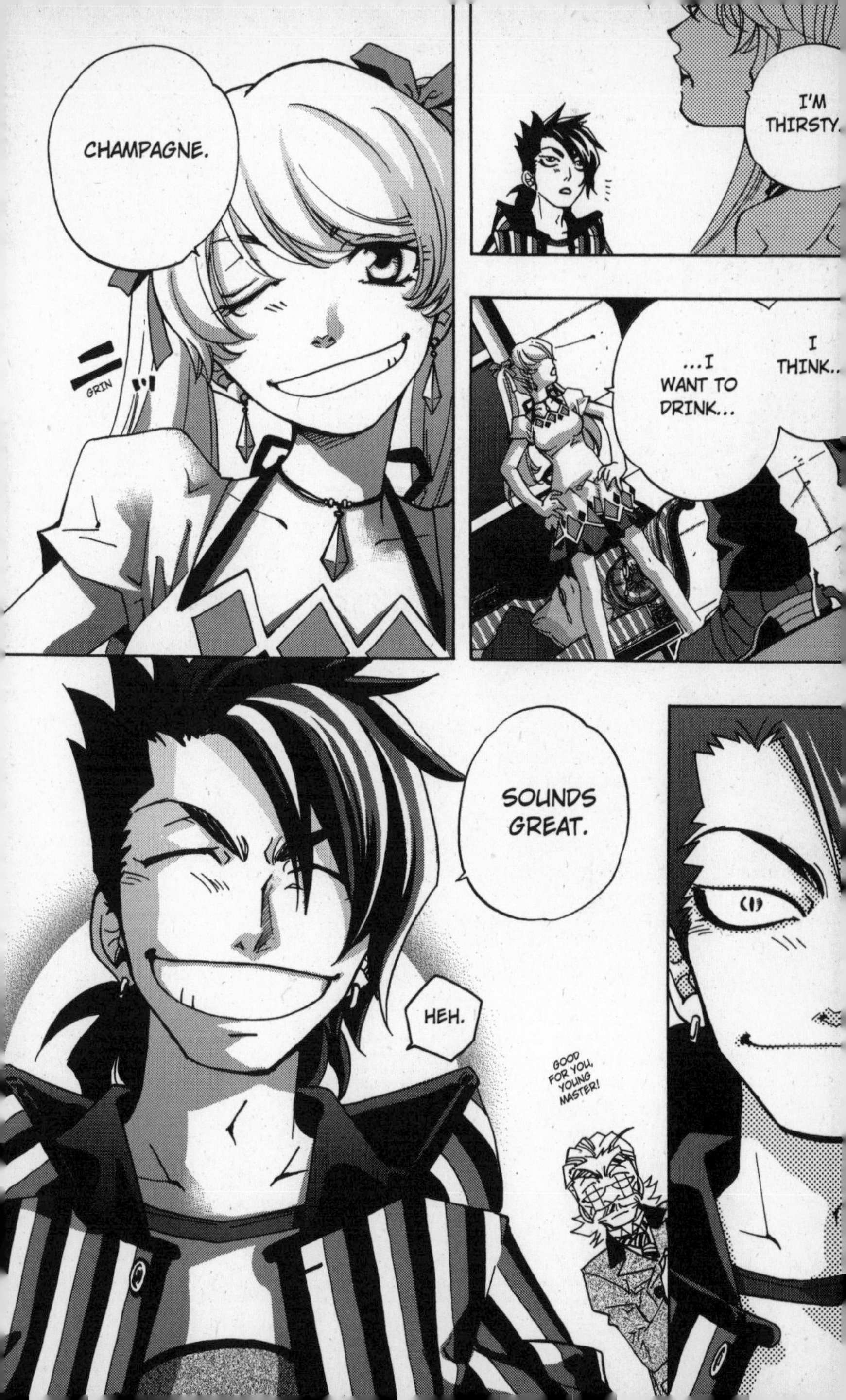
I'M THIRSTY.
I THINK..
...I WANT TO DRINK...
CHAMPAGNE.
GRIN
SOUNDS GREAT.
HEH.
GOOD FOR YOU, YOUNG MASTER!

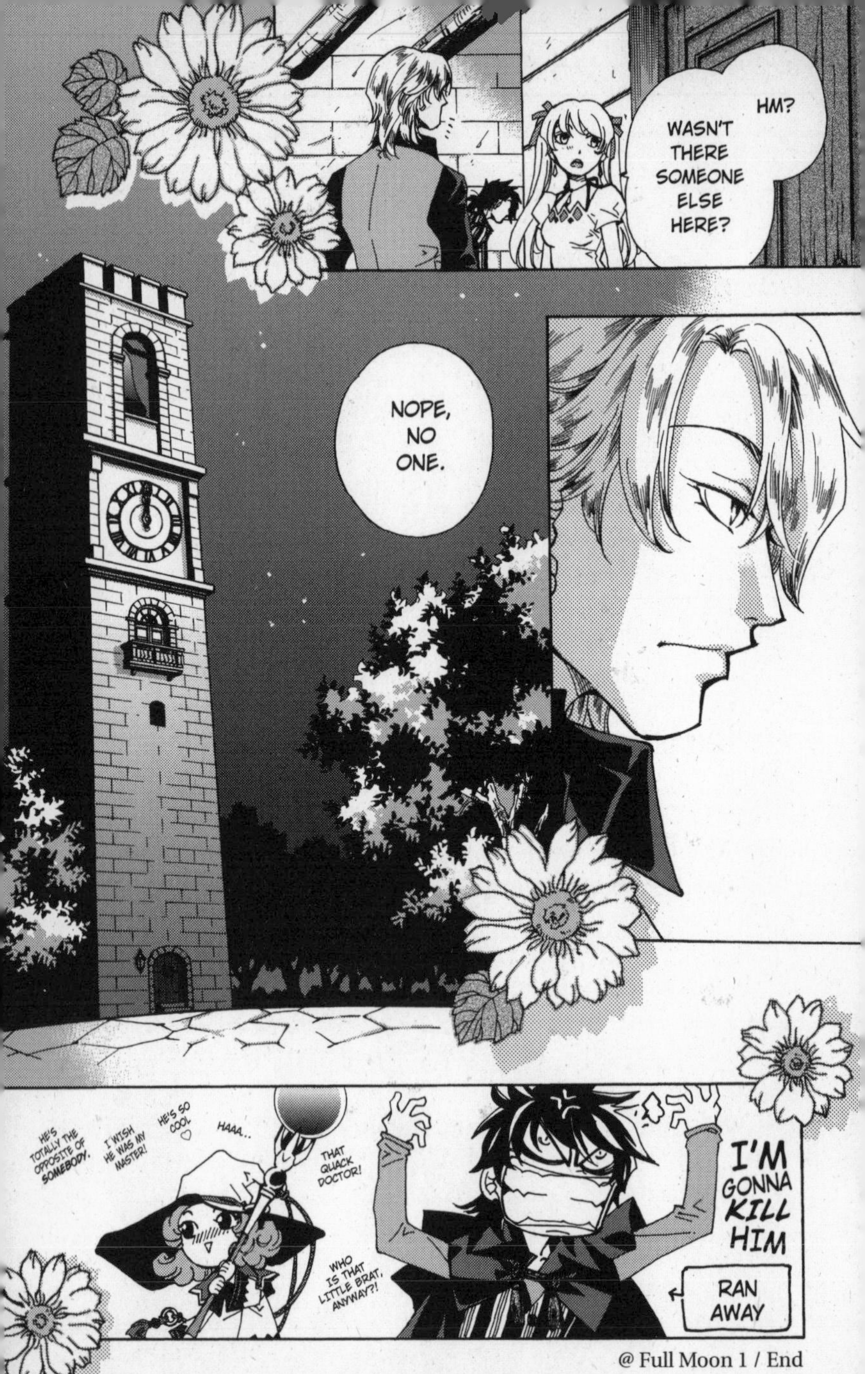
HM? WASN'T THERE SOMEONE ELSE HERE?
NOPE, NO ONE.
I'M GONNA KILL HIM
RAN AWAY
THAT QUACK DOCTOR!
WHO IS THAT LITTLE BRAT, ANYWAY?!
HAAA...
HE'S SO COOL ♡
I WISH HE WAS MY MASTER!
HE'S TOTALLY THE OPPOSITE OF SOMEBODY.

@ Full Moon 1 / End

Thanks for buying @ Full Moon.

This volume is a sequel to "Under Full Moon."

The magazine it previously appeared in shut down, so I was grateful when I was contacted by the editor at MiChao!

They suggested I write this sequel, and I agreed.

Since it's being published by a different company, I had to change the title. I had a really time trying to think of one, but the editor suggested I go with something similar to the previous series, so I went with an internet theme and chose "@Full Moon." ♡

So far fans seem to be really pleased with it! The editors have also complimented me, although they seem to want me to work at a faster pace (sorry! [sweat])

I hope you enjoyed this first volume.

I hope to do more new series besides Full Moon. I haven't thought of any specifics yet, but I know I'll writing it. I hope you pick up a copy when it gets published!

Thank you for your continued support.

See you next time!

@ Full Moon volume 1 is a work of fiction. Names, characters, places, and incidents are the products of the author's imagination or are used fictitiously. Any resemblance to actual events, locales, or persons, living or dead, is entirely coincidental.

A Kodansha Comics Trade Paperback Original

Published in the United States by Kodansha Comics, an imprint of Kodansha USA Publishing, LLC, New York.

Publication rights for this English edition arranged through Kodansha Ltd., Tokyo.

First published in Japan in 2009 by Kodansha Ltd., Tokyo.

ISBN 978-1-935-42920-3

Printed in the United States of America.

www.kodanshacomics.com

9 8 7 6 5 4 3 2 1

Translator: Andria Cheng
Lettering: Janice Chiang

TOMARE!
STOP

You're going the wrong way!

Manga is a completely different type of reading experience.

To start at the beginning, Go to the end!

That's right! Authentic manga is read the traditional Japanese way—from right to left, exactly the opposite of how American books are read. It's easy to follow: Just go to the other end of the book and read each page—and each panel—from right side to left side, starting at the top right. Now you're experiencing manga as it was meant to be!